CORP
CANN

D1535447

Colleen Ryan has a background in economics and accounting and has been a business reporter on the Australian corporate world for fifteen years for the *Australian Financial Review*, the *National Times*, where she was business editor for five years, and now the *Sydney Morning Herald*. In 1990 she was awarded the Australian Shareholders Association Award for excellence in financial journalism.

Glenn Burge graduated with an Arts/Law degree in 1981 from Macquarie University, NSW, and completed the College of Law in 1982. He began his career in journalism at the *Daily Telegraph* in 1983 and then in 1985 worked for two years for the *Sun*. He has since been working for the *Sydney Morning Herald* as a business reporter, including positions as investment editor and editor of the CBD column.

Colleen Ryan & Glenn Burge

CORPORATE CANNIBALS

A gripping story of power, prejudice and corruption in the brutal battle for Australia's biggest newspaper group

Mandarin

A Mandarin Paperback
CORPORATE CANNIBALS

First published in Great Britain 1993
by Mandarin Paperbacks
an imprint of Reed Consumer Books Ltd
Michelin House, 81 Fulham Road, London SW3 6RB
and Auckland, Melbourne, Singapore and Toronto

First published 1992 by William Heinemann Australia

Copyright © Colleen Ryan and Glenn Burge

A CIP catalogue record for this title
is available from the British Library

ISBN 0 7493 1609 8

Printed and bound in Great Britain
by Cox & Wyman Ltd, Reading, Berks

Contents

Authors' Note

WE WOULD like to acknowledge, with gratitude, the generous co-operation of many of the parties involved in the Fairfax sale. In over 100 hours of interviews, we disrupted their working lives and weekends as they retraced for us their steps during 1991 and carefully explained the nuances of negotiations and the technical, legal and political aspects of the various bids.

We have attempted where possible to reconstruct key conversations. In some cases this has been done with the help of transcripts and detailed minutes. In others we have relied on people's memories and have checked the recollections of as many as possible of those present in meetings. Where recollections or interpretations differ in a major way we have footnoted the alternative or dissenting version of events.

Prologue

BILL BEERWORTH arranged his papers on the table in front of him. He was fiddling to keep his hands occupied. The atmosphere was strained. Five men sat at a table big enough for twenty. They were in one of the larger meeting rooms of the Los Angeles office of US law firm Coudert Brothers. Beerworth had his back to the room's only entrance—a large set of double doors. He felt peculiarly vulnerable. Beerworth was impeccably groomed in his English-cut woollen suit, his neatly clipped brown hair framing a broad face, his jaw jutting forward. Beside him sat his Los Angeles attorney Ted McAniff of O'Melveny & Myers. Beerworth was representing Warwick Fairfax and his Fairfax Group. Opposite them was Tom Brislan, a partner of Couderts, the legal advisers to a group of US investors who held $450 million worth of junk bonds in Warwick Fairfax's company. Next to Brislan was Steve Ezzes and Mark Atanasio, representatives of two of the largest bondholders. They were present to discuss the appointment of Sydney investment banker Malcolm Turnbull as financial adviser to the bondholders. It was an appointment the Fairfax team had objected to violently.

Brislan opened proceedings. Without pleasantries he launched straight into an attack on Beerworth. His words stung. It was as if Beerworth were being slapped across the face. Brislan shouted: 'It is not your right to choose our financial adviser. We will choose whomever we like. Who do you fucking think you are?'

Beerworth was shocked. This was not how lawyers should speak to each other, even if on the other side.

'Mr Brislan this is outrageous behaviour for an attorney.'

Beerworth, who can be prudish at the best of times, was at his most proper. But he was putting himself straight on the back foot. Ezzes intervened. Warwick Fairfax had to realise that he didn't hold all of the cards any more, Ezzes told him sharply. He had no right to interfere with this decision. At this point the large double doors behind Beerworth were shoved open. Pandora Pang, a finance executive with Executive Life (an investor which held a sizable parcel of Fairfax bonds), burst in.

'Fuck you. I am going to sit here and listen. My clients are owed $87 million. I haven't voted for anyone to represent me. I am staying.'

She sat down, throwing her briefcase on the table. Beerworth was stunned and Ezzes and Atanasio looked uncomfortable and embarrassed. Brislan, however, continued to berate Beerworth, appearing to enjoy the presence of a larger audience.

The double doors flew open again. Beerworth half turned, glimpsing a well-dressed man stride into the room. He too demanded that he sit in on the meeting—he was damned if the meeting would go on without him. He had barely finished an agitated monologue when the doors burst open again. The procedure was repeated.

Over minutes the room began to fill. It was becoming impossible to continue as people barged in, grabbing chairs, slamming briefcases and pulling out papers.

This was too much. Beerworth felt he had been set up. Soon there were about thirty people in the room. All angry, all performing. Some stood at the table, some leant on the back of chairs, most sneered at his every word. The script for each of them was almost identical—why wouldn't Fairfax let them choose their own financial adviser? Every time Beerworth opened his mouth, someone yelled at him, demanding their money back. One bondholder demanded: 'Will the company pay our fees?'

'No it will not,' Beerworth replied curtly. It was an unwise response, bringing only another barrage of shouting.

Finally in desperation Beerworth tried to regain some order in the meeting. He asked Brislan if the letter outlining Fairfax's objection to the appointment of Turnbull & Partners had been circulated. Various people looked at each other and shook their heads.

No, Brislan admitted, the letter had not been circulated. Beerworth demanded that this be done immediately, but Brislan didn't have a copy. He asked Beerworth if he did, pointing at a large, yellow package in front of him. What was in it?

There was no letter inside; the bulky package contained dozens of press clippings from Australian newspapers collected by Macquarie Bank. It was a potent collection of clippings—the carefully edited Turnbull file.

Each clipping documented concerns about Turnbull's role as an adviser to Westpac Banking Corporation on the recent decision to put the television group Ten Network into receivership and plans for its future operation—perhaps as a no-frills network, perhaps using Nine Network's transmitter. The clippings also quoted misgivings about Turnbull's connection to Kerry Packer's Nine Network (Turnbull had recently been a director of the network): the Federal Communications Minister Mr Kim Beazley warned that the Government would not accept any plans by Turnbull and Westpac to allow Ten Network to take programmes from Packer's Nine Network; the Trade Practices Commission threatened to go to the Federal Court and seek an injunction against Turnbull having any say in the running of Ten Network.

Mark Johnson, the Macquarie Bank adviser who had accompanied Beerworth and Warwick to Los Angeles, had handed the package of clippings to Beerworth that morning. The evidence was to be given to Ezzes and Atanasio, to demonstrate that politicians and others were also suspicious of Turnbull's connection to Packer. It was not just Fairfax advisers raising concerns.

There was nothing to lose. Beerworth decided in a split second to circulate them. It was not an ace, but he hoped it might calm things down. As the clippings were handed around the table the doors were flung open again.

It was Turnbull. He had been left cooling his heels in an empty room as the bondholders raided Beerworth's meeting. Turnbull's timing was impeccable. Beerworth had been caught handing around the corporate equivalent of dirty pictures.

When Turnbull—pudgy-faced, his gait pushy, his demeanour

prickly—walked in, Beerworth's stomach turned. Turnbull was the last person he wanted to see. Why was he here? Was this some sort of trap? A set-up?

Beerworth could feel his anger rising. How could he have slipped up? He was always a stickler for controlling the environment of a meeting—imperative for a corporate adviser—and he had broken his own rules. This was an unfamiliar office in downtown Los Angeles, an unfamiliar city.

Turnbull paced around one end of the room, theatrically asking what Fairfax had against him.

'Why are you opposed to me?' he pleaded. 'Why are you defaming me?'

Beerworth decided things were getting out of control. He'd had enough. He had gone to Couderts on a conciliatory note, to talk to Ezzes and Atanasio specifically. Now he was stuck in a room full of belligerent bondholders hurling abuse at him.

He angrily told Brislan that he had been brought here under false pretences. He regarded the whole meeting as offensive.

'This is totally unproductive,' he shouted above the din.

Turning to Atanasio and Ezzes, Beerworth said he would quite happily meet them at another time if they contacted him at O'Melveny & Myers. Beerworth and McAniff—who had sat silent throughout the confrontation—left hurriedly, facing a barrage of obscenities as they departed. They walked back through the windswept streets of downtown Los Angeles's business district to the attorney's office.

Beerworth was grim-faced as he began to recount the extraordinary events to the waiting team of lawyers and advisers. To his consternation his account only produced howls of laughter.

Beerworth had unwittingly walked into his first meeting with a group of bondholders.

CHAPTER ONE

BATTLING THE BONDHOLDERS

BEERWORTH WAS in Los Angeles only because he had little choice. For the past two weeks he had been trying desperately to ensure Turnbull had nothing to do with Warwick Fairfax's newspaper company.

Malcolm Turnbull is one of the most feared and, at times, most talked-about corporate advisers in Sydney. A talented barrister, he briefly seized the international spotlight in 1987 by his successful challenge of the British government in the Spycatcher publishing trial. But, like so many others during the 1980s, Turnbull branched out from a legal career into the lucrative corporate advisory business. The difference with Turnbull, though, was that he was impeccably connected. His partners were Neville Wran, former New South Wales Labor Premier, and Nicholas Whitlam, high-profile banker and son of former Australian Prime Minister Gough Whitlam. Turnbull had also been bankrolled by Australia's richest man—his long-time supporter and media giant Kerry Packer. Packer had sold his interest in the firm some time ago and Whitlam had left after a fight with Turnbull, but the association with Packer's Consolidated Press Holdings had remained close. In the tight-knit advisory business Turnbull is seen as a johnny-come-lately—someone who has muscled his way in, relying for much of his credibility on his Packer and his political connections.

Turnbull's tousled black hair and slightly overweight frame are well-known to Australians outside the business pages of newspapers.

He has a likeable, boyish face and a keen interest in politics. He once stood, unsuccessfully, for preselection as a Liberal Party candidate in a blue ribbon seat, and has taken a well-publicised stance on the drive to make Australia a republic. In fact Turnbull has maintained a high profile since his teenage years when he was a Rhodes Scholar and a journalist.

Turnbull is also well-known, however, for his abrasive personality—a minus when fostering long-term client relationships. Competitors recount with delight the stories of Turnbull breaking his computer diary in anger and his threats to sue for defamation at the slightest insult.

What competitors can't laugh about, however, is how Turnbull has captured the corporate advisory business. When in need of a tough guy, call in Turnbull. He is willing to take on the hard cases—those that run the risk of upsetting a lot of people in the ferocious fight for a client's interests.

The holders of $450 million worth of subordinated debentures—known derisively as junk bonds—in the struggling Fairfax Group needed a fighter. They no longer wished to talk to some rich, young kid who was in a perilous financial situation. They felt Warwick Fairfax had conned them into investing their cash in his company less than two years earlier in January 1989. Certainly there was nothing to lose if they appointed a maverick, someone who didn't care who he upset. So on the previous afternoon the representatives of two of the largest junk bondholders, Mark Atanasio from Drexel Burnham Lambert and Steve Ezzes from the Airlie Group, engaged Turnbull as the bondholders' financial adviser—above other major advisory firms and despite Beerworth's strong advice against Turnbull's appointment, which he predicted would see Fairfax go into receivership. They had appeared to listen to him, but had then gone ahead, completely ignoring his warnings.

Beerworth still couldn't believe the bondholders could be so stupid. He was enormously frustrated. This was becoming an increasingly familiar emotion since he had been appointed as a director of the Fairfax Group—just three months earlier in August 1990, when the Group was already in its death throes. Warwick had just sacked two directors and a third (his chief executive) resigned in protest. The company was struggling under a debt load it couldn't service. Beerworth had the near impossible task of restructuring the Group's finances and keeping it one step ahead of receivership.

This job was important to Beerworth. He had been in his own business at William J Beerworth & Partners for just over a year. Keith Halkerston was his partner but was based in London and it was very much a part-time proposition. Halkerston lent his name to the firm rather than all his efforts. Beerworth was trying to establish himself in the post-1980s environment.

Some would argue that Beerworth chose the wrong path during the 1980s, working with Wardley Australia—one of the most active investment banks of the decade, which numbered among its clients Alan Bond and Christopher Skase. Now Beerworth appeared to have done a backflip—he had left Wardleys in October 1989 and was pitching himself very much in the establishment mould. This in fact was his more natural milieu. He is a Harvard MBA who spent three years on Wall Street before joining Canberra's public service mandarins as a senior assistant secretary of the Attorney-General's department. While there he worked on new national companies' legislation. In 1976 he joined law firm Mallesons Stephen Jaques. He spent ten years there and was a senior partner specialising in mergers and acquisitions. He was considered one of the best in his field before joining Wardleys in 1986 at the age of forty. Now in 1990 the Fairfax role was Beerworth's most high-profile commission in his new firm. It was important that it was handled well, and that meant keeping the Fairfax Group out of receivership.

That was why Beerworth was in Los Angeles in late October— to spearhead a desperate re-financing effort. With him was a top-level Fairfax team. Also there as an adviser was Luis Rinaldini of Lazard Freres. This Wall Street investment bank had been retained to find a new, large foreign shareholder for Fairfax to inject much needed capital. Warwick was in Los Angeles too, preparing for his presentation to cajole and coax the bondholders into taking part in some sort of restructuring.

For Beerworth the Turnbull appointment was a major problem. A court battle with the bondholders now seemed inevitable.

Turnbull's tactic book must have litigation as a main weapon. And Turnbull's presence would lead to suspicions that the giant frame of Kerry Francis Bullmore Packer was lurking somewhere in the background. This, as far as Fairfax's advisers were concerned, would probably scare off potential new investors in Fairfax. In fact Beerworth feared that Turnbull's appointment could signal the end of the road for young Warwick Fairfax's shaky hold on the family company. Such fears were based on more than gut instinct. Beerworth had it all but confirmed the previous night when he telephoned David Craig of the ANZ Bank and Jim Featherstone of Citibank.

Fairfax's two key bankers led a syndicate owed $1.25 billion in loans. The news was important and, because of the time difference, Beerworth disturbed them at their homes. The response was unmistakable. They were deeply disappointed. Their patience with the troublesome Warwick Fairfax was almost exhausted. Since January they had sat through dozens of meetings as Warwick and his legion of advisers had worked at snail's pace toward another restructuring. Then in August Warwick had sacked his board of directors. Now Malcolm Turnbull was in on the act and any push he launched on behalf of the Fairfax bondholders could only be detrimental to Warwick's attempts to secure a cash injection.

■　■　■

That day's confrontation at Couderts had shaken Beerworth, but he knew exactly why Turnbull and the bondholders were so agitated. The last twenty-four hours had been tortuous. After being informed of Turnbull's appointment, Beerworth and the Fairfax team decided on an aggressive strategy. He and Mark Johnson drafted a letter to Couderts, pointing out that the briefing planned for the next day—a two-hour detailed rundown on the Fairfax Group's finances and performance would only proceed after the signing of confidentiality agreements.

There was also another hitch. Fairfax would not foot the bill for the bondholders' financial adviser—traditional in these circumstances when the issuer of the junk bonds is threatened with receivership and the bondholders face the prospect of only partial repayment of their funds—unless the agreements were signed. In the arcane world of corporate advice, confidentiality agreements are a key part of the weaponry. In a corporate stoush they work rather like strong rope—you can tie up your opponent with them, restricting their ability to fight back. For hours Warwick's advisers pored over the wording of the agreements, adding some tightly worded clauses directed specifically at Turnbull. The bondholders would be asked not to pass on any of the information they gleaned from the financial briefing to anyone—including Turnbull—unless there was a clause in the confidentiality agreements that specifically excluded him from giving information to others, including Kerry Packer. It was tough tactics, but if the bondholders had Turnbull, then they must know that any negotiations would now be a lot more brutal. Or so the Fairfax team reasoned.

The tactics backfired. Turnbull turned the confidentiality agreements to his own advantage. He used them as further evidence of the vindictive nature of these Fairfax people. How they were targeting him personally because they knew he would not let the bondholders down. The company didn't want the bondholders to have a strong adviser. They wanted them to be in a weak negotiating position. Turnbull was convincing. Ezzes and Atanasio agreed. If the Fairfax team wanted to play hardball, they would too. The message went back—no signed confidentiality agreements, so no financial briefing session. The game was cancelled. The Fairfax team could go home.

The Australians were stunned. What now? Luis Rinaldini and Ted McAniff were much more blasé. They had been down the junk bond buyout route several times before. They tried to console Beerworth and Johnson. Something could be worked out. This sort of disagreement was to be expected. People stood to lose hundreds of millions of dollars. Someone had to take the rap. Some of the executives of these junk bondholders had made bad career decisions in buying the bonds in the first place. They could lose their jobs. Early negotiations were always marred by bitter confrontations and, in some more colourful cases, by screaming, jostling and even pizza throwing. The bondholders, Rinaldini explained, would then resume some sort of negotiations. Sit tight; wait for them to make the next move.

For Rinaldini these negotiations were small beer. A hard-driving Argentinian, he was well-known in the USA for his role as financial adviser to the board of RJR Nabisco in the country's biggest takeover—a staggering US$25 billion. The Australians had confidence in him. Rinaldini's advice seemed vindicated when Tom Brislan telephoned back an hour later. Would Beerworth and McAniff be prepared to meet at 11 am with him, Ezzes and Atanasio?

Beerworth and McAniff had no fear of the latter two. Ezzes is young, in his mid-thirties, bright, a typical Wall Street finance executive and a reasonable negotiator. Atanasio is less stylish but a very courteous and calm operator. He inherited the daunting task of sorting out Drexel's portfolio post-Mike Milken, the junk bond king whose lending exploits fuelled the Wall Street takeover boom of the 1980s. Milken was later indicted for insider trading and imprisoned. Drexels collapsed in early 1990 and Atanasio was left sifting through the dozens of collapsed companies in which Drexels had junk bonds. His days were filled with pressured, acrimonious negotiations trying to salvage something—anything.

Drexels was the largest Fairfax bondholder. However, the other major holders included Drexel's inner sanctum of clients. The Fairfax bonds hadn't been easy to offload. Only their best clients could be cajoled into purchasing them—companies like First Executive Corporation, now in deep financial strife; the California-based Columbia Savings & Loan Association; the Airlie Group, a former partner of Drexels but now backed by Texas' wealthy Bass Brothers; and Prudential-Bache High Yield Fund Inc. Australian tycoon Robert Holmes a Court had also emerged as a bondholder, picking up a small parcel just two months before. Fairfax was due to make an interest payment of US$15 million to the junk bondholders in January 1991, but the escalating financial troubles confronting Fairfax meant it faced problems meeting the commitment.

The company knew it had to convince the bondholders that their loans had little hope of being repaid. Then Fairfax could offer them a discounted buyback, offering perhaps twenty-five cents in the dollar. But the meeting with Ezzes, Atanasio and Brislan had been a disaster—the rift between the Fairfax Group and the bondholders was larger than ever.

The row with Beerworth only reinforced Steve Ezzes' view that this new bunch of Fairfax directors and advisers were no more co-operative than the last. They didn't seem to have a grasp on reality—the company was heading for collapse: Warwick and his directors had to realise that their days of control were virtually over. Ezzes' anger about the Fairfax situation had escalated for nearly six months now. It wasn't a huge part of the Airlie Group's portfolio—just $62 million out of $2 billion of investments—but it was still a lot of money to do cold. It made him nervous.

Ezzes' handsome, yuppie image, his gentle manner and gold-rimmed spectacles disguised a fairly hardened and cynical investor. He had spent the 1980s at Goldman Sachs, New York, in the high-yield or junk bond division and then with the Airlie Group, a specialist high-yield investor. Warwick was not the first deluded potential bankrupt he had come across. He knew the type—they could not comprehend that once the company went into receivership, they were out of the picture ... forever. What worried Ezzes was that the bondholders might be out of the picture too. These assets were a long way away in a different jurisdiction with different laws. He had hired Coudert Brothers in New York and Sydney in April to look into the debenture agreement and to establish the Airlie Group's rights.

Ezzes had also been trying to get the other bondholders interested in joint action. He had only succeeded in doing that in September. And that was after his best plan had collapsed. It had died with his partner Robert Holmes a Court. Beerworth and Warwick didn't know it, but Ezzes had joined up with Holmes a Court to work out an audacious plan to solve the whole Fairfax situation two months earlier. In mid-August Ezzes spent five days in London with Holmes a Court making the final touches to a plan to seize control of Fairfax. Ezzes and his partner at Airlie Group, Dort Cameron, knew Holmes a Court socially. Dort's daughter and son attended Middlebury College, a private US university. So did Peter Holmes a Court, Robert's oldest son. At social gatherings conversation often turned to common ground— Australian business. Airlie Group had a large amount of Fairfax junk bonds and Holmes a Court loved the power and prestige of the media.

If the stockmarket crash hadn't intervened in 1987, Holmes a Court might have been one of Australia's media moguls by the time he met with Ezzes in London. He had owned the *West Australian* and had undertaken to purchase the *Australian Financial Review* and the *Times on Sunday* from Warwick Fairfax when the young media proprietor was desperately seeking to sell assets to reduce borrowings after his $2.1 billion takeover. The stockmarket crash and Holmes a Court's post-crash problems saw that deal fall through and most of his media assets divested. Now, however, Holmes a Court was ready to hit the takeover trail again. Fairfax was a jewel waiting to be plucked.

Amid the splendour of Holmes a Court's London mansion (Grove House), Ezzes and Holmes a Court plotted to gain control of around $200 million of the Fairfax junk bonds—about half the portfolio. Holmes a Court would then approach ANZ and Citibank to arrange a rational debt-for-equity swap—all of the junk bonds would be swapped for equity. Warwick and Mary Fairfax would retain some equity but control of the Group would rest with Holmes a Court and the Airlie Group. Airlie already had $62 million of bonds and Holmes a Court $8 million. They believed the remaining $130 million needed could be purchased for about $60 million, and Holmes a Court would provide the funds.

But on Saturday night, 1 September 1990, on his property outside Perth, Robert Holmes a Court died instantly from a massive heart attack. With Holmes a Court dead, a venture of this nature was too huge for Heytesbury, the Holmes a Court family company, to take on. It put Ezzes back at square one and keen to get the bondholders moving to make sure they weren't screwed down by the new batch of Fairfax directors and advisers. Ezzes' dealings with Holmes a Court made him acutely aware that the Fairfax situation was a powder keg and the bondholders could be left with nothing.

In September the bondholders began to plan the appointment of a financial adviser. It co-incided with an approach by Turnbull to Drexels. A list was drawn up and ten firms were asked for a written submission, including three from Australia—Turnbull & Partners, Bankers Trust Australia and Schroders Australia. The list was eventually culled to four who were invited to Los Angeles to make an oral presentation. To Ezzes and the others on the selection committee, Malcolm Turnbull was the clear winner and meeting him face-to-face reinforced their view. In his written submission Turnbull showed the most media experience and intimate knowledge of Fairfax from his days as adviser to the company. When it came to personal credentials, Turnbull was not bashful. His CV boasted that he was a lawyer and, following his defence of Peter Wright in the Spycatcher case, was 'probably the best known trial advocate in the British Commonwealth'.

Turnbull's submission went on to state how he and Wran were nationally known public figures with the ability to access the most influential figures in banking, government and business. He was energetic, he had a passion for the media industry, and Ezzes and Atanasio felt confident he would fulfil his commitment to give this fight everything he had. Bill Beerworth's and Warwick's violent objections only confirmed their judgement. They must be intimidated by Turnbull—he was just what the bondholders needed. This was going to be a good stoush.

CHAPTER TWO

WARWICK FACES FAILURE

IT WAS a bitterly cold November day in Toronto just ten days after the humiliating confrontation with the bondholders in Los Angeles. Warwick Fairfax sat like a shy, defenceless child as he listened to Conrad Black give a brusque and fairly brutal run-down of how Warwick had blown his $500 million family inheritance. Warwick had ruined the Group by overloading it with debt. Clearly it would go into receivership or, if Warwick was extremely lucky, the company might get new equity.

Black was the latest entrant into the ranks of international media moguls and he made no allowance for embarrassment, did not soften words to protect Warwick's feelings. Not that Warwick cared. It was too late to dent the young man's pride—it had already gone.

Bill Beerworth was with Warwick in Toronto on this final sales mission before the young media proprietor returned to Australia. It was yet another search for an equity partner—with the Los Angeles debacle still fresh in their minds. Beerworth bristled at Black's sneering speech. He wished he could come to the defence of his client. But it was they who had come to see Black and, after all, Warwick needed someone to inject new equity into Fairfax.

Beerworth looked at Warwick. He was not surprised that Warwick seemed insensitive to the barbs. He had retreated into his own perception of himself a long time before Beerworth had met him.

The Canadian finished his spiel. There was little Warwick could say. He was not the sort of person to show anger.

But if the Canadian thought his carefully chosen language was impressive, it was a jury of one. Warwick didn't care. Corporate power games were not his scene. Beerworth sensed it was time to go. Politely thanking Black for his time, he said Lazard Freres would forward the information memorandum containing financial data on Fairfax shortly. Beerworth hurried out onto the street, eyes darting as he looked for a cab to rush them to Toronto Airport to take a direct flight back to Sydney. It was a chance to catch up on some lost sleep from a hectic and emotionally draining trip.

* * *

Beerworth had known that this job would be tough, with the added burden of a difficult and idiosyncratic Warwick. Warwick is not an easy person for merchant bankers and corporate lawyers to understand. Money seems to mean very little to him. Religion is his first love—his God is the traditional one. His participation in high finance was an accident of birth. He is a Fairfax, the oldest of the three great Australian media dynasties, more recently joined by the Packers and then a brash, young Rupert Murdoch.

Warwick seems to lack the focus that dealmakers thrive on. He lived a sheltered life at Fairwater, the Harbourside home of his side of the Fairfax dynasty. His father, Sir Warwick, favoured intellectual pursuits, while Sir Warwick's younger third wife, Lady Mary, concentrated on the whirl of the establishment social scene.

Warwick became a devout Christian and shied away from the trappings of a rich, young man who one day would be a media baron. He avoided the corporate world of first-class airfares, expensive restaurants and multi-million dollar acquisitions—the normality of big business in Australia during the 1980s. Although Warwick is intelligent by any traditional analysis—he graduated from both Harvard and Oxford Universities—he intrigued the revolving door of advisers he retained because he appeared incapable of concentrating on more than one thing at a time. He couldn't prioritise. If he was tying his shoelace, that was all he could do. And he would do it meticulously. He had extraordinary tunnel vision. He could not think three-dimensionally. This was a problem Warwick was aware of and he discussed it with others, envying their peripheral vision, as he called it. Character judgement was another area where, he was prepared to concede, he had clearly failed dismally.

Warwick's is not just a household name in Australia. His is the name that in many ways encapsulates the 1980s: Australia's decade of greed. His takeover of John Fairfax topped, by a factor of five times, the highest takeover advice fee ever paid in the country—$100 million to one of the most discredited businessmen in Australia—Perth financier Laurie Connell, the driving force behind the disgraced Rothwells merchant bank.

The timing of Warwick's takeover was poor: he chose the weeks prior to the greatest stockmarket crash since 1929—October 1987—to launch the takeover for the Fairfax family empire—an empire he would have controlled without lifting a finger if he had been prepared to wait another few years—to wait his turn.

It was Warwick's fatal flaw—he simply couldn't wait. A simmering family feud; the death of Sir Warwick a few months earlier in January; and the vengefulness of his mother, Lady Mary, who felt spurned by her husband's family and ignored by arrogant company management all combined to place Warwick in a vulnerable position. Finally his own personal ambition and naivete pushed him over the precipice. He was only twenty-six when he made his $2.1 billion bid.

The Fairfax family, through its controlling share in John Fairfax & Sons, had dominated Sydney newspapers for almost 150 years. For the ten years before the takeover it had also dominated the Melbourne print media when it moved to full control of David Syme & Co., the venerable Victorian company that owned the *Age* newspaper. Fairfax had the Sydney, Melbourne and Canberra quality broadsheets—the *Sydney Morning Herald*, the *Age* and the *Canberra Times*; it had Australia's only financial daily, the *Australian Financial Review*, which it started from scratch in the 1960s; it had twenty-five per cent of the national magazine market—including *Woman's Day*, *Cosmopolitan*, *Business Review Weekly*; and also Macquarie Broadcasting, the largest radio network in the country.

Until just before the takeover, it also owned Seven Network, Australia's number two rating television network. If a prototype of the Fairfax Group had existed in the USA, in early 1987 it would have controlled the *New York Times*, the *Washington Post*, the *LA Times*, the *Wall Street Journal* and CBS.

In 1987, the year that Warwick launched his takeover of the Group, his half-brother, James, was chairman of the company. He had replaced Sir Warwick in 1976. Warwick's cousin, John, was deputy chairman. Warwick had just returned to Australia, after completing his MBA at Harvard, to be groomed to take over the helm from John. When James died, Warwick would be bequeathed most of his shareholding in the Group. His position was assured.

Warwick saw things differently, however. He could not afford to be so blasé. His sense of history tended towards the short-term perspective. He saw Fairfax Group as weak and vulnerable. He had watched the Fairfax board of directors get badly beaten in January 1987 as Rupert Murdoch swallowed up the Melbourne-based Herald & Weekly Times (HWT) group. Murdoch rose from third place in the Australian print media to control sixty per cent of the country's metropolitan and national newspaper circulation in one takeover. Then a few months later Robert Holmes a Court was rumoured to be stalking Fairfax. Warwick was concerned that the family's hold on the company of just over fifty per cent could be prised apart by a corporate raider. So with the assistance of his mother Lady Mary and family friend Martin Dougherty he decided to move first and seize control.

The October crash came in the middle of his offer and made the price he paid out to other shareholders—including his relatives—much too high. It also cut the prices expected for asset sales and killed the planned public offering of up to fifty-five per cent of David Syme.

Warwick's takeover consequently left Fairfax with an extremely high debt burden and serious problems with management. The new team he brought in when he took over the Fairfax boardroom in early December 1987—Laurie Connell and Martin Dougherty—caused major rifts with staff within a few months. Fears of editorial interference by Connell, who was unhappy with the

Fairfax's press coverage of his business affairs and those of friends like Alan Bond, unsettled staff. And there was an expectation that Connell and Dougherty would move in editors more compliant to their wishes.

These concerns culminated in the bloc resignation of some senior staff members of the *Sydney Morning Herald* after the newspaper's editor-in-chief, Chris Anderson, resigned. Journalists in Sydney went on strike, and Warwick was forced to back down. Dougherty and Connell were sacked in early 1988 and a new management team, including Anderson, was brought in. This ensured industrial peace. And thanks to a property boom and an overheated economy, Fairfax's revenue continued to improve.

But there were further problems for Warwick. Connell's departure in acrimonious circumstances and Warwick's belated misgivings about the quality of Connell's advice prompted Warwick to refuse payment of the infamous $100 million fee. The resultant legal action dragged the young proprietor into the NSW Supreme Court. Sydney business and media circles were titillated by tales of the feuds between members of the Fairfax dynasty and the influence of Lady Mary. It was public humiliation.

Dougherty's barrister George Palmer QC told the Court how Warwick had said he was the intelligent one in the family. Palmer related how Warwick, in conversations with Dougherty, had labelled his half-brother James 'ineffectual' as chairman, and claimed his cousin, John Fairfax, although a pleasant person, had no business ability. The Court was told how Warwick was resentful of the ousting of his father, Sir Warwick, from the chairmanship of the company during the 1970s, and this was a factor behind his ambitions to secure control of Fairfax. Some of the most damaging testimony came from Warwick himself, who told the Court dispassionately: 'Now I have had experience in a takeover myself, there are many risks that I appreciate that I did not then ... There is also a risk when hiring a merchant bank you will get people who focus on the minimum required to earn the fee and not on what needs to be done to make sure the takeover proceeds successfully.'

■ ■ ■

Warwick was not an active proprietor. He moved to Chicago and, although he visited frequently, he essentially left the running of the highly leveraged Group to the board and management. But within two years it all came unstuck again. Warwick felt betrayed by his board, by people he had trusted.

The 'new' board was blue chip. The chairman was Bryan Kelman, former chief executive of one of the country's largest industrial companies CSR. The directors were Bob Johnson, the former head of the Reserve Bank, and Anderson. In Warwick's eyes their act of betrayal was that they entertained a proposal to ensure the financial survival of Fairfax that would be at the expense of Warwick's and Lady Fairfax's shareholdings. This proposal came from US merchant bank Goldman Sachs. It had been retained primarily to work on strategies to secure the discounted buyback of the junk bonds. And it had come up with some horrific options for the bondholders—under one proposal an offer as low as three cents in the dollar for the senior bonds and two cents for the junior bonds was contemplated. These proposals had found their way back to bondholders such as Ezzes and Atanasio and had infuriated them.

But more damaging than the reaction of the bondholders to the Goldman proposals were the reactions of Warwick and Mary. One proposal being entertained by management particularly upset Warwick. Under this scenario Anderson and unnamed Fairfax staff would gain up to sixteen per cent of Warwick's company, while leaving Warwick and his mother with only 2.5 per cent each. Warwick was devastated. As he saw it, Anderson, the man he had trusted to be a senior executive of his company, was looking at ways to end up with more equity than him, the owner of the company.

At a loss for whom to turn to, Warwick arrived one day unannounced in the foyer of Beerworth's Sydney office. He needed help. When Beerworth's secretary told him Warwick Fairfax was outside, he thought it was a prank. It wasn't.

As Beerworth sat and listened, still amazed at the circumstances of the approach, Warwick poured out his problems, making clear the extent of his anger about the management plan. He then retained Beerworth and Halkerston to assist. By late

August 1990 Warwick had sacked the board. Beerworth and Halkerston were appointed directors and Warwick became chairman and chief executive.

* * *

The banks that had lent Warwick $2.1 billion to make his takeover had observed the events at Fairfax over the three years with increasing alarm. By November 1990 Warwick's boardroom antics, his refusal to face reality and now the threat of angry junk bondholders advised by Turnbull was hardening the resolve of the Fairfax banking syndicate against Warwick. The Fairfax loan was now definitely on the alert list, and it could not have come at a worse time for Australia's banking sector.

The onset of the recession sparked an alarming number of high-profile corporate collapses as the cavalier lending practices embraced in the 1980s were driven home. Bank executives panicked as the entrepreneurs' cash flows evaporated. The property market bubble burst as the then Federal Treasurer, Paul Keating, attempted to slow the economy by lifting interest rates. Instead of slowing it, he crippled it. Bad and doubtful loans in the banking systems shot towards $30 billion. Household names like property group Hooker Corporation, Alan Bond's Bond Corporation Group, and television mogul Christopher Skase's Qintex crashed. John Spalvins' Adelaide Steamship Company Group (controller of retailers Woolworths and David Jones) and food group Petersville Sleigh (Edgell; Four 'n' Twenty pies) imploded when share prices collapsed due to nervous foreign banks pulling credit lines. The once mighty Elders IXL Ltd, the pastoral and brewing giant led into mining and high-risk financing by Melbourne businessman John Elliott, was floundering. Elliott's grand plan to go from employee to owner backed by loans from generous bankers and a coterie of his Melbourne friends was coming badly unstuck. Citibank was in deep trouble. Apart from the Fairfax exposure, it had lent the failed Abe Goldberg about $100 million and the failed Northern Star Holdings $40 million. These were just two of the bad loans. Citibank's provision for bad and doubtful debts rose from $63 million in 1989 to $203 million in 1990. With bank executives under extreme pressure, the bumbling Warwick Fairfax was the next accident waiting to happen. The company's advertising revenues had begun to shrink, thanks to the onset of the recession, and the banks knew that Warwick would be unlikely to continue to meet the conditions or covenants on his loans until the end of the year.

It was clear that Warwick could not retain control. The numbers were so simple, even if Warwick didn't want to believe them. He owed the banks $1.25 billion. He also owed the unsecured bondholders $450 million. So if Fairfax was worth one cent less than $1.7 billion (and various advisers were placing the value at between $900 million and $1.4 billion), Warwick's seventy-five per cent shareholding and Lady Mary's twenty-five per cent were in theory worthless.

Beerworth came into Fairfax very late. His task was almost impossible. The first obstacle to overcome was the most sensitive. This was to convince Warwick and Lady Mary—who were fighting over their Fairfax shareholdings—that their scrip was worthless. There was, however, a slim chance that they could retain some shareholding. But only if they could find a new major shareholder with enough credibility to convince the banks to stave off receivership. And then for the Fairfaxes to secure any sizable shareholding, the angry bondholders needed to be persuaded to accept around twenty-five cents in the dollar for their debt.

Beerworth and Johnson were making slow progress finding a new shareholder. The lengthy information memorandum needed to be compiled. That could not be done overnight. Another problem was the Federal Government's media policy. All indications were that it was extremely unlikely that a foreigner would be permitted to own fifty per cent or more of Fairfax. Unless some major Australian company with no interests in the media suddenly decided to diversify its line of businesses, Australia's richest man, Kerry Packer, seemed the only possible option. Any invitation for Murdoch to join in a carve-up of Fairfax was cancelled by his bankers. His News Corporation newspaper, magazine and television empire was on the brink of collapse. Murdoch owed nearly $12 billion to his bankers. High interest rates and a dwindling cash flow as the world's major economies plunged into recession had him begging for mercy from his bankers.

With Turnbull on the scene, and no restructuring imminent, bank executives suddenly became worried about what Warwick might do next. As secured lenders they didn't want anything done that might further erode the value of their security. ANZ chief executive Will Bailey and his counterpart at Citibank Michael Cannon-Brookes were rapidly reaching the conclusion that they needed an outside adviser to co-ordinate the management of the deteriorating Fairfax account.

· · ·

Mark Burrows, principal of Baring Brothers Burrows, loves a good corporate dogfight. And he likes it most of all when he is at the centre of a transaction. The forty-eight-year-old adviser would qualify as a newspaper junkie too, thanks to his appetite for breaking business news and his fascination for every major corporate transaction, even when it is somebody else's client. His enthusiasm for deals can be infectious. Another member of Sydney's close-knit corporate advisory network tells the story of how he was following Burrows' Porsche down Sydney's William Street one morning. He waved to his friend in greeting. Much to his astonishment Burrows jumped out at the next red traffic light and raced back to his friend's car to share a hot piece of business news. For Burrows, Fairfax had all the elements of a deal to set his adrenalin rushing. He had kept a close eye on the company's affairs.

Sandy-haired and fair skinned, Burrows is a tall, big man who keeps fashionably fit by cycling. He is always impeccably groomed, exceedingly confident and, above all, proud. He wouldn't know how to slouch—or to take second place. He is a prodigious worker, but far from remaining closeted in his office, he maintains a high profile in community affairs as well, particularly in the arts. He is on all the right boards—he is chairman of the Sydney Theatre Company, chairman of the Foundation for the Museum of Contemporary Art and is on the board of Film Australia. He is also a member of the right clubs—the Union Club, Royal Sydney Golf Club and Royal Prince Edward Yacht Club.

A good part of Burrows' spare time, however, is devoted to corporate law reform. Burrows has clear ideas on how business should operate and was a noisy critic of the excesses of the 1980s. He, perhaps more than any other member of the private sector, threw himself into the push to transform the struggling corporate regulatory authority The National Companies and Securities Commission into a new body better equipped to regulate the corporate sector. Burrows was given the key role of chairman of the advisory committee to the Attorney-General on the establishment of the Australian Securities Commission. He is very much business establishment, proper without being stuffy and highly competitive.

For three years Burrows had watched the saga of Warwick's reign at Fairfax intently. The takeover, the Fairfax family history and the huge fees paid to a succession of advisers and bankers made this a very special situation in Australia.

But Burrows had another interest. In March 1987 Warwick asked his firm for advice on the possibility of making the takeover. Burrows and his then partner Keith Halkerston gave short and sharp advice. Don't do it. They were adamant that Warwick could not pull it off without facing enormous financial strain afterwards as he attempted to sell assets to repay borrowings. The takeover was fraught with unjustifiable risks. They were right.

When Warwick appointed Beerworth and Halkerston to the Fairfax board in August, Burrows became even more interested in the fate of Fairfax. Halkerston had been Burrows' mentor since he joined him on the establishment of Baring Brothers Halkerston in 1982.

Halkerston, eleven years Burrows' senior and a former partner of Potter Partners, was already well-established in the corporate advisory industry at that time. Burrows was a relative novice. A lawyer by training, he had worked for Baring Brothers in London and then returned to Australia and worked at Martin Corporation, a Baring associate.[1]

---

[1] Two other notables at Martin Corporation in that period were Laurie Connell and Brian Yuill. Their careers took a different tack to Burrows—they went on to head Rothwells and Spedley Securities, the two controversial finance groups which collapsed in the wake of the sharemarket crash. It gave Burrows an early insight into the sharp end of Australian business.

When Baring Brothers sold out of Martin Corporation, they formed an advisory business with the well-connected Halkerston. By joining up with Halkerston, Burrows received an entrée into the boardrooms of Australia's leading companies. He was not without his own connections. He came from an establishment Sydney stockbroking family—his father was principal of brokers E L Davis and his younger brother, Peter, was rising through the broking ranks. But the Halkerston link helped immensely. With the added kudos of the frightfully proper Baring name, Halkerston and Burrows quickly built up an impressive client list: transport group Brambles; trading and hardware group Burns Philp; white-goods manufacturer Email; Woolworths; Queensland Coal Trust; and Ashton Mining headed the list of clients. Halkerston and Burrows pitched the firm as a boutique establishment operation. They stressed the importance of long-term client relationships.

In this they stood apart from many of the hungry stockbrokers and investment bankers of the 1980s who had begun to shop around for deals with little regard to client loyalty. The fees during this period were extraordinarily lucrative. Young men and women equipped with accounting, economic and legal skills found themselves making huge salaries with large bonuses—$200 000 to $300 000 a year was *de rigueur*.

It was a tougher competitive environment for Baring Brothers, but the company maintained the establishment culture and stayed at the top of the corporate advisory tree.

The last three years had been difficult for Burrows, however. In late 1987 Halkerston suddenly quit the firm after doctors discovered he had lung cancer. Four of Burrows' key executives then defected in 1988 to Potters, which was lifting its presence in Sydney corporate advice. Then in 1989 Halkerston, in a recovery phase after cancer therapy, re-entered the corporate advice scene as a London-based partner to Bill Beerworth.

Despite all of this, the doubters in the bitchy, incestuous corporate world who said Burrows was finished without Halkerston were proved wrong. Burrows worked incredibly long hours to demonstrate that he was one of the best advisers around. The firm continued to secure lucrative corporate clients. If there was a major transaction being contemplated by either his existing clients or an establishment company, Burrows was usually on the short list for a role somewhere. He also fostered close links with the Federal Labor Government—connections which were to prove invaluable as the privatisation programme began in earnest. It was Baring Brothers that gained the prestigious advisory appointments for privatisations like the Commonwealth Bank and Qantas.

As he moved into his forties, Burrows began to collect corporate board seats—Brambles, National Roads and Motorists Association (NRMA). With Baring Brothers earning rich fee income during the 1980s, he was able to buy a country property at Bowral and in 1991 moved into Trahlee, a mansion in Bellevue Hill.

In early October 1990, as Warwick struggled to survive, Burrows began to look at the Fairfax Group's problems more intently. After all, this was going to be the biggest corporate game in town. And the recession had ensured that the high-profile, private sector transactions, and of course the large fees, were a thing of the past. Burrows discussed Fairfax's position with ANZ Bank chief executive Will Bailey and Citibank chief executive Michael Cannon-Brookes at ANZ's headquarters in Melbourne.

His pitch was blunt—the banking syndicate should consider the appointment of an outside adviser on any proposals presented by Warwick. If the banks didn't, the syndicate members would spend too long arguing among themselves. They had to be focused. Co-ordinated action was the only way to handle what could be a messy and potentially litigious process. He didn't need to remind them that the bondholders were a potential problem, or that there were rumours that Turnbull was pressing hard to represent them.

The banks were not the only parties Burrows was trying to coach on Fairfax. Coudert Brothers had asked him if he was interested in pitching for the advisory role to the junk bondholders, but he declined. And Hellman & Friedman, a San Francisco-based investment fund, had approached him to act as their adviser. He agreed, but this was short-lived. For, soon after Turnbull was appointed by the bondholders, Cannon-Brookes and Bailey told him they wanted him to be the adviser to the banking syndicate. The banks agreed to give Burrows a wide mandate.

On 9 November 1990, while Warwick and Beerworth were in New York preparing material to present to Conrad Black, it was announced in a short statement that Burrows had been appointed as adviser on any restructuring proposals put forward by Fairfax.

■　■　■

Bill Beerworth watched from his plane window as Sydney Harbour came more sharply into focus. He reflected that the next month would be critical for Warwick and his mother. The trip to the USA had been a disappointment—no deal with the junk bondholders, no new equity investor. And Mark Johnson, who had returned to Australia several days earlier, had told him by phone that the attitude of the banks was now very frosty. Dealings were suddenly and decidedly curt. Warwick Fairfax seemed to be rapidly running out of time and options.

Any doubts that the banks were now seriously contemplating receivership were dispelled the following week at a meeting with Fairfax's bankers. As Beerworth, Halkerston—who had flown in from his home in the UK—and fellow adviser, Mark Hodge, joined Johnson in the walk across town to Citibank's chrome and glass tower on the edge of Sydney's central business district on 15 November, they each knew that this meeting would be far from routine.

Instead of the familiar faces of the representatives from the banking syndicate, the four walked in to find a smiling Burrows occupying a seat in the middle of the table.

There was not a lot of good news for the Fairfax team to report. Beerworth explained how Fairfax had vigorously opposed the appointment of Turnbull as adviser to the junk bondholders and ran through the list of objections. 'His approach is high aggression,' Beerworth explained. The association with Packer, the Federal Government's response to the Ten Network situation and his litigious nature were added to Turnbull's sins. There was also still a dispute over the terms of the confidentiality agreements. 'We will only be giving the bondholders the information they are entitled to,' Beerworth added. But he was optimistic the confidentiality agreements could be worked out, allowing the bondholders only limited information.

In measured tones Beerworth then ran through the progress being made by Lazards on securing a major foreign media group to invest in Fairfax. 'We are confident they will find one. It will be some weeks before we get serious expressions of interest,' Beerworth concluded.

Burrows wasn't impressed with these hopes of a foreign white knight, since he didn't like the chances of the Federal Government allowing a single shareholder to take perhaps thirty to fifty per cent. To Burrows, Beerworth and Halkerston seemed to be curiously indifferent to this fundamental block to their plans.

'We have seen Keating [the then Australian Treasurer],' Halkerston offered. 'And the discussions were not unhelpful. Keating has some strong views about Fairfax newspapers—he thinks anything gets in the papers. If we can get him on-side, then forty per cent is possible.' Halkerston explained how, without foreign investment, the print media could end up in the hands of Murdoch and Packer.

These issues were important but were not those weighing most heavily in the minds of Beerworth and Halkerston. Before the meeting, the two had discussed how it was essential that they get some sort of indication from the banks that they would continue to support the Fairfax Group. Cash flow was dwindling at an alarming rate. There were a number of conditions of the bank loans—loan covenants—such as the ratio of earnings to interest payments which were going to be under pressure shortly. They might even be broken soon. This placed tremendous focus on directors' responsibilities. It went right to the personal positions and the personal assets of Beerworth and Halkerston. If they allowed the company to trade when it was insolvent or to make certain undertakings to the banks on the renewal of financing—undertakings they knew might not be fulfilled—they were culpable under company law. For Fairfax D-day was 10 December, when a ninety-day bank bill facility for $800 million was due to be rolled over, or renewed. If this wasn't worrying enough, there was the interest payment due to the junk bondholders in January and a loan condition, a covenant, requiring asset sales to repay $27 million.

Both men were worried that unless the banks agreed to give a letter of support or a moratorium, they wouldn't be able to legally sign for the bank bills because of the section of the Companies Code (section 556), which covers directors' responsibilities. It was a frightening prospect—risking your home and other assets for Warwick Fairfax.

Beerworth took a deep breath. 'Fairfax will require a moratorium, an accommodation or a letter of support,' he told Burrows and the bankers. Glancing around the table there was no reaction as the bankers sat stony-faced.

As the meeting wore on, it was clear that Burrows was in control, and his tone and tough line of questioning made the Fairfax advisers uneasy. A certain level of tension existed between Beerworth and Burrows. It was not just related to the Halkerston relationship. Despite their different stands, Beerworth and Burrows respected each other—to a degree. They were on opposite sides of the debate on corporate law reform: Burrows pushed strongly for a new national body; Beerworth argued to retain and improve the Federal State system. Both considered themselves to be on the intellectual end of their profession and both had extremely competitive personalities. When they met the sparks were only barely concealed. Beerworth didn't particularly enjoy being interrogated by Burrows, but in this instance he had little choice.

In front of Burrows was a foolscap piece of paper, containing a long list of questions. He had spent hours carefully working them out, each question loaded. It was not just for his own benefit—he wanted Cannon-Brookes and ANZ's Rupert Thomas and David Craig and the representatives of the other banks present to know what the critical issues were in his strategy. This way, he hoped, their perceptions of what should be done would mirror his own.

Burrows wanted the bankers to see the weaknesses in Fairfax's arguments that the company should handle its restructuring alone, and how he planned to deal with Turnbull. The banks would be the only losers if they didn't take the initiative. Why were the bankers silent, Beerworth asked himself. In the past, meetings had been cordial and constructive. Now it was clear that their attitude had changed. His fears about how the banks would react to Turnbull's appointment were being realised.

Burrows glanced at his list. There was one thing he wanted answered, now that Beerworth had raised the solvency questions.

He turned to his former partner: 'Keith, in your opinion, is Fairfax worth $1.2 billion?'

Halkerston paused. He knew exactly what his protege was trying to do. 'In my view the company is safely worth that amount if it is not in receivership—and I'd love to own it at that price. If it were in receivership, the effects could mean the value was below that figure.'

Burrows turned to Johnson. What was his view? Johnson paused. 'We haven't got any formal valuation. Macquarie Bank believes it is worth $1.26 billion-plus.'

Neither answer was what Burrows or the banks wanted to hear—the Fairfax advisers were basically admitting that the litigious bondholders' loans and Warwick's shareholding would probably be worthless unless a foreign investor paid a very high price.

As the meeting wound up they discussed management issues—the lack of a chief executive was a concern for the banks. Halkerston and Beerworth received some more worrying news when Burrows announced that from now on all dealings on Fairfax were to be conducted exclusively through his office. The shutters were coming down fast.

As the Fairfax advisers walked back through the city to Beerworth's office, they knew Warwick was in deeper trouble than they had thought. They agreed that the banks were probably already talking with their lawyers on the legalities of allowing Warwick to slide into receivership.

Beerworth had been contemplating the R word himself; he had even approached Ian Ferrier of Ferrier Hodgson & Co., Australia's most high-profile receivers, with the prospect of becoming a consultant should Fairfax go under. He kept it very quiet—the last thing he needed was a blaze of publicity that Warwick Fairfax was contemplating receivership.

Despite the bad reception there was one thing that would probably work in Warwick's favour. The banks might want him out, but they were likely to be too frightened to actually push him under. There was a risk of a bitter legal wrangle, which would also be severely damaging in terms of publicity. They would be reluctant to take that risk.

Back in his office Burrows was happy with the meeting.

Thankfully Beerworth was thinking about directors' obligations, as Burrows would expect from a top-flight former lawyer. Beerworth would be extremely reluctant to run the gauntlet of breaching the Companies Code. Forget litigation, Burrows mused. Beerworth might end up with no option but to put Fairfax under himself. This would be a good result for the banks. If they tried to push Fairfax into receivership, the company and Turnbull would certainly litigate. The whole thing could drag on for twelve months or more—in the meantime the value of Fairfax would deteriorate. Letting the Fairfax board fall on its own sword, effectively doing the banks' dirty work for them, was by far the best alternative. But would Beerworth actually do it when push came to shove?

■   ■   ■

Jeff White rubbed the dirt off his hands as he walked from the garden into the kitchen of his Roseville home on Sydney's leafy and tranquil North Shore. White looks more like a scholar than an investment banker. His horn-rimmed glasses and thoughtful demeanour seem at odds with the tough world of takeovers in which he works. But he thrives on it, and joining Baring Brothers recently meant he was right at the centre of the action. He picked up the telephone, wondering who had disturbed his Saturday afternoon break from a hectic week assisting Burrows in seemingly endless meetings on the Fairfax saga.

'Jeff, it's Warwick Fairfax here. Why are you trying to put my company into receivership?'

White was shocked. What the hell was Warwick Fairfax doing ringing him and asking that question?

'Well, why are you doing it?'

Struggling for words, White stuttered: 'What are you talking about? And anyway,' he continued indignantly, 'this is most improper ringing up like this.'

There was a short pause before Warwick began laughing. 'Ha! Tricked you. It's Malcolm Turnbull here. What's happening?'

Since his appointment to represent the bondholders, Turnbull had become increasingly frustrated about the attitudes of Fairfax, the banks and Burrows. Fairfax's advisers were still shutting Turnbull out, deciding it was best if he was made the equivalent of a bee buzzing around in a bottle. The row over the confidentiality agreements continued and didn't look like being resolved for some time. Both sides were playing it tough—Ezzes was still angry that Fairfax could seriously believe it had any say in who advised the bondholders. Couderts had fired off a tough letter to the Fairfax lawyers stating that the bondholders would not fire Turnbull and would not sign confidentiality agreements that stopped them passing on information to their financial adviser.

As December approached, drafts of the confidentiality agreements still sat in an open file in Beerworth's office. One was for the bondholders to execute; another was for Turnbull. Burrows adopted the same approach as Beerworth and avoided contact with Turnbull. He delegated Jeff White to stonewall Turnbull, a task he didn't relish. Burrows simply refused to take the calls. He could see no point in it commercially, nor did he favour the idea of meeting someone he didn't have much time for. Turnbull's efforts to discover from the banks what was going on were proving fruitless. Although bank executives in telephone conversations with Neville Wran stated they were happy with the bondholders' appointment of Turnbull, their actions now indicated they were being polite to the influential former New South Wales Premier. They were ignoring Turnbull. Burrows had stepped in to avoid any schisms developing between the banks in the syndicate. Apart from ANZ and Citibank, the syndicate comprised the State Bank of NSW, Bank of Tasmania and State Bank of Victoria. This left Turnbull relying on rumour and endless telephone conversations to learn what the banks or Fairfax might do. There was also the stand-off with Beerworth and Fairfax management.

Faced with this wall of opposition Turnbull's only tangible progress was the plot for legal action against the banks on the bondholders' behalf. It was a bargaining tactic revolving around the claim that the bondholders were misled in their decision to invest in Fairfax. The litigation was designed to force Fairfax to deal with his clients.

* * *

The banks and Turnbull were only two of the pressing problems Beerworth and Johnson were facing as the days wore on. There were two people still requiring delicate personal skills—Warwick and Lady Mary. For weeks Beerworth and Johnson had been gently trying to convince Warwick that he was in deep trouble. They warned him there was absolutely no chance of him maintaining 100 per cent of Fairfax. In endless meetings and telephone calls as they brought Warwick up to date on events, they tried to make him understand that if he retained over twenty per cent, he would be very lucky.

Warwick still needed to be handled very carefully, however. Rinaldini from Lazards brought the bluntness of Wall Street to Warwick one Saturday afternoon soon after Beerworth became involved. He told Warwick that the prospect of retaining any— not just a diluted—shareholding in Fairfax was potentially at serious risk. Warwick suddenly went silent and then excused himself from the meeting at the first opportunity.

The next day Warwick refused to take telephone calls at his modest bungalow in Chatswood where he lived with friends, his red Toyota Camry sitting in the driveway. His wife, Gale, spent the day fending off calls from Beerworth, while her husband sulked for a few days. Beerworth and Johnson had come to recognise these defensive reactions. They could almost see the mood descending—like shutters closing over his eyes.

Finally on the eve of the company's 150th anniversary, Warwick appeared to have become more philosophical about losing his family's control of Fairfax. Not so Lady Mary and her legion of lawyers and advisers. For over eighteen months she had been arguing with Warwick over her investment in Fairfax. Apart from her twenty-five per cent shareholding, Lady Mary was also receiving an inflation-indexed $3 million a year annuity. Despite her protestations about her love for her son, she was fighting hard for her rights, prompting complex manoeuvres in a group of family trusts. As Warwick's problems escalated, Lady Mary still pursued her own agenda. She wasn't keen on the idea of a serious dilution of her equity, and the lack of information about where mother and son stood with each other exasperated the banks.

As November 1990 wore on, the banks were becoming increasingly agitated over Fairfax, and Burrows was quickly realising that the uncertainty about the whole Fairfax saga—Warwick fighting with Lady Mary, and Fairfax fighting with the bondholders—should be resolved. The whole matter could easily develop into a shambles, or worse still, litigation.

Before any precipitous action was taken, however, the banks wanted to make sure that Warwick and Lady Mary understood the gravity of the situation. This meant a personal confrontation. The days of dealing only with intermediaries were gone. The bankers wanted to hear Warwick's and Lady Mary's plans for the company from their own mouths.

CHAPTER THREE

THE END OF A DYNASTY

THE ROLLS Royce glided to a halt in Kent Street outside Citibank on a warm Friday afternoon. It was the last day in November 1990. Lady Mary walked through the revolving door and was guided by a security guard to a desk where she was issued with a security pass. She took the elevator to the eleventh floor and was escorted into the conference room where Warwick and Beerworth mingled with representatives of the major lenders. The Citibank contingent was large—Gerry Van der Merwe, Jim Featherstone, Mary Reemst and Ken Cambie. ANZ's David Craig, Peter Meers and Rupert Thomas were also there for this critical gathering.

This wasn't just another question-and-answer session; it was the make-or-break meeting for Warwick Fairfax. Burrows had spent several hours preparing his list of questions. It was critical that he draw Warwick and Lady Mary out, get them to tell the bankers in their own words where they stood, how they planned to deal with their financial problems and even how they viewed them. It was only when the bankers saw the situation from the same perspective as Burrows that they would be likely to act confidently on his advice.

Sitting down opposite Warwick, Lady Mary and her lawyer Jim Momson of Minter Ellison, Burrows pulled out the list of questions from his briefcase. If Beerworth and Johnson didn't have some sensationally positive news, he was certain Fairfax would be in receivership by Christmas. Burrows peered over his reading glasses sitting on the end of his nose. His jaw set, he was in no mood for pleasantries.

'This meeting is crucial in the answers you give,' Burrows said bluntly as he opened the proceedings. 'The banks are very worried and are considering all their rights. I don't want any of you to have false hopes. They have no intention of giving a moratorium and they have no intention of giving a letter of comfort. They reserve their position and they want no doubt as to the seriousness of the matter. The banks want direct answers on a number of matters.'

Beerworth was disconcerted by this abrupt manner. He gritted his teeth, however, as he realised he was in for some fierce cross-examining.

Permitted to give an update, Beerworth related how Lazard Freres was confident about finding a new shareholder. 'Rinaldini says there is one group that is very serious and he believes it will lead to an offer,' he began confidently. He mentioned Pearsons PLC, the UK group, adding that it would eventually want to acquire the *Australian Financial Review* if earnings forecasts were not met. 'Rinaldini also advised me that he is talking to Associated Newspapers and Conrad Black,' he added.

When Beerworth mentioned Associated, Burrows raised his eyebrows. The UK group was a client of his firm, and Lord Rothermere had told Burrows that the group wasn't interested.

Burrows returned to his central goal. 'Bill, what do you think Fairfax is worth?' The same old question Halkerston had to fend off two weeks earlier.

'Lazards is confident there is a seventy per cent chance that the value is between $1.4 billion and $1.6 billion,' Beerworth replied.

This was all very well, but whether the Federal Government would allow a foreigner a large holding was another matter and Burrows didn't hide his scepticism.

Beerworth explained that Keating had indicated that twenty per cent would be allowed for certain contenders, and that suggested flexibility. The Treasurer also noted that there was a difference between a Maxwell and a Pearsons, which seemed to suggest that the foreign component could depend on who the foreigner was and how well respected the applicant was in international circles. So forty per cent in an application was possible.

'Forty per cent seems high, Bill,' Burrows said quickly. Interrupting, Beerworth reiterated what Halkerston had explained at the previous meeting—Keating told them any decision would be political and he wanted to know before anything was agreed.

Burrows was sceptical about Lazard's search for a foreign saviour. And if there were no foreign investors, where did this leave Fairfax? The only hope for a cash injection was then an industrial company that wanted to diversify into media ... or Packer or Murdoch.

Just when the foreign equity might eventuate was another worry for the banks, even aside from the political hurdles. Beerworth told how Lazards believed there would be expressions of interest by Monday, 10 December, or by Christmas at the latest.

What was happening with the bondholders was also raised. Beerworth was able to say that the bondholders were now close to signing the confidentiality agreements, and that he expected three-way talks—the shareholders, banks and bondholders could begin in January.

Throughout the meeting Lady Mary and Warwick sat quietly. Now it was their turn for interrogation.

'Warwick, have you reached any agreement with your mother? Are you going to be comfortable with a dilution of your equity?' Burrows asked.

Leaning forward, Warwick nodded. 'We both realise the company has a lot of problems. We don't quite know what shareholding we will be left with, and what I want to do is find something that is fair for all of us. I want the company to survive, and we need something to be done.'

Pointing his biro at Lady Fairfax, Burrows asked for her feelings. 'We need to be realistic and I'm happy that Lazards thinks something can be done—it wouldn't be going to all this trouble if it were not confident. I am aware that we both will have a lower shareholding. It would be good for the company though I think if some Fairfaxes still had a shareholding.'

A more specific answer was wanted and Burrows tried again. 'Look, have you reached a position on how you will divide any remaining equity?'

Warwick blinked: 'Well, not exactly. We wouldn't want to hold up a re-financing, of course.'

Beerworth quickly tried to elaborate, saying he was confident the two shareholders would not stop any restructuring.

Yes, Burrows went on, but if they are fighting over some family trusts, how could they possibly focus on the big picture?

Lady Mary's lawyer Momson spoke up. 'The Oriolo Trust has other people involved in it. Anyway, the shareholding issue doesn't come up until there is a proposal and the issue of what is left is outside the banks' security—the question is irrelevant.'

Burrows was cynical. Trying to show a united stand on share-holdings now was all very well, but hadn't Warwick sacked his board over the Goldman Sachs plans that would have left them with perhaps five per cent of the company?

'No, it wasn't just if the five per cent was fair,' Warwick replied to Burrows. 'Both of you banks weren't keen because you didn't think the plans for a low tender offer for the bonds had much chance of success. And the plans meant receivership if the plan didn't work. I don't care about my shareholding percentage if the process to reach it is fair and reasonable.'

Pursuing the line of argument, Burrows asked Warwick what Fairfax was worth. Warwick dodged the question, saying the value would be determined by a new shareholder. However, Lady Mary now wanted her say. 'Something is only worth what people pay for it and they are striking a bad time in Australia,' she said in a classic understatement. 'The sharks are circling and I can understand the banks wanting to protect their position.'

The meeting was going badly, and Beerworth knew it. There was little he could do. Every question was framed to force them to admit a restructuring was impossible.

Turning to loan convenants, Burrows raised the critical issue— the solvency of Fairfax in the next few weeks. Burrows knew from the last meeting that Beerworth was worried about his respon-sibilities as a director under section 556 and he wanted to find out where Beerworth and Warwick stood. If Fairfax was going to go under, it was still preferable that the board did it themselves.

Beerworth explained he needed an indication from the banks that funds would be available. 'There may be a breach of cov-enant today. There is a distinct possibility, but we won't know for a few weeks. We will not wait until the last minute to tell you and we are not going to fight you. If we believe there is an event of default and there is no letter of comfort, we will be in difficulty under section 556. If I have to make a declaration under section 556, I need to give notice to the directors of subsidiaries and I feel I have until next Friday.'

Burrows wanted Warwick's reaction to his fellow directors' willingness to put Fairfax under to protect themselves under section 556. Turning to Warwick, Burrows said pointedly: 'I suppose if Bill refused to sign the roll-over, on your track record you would sack him.'

Warwick didn't look Burrows in the eye, focusing on the papers in front of Burrows. 'No, I wouldn't. I respect Bill's views on that. I do not do anything capriciously. I have confidence in Bill's, Keith's and Macquarie Bank's opinions. If they say there is a problem, I can't see myself going against that view.'

The answer hit Burrows like a bullet. It was the one he had been waiting for! Beerworth would be cornered; he would be forced to put the company into liquidation if the banks refused to roll over the bank bill financing in December. Warwick said he wouldn't sack him. The significance of the answer had not yet gelled with the other participants. Beerworth looked around the room, the stiff body language of the bankers who had sat silent for most of the meeting said it all as Burrows pressed him on the roll-over.

Clearly, Beerworth responded, there were problems. He elaborated on the importance of finding an equity investor. The other alternative was simple—if the banks agreed to give Fairfax a fourteen-day roll-over, he might be able to sign off on the roll-over if Lazards had found an investor. There would be a problem, though, on a ninety-day roll-over: 'You banks will probably have the opportunity to put in a receiver before we find a foreign investor,' Beerworth said. 'If the bondholders waive their interest payment, there probably will be no default until the asset sales convenant. We have a realistic time frame to find an investor.'

Lady Mary cut in, speaking about the bondholders. 'I have talked to John Shad at Drexels for some help, and they have $101 million of the bonds. I think that if fifty-one per cent support our plans, then we can all breathe a sigh of relief.'

It was a brave statement, and it was heartening that Lady Mary was moving into the front trenches and putting her skills toward sorting everything out. The bankers present and Burrows were not, unfortunately, convinced that Lady Mary could triumph.

'I must admit that I am sceptical about the ability of any proposals on a restructuring,' Burrows said, fixing a steely look at Warwick, who again avoided eye contact. 'I have a high regard for Bill, Keith and Macquarie. However, the task of bringing in foreign equity and an accommodation with the bondholders seems too hard. This is only my opinion; I haven't spoken with the banks and they might not share my scepticism.

'Your answers here today were important—it is important for the banks to know what is happening since they have to make a judgement. However, the bank's have been in the dark about the plans and have seen boards come and go.'

Having listened to Burrows interrogation intently, the bankers were even more sceptical than Burrows. For twelve months they had watched Warwick dither. They might have been silly to lend so much money in the first place to Warwick—the only consolation was that they had the power to foreclose on him.

Any hopes Beerworth might have had that Burrows was speaking with no authority were shattered immediately. Van der Merwe had heard enough and he clearly didn't like it. 'Citibank is sceptical—the company has been working on a restructuring all year and it doesn't appear to be any further advanced than in January. The loss of King and Anderson worries us. We are worried about the erosion of value.' His next comments, said with such feeling, left Beerworth stunned. 'There will not be any change to our position. There is no moratorium and no letter of support. There will be no concessions.'

Some of the other bankers winced—these were stronger and more definite words than they would have used. No one wanted to give Beerworth and the Fairfax lawyers any fuel for litigation.

'Is that your final position?' Beerworth retorted. 'If it is, then we might as well make an application [for a provisional liquidator] right now.'

Van der Merwe replied, toning down his comments to the relief of the other bankers: 'Look, there will not be any concessions within the constraints of the legal position, the structure and the documents. We will not do anything to detract from the value of the company but we are not going to make concessions on our legal position.'

David Craig of ANZ chimed in to put the position of the largest lender: 'If you can't show progress on the restructuring, it is difficult to give you a letter of support,' he said frankly. 'The banks don't want to inhibit discussions. On the other hand, if there is no demonstrable progress on a new shareholder, then we can't consider a request for support.'

They are being so unreasonable, Beerworth thought. 'I can't produce an investor in a week ... and you should all consider that very carefully,' he warned.

'And what about Turnbull?' Burrows asked. 'You are seeing him next week.'

'I don't think he can add much,' Beerworth shot back.

'Well, I hear he has a plan,' Burrows retorted, barely concealing his wicked delight now he knew Beerworth would finally need to deal with Turnbull.

Walking back across town, the peak-hour commuter rush to Wynyard station escalating, Beerworth was acutely aware that the meeting had not gone well. He hadn't expected such an onslaught, so many detailed demands for immediate answers. And Van der Merwe's cutting statements chilled Beerworth. It was one minute to midnight and the banks had their fingers on the large hand.

. . .

Contacting Johnson that Friday evening, Beerworth ran through what had happened. The banks were being unreasonable. They were told back on 15 November that it could take as long as January to find out who the new investors might be. Now they were indicating strongly they wouldn't wait.

Johnson and Beerworth agreed they had to strike some sort of deal with Turnbull quickly, unpalatable as that was, if there was to be any chance of Warwick surviving. Turnbull had been breathing fire about screwing everybody, but Beerworth knew that Turnbull's only chance was to deal also, or his clients as unsecured lenders would probably lose most of their $450 million.

The previous evening shortly after 9 pm, Beerworth had called Turnbull and explained how the loan covenants were becoming a major concern. He raised the issue of the bondholders granting a waiver on the January interest payment.

Turnbull was not interested. As far as he was concerned, this couldn't be considered until financial information was handed over and Fairfax agreed to come to some arrangement on the bondholders' fees. Remaining defiant, Turnbull added he wasn't inclined to recommend any waiver unless the banks agreed not to exercise their rights to appoint a receiver for a defined period. Despite Beerworth's warning that time was running out, Turnbull was in no mood to be sympathetic. To suddenly be told the banks were restless and receive a request for urgent assistance, after being ignored for weeks, was mystifying. Still, Turnbull was prepared to talk and suggested some triparte talks including Burrows. But Beerworth didn't think this was warranted, since he didn't know what the banks planned to do.

Now, however, the events of the last few hours had changed everything. Beerworth was back on the telephone to Turnbull, knowing that an uneasy alliance must be forged urgently.

Beerworth might have been opening up, but Turnbull still wasn't getting very far with his efforts to talk to Burrows. His latest letter from Baring Brothers, received on Monday morning, 3 December, was another knockback. In it Jeff White informed Turnbull that there was no point meeting until something was worked out on the bondholder interest rate payment. How could Turnbull expect to come to the negotiating table if he couldn't even get his clients to agree on waiving the interest payment? The punch line in the letter was that Baring Brothers would contact him the following week. It might be too late by then.

Since Turnbull was now talking to Beerworth and Johnson, he replied to Burrows that the bondholders were now prepared to discuss a waiver. He was also putting the finishing touches on his proposal to the banks for salvaging the situation—and leave his clients in control of Fairfax under his guidance.

To Turnbull, one thing was clear—Warwick and Lady Mary would never end up with much. After all, their shareholding ranked behind his clients'. They really deserved nothing. Anything that they got would be a bonus.

With his proposal coming together, Turnbull headed off for a meeting to put the heat on Lady Mary and Warwick. Turnbull sat down opposite Lady Mary's advisers Momson and Gerry Gleeson, the former head of the New South Wales Premiers Department under Wran. Turnbull's message by now was simple and blunt. The shareholders must get together with the bondholders and strike a deal—otherwise the banks would be tempted to take the uncertainty out of the process by appointing a receiver.

■ ■ ■

Late in the afternoon Burrows received a telephone call from Rinaldini in New York to update him on the progress of the foreign investor hunt. His broad assertions that everything was going well amused Burrows. 'Now, Luis, do you really think Fairfax is worth over $1.6 billion?'

The Argentinian went silent before admitting his own doubts. 'Maybe not. I would be very disappointed if it wasn't worth $1.4 billion.'

It was still confident feedback, and Burrows remained unconvinced that the lower valuation wasn't actually at the top end of the range.

■ ■ ■

Steve Ezzes was really finding out what the word frustration meant. Nothing was happening anywhere and cracks were starting to appear among the bondholders' group. Since the Los Angeles meetings at the end of October, two more of the bondholders—Far West and Columbia Savings & Loan Association —had been taken over by the US Government (the Resolution Trust Corporation [RTC]). The meetings to decide on legal action had been appalling. The RTC lawyers thought the whole Fairfax situation was a doddle. What seemed to really interest them was getting the dirt on Drexels for other legal actions they had underway. And what an opportunity! A thorough legal discovery process would turn up reams of valuable documents. The agonising debate centred around whether Drexels should be in a separate action from the rest of the bondholders or whether the RTC lawyers should be terminated. The latter course was taken

—the lawyers were replaced and it all started again.

The vibes Ezzes was getting from Turnbull did not augur well either. Turnbull's latest fax on Tuesday outlined his version of a conversation with Burrows, who told him that Beerworth would put Fairfax into receivership to 'save his house, car and boat' if the banks didn't waive covenants. He noted that Burrows said he was sceptical about Lazard's strategy.

From Turnbull's fax and conversations Ezzes knew that the banks were freezing out the bondholders also. Ezzes and the Drexel team (Atanasio in Los Angeles and Doug McClure in New York) decided to take some action themselves. A Drexel partner Fred Zuckerman arranged a meeting with Steve Gerard, the head of credit at Citibank in New York. They would go to the top and see if they could get some sense out of somebody who mattered. Gerard was pleasant and fully abreast of the Fairfax situation—it was a huge problem loan for them. He would look into the situation further—but at this stage he was comfortable with the way it was being handled. The bank was nervous about Warwick continuing as chief executive of the company. The pressure kept coming through from Beerworth to waive the January interest payment for the bondholders. Ezzes managed to convince the others to sign waiver sheets, just in case, and then hopped on a plane to Australia. He could not stand the frustration any more. He had never been to Australia and it was time he found out what it was like. His company had $62 million invested there in a dud company.

∎　∎　∎

By Wednesday, 5 December, Beerworth had become exasperated. He knew his request for a fourteen-day roll-over was being ignored. His letters seeking an urgent response got nowhere. He faxed them, he had them couriered to ANZ and Citibank; he tried everything. He was getting tired of bankers' secretaries stonewalling him, refusing to put his calls through. It was humiliating, leaving message after message. His last request was for an answer on the roll-over by midday Friday, moved from Thursday morning. What was even more galling was the need to start preparing to place Fairfax into liquidation. If Beerworth had no option, it was a legal and accounting nightmare. Documents were now being prepared to put every company in the Group into liquidation. The banks had not agreed to a request that just one company be symbolically placed in liquidation. Hundreds of companies, obscure subsidiaries stretching from Warrnambool in Victoria to Newcastle in New South Wales, would have to be put through the legal process. There were thousands of pages of documentation, enough to keep a team of lawyers busy for days and nights. By the time Beerworth dragged himself home late in the evening, the costly preparations were well underway.

The next morning Johnson and Beerworth continued discussions with Turnbull over his proposals for Fairfax. If something was worked out, Turnbull agreed the interest payment waivers would come through. It all sounded good in theory.

Beerworth, however, was still concentrating on the more important solvency issue. There still wasn't any answer from the banks. Sitting in his office, he dictated yet another letter to Burrows, sending copies to the senior bankers. He must know the intentions of the banks before Monday morning—it was just too late to do anything then. He was also worried about any debt incurred on the weekend; Fairfax was a twenty-four-hour-a-day operation and debts might be incurred in breach of section 556.

. . .

While Beerworth steamed, Burrows knew the end play was fast approaching. On Thursday morning he finally met with Turnbull—getting an audience with Burrows was harder than one with the Pope. Burrows curtly replied to Turnbull's questions, his face stony. If only Turnbull knew what was going on; if only he knew the way everything was moving.

'My clients would be crazy to unilaterally waive their interest payment,' Turnbull exclaimed as he pushed the need for the Fairfaxes to come to the negotiating table. There was another way, he continued, outlining in broad terms a plan that wouldn't require fresh cash from a new investor. He explained he had been working on a plan for the banks to convert perhaps $300 million or one-quarter of their debt into redeemable notes. The bondholders could convert half of their bonds to redeemable convertible notes, which ranked behind the bank's notes. They would then convert the rest of their debt into a shareholding. A token amount would be given to the Fairfaxes. A serious cost-cutting programme would then begin to lift the media group's profits.

'Sounds interesting, Malcolm,' Burrows responded. 'Go and work something out and then get back to us.'

Turnbull had been dismissed.

■　■　■

On Friday morning, 7 December, Beerworth telephoned Burrows again to find out what the banks planned to do. This time he actually got through. It was crucial, he said, that he know what the banks were considering because of the 12 noon deadline he had set in view of the directors' duties problem.

'Bill, could you extend the deadline till 2 pm?' Burrows asked. Beerworth agreed in good faith. Unfortunately it was just another stalling tactic. When Burrows replaced the telephone handset, he left to walk across town to the banks' legal firm, Mallesons Stephen Jaques. Everything was going according to plan, as long as the banks and their lawyers didn't lose their nerve. It had to be done properly. A team of lawyers was poring over the boxes of loan documents, looking for every possible loophole or potentially litigious covenant. The banks needed to be confident that they would be covered if the Fairfax board didn't collectively fall on its own sword and place the group in voluntary liquidation.

If Beerworth had known why Burrows was going to Mallesons, he would have had a very good indication of just how far down the track the banks were. Burrows was there to interview potential receivers for the Fairfax Group. It was a tedious three-hour process. Some interviews were very short—the firms were ruled out because of potential conflicts of interest. In the end the firm Deloitte Ross Tomahtsu appeared to be the best candidate. Partner Des Nicholl was their nominee.

By Friday evening Beerworth was under extreme pressure: his 2 pm deadline had come and gone. Fairfax's lawyers from Free- hills were still pushing Mallesons, the bank's lawyers, for answers. But the banks were ducking and weaving, conceding nothing and limiting the options for Beerworth with the roll-over now due on Monday morning at 11 am.

Beerworth telephoned Warwick and told him that things looked bad. He couldn't possibly sign the roll-over on Monday unless a moratorium or letter of support was received. The only positive development had been that Turnbull had secured the support of the bondholders for a waiver of the interest payment. Steve Ezzes was on his way to Australia and the waiver documentation was coming by fax. Negotiations would continue the next morning for the bondholders to swap a portion of their debt for equity in Fairfax.

But for the key bankers and Burrows, there wasn't going to be a next week for Warwick Fairfax and the bondholders.

●　●　●

Sydney's central business district is almost deserted on Saturdays. But on this particular Saturday morning there was a string of taxis delivering casually dressed bankers to the skyscraper at 50 Bridge Street—the headquarters of Mallesons Stephen Jaques. The Fairfax bankers were sacrificing their weekend social engagements to meet with their lawyers. It was an attempt to convince themselves that a decision to allow Fairfax to slide into receivership was fail-safe.

While they deliberated with the lawyers, Turnbull was in his office, one block away next to the Sheraton Wentworth Hotel, finalising his proposal. As far as Turnbull was concerned, it would be a gift if Warwick and his mother ended up with even five or ten per cent of Fairfax. The bondholders really owned Fairfax now and this had to be made clear to Burrows. The bondholders ranked second in line after the banks, and it was the way all negotiations in the next few days must proceed.

The banks were also going to have to be realistic. Under Turnbull's plan, the banks would be required to convert about $300 million of their loans into A Class, fourteen per cent redeemable notes, leaving $900 million of debt with interest at the rate of thirteen per cent a year. This meant that interest on one-quarter of their loans would be suspended—delayed until the notes matured. His clients' total claims were assessed at $A555 million, and they would convert $200 million into B class, twelve per cent redeemable convertible notes (these had the same effect as the bankers' notes, but the interest rate was two per cent less, and the notes could be converted into shares). The balance of $355 million would be converted immediately into a controlling shareholding in Fairfax. As for Warwick and Lady Mary, they would be given a shareholding worth $20.9 million—a mere 2.5 per cent.

With the financial structure in place, Turnbull intended to head down to the Herald Building on Broadway and give Fairfax a shake-up. The company would need a chief executive, and he had a candidate in mind to impose on the banks: Trevor Kennedy, the chief executive of Kerry Packer's Consolidated Press. For weeks Turnbull and Kennedy had discussed this option. Kennedy had been looking for a way out from under the thumb of Australia's richest man, and the prospect of running Fairfax appealed to him. In fact he had rung Mark Burrows in November, the day after he had been appointed by the banks. Kennedy was overseas at the time, but he wanted Burrows to know that he had a special interest in Fairfax.

With Kennedy in charge, a savage cost-cutting exercise would be started. Under one cost-saving scenario salaries and wages would be cut by fifteen per cent over the first two years. Under a second scenario cuts of up to twenty per cent were achievable in all areas except newsprint. It was tough stuff. With Fairfax shaved to the bone, Turnbull and Kennedy would then oversee the devotion of the bulk of the company's cash flow to repaying the A class notes. Under Kennedy's strict cost-cutting plan, the $300 million in notes would be repaid to the banks by the 1993–94 financial year.

When Beerworth and Johnson first met with Turnbull and saw the plan, they were staggered by its stringency. There was no time to worry about it too much, however. Turnbull was posturing; it was only an ambit claim and the basis for starting negotiations, they reasoned. A better plan could be worked out later, giving Warwick and Lady Mary a higher shareholding. But this could only be done if the roll-over went ahead on at least a fourteen-day basis.

Their confidence was mistaken. What Beerworth and Johnson didn't count on was the way Turnbull would present the plan to Burrows. He would make the fatal mistake of contradicting Beerworth's and Johnson's views. This would convince Burrows that the shareholders and the junk bondholders were not of one mind. The Turnbull plan could not be relied upon.

Turnbull ran through the basis of his plan early on Sunday morning to Burrows and Jeff White, with a jet-lagged Steve Ezzes listening intently. 'Lazards and Beerworth haven't convinced Lady Mary and Warwick yet,' Turnbull opined. 'You should give Beerworth two weeks on the basis that the bondholders and the shareholders agree in that period. If they don't back the deal, the banks and my clients should then work together.'

Burrows thought to himself, so much for a unity of purpose between shareholders and bondholders. Turnbull would cut them out at the first chance he had!

'Just give them a fourteen-day period of grace,' Turnbull continued. 'The waivers will only be given if there is a two-week extension and they are committed to the deal.'

There was a knock on the door and Mark Johnson came into the room to join the meeting. His view—that there was a broad basis for an agreement with the bondholders—was at odds with the comments that Turnbull had just made.

There were just too many imponderables for Burrows. There was no agreement on the level of equity for Warwick and Lady Mary, no feeling for how the Federal Government would take to a bunch of US junk bondholders ending up in control of Fairfax, and no detailed management plans. The more Turnbull and Johnson talked, the more Burrows decided they were running around in circles.

When Turnbull and Ezzes left, Johnson had some grim news. He explained that the chances of foreign equity had been reduced after Beerworth had spoken to Rinaldini the previous evening. With Turnbull gone, Burrows vented his misgivings about Turnbull's plan. 'Turnbull looks like he wants to run Fairfax,' he said. 'The banks won't participate in an unstable structure. Turnbull's schemes on a structure for the bondholders' foreign equity will get nowhere with the Government.'

Before Johnson departed, Burrows told him that he must convince Turnbull and the bondholders that they couldn't run Fairfax.

Mark Johnson's style is deliberate and calm. Although at fifty he is only a few years older than Beerworth and Burrows, his demeanour is one of the wise owl in comparison to the competitive youngsters. His career in Australian finance has been a roller-coaster ride—he has known the elation of seemingly endless success and the pain of failure. He was joint managing director of Hill Samuel Australia—one of Australia's most outstandingly successful merchant banks in the 1970s (later to become Macquarie Bank in the early 1980s). Johnson moved on from Hill Samuel Australia to the bank's head office in London and was later headhunted back to Australia to become managing director of the Australian Bank—Australia's first new trading bank in decades. As it tried to claw market share from the established banking cartel, the new bank faltered on a few adventurous loans. Johnson resigned and rejoined Macquarie Bank in corporate advice, no longer head honcho. Nevertheless he is considered one of the true seniors of the corporate advisory network. And he knows Fairfax intimately.

* * *

As Johnson trudged up Bridge Street towards Mallesons' office early that Sunday evening on 9 December, he knew that this was just about it. Tired, he had lost the spring in his step. Lazards had no saviour and the banks were unyielding on the options put to them. This would be the final plea for leniency—for just a few days to go through the Turnbull proposal again. He had discovered only minutes before from Burrows' office that the banks' representatives were meeting again. So he had asked for one final chance to argue his case for a roll-over—just one more hour to take them through Warwick's case again. A little more time and perhaps it could all be salvaged.

As he walked into the conference room, Johnson was confronted with nearly two dozen men sitting at a table. It was an odd sight—all of these bankers and lawyers dressed in casual clothes. Johnson sat down, conscious that he didn't have his corporate armour on either. There was silence as Burrows asked him what he wanted. Johnson glanced around—he felt he was in the dock. And as he realised exactly who was in the room, he knew this was serious.

When Johnson left at about 8 pm the discussions continued.

Each of the bankers had been shown the Turnbull plan. One broke the mood when he threw his copy on the table with a thump. The Turnbull option wasn't palatable. The bankers were being asked to take a haircut on their loans by a group of bondholders who ranked behind them—the bondholders were nothing more than unsecured creditors. Turnbull's plan would mean that the banks' outstanding loans would effectively be transferred from the Fairfaxes to the new shareholders—the junk bondholders, the banks themselves and Warwick and Lady Mary being left with a token few per cent.

By 10 pm it was all resolved. The banks agreed to take the tactical route of forcing the board to place the company in liquidation. The bills would not be rolled over for fourteen days; only a ninety-day option would be available. Mallesons immediately contacted Freehills and delivered the verdict.

●　　●　　●

Steve Ezzes had enjoyed a pleasant Sunday night at Malcolm Turnbull's $2 million home in Paddington. Ezzes and Turnbull agreed over dinner that the day had gone well. They weren't through the worst of it yet, but at least the banks must decide to give them more time. Ezzes was looking forward to a long-delayed sleep as he walked to the door of his hotel room. His first day in Australia had been exhausting. As he got closer to the door, he realised the telephone was ringing.

'It's Malcolm, Steve. The banks have refused the fourteen-day roll-over.'

●　　●　　●

Beerworth replaced the phone after talking to Fairfax's lawyers. He knew he had to make this final telephone call. Alone in his office, he dialled Warwick's number. He glanced at his watch as it rang. It was after midnight. He had spoken to Warwick at his home during the afternoon, keeping him informed about the progess of the talks. Warwick seemed calm, almost fatalistic. He had tended to treat Beerworth almost as a father figure these past few months. They had become quite close. The young man answered the telephone and Beerworth apologised for ringing him so late. He then got straight to the point: 'The banks have refused the roll-over, Warwick. We will have to put the company into provisional liquidation in the morning.'

It was as simple as that. Just a few sentences to tell him that it was all over. The end of a media dynasty.

▪   ▪   ▪

When Mark Burrows arrived home on Sunday night, there was a telephone call from Mark Johnson. He knew the outcome of the meeting from Fairfax's lawyers, but could they have another chat? Burrows agreed to meet him at the Macquarie Bank office at 8 am on the Monday morning.

Johnson tried hard. Although Burrows and Johnson got on well, there was a certain amount of unease in the relationship. Each was wary of the other's judgement. Johnson, however, had little hope of influencing Burrows on this occasion. It was a mere formality when they sat down in the small conference room. Burrows outlined the banks' reasons for refusing to give any concessions. There was no going back now. At least that is what he decided to tell Johnson.

But Burrows was nervous that one of the bankers might still baulk at the enormity of what they were doing—placing the country's oldest media dynasty and its major quality newspapers in receivership. It could be a public relations disaster for the banks, still reeling from the flack from their 1980s lending practices. Just after 9 am Burrows and White walked the five blocks across the city, dodging the office workers scurrying to commence another working week, to the Citibank offices in Kent Street. The bankers were gathering there and Burrows wanted to make sure he was ready if there was any unexpected hitch as the Fairfax lawyers and the banks finalised their respective move to the courts.

▪   ▪   ▪

Steve Ezzes had had a restless night. He was awake early—his body clock out of kilter. Four am in Sydney was lunchtime in New York. How could anyone expect to sleep? He got down to Malcolm Turnbull's office by 8 am.

But what was the point in sitting around waiting for the bad news? Ezzes was tetchy. They still hadn't had a decent hearing from Cannon-Brookes at Citibank. 'Let's just front up there,' Ezzes suggested.

Turnbull was a little reluctant—they would be lucky to get a hearing—but what the hell? Arriving at Citibank, the first port of call was Jim Featherstone's office. Ezzes couldn't believe what he saw. There above the photocopier, in the middle of the open-plan office, was a huge blow-up copy of the cheque to buy Fairfax. It was like a trophy. What a laugh.

Featherstone wasn't around and they were told to wait. Turnbull wanted to get on to Cannon-Brookes to see if he could arrange a meeting. He walked across and picked up Featherstone's phone. While Turnbull was dialling the internal number, Ezzes looked at the wall full of tombstones, advertising each of the Citibank financing deals Featherstone had been involved in. He saw that a couple of the tombstones had been turned upside down. Ezzes worked out that each of the companies involved had gone belly up. Featherstone had been scrupulous. The Fairfax tombstone was already turned.

'I know what today's decision is going to be, Malcolm,' Ezzes said drily.

Turnbull wasn't having any luck getting through to Cannon-Brookes. He looked up at where Ezzes was pointing. They decided to wait outside Cannon-Brookes' office.

■　■　■　　　●

Burrows and White walked out of the elevator at the eleventh level, chatting together as they headed towards Cannon-Brookes' office. As they turned the corner their footsteps froze. Instinctively they both did an abrupt about-turn and scrambled for the fire escape. 'That's them!' They felt like schoolboys. It was ludicrous.

Downstairs a breathless Burrows grabbed a phone and rang Cannon-Brooks. 'Malcolm Turnbull is outside your office. Can you get rid of him?'

It did not have to be quite that dramatic. Directions were given to an alternative entrance. Turnbull and Ezzes kept up their vigil uninterrupted, unaware of the fracas they had caused.

At 11 am Beerworth rang. The expiry time for the roll-over had passed. He had no choice. He was leaving for the courts to request that a key company in the Fairfax Group be placed in provisional liquidation (the banks had agreed at the last minute to allow one company, rather than hundreds, to be placed in liquidation). Once that was done, the banks legal representatives were free to appoint a receiver uncontested. The tension in the Citibank offices broke.

Someone had to go out and tell Turnbull. Amid laughter Burrows was appointed. 'You got us into this, Burrows. You go and do it.'

Burrows stood before Turnbull and Ezzes. He was direct. 'Malcolm, Bill is applying for a provisional liquidator.'

He turned around and left.

■ ■ ■

Turnbull was convinced that this receivership would be the end of Beerworth's career. When he and Ezzes sat back in his offices later that afternoon, he put in an anonymous call to William J Beerworth & Partners. 'Is there any spare office space there available for lease?' he asked mischievously.

But Turnbull received an odd call himself a little later. The caller was Lady Mary Fairfax. Turnbull put her on speaker phone so Ezzes could listen in. Warwick had clearly performed badly— the company was in receivership, she began. Now it was important that Charles (Lady Mary's twenty-one-year-old adopted son) take over the reins of the family company. Could Turnbull help?

Turnbull was gentle. 'Lady Mary, the company is in receivership. You can't make those sorts of decisions any more. If it will help, I will speak to Warwick. Could you arrange a meeting?'

Lady Mary's reply left Turnbull amused. 'Oh no, Malcolm. Warwick won't see you. He is afraid of you.'

■ ■ ■

There were more tense moments still to come for Burrows that day. He had to face Bill Beerworth again and endure too a bizarre encounter with Lady Mary. At 5 pm Des Nicholl and Burrows headed for the Herald Building for a joint press conference with Beerworth. Burrows was anxious that Beerworth and Mark Johnson hold their fire on the banks. Both were deeply angered that the banks had closed off their options so conclusively.

There was compassion for Warwick too. Burrows knew that if they chose to focus on the role of the banks in this collapse, it could be a public relations nightmare. Burrows was charming. There could be a role for Beerworth and Halkerston, the old directors, under the new restructuring, he told the conference.

After the journalists left, Beerworth, Nicholl and Burrows were chatting amid the dreary, black leather decor of the chief executive's office at Fairfax, when a call came through for Burrows. It was Lady Mary Fairfax. Her request left Burrows speechless. 'Oh, Mark, I just wanted to put a word in for Warwick. He is really interested in journalism, you know. You have some influence with the banks. Could you just pass it on to Will [Bailey of ANZ]? Warwick would like to work at Fairfax.'

CHAPTER FOUR

THE SHARKS ARE CIRCLING

CHRIS CORRIGAN was ready to pounce as soon as the receivership of Fairfax was announced. It was his face that graced the *Herald* the next morning as the first to express interest as a potential buyer.

'This is the one we've been waiting for,' he stated confidently.

If Corrigan could pull off the Fairfax deal, the future of Jamison Equity was assured. Fairfax was now in receivership and fair game for financial engineers like Corrigan. The banks would have to sell the media group to get their money back. There were huge profits to be made if a bid for Fairfax was handled right.

Jamison was a brand new company—a cash box formed just seven months earlier at the end of the 1980s boom. Corrigan had it poised to take over the oldest (the Fairfax family control of the *Herald* stretched back to 1841) and most profitable media company in Australia.

For Corrigan, snaring Fairfax would propel him right back into the centre of Australian business. Tall, angular and sandy-haired, Corrigan's characteristic slight frown hides a dry sense of humour, often delivered with a crooked grin, and a deep passion for a good punt. He is also a staunch Labor voter and supporter of Paul Keating.

There is an element of the larrikin in Corrigan. He could be running one of the most respected merchant banks in the country, as he did when he headed Bankers Trust Australia (BT Australia) in the early 1980s, but at home have a garage full of terracotta pots.

Always with an eye for a good deal, he had bought them for a song at auction but hadn't calculated the difficulty of offloading them.

Corrigan had spent the past year establishing Jamison. He had managed to get the backing of AFP—one of the most entrepreneurial of companies controlled by John Elliott's Monaco tax-exile friends—in a country where the epithet 'entrepreneur' was no longer a compliment. He then set about balancing this by coaxing nearly $200 million from Australia's institutions, the large insurance giants including the two biggest—Australian Mutual Provident Society (AMP) and National Mutual.

Corrigan's plan was to be counter-cyclical—snap up the bargains that a depressed economy and the collapse of high-profile companies offered. There was a certain irony in this plan and the presence of AFP.

Executives with companies like AFP had become multi-millionaires as they pocketed huge fees advising companies to borrow big for corporate takeovers during the frenzied 1980s. Now, as many Australian conglomerates lay in tatters, with the economic downturn making a mockery of their debt repayment plans, there was even more money to be made buying the companies cheaply and waiting for economic recovery.

Corrigan's ability to meld in Jamison an unusual mix of high rollers and conservative investors was a coup. The press called Jamison a vulture fund. Corrigan demurred on semantics—vultures destroy their prey; Jamison would rebuild companies—but the description was pretty close.

Picking the right investments would be the key for Corrigan, and Fairfax was the big play. He had at least $200 million in Jamison's bank account and he wanted to deal himself into the Fairfax boardroom.

The forty-four-year-old Corrigan already had a strong reputation in the Australian finance world, built while he was managing director of BT Australia for six years to 1985. He had been out of the action for the past five years, however, trapped in Asia as regional manager for Bankers Trust.

It had not been a particularly happy sojourn. The bureaucracy of a large international bank weighed heavily on Corrigan when he was trying to forge ahead in the Asian equity markets. The independence he had managed to establish as head of the bank's Australian operation had proved impossible to achieve in Asia. The clash of Australian and US cultures was much more evident and Corrigan's occasional black temper rose a little too often. He quit the bank in September 1989, after twenty-two years with BT and returned to Australia to set up Jamison.

To Corrigan, Fairfax was a wonderful opportunity. If he could tie up the main providers of funds—the insurance and super-annuation giants—and put in a reasonable offer, he might just force a quick and cheap sale, avoiding an auction.

Corrigan was particularly well-placed for Fairfax. Apart from having the confidence and backing of the country's largest institutions, he had good contacts within the Group. Corrigan is a close friend of John Alexander, editor-in-chief of the *Herald*. They first met when Alexander, then a finance reporter, profiled him for *Australian Business* magazine in the early 1980s. They clicked and stayed close. Partly due to the Alexander connection, Corrigan became a keen observer of the Fairfax imbroglio.

Alexander, in turn, was close to Anderson, who clearly thought his departure from Fairfax was temporary—he had not taken a new job but was waiting in the wings to be called in by the new owners, whomever they might be. Alexander kept Corrigan well-informed of the Fairfax machinations. Corrigan felt confident that Anderson and Alexander could deliver him the good will of the management and the journalists at Fairfax.

What Corrigan believed he could offer was a smooth transition—an attractive option for the banks. And, he hoped, a quick, cheap sale would be an attractive option for the institutions. From the beginning Corrigan had been mouthing the right sentiments about the requirements to run Fairfax. It was more than just a business. He spoke about Australian ownership, editorial independence and keeping the Group intact.

Corrigan believed that the institutions would back Jamison above any other bidders that were certain to emerge. The AFP connection, however, was a potential problem. AFP did not fit the image of a stable newspaper owner with respect for operating quality newspapers. AFP's historic philosophy had been to get something cheaply, try and improve the assets value and then sell it to the highest bidder. Critics immediately argued that Fairfax didn't need such an owner.

AFP was also considered a satellite of the John Elliott–Elders camp during the 1980s. Its executive team included a number of former Elders directors. There had been times when the young operators behind AFP—Basil Sellars, Peter Scanlon, Robin Crawford and John Gerahty—were considered clever operators.

They had since been participants, however, in some very controversial corporate manoeuvres with Elders and food giant Goodman Fielder. Some of the AFP team also got involved in Ten Network, one of Australia's three commercial television networks that went bust during 1990. By the time Fairfax went into receivership, AFP's track record was patchy. To make matters worse, the Federal Labor Government didn't take kindly to Elders' and AFP's low tax-paying habits. The AFP men had made themselves a packet of money, but some of what they had touched had turned to clay.

• • •

Chris Corrigan was confident he could seize control of Fairfax by tying up the major source of funds for any offer for Fairfax, despite the inevitable strong competition. As Warwick's passing parade of directors had each tried to restructure the financing of the hopelessly overgeared Group, they had trawled the world over, searching for equity partners. By the day Warwick went under, there was a long list of interested potential buyers, some of them already just as active, if not as noisy, as Corrigan. One of those was Tony O'Reilly—a man who, as much as anyone, encapsulates the odd intimate relationship between the Irish and Australians.

Almost twelve months before the receivership O'Reilly had attended a special function at Fairwater, Lady Mary's mansion. It was a garden party for the Ireland Fund, established by O'Reilly in 1976, and an occasion at which O'Reilly felt exceedingly comfortable. It was through his influence that each of the organisers on the Garden Party Committee had come together. He was a networker *par excellence*. His social skills were unparalleled at that gathering.

O'Reilly is charming company and, a rare commodity in Sydney, an internationally successful businessman. Much of the chatter was inevitably about the fate of the Fairfax Group. In smoke-filled Darcy's restaurant in Paddington later that evening, as he sat with his son Cameron and an old friend Kevin Luscombe, the former executive of Heinz in Australia and now an advertising and marketing industry executive, O'Reilly could not get the newspaper group out of his mind.

He took a breath and leaned toward Luscombe, a look of obsession in his eyes. 'I want Fairfax,' he said.

Although O'Reilly spends most of his time running US-based food group H J Heinz and Co. and lives for much of the year in Pittsburgh, he also has his own business interests, including a controlling stake in Independent Newspapers PLC. This Ireland newspaper group accounts for sixty per cent of Ireland's print media. O'Reilly is Ireland's equivalent of Rupert Murdoch.

His connection with Australia is through his former wife, an Australian Susan Cameron, whom he met on a Rugby Union tour of Australia in 1959. Their six children carry Australian passports, an asset in 1987 when Independent used a network of trusts dominated by the children to buy from Rupert Murdoch, Australian Provincial Newspapers (APN) — the largest regional press group in Queensland and northern New South Wales.

Now O'Reilly wanted the Fairfax Group as well.

His son, Cameron, who had been living in Australia since the purchase of APN, announced the day after the receivership that Independent was very keen to examine an offer for Fairfax. Independent had been working on the possibility of a Fairfax purchase for at least a year — O'Reilly's name had appeared in Fairfax board papers mid-year as an interested party. Independent retained BT Australia as financial adviser.

BT had finally secured a client in the Fairfax saga. Peter Hunt, who had returned to Australia looking for a new start in the corporate advisory industry after an unfortunate few years working for failed New Zealand entrepreneur Allan Hawkins, had pitched for the junk bond adviser role as well.

* * *

In Melbourne there was another Fairfax Group aficionado — Robert McKay. The day Fairfax went into receivership he began to work full time on the media group. Four months earlier he and a close friend Tom Harley had predicted the week of the receivership. But they had got the day wrong.

Their interest in the Group pre-dated Corrigan's and O'Reilly's by just over three years. But their names were not mentioned in the speculation about the possible buyers for Fairfax in the days following the receivership. Their strategy involved keeping a very low profile.

Neither McKay nor Harley was well-known in Australian business circles. McKay is a publisher, the chairman of Macquarie Library, which publishes the *Macquarie Dictionary*, and a business consultant. Harley is a Treasury executive with BHP. Each fits to a tee the description of a city gentleman. While they blend well into the Collins Street business scene in Melbourne, in Sydney they tend to stand out starkly among the brassier, more aggressive elements of the finance community.

Their backgrounds and their track records couldn't be more different from people like Corrigan and O'Reilly. They didn't run companies, had no access to large sums of cash and had no experience in newspapers. Their interest in newspapers stemmed from an involvement in a consortium plan to buy the *Age* newspaper in 1987 when Warwick Fairfax was considering a sale. Many hours were spent together with well-meaning journalists, businessmen and others passionate about the Melbourne newspaper's tradition and commitment to quality journalism.

The consortium couldn't compete with the crazy offers made for the newspaper, and the concept lay dormant as Warwick stumbled. With Fairfax in receivership, the two men began to activate the Melbourne network again. Despite their good intentions, it seemed like they were just a couple of well-bred dreamers.

They were much more than that, however. Both were passionate about quality newspapers and the need for editorial independence. Exceptionally well-connected in Melbourne, they had already struck a chord with many investors on the basis of the perceived need for Australian ownership of Fairfax, and the need to retain diversity in Australia's print media.

■ ■ ■

One of the options the banks knew they would have to consider to extricate themselves from the Fairfax mess was a public float of the media group. They could secure a stockbroking firm, which would then underwrite an issue of shares to large institutional investors and the public.

The funds raised could be used to retire a large portion of the $1.25 billion owed to the banks. A new board of directors and chief executive would be arranged also. This possibility was not lost on the stockbroking community, which began to work on proposals.

One energetic stockbroker who had been closely scrutinising Fairfax for months was Neville Miles, a director of the stockbroking firm Ord Minnett Securities. He had spent fourteen months trying to get a role in the biggest game in town. His first approach to Fairfax offering Ord's services to raise capital was in January 1990, just as Drexels finally collapsed. Since then he had spent seemingly endless hours examining it. Even to the extent that it had become embarrassing among his colleagues. 'How's the Fairfax deal going, Nev?' they would chide him. Under his first proposal, when Drexels was struggling, Miles agreed with one of the Fairfax board's strategies to try a discounted buyback of the junk bonds with a cash-raising through Ords. His approach to Fairfax executives got nowhere.

Then in early August 1990 Miles tried again. Chris Anderson and Peter King, the then chief executive of Fairfax, were invited into the offices of stockbroking firm Ords for a silver service boardroom lunch, where Miles went through a similiar proposal. They needed to buy the junk bonds back at a discount, find some new equity investors, possibly through a public listing, and convert some of the bank debt to shares. Although obviously an obstacle, the need to substantially dilute Warwick's equity was clear, he told them. There were no arguments from King and Anderson on that point; this option was already being considered.

Miles explained that perhaps Warwick's holding could be reduced as low as twenty per cent. This could be made more attractive by giving Warwick an option over the part of the bank debt that would be converted into shares. When the banks sold out after the company was back on its feet, they would have to sell to Warwick. He could thus still keep his family's grip on the company.

Miles' proposal was ill-timed. In the next two weeks, while he was poring over financial information on Fairfax for a draft proposal, Warwick was busily dumping King ahead of Anderson's exit.

Despite the knockbacks, however, Miles knew that Fairfax was the main game and that at some stage a stockbroking firm would secure a lucrative role. Any foreign bidder would require Australian institutional investor support, since it was clear the Federal Government was extremely unlikely to allow 100 per cent foreign ownership.

Nor did there seem to be any logical Australian buyer who could afford to own 100 per cent. So, Miles reasoned, whoever grabbed control of Fairfax would need a stockbroker to underwrite the issue of shares to the institutions.

Naturally the fees would be exceptional. Probably four per cent of the amount raised. As it was reasonably certain that around $400 million would need to be raised in fresh equity from institutions, that was over $15 million in potential gross underwriting fees.

Being the executive who delivered this prize to Ords would give one tremendous kudos. Miles, a South African who had joined Ords from Westpac Banking Corporation's subsidiary Partnership Pacific, knew that if he was that executive his career would receive a significant boost.

The firm needed it too. Ords, owned by Westpac, had been having a lean time since the October 1987 stockmarket crash. While the firm was involved in some large floats during the bull market run, the fee income generated by the corporate division had dried up considerably since then. Competition was tough, and there was nothing worse for a firm than missing out on a role in big transactions. It was more than just the foregone fee income, it was the prestige of having the role. Once a firm began slipping down the ranks, it was hard to recover.

Those broking houses running hot and securing roles in the larger deals had the distinct advantage of clients and potential clients believing that they were the best bet for efficient service or that they had the best ideas on offer. So the exit of King and Anderson did not sap Miles' enthusiasm for a role on Fairfax. When Halkerston and Beerworth took over, Miles approached them with the same plans. But they were not very interested. The search for foreign equity was in full swing, and there was no pressing need to involve a stockbroking firm at that stage.

Once Fairfax went into receivership, Miles sent off another letter, this time to Burrows. It offered Ord's services to underwrite a public float, putting the firm's name alongside Melbourne-based firms Potter Warburg and J B Were & Sons.

Another stockbroking firm with the same ideas was James Capel. Capel's managing director Kerry Roxburgh decided he would pursue a public float idea and also look for an overseas investor as a core shareholder. A former accountant, Kerry had been around the financial community for over two decades. In recent years he had been at the Hongkong Bank, one of the largest lenders to Alan Bond.

When the corporate advisory division began to break up, Roxburgh transferred to run the bank's stockbroking affiliate. Also attracted by the fees that could be generated from being involved in a sale of Fairfax, Kerry ordered his staff to do some research on the Fairfax Group. Like all the other advisory firms and stockbrokers, there wasn't much point in pushing for a role unless you knew at least something about the business.

Roxburgh's staff duly bought a dozen copies of finance journalist Trevor Syke's book on Warwick's takeover of the media group, *Operation Dynasty*. Armed with a little knowledge of the Fairfax family and business, the firm then searched for potential core shareholders.

• • •

As corporate advisory firms and stockbrokers began jotting down the names of the likely participants in the sale of Fairfax, one of the first names to come to mind was John B Fairfax, Warwick's cousin.

In the weeks after receivership John was deluged with telephone calls and letters.

One approach was from a former *Herald* newspaper distributor who claimed he had access to $2 billion in Arab funds to finance the purchase. The French group Hachette and UK group Pearsons PLC made approaches. Corrigan, Miles, Roxburgh and stockbroker County Natwest Securities sent letters. Rob McKay paid a visit to John, although he was secretive about the plans of an unnamed group of prominent Melbourne investors. Sir Rod Carnegie, the Melbourne businessman and former chief executive of mining company CRA visited John on behalf of US investment fund Hellman & Friedman.

John, perhaps more than anyone in the family, was devastated when Warwick unleashed his plan to privatise the Fairfax Group in 1987. He had been working his way through the management of Fairfax for twenty-seven years, from relatively humble beginnings as a cadet reporter to the board in 1979 and eventually deputy chairman in 1985.

A polite and gentle man in his late forties, John started work at the family company a year before Warwick was born. It was widely expected that he would become chairman of the Group in 1993 when James, his cousin and the current chairman turned sixty. Warwick ruined that simple plan. John reacted emotionally and publicly.

The day after Warwick dropped his takeover bombshell to the market, John told the *Herald*: 'Warwick dropped around to my home at 10 pm on the night of Sunday, 30 August and informed me he was making a bid at 9 am the next day for all public shareholdings. It was the first we knew of it. From your point of view [as an employee] you must now wonder what on earth is happening. I am just as shocked—totally shattered. And I don't need to tell you how my father feels—a marvellous man.'

John's father is Sir Vincent Fairfax, cousin of Sir Warwick Fairfax, young Warwick's father. Sir Vincent is a former chairman of AMP, which was the single largest investor and a key shareholder in Fairfax when it was a publicly listed company. Sir Vincent's connections with AMP were not lost on the advisers scrambling for a role in the Fairfax deal.

Each of the players knew that the support of the institutions was going to be crucial for an acquisition the size of Fairfax. This had been confirmed within days of the receivership when Leigh Hall, AMP's investment manager, said that AMP could possibly take up to twenty per cent equity in a new Fairfax.

Who better then to get into your consortium than the son of the former AMP chairman and the great-great-grandson of the founder, the former deputy chairman of the Group, and a man who commanded the admiration of journalists across the country for his outspoken support for an independent press?

This only helped exacerbate John's discomfort. This was his chance to regain the family jewels, to recommence the Fairfax dynasty and protect Fairfax's unique role in Australian society. However, he didn't feel it was possible to seek such goals. The whole concept was doomed to failure.

John couldn't bring back the old Fairfax, no matter who went into partnership with him. If he and his family (father Vincent, brother Tim and two sisters) could afford to buy the Group, he had a big chance of continuing the Fairfax editorial culture. But they couldn't afford it.

Any partnership was going to be a compromise and John's very presence would promise a nirvana that he knew he couldn't deliver.

When Warwick made his takeover offer, John and his father and siblings accounted for seventeen per cent of the Group. They had the option of remaining with Warwick as minority shareholders, but from the outset that was clearly a potential nightmare.

They sold their shareholding for $306 million and negotiated with Warwick and his advisers the purchase of some of the smaller Fairfax publishing interests, including its share in the *Land* newspaper; the half share of the Sydney suburban publishing and printing group Eastern Suburbs newspapers; a swag of regional and rural newspapers; and a share in Brisbane's FM station.

In total the assets cost about $78 million. It provided the genesis of an independent publishing group Rural Press, which was performing extremely well by the time Warwick collapsed in 1990 and left John's side of the family comfortably wealthy and quite content.

It had always been much less flashy than the Warwick Fairfax Snr arm of the family, which lived in ostentatious style at Fairwater and, thanks to Lady Mary, took a prominent role in Sydney's social life.

Sir Vincent, on the other hand, lived on the Elaine estate, just along Sydney Harbour's Seven Shillings beach from Fairwater. And while his son John remembers his father dressing in a dinner jacket each night for the evening meal, he kept a low profile in the eastern suburbs society.

The Vincent Fairfaxes were best known for their philanthropy.

Buildings for the homeless, camping facilities for the Anglican youth service, walking tracks in the mountains specially engineered for the disabled, all came courtesy of the Vincent Fairfax Foundation. The family gave in big licks of cash, often a quarter of a million dollars at a time. In a country like Australia, where a tradition of philanthropy among the wealthy barely exists, the Vincent Fairfaxes were a large exception to the rule.

John was even more low key than his father. He had gone to the right school, Geelong Grammar in Victoria, and studied at Australian National University. When he worked his way through the firm he was treated like any other employee—as much as one could being a Fairfax. He was suspended without pay for a week during his cadetship when he made an error in a court report. He worked in London as assistant to the general manager, and then in the marketing department of the Group before becoming deputy chairman.

John was so unpretentious that many executives found it tempting to dismiss him as amiable but without the drive to run a large company. They were proven wrong. Once out on his own at Rural Press, he showed that he was an adept businessman. He shocked even his supporters with forthright speeches on the Australian media and his outspoken criticism of the new media barons and their close political connections.

John was therefore a perfect cornerstone shareholder in a consortium to buy Fairfax. He wouldn't contemplate this role, but he was receptive to lending his support in some way, provided there was something in it for his business interests.

John felt that Fairfax's *Newcastle Herald* was a suitable acquisition at the right price. It would fit well with his other regional publishing interests. When it came to sorting out what role he would finally take, his own commercial interests were going to be paramount.

On the periphery of the circle forming around the Fairfax carcass was Pearsons PLC of London, publishers of the *Financial Times* and the *Economist*, with, as it happened, Rupert Murdoch as a shareholder. Pearsons' executives had visited Australia during the first week of December—the week before the receivership. They made it clear that they were particularly interested in the *Australian Financial Review*.

Also visiting Australia that week was Warren Hellman from Hellman & Friedman. This advisory and investment fund group had been set up by Hellman and Tully Friedman in 1983 when they became disenchanted with the direction Wall Street firms like Drexels were taking.

To put the fee before the long-term interests of a client was quickly becoming the rule on Wall Street. Hellman had worked for the investment bank Lehman Brothers until 1977 before setting up a venture capital firm in Boston. Friedman worked for Salomon Brothers during the 1970s. In 1981 they met and became friends. They agreed to set up their own small, leveraged buyout firm and provide advice for relationship clients. The buyout fund business received a major boost in 1984 when it arranged the US$1.8 billion privatisation of Levi Strauss. The venture was successful—the 1.3 million shares the firm received grew to a value of over US$60 million.

By 1987 Hellman & Friedman's reputation as canny, conservative investors allowed them to raise about US$325 million for an investment fund from corporate pension funds, private foundations and financial institutions. A second US$280 million fund was being set up as Hellman looked closely at Fairfax.

Focusing on the Pacific Rim, the firm was involved in a consortium that sought to bid for Nine Network when Alan Bond was a forced seller. They got trounced by Kerry Packer, however, whose lobbying in Canberra was rewarded when a law was passed that foreign investment in television stations was limited to twenty per cent.

This counted out the US consortium, which included television group National Broadcasting Company (NBC). Hellman had been taking a close interest in Fairfax for over a year. He had met Lady Mary Fairfax at a function at Harvard Business School and kept in touch. As a specialist in turn-around situations, Hellman could see that a recapitalised Fairfax was likely to be a lucrative investment.

One other foreigner paying close attention was Robert Maxwell. His bid for the *Age* that was rejected by Keating in 1988 hadn't deterred him. He told ABC radio in December that he intended to come out to Australia to watch the cricket and check out the Fairfax assets over summer.

New Zealand corporate raider Brierley Investments quickly expressed interest in Fairfax. Founded by Sir Ron Brierley, this group was a crucial player in the 1987 carve-up of the Herald and Weekly Times group when its shareholding was the catalyst for Rupert Murdoch's takeover.

Brierley Investments had no intention of being a long-term, conservative owner of Fairfax. The Brierley executives in New Zealand cut a swathe through the media in the 1980s, the upshot being a lot less newspapers and plenty of cash in the company's bank acccounts.

New Zealand media group, Independent Newspapers, was also keen on Fairfax, despite one small problem. It is forty-nine per cent owned by Murdoch's News Corporation—the Kiwi executives, however, didn't seem to think this was an insurmountable problem.

∎ ∎ ∎

For the potential foreign groups, the interest level could be narrowed down very quickly by the Federal Government. So much hinged on the level of foreign ownership the Hawke Government would allow. The Government had set a precedent when it quickly introduced the twenty per cent foreign ownership for television stations. The position on foreign ownership of newspapers was yet to be clarified, however, despite one classic example of how the Government decided who was and was not an acceptable foreigner.

The controversial Maxwell had made an offer for David Syme in February 1988 of over $800 million. The offer caused an outcry among journalists at the *Age*, who fiercely guard the independence of the newspaper. They quickly garnered support from across the political spectrum and the business and general community in a campaign against a sale to Maxwell.

Keating at first told Chris Anderson that if there was to be a sale to Maxwell, it should be done quickly to avoid a backlash. Keating then did a backflip as public pressure grew, and Hawke came out and made it clear Maxwell was unacceptable.

Maxwell had a second rebuff when he expressed interest in purchasing the *West Australian* early in 1990. David Syme can be grateful for Keating's change of heart about allowing Maxwell into the Australian media club. In late 1991 Maxwell died in mysterious circumstances when he went overboard from his luxury boat. It was subsequently discovered he had perpetrated a financial swindle on his bankers and raided the pension fund of his staff.

Even the laws regulating foreign ownership of newspapers are fuzzy in Australia. Under the Foreign Acquisitions and Takeovers Act (FATA), a foreigner can hold 14.99 per cent ownership of an Australian company without being subject to Foreign Investment Review Board approval.

However, a Treasury department booklet 'Australia's Foreign Investment Policy' states that 'all proposals by foreign interests to establish a newspaper in Australia or buy an existing newspaper business are subject to case-by-case examination, irrespective of the size of the proposed investment'.

Although this policy is not enforceable under the FATA legislation, it does give the Treasurer the power to rule out an acquisition as contrary to the national interest. Lawyers may search for reasons this policy might be unenforceable. Challenging it is another matter. These combined regulatory and discretionary powers ensure that approval of the Government is crucial for any important media acquisition.

Prime Minister Hawke put his position forward the day the receivership was announced, saying that he would prefer that the Fairfax Group stayed in Australian hands. He followed up gratuitously with the comment that the actions of Australian media proprietors in recent years had been 'absolutely bloody crazy'.

He neglected to add that some of the financial problems were created by his own government's media policy shuffles.

* * *

Des Nicholl is used to walking into companies and taking over the reins. It is his job as a receiver. And he has that no-nonsense approach which generally works well with hysterical employees who can see the mortgage payments mounting while they're on the dole.

In his fifties, balding, conservatively and unimaginatively dressed, Nicholl has a gruff manner, full of machismo. He is a quintessentially Aussie bloke—straightforward and unsympathetic to any form of corporate nostalgia.

Nicholl was in damage control mode when he arrived for his first day on the job at Fairfax's Broadway headquarters. The Herald Building, as taxi drivers refer to it, is a grey, ugly cement tower that straddles a whole city block at the seedy end of town near Sydney's Central Railway Station.

From the moment you walk through the large double doors and into the marble foyer, however, the Fairfax family icons surround you. On one wall is a huge wooden scroll upon which is inscribed in gold the editorial policy laid down by the first John Fairfax.

Above the bank of lifts is a large mural, some twenty metres in length depicting a day in the life of a newspaper and commissioned by the Fairfaxes in 1981 to mark the *Herald*'s 150th birthday. Such was the sense of tradition and the hierachical nature of the Fairfax Group, that one of the elevators, the last one in the bank in the far right-hand corner, was reserved for management until the 1980s. It went straight to the fourteenth floor—the mahogany-walled and parquetry-floored precinct of management —and spared the occupants any view of the printing presses, the editorial floors or the advertising sales offices.

Seven oil portraits of five generations of Fairfaxes watched over Des Nicholl as he took up residence on the fourteenth floor the day after the receivership was announced—the day after the Fairfax family was banished from the building forever. Fairfax without the Fairfax family was a bit like heaven without God for some of the long-term staff members.

But that wasn't Des Nicholl's problem. He was there to do a job. As he addressed gatherings of union representatives and meetings of management staff he used the same phrases—stability, no changes, restructuring. But there was more than jobs at stake.

The journalists were pushing editorial independence and asked Des, as he became affectionately referred to by staff, to sign a charter ensuring its continuation. Warwick Fairfax had already signed the *Age* Charter and was preparing to sign a similar document to cover the three Broadway newspapers when the banks pushed him out.

The Fairfax family, most particularly under Warwick, and before him under James, had been the least interventionist of any of the Australian media proprietors. A journalistic culture had grown to represent a stable of newspapers whose reporting was not compromised by the other business interests of their proprietor—they had none. Nor was it compromised by succumbing to political pressure. At least that was the theory.

And while there might have been some trangressions over the years, journalists generally felt untrammelled by the political and business alliances of the Fairfax family. They also saw a charter of editorial independence as one way of trying to ensure that the Fairfax tradition, or at least remnants of it, continued under the new proprietors. Journalists strongly believed that a proprietor should never be allowed to push outside commercial interests or political agendas through the respected Fairfax newspapers.

It was a concept that had been alive in the Fairfax Group since Maxwell's bid as one that required a stand on principle. And there were plenty of international precedents, much to the chagrin of executives at Murdoch's News Corporation and Packer's Consolidated Press, who dismissed the concept as ludicrous. It is adhered to by the *Washington Post*, the *Observer* and *Le Monde*, for example.

At Time Inc. in the USA the concept was even further advanced. There was such a separation of church and state (editorial and management) that the editorial chief was not even required to report outstanding defamation actions to the board; he also chose his own successor without any interference from the chief executive.

For the Fairfax journalists the charter issue served a purpose other than assured editorial independence. It took their role in the sale of the company beyond the usual negotiation of job losses and redundancy packages. They believed it was crucial. Des had taken the charter plea on board and promised to consider it.

But the weight of taking on a receivership that covered the country's most influential newspapers was beginning to show— and it showed on the pages of the newspapers. On his second morning on the job—Wednesday, 12 December—Nicholl opened the *Herald* to find a letter to the editor from Ross Langford of Wollstonecraft, headed 'Corporate Tragedy'.

The letter warned '... if you start mucking with the *Herald*, that will be felt [by us] every day. We the people are watching.' And in the news pages there was an open letter to Nicholl by columnist Peter Smark. This drove home the point that newspaper receiverships were different and Nicholl had to watch his step: 'Tread gently when you walk on our souls, Des.'

But there were a few laughs too. Smark said: 'Let's look first at the factors in your favour: 1. Compared with some so recently operating at board level, yours seems to us a renaissance mind. I'm sure you won't be hurt if we say so would the mind of Skippy, the kangaroo. 2. As far as we could tell, you didn't seem to bring with you another half-dozen advisers being paid huge fees to achieve nothing. 3. You give every evidence of being able to count. Don't act surprised. We're pretty used to people who can't.' Later came the knife: 'These newspapers aren't just products or factories, Des, they're ideas generators, they're manufacturers of challenge, they're checks on governments, they're stimulants and, just rarely when everything works, they're movers of mountains. And politicians aren't comfortable with them, Des, don't like them at all, because they can't do deals with them. We think that's a huge plus on our balance sheet, Des, but I don't know how it computes.'

Des fared better than young Warwick. On that same Wednesday in the *Australian Financial Review*, columnist Peter Ruehl was giving Warwick plenty of stick. 'Tough break kid. I heard they also took you off the subscription list for the *Harvard Business School Alumni* magazine. Well, er ... ah ... you weren't exactly a walking advertisement for the place. On the other hand you could say to yourself, think how bad it could have been if you hadn't gone to Harvard. You might have come back here and just donated the whole thing, half to Murdoch and half to Jim and Tammy Fay Bakker.'

Being receiver of the Fairfax Group was clearly going to require more skills than bean counting and diplomacy.

■　■　■

Nicholl did not need to concern himself too much with the task of finding a new owner for the Fairfax Group. On Christmas Eve the banks announced that Burrows would be advising on the sale or recapitalisation of the Group—all negotiations would be done through his firm and he was given broad powers. He would handle the sale process, and Nicholl would run the operations with the view of not allowing any further deterioration in the Group's value.

Burrows was ecstatic. He had secured the plum advisory job and negotiated a significant fee if he could retrieve the banks their funds. He would be the kingmaker at Fairfax. With some bank executives worried that Fairfax was only worth $800 million to $900 million, Burrows was given a huge incentive to make sure he could sell Fairfax and cover the bank debt. If he could achieve this, his firm would receive a fee related to the sum over the $1.25 billion he achieved as the auctioneer.

Summer holidays were cancelled and Burrows got to work. This one job could be worth ten, twenty, thirty million dollars, depending on how successful he was, on how far he could drive up the price. It was the assignment of a lifetime.

Burrows had seldom felt more motivated. But he knew that he couldn't afford too many errors. This auction had to be well-orchestrated. There was a mountain of work to do. Burrows delegated to Jeff White and Peter Breese the task of thoroughly analysing the Fairfax finances. Potential buyers would need an information memorandum on Fairfax with complex financial data. Breese is another senior executive at Baring Brothers and an excellent 'numbers man', whom Burrows had coaxed across from his sinecure with Pancontinental Mining two years earlier to the uncertain world of corporate advice. Lawyers and accountants had to be retained for the sales process, both in Australia and the USA.

Burrows, Nicholl and White all made the trek to New York in the first week of February. Nicholl settled in at the Waldorf Astoria; Burrows and White made themselves at home at The Plaza. These are two of New York's most salubrious hotels—this receivership was not being done on the cheap. They stayed six days interviewing representatives of top Wall Street advisers—Morgan Stanley, Merrill Lynch, Goldman Sachs, Rothschilds and Lazard Freres—to advise them on dealing with the junk bondholders. Karen Bechtel at Morgan Stanley was chosen.

Bechtel is a tough negotiator and she had no conflict of interest with any of the bondholders. As legal adviser Burrows and Nicholl chose Citibank's law firm in New York, Sherman & Sterling, and partner Fred Cohen was designated to handle the Fairfax account. The trio was conscious that while they went up and down Manhattan employing high-priced advisers, Malcolm Turnbull was back in Sydney plotting his strategy.

New York wasn't all numbers, lawyers and plans to outfox Turnbull, however. One night after a tiring round of interviews, the three Australians dropped into the famous Harry's Bar for a drink. Burrows and White were to see their no-nonsense receiver in a new light when the maître d' greeted Nicholl with: 'Good evening, Mr Nicholl.'

CHAPTER FIVE

MALCOLM HEADS
TO COURT

AS BURROWS and Nicholl selected their advisers and began gearing up for the mammoth auction of Fairfax, Malcolm Turnbull confronted the awesome fact that the company in which his clients had invested US$450 million had gone bust. His role as financial adviser to the junk bondholders had not gone as he would have liked to date. Only one month into the assignment Turnbull and his clients had been factors in the banks' decision to end Warwick Fairfax's hold over the newspaper empire. Certainly Turnbull could angrily tell Mark Atanasio and Steve Ezzes that the conduct of the banks, Burrows and the lawyers had been appalling or that Warwick and his advisers and the banks were crazy not to agree to his plans. But that didn't change anything. Fairfax was in receivership and up for sale.

The Americans were livid. To some of them the receivership had come as a total surprise. Until the last few days they had had no idea that the banks were so far down that road.

This would never happen in the USA, Mark Atanasio mused. He had spent hours on the phone to Turnbull complaining. What on earth *are* the bankruptcy laws in that country? Don't they have Chapter 11—a US law that allows a moratorium on debt repayments while the company attempts to get out of trouble? How can the banks place a company in receivership without committees that include the other creditors?

Atanasio had been involved in countless other restructurings that included junk bondholders, and this had never happened before. Some of these bondholders, like Prudential, were big US investors. They didn't like to lose millions of dollars unnecessarily, Atanasio argued. What was this going to do to Australia's reputation among investors?

Atanasio was flummoxed. You play these deals like a game. You work out what is in the other side's best economic self-interest and you negotiate accordingly. But this time he had blown it—completely misread the situation. The equity holders were now totally wiped out.

The banks could have done a debt-for-equity swap with the bondholders. Atanasio was willing to let control stay with Australians—he didn't want to run a newspaper company. No, Atanasio was convinced there were personalities involved here—the money side had been overridden.

■   ■   ■

The day before the receivership became reality, the Drexel team had tried one last shot for a reprieve from Citibank. Doug McClure, the abrasive partner of Atanasio on the Fairfax matter, had called Steve Gerard of Citibank, the chief of credit worldwide, at his home on Sunday afternoon.

He wanted to make absolutely sure Gerard knew that the bondholders had proposed through Turnbull a complete debt-for-equity swap. Gerard pleaded ignorance and delayed to confer with his team. He rang back to confirm that they knew of the proposal, but still considered receivership the best option.

Lack of knowledge of Australian company law was part of Atanasio's problem. Had he misread the banks' assessment of Turnbull too? From where the bankers sat it seemed Burrows' suggestion that Turnbull would have liked a large say in controlling the Fairfax Group might have been correct.

Perhaps as a director or, at the very least, financial adviser to the bondholders, Turnbull was set under his draconian, cost-saving plan to be an important force at Fairfax. With his friend Kennedy as the likely chief executive, it would have been a dynamic and influential combination.

Over the Christmas break Turnbull continued to mull over the options. He was giving this deal every ounce of energy he had. It was obvious that his bargaining position was now very weak and he was becoming more and more angry about the treatment meted out by Burrows and the banks.

The day after receivership, Turnbull, his wife Lucy and Ezzes met with Rupert Thomas from ANZ, and Jim Featherstone and Mary Reemst from Citibank. Burrows and White also sat there quietly.

Opening the meeting, Thomas complimented Turnbull on his attitude since the receivership. However, as Turnbull spoke, his ideas were obviously contrary to those present. Explaining that he wanted to work with the banks, he suggested that a committee be formed. He then reiterated his proposal delivered on the eve of the receivership.

Turnbull's ideas of working with everyone prompted some heavy body language from Burrows. He left the room shortly after Turnbull began his pitch.

'As long as the banks' economic position is protected, they should be indifferent to proposals in which the bondholders get a higher return,' Turnbull extolled.

As the meeting wore on, there were some tense moments. Turnbull's suggestion that Fairfax was mismanaged and the suggestion of cost cuts didn't go down well with Featherstone.

'Fairfax isn't mismanaged,' he curtly replied.

Turnbull suggested that cost cuts were necessary ahead of any sale to maximise the return to the bondholders. Ezzes fully supported Turnbull's ideas.

'I realise the receiver is not an expert in the media. Malcolm has a lot of experience,' he chipped in.

Following the meeting, Turnbull thought everything was fine. Thomas and Featherstone had said they were happy to involve Turnbull and his clients in the process and hand over financial information. Also just after Christmas, when Burrows was appointed to advise the receiver on the sale process, he also seemed co-operative.

In a fax to Ezzes two days after Christmas, Turnbull said that Burrows was all 'sweetness and light' and they agreed to do lunch the next day. Unfortunately Burrows wasn't around the next morning.

By the end of January Turnbull had no doubts the banks and Burrows had decided not to co-operate. His telephone calls were not returned and faxes requesting financial information went unanswered. The banks slammed the door in his face. Turnbull had to turn that right around now.

■ ■ ■

Turnbull had no doubts that Fairfax was worth well below the $1.25 billion secured bank debt. Perhaps even as low as $900 million. The tough economic climate was biting deep into the rich classified advertising revenues of both the *Herald* and the *Age*.

There was no upturn in sight and Turnbull was well aware that any sale at below the bank debt level would leave his clients with nothing. It would also leave Turnbull with nothing.

His fee arrangement with the bondholders was out of pocket expenses plus $20 000 a month and three per cent of anything the bondholders got back. If they got nothing, he got next to nothing as well.

Sitting back and watching the banks sell Fairfax and shut out his clients was an option Turnbull was not prepared to entertain. For Turnbull, there is nothing worse than being ignored. If no one would deal with him, Turnbull had to make sure that he was a force to be reckoned with.

He had promised the bondholders back in Los Angeles that he was a brilliant lawyer and it was time to show them that he was not just bluffing. Burrows could continue to ignore him at his own peril. Turnbull decided that the best recourse was to enter the arena he knew best—the courtroom.

The rationale was simple. A messy court action against the banks and Fairfax had the potential to make Burrows suffer—his auction would become extremely difficult. What buyer would be willing to pay a decent price for Fairfax if there was the cloud of litigation threatening to bog down the sale process and also jeopardise any sale of the existing corporate shell?

And the key to Turnbull's thinking was the banks' ability to sell the company as a whole. Fairfax might be in receivership, but there were going to be numerous benefits to the banks in selling the existing company structure, instead of just selling the assets out of the company.

The main consideration was the heavy tax losses. As Fairfax's profits after interest evaporated, it accumulated significant tax losses that could be used in the future by a new owner. Such tax losses have value, since the buyer would probably not have to pay any tax for the first few years.

This would assist repayment of borrowings, or even better, the payment of attractive dividends to shareholders. If the banks were thwarted from selling the company shell because of the multi-million-dollar litigation outstanding by the bondholders, the only alternative would be to sell all the assets individually.

This would be a nightmare for the banks and any buyer. It would also mean huge stamp duty costs, possibly over $50 million, not to mention the legal and accounting costs. The buyer would not be able to take advantage of the tax losses either, and this would lead to a lower price.

On top of this, an indemnity against the bondholders' legal action would be required. Then there was the issue of staff entitlements on holidays, redundancy, union awards and a long list of other matters.

Under Turnbull's analysis, the banks could not possibly justify taking on these sorts of problems as an alternative to dealing with the bondholders. A messy and drawn-out legal battle would also hang over the banks.

The banks could find themselves selling the assets for below their loan values, and then later losing the court case and paying out huge damages to the bondholders. Turnbull therefore had good cause to believe that the banks would have no option but to deal with his clients if they wanted a smooth and easy sale. His clients would need to be paid out something for their co-operation.

Ever since Turnbull was retained, he had the possibility of legal action at the back of his mind. Coudert Brothers, the bond-holders' US legal adviser, was very receptive to the argument that there was plenty of evidence to support a case that the junk bondholders had been misled when investing in Fairfax. Turnbull was acutely aware that the junk bond raising finished in early 1989 had been a necessary band-aid solution to Warwick's debt problems.

Turnbull went back through the history of the junk bond raising in fine detail in order to assess the strength of the legal action. It started back in early 1988. Warwick's programme of asset sales to reduce borrowings after the takeover had not gone according to plan. However, he had still managed to raise over $900 million through the sale of a range of assets, including the *Canberra Times* and most of Fairfax's magazines to Kerry Packer for about $212 million.

But the two major mooted sales had collapsed. Robert Holmes a Court had signed a contract in September 1987 to buy the *Australian Financial Review* for about $300 million. The sale fell through after the sharemarket crash.

With the sharemarket fall ruining the float plans for David Syme, attention turned to sell its major asset, the *Age*. In the end the only serious offers for the *Age* came from Maxwell, who indicated he would pay $850 million. This was a very attractive price. But the plan failed on a political level before it had been properly assessed.

. . .

The failure to retire debt through asset sales forced Warwick to look at other options, and a new refinancing was the only real solution. It was clear that Fairfax didn't have enough buffer between profits and interest repayments. Unless a more suitable arrangement was reached, which lowered the annual interest bill before the ANZ syndicate and Citibank facilities fell due, Warwick was again in deep trouble.

Both major banks were willing to give him another chance when Fairfax executives announced they were favouring a re-financing involving the issue of junk bonds through Drexels. In simple terms a group of financial institutions would provide the funds in return for an attractive rate of interest. If the Fairfax Group failed, these new lenders would rank behind Citibank and ANZ.

With the earnings of Fairfax moving ahead strongly in 1988, the bankers felt more relaxed. It was always going to be a tough re-financing, although there was a pleasant consolation for the banks—the re-financing would generate huge fees.

Both banks agreed to two new facilities—a $350 million seven-year loan and a $750 million five-year zero coupon loan. This structure gave Warwick some breathing space. The interest on the $750 million loan was rolled up.

By deferring this interest payment Fairfax could hope that a better economy and probably asset sales later on would leave Warwick with some equity in the Group and some cash to pay the balloon interest bill, expected to be $700 million by 1996.

Drexels was keen to help arrange the issue of another $450 million in junk bonds to pay down facilities owed to the major lenders. Although Drexels was the largest junk bond issuer in the world, organising junk bonds for an Australian company was a rarity. The only other deals Drexels had done in Australia were Alan Bond's financing of his brewery interests—Castlemaine, Toohey's and Swan; and textile king Abe Goldberg's Linter Group. If Drexels had any misgivings about lending in Australia, the Fairfax team's agreement to its request for a fee of $33 million was enough to encourage them to try and pull the deal off.

The fee was large, even by avaricious Wall Street standards. Armed with extensive financial data about Fairfax, Drexels began a roadshow, seeking investors for the tranches of bonds.

The first package of $300 million involved eleven-year bonds, called senior subordinated debentures because they would be repaid first if the company was wound up. This did not mean they would be repaid ahead of other creditors, but ahead of the shareholders and other junk bondholders.

The other package of bonds amounted to $150 million and ran for twelve years. They were called subordinated debentures. The issue proved tougher to offload than Drexels had anticipated. It had to work hard for its fees.

An extensive roadshow through Australia's institutional investors, conducted by Ord Minnett, was a serious flop. The Australian financial community was very sceptical about Fairfax. Even if the issue looked attractive in terms of the interest rate on offer, the misgivings about Warwick as a proprietor overshadowed the potential gains. It was just too much of a risk.

The poor reaction from the institutional investors was bad enough. But even some of the executives of Fairfax had grave misgivings about the issue. Chris Anderson, in particular, was nervous. He complained that the Drexel offer document did not give enough prominence to the risks attached. He put his objections in a memo to chief executive Peter King, stating that he was unhappy 'about the disclosure values of the document and, in my view, the downplaying of the potential risk'.

Anderson was not alone. William Simon, the former head of the US Treasury, who had befriended Lady Mary Fairfax, suffered a bad case of cold feet over the issue. Simon was one of the parties responsible for introducing Warwick to Drexels. His firm WSGP Inc. agreed to take a small parcel of the bonds, and Simon agreed to Warwick's offer of a board seat in August 1989.

On closer examination, however, Simon decided that the whole refinancing was too risky for him to be involved. Simon joined the September 1989 board meeting at Broadway and informed his fellow directors that he was resigning.

He cited the difficulty in insuring himself against legal actions that might ensue from being a member of the board. Simon was petrified that he might be the subject of a legal action for damages from the bondholders in the future. The $8.64 million fee that Fairfax paid him for his assistance in match-making Drexels with Warwick apparently didn't help allay his concerns.

As a parting gift Simon had advice to offer Warwick when the details of the bond issue were explained.

'Warwick, you are in deep shit,' he said.

Drexels finally concluded the bond issue in January 1989, but only after convincing Fairfax that the issue must be sweetened to attract wary investors. Not only would Fairfax have to pay high interest rates on the bonds, but it was forced to take on the foreign currency risk for investors as well. The bonds would come equipped with Foreign Exchange Appreciation Rights (dubbed FEARS), which protected US holders against adverse movements of the Australian dollar against the US dollar.

This was a potentially bottomless pit for the company—a currency shift nightmare. In addition the bonds would also have equity appreciation rights (EARS), which could be converted into either cash, non-voting shares or more bonds.

Even with these sweeteners, Drexels still had problems getting rid of the bonds—it was left with a shortfall of over twenty per cent. So Drexels itself became the largest bondholder with a parcel worth $101 million.

Warwick got breathing space until 1993 under the package, but the sheer size of the future debt repayments meant there was no guarantee of survival. When the first lot of debt fell due in 1993 he faced either major asset sales or the possibility of a partial public float.

In the meantime any downturn in the economy would put everything at risk. The buffer between annual interest payments and gross earnings was not large enough given the volatility of Fairfax's earnings.

The junk bond issue documents were very rosy about the future earnings potential—they forecast continued strong revenue growth and profit growth, paying little attention to the dangers of an economic downturn. Drexels wouldn't have got the fee, and executives their bonuses, if reality had prevailed.

* * *

As Turnbull sifted through the information provided to the bondholders by Drexels, he was convinced that there was fertile ground to mount his argument that the bondholders had been misled about the financial health of Fairfax when they committed their money.

In January Turnbull managed to convince Ezzes that there was enough material to mount a credible court challenge in Australia under the Trade Practices Act provisions on false and misleading conduct.

Couderts was encouraging on the US side. Under its assessment, there would be no problems in fighting a case at the same time through the US court system. Although Turnbull and Couderts were keen for the case to go ahead, some of the bondholders were reticent. They couldn't see the value in spending more money fighting the case. Others simply couldn't find the time to give the matter much attention as they grappled with other more pressing financial problems.

Finally Ezzes was able to coax three others, holding bonds worth about $133 million, to join his Airlie Group. The other original plaintiffs were the Florida-based Guarantee Security Life Company, Prudential-Bache, and Luxembourg-based US High Yield Fund SA.

* * *

Eventually a deal was done on the cost of the legal battle. If the legal battle was successful, any bondholder who had put up funds to fight the case would receive from the proceeds three times the amount of funds committed before any of the other bondholders got back any of their money.

It was not possible for Turnbull to undertake the litigation himself; he was the financial representative of the bondholders and in the end it was decided that it would be unwise to mix up the litigation with his advisory role on commercial matters.

So he decided to call in a former colleague, young Englishman Colin Winter—a partner at legal firm Phillips Fox. Winter had worked with Turnbull in 1986 when he ran a legal firm Turnbull McWilliam. Winter came to Australia from the UK when in his late twenties to have a break from the world of commercial law. He had planned a six-month holiday, working his way in pubs.

He found it particularly difficult getting a job, however. Pommie lawyers with little bar experience weren't in great demand in Sydney pubs. He turned to Phillip Mason, the then publisher of *Australian Playboy*, whom Winter had represented at one stage in the UK. Mason introduced him to Turnbull.

In a brilliant piece of luck Winter scored a job assisting Turnbull in the Spycatcher litigation. It was a fascinating case, made even more attractive by the fact that Turnbull won and won against the legal might of the British Government. Winter liked working for Turnbull. There was an infectious, hard-working atmosphere in the firm.

Turnbull encouraged the younger lawyers around him, and life was never as dull as working for a traditional UK law firm. Winter went back to the UK, but later decided to return to Australia. By this time Turnbull McWilliam had dissolved, and Turnbull had joined Nick Whitlam and Neville Wran to form Whitlam Turnbull.

Winter joined the legal firm Gadens. Later he defected with colleague Mark O'Brien, who did defamation work for Packer's Consolidated Press, to competitor Phillips Fox. In January 1991 Turnbull contemplated enticing Winter to come to his investment bank and run the junk bond litigation from there. But Winter was very happy at Phillips Fox and was unwilling to give up his partnership.

So Turnbull sent Winter to talk to Bob Seidler at the Sydney office of Couderts and commenced preparation for the litigation. It didn't take long for Winter to realise that it was a huge task with few resources. Trying to co-ordinate the involvement of the bondholders was a nightmare.

Each financial institution had its own views on the merits of taking court action. When their lawyers became involved it got even messier. There was also fierce rivalry between some of the bondholders—they were often on different sides of other battles in the USA, and now they had to form an uneasy alliance to litigate.

A few were financially crippled, facing severe financial pressure, teetering on the brink of bankruptcy. Then there was Drexels.

Legal actions hung over the failed financier, and there were grave doubts whether to allow the firm to join litigation over Fairfax, since it was the firm that conducted the issue.

In a few weeks Winter found himself taking telephone calls at home in the early hours of the morning. These were marathon conference calls involving several parties arguing about the benefits and intricacies of litigation. It got to the point that Winter would wake in the middle of the night with voices in his head— was it the vestiges of a dream or was it another bondholder talking into his answering machine in the next room? Many times Winter trudged off to work the next morning after little or no sleep to face another long day.

. . .

In the second week of February a handful of the disgruntled bondholders filed a claim in a downtown New York court seeking $450 million plus damages.

The lengthy filing accused the defendants—Fairfax, the banks and auditors—of fraudulent conveyance, common fraud and breach of fiduciary duty. It was not pleasant reading for ANZ and Citibank executives. The claim alleged that the banks and Fairfax had misrepresented and withheld information about the market prices for Fairfax's assets.

The documents had under-provided for capital expenditure requirements and exaggerated cash flow forecasts. It was alleged that the banks had put a valuation figure on Fairfax of between

$2.04 billion and $2.16 billion, when there were independent valuations at the time which produced numbers much less.

They had also underestimated capital expenditure over the next ten years by $200 million. The statement of claim said that the banks had encouraged various misrepresentations in an effort to lower their exposure to less than the true asset value of the company. This exposure was then transferred to the 'uninformed' US junk investors. The statement honed in on the misgivings about the issue among directors, claiming directors discussed their liability for taking on the additional junk debt and tried to get the banks to protect them against any future liability.

In Australia a case alleging misleading and deceptive conduct was commenced in the Federal Court in mid-February. With the case underway, executives from the other junk bondholders began to join the action; Drexels also came in.

The appearance of Drexels left executives at ANZ and Citibank dumbfounded. It was a bizarre twist, considering the firm had sold the bonds to the other investors.

Drexels alleged, however, that all it did was receive financial information from Fairfax, which was misleading, and made similar allegations to those of the other bondholders.

With the legal actions commenced, Turnbull could finally claim to have got somewhere. As far as he was concerned, the banks and Burrows would have to deal with the bondholders to get their co-operation on any sale of Fairfax.

His clients would either end up with a cash payout or would demand equity in any reconstruction. If the banks tried to sell the assets out, the bondholders would pursue the banks relentlessly. The strategy seemed water-tight. The banks would pay for their treatment of the bondholders and, of course, Turnbull.

■   ■   ■

The commencement of the litigation pleased Turnbull. His efforts to coax Kerry Packer into his other grand plan, however, had received a cold response. Sitting in Packer's office at the Consolidated Press headquarters in Park Street, Sydney, Turnbull's badgering got nowhere.

Despite their long friendship and Turnbull's membership of the House of Packer, Australia's richest man still played very tough.

Turnbull had discussed Fairfax at length over the last few months with Kennedy, who didn't need much convincing about plans that might see him become the Fairfax chief executive. But the meetings with Kennedy's boss didn't go well.

Turnbull enthusiastically outlined his idea for Packer to take 14.99 per cent in a consortium offer for Fairfax. This was all Packer could hold in Fairfax. Australia's cross-media ownership laws banned him from owning or controlling Nine Network and also Fairfax. Turnbull argued that he could still have 14.99 per cent as long as he didn't control Fairfax—if the right structure was set up and independent directors were brought in.

The bondholders would be involved and would sign an exclusive agreement with the core shareholder. An offer for Fairfax would be made, and the bondholders would agree to drop the litigation against the banks if it was successful. If the banks tried to sell to another bidder, however, the litigation would continue.

Packer was derisory about the value of Fairfax, saying that it was worth much below the bank's $1.25 billion in borrowings. If that were the case, the bondholders would have no leverage, nothing to offer Packer. The only important people were the bank executives. All Packer had to do was call Will Bailey at ANZ.

Packer didn't seem overly interested in doing anything with Turnbull. The only other option open to Packer was to sell his share of Nine Network and bid for 100 per cent of Fairfax.

There were problems in this approach. When Packer regained control of the television network from Alan Bond, he promised institutional investors that he would remain as executive chairman of Nine Network for a number of years, providing management expertise to shake up the network and return it to profitability.

Breaching his agreement with institutions would be a poor move. And any sudden moves to sell a majority shareholding in Nine Network would depress the share price. Packer wasn't noted for selling at fire-sale prices—his rule was to buy assets cheaply and sell at high prices.

Turnbull seemed to get nowhere. Nor did Packer let on in the early meetings whether he had other ideas. Turnbull was uncertain whether Packer wouldn't come around later. In the meantime he would look at other options.

ANZ and Citibank were angry at Turnbull's pre-receivership antics. Now Turnbull had taken an action that elicited cold, white fury. How could Turnbull of all people sue Fairfax and its bankers? Turnbull had been one of Warwick's advisers in late 1987 and early 1988 and helped clean up the mess from the takeover.

Along with Whitlam he had been integrally involved in pulling together the urgent $500 million loan from Citibank in mid-January 1988 that saved Warwick from imminent collapse—just months after the takeover.

Turnbull was critically involved in the asset sales programme, negotiating on the failed sale of the *Age* to Maxwell. The firm racked up $9.88 million in fees for its efforts. Nicholas Whitlam had bought himself a holiday house at Whale Beach, Sydney, on his cut of the proceeds, wittily naming it 'Wokka Waters'.

As part of its role in early 1988 Whitlam Turnbull put out its own valuations on assets. This was not that different from the valuation given to the bondholders—the valuation that Turnbull was now calling fraudulent.

There was general agreement among the banks that if Turnbull wanted to fight it out in court, he would have to defend some of his own valuations and advice given in 1988. There would be a cross-claim against Turnbull: if the court found the banks guilty of misleading and deceptive conduct, they would claim they relied on representations on asset values made by Turnbull in April 1988.

While the lawyers mulled over how to attack Turnbull, he was busy keeping up the heat. An opportunity to fire another shot at the banks and Burrows for refusing to deal with him could not be missed.

On 27 March Turnbull was invited to make a lunchtime address at the Institute of Directors and he chose his favourite topic: Fairfax. Strutting the dais and savouring the opportunity to have his say before an influential audience, Turnbull was at his oratorical finest.

He lambasted the banks for putting Fairfax into receivership in the first place and accused them of then doing nothing.

Turnbull said that everyone's interests would have been better served if the banks had allowed more time for Beerworth and Halkerston to produce a financial restructuring. Because of the receivership, the value of Fairfax had now fallen to $900 million.

'Given the lack of activity on the part of the receivers and their advisers it would seem when the banks put Fairfax into receivership they had no plan of action. No doubt they hoped to sell the assets for more than their debt, but they clearly had no particular idea how they were going to do this, or what they were going to do with the assets in the meantime.

'Nearly four months later Fairfax has drifted ... no strategy for a sale or reconstruction has been decided, no changes to management or directions of the company have been implemented.'

The speech was scathing. Turnbull performed at his best. But even Turnbull excelled himself with a one-liner that infuriated Burrows and bank executives: 'Talk about lunatics being in charge of the asylum.'

■   ■   ■

Turnbull got his response the following week. The cross-claim against Whitlam Turnbull, the old firm name before Whitlam's acrimonious departure, was filed, dragging Turnbull into a legal morass.

For Burrows this move was not much consolation since he knew that it was yet another obstacle to the smooth sale process he had hoped to run.

Getting under Turnbull's skin was one thing, but the main task was to encourage as many bidders for the Fairfax Group as possible.

The bondholders' litigation was a problem and had distracted attention away from getting the information memorandum together to start the sale process. But Burrows knew that the bondholders would have to be dealt with at some stage, either through Turnbull or individually.

■   ■   ■

Mark Burrows also knew it was essential that Fairfax should run smoothly during the receivership. The Group had been traumatised for over three years. The staff were shell-shocked.

Warwick's takeover was bad enough when it ruined just under 150 years of stability. It was followed by the walkout of senior staff in protest at the new management team in February 1988. The sacking of that management team followed in response. The subsequent closure of two newspapers, the *Times on Sunday* and the *Sun* in Sydney, in a cost-cutting drive, threw several hundred out of work.

The heavy asset sales programme of magazines, regional newspapers, property and other businesses further depleted the Group. Many of the existing senior management in 1987, some of whom had been at Fairfax for decades, departed following the takeover.

Warwick's boardroom shuffles in 1990 also left a pile of casualties. When the company finally went into receivership, it was Warwick who occupied the chief executive seat in Sydney.

Greg Taylor, the long-serving managing director of David Syme, had ensured stability in Melbourne, although staff collectively waved their fists at what those Fairfaxes had done to the Melbourne subsidiary.

When Des Nicholl moved into the fourteenth floor at Broadway, the brief was simple. Keep the place running smoothly, the bank executives and Burrows told him. Don't do anything to further destabilise it. Burrows was acutely concerned about avoiding any industrial action. Fairfax wasn't like the hundreds of companies where it was easy to send in the receiver to look after the books, perhaps cutting some costs ahead of a resale.

The value of the business was more than just the printing presses and other equipment. A crucial factor behind the value of Fairfax was the staff. As long as the paper rolled off the presses, everything was fine. But if there was any industrial action, it would jeopardise the amount of advertising revenue and the value of the titles in any resale.

Burrows had to ensure that the businesses were not damaged during the receivership. One idea was the appointment of an interim chief executive reporting to Nicholl. The banks had no real problems with this idea, but decided to see how things went over the quiet summer months.

There didn't seem to be any urgency until an unexpected hiccup.

Alan Deans, the *Herald*'s business editor, was perplexed at the request. Who was Jim Grant, what was he doing on the fourteenth floor, the inner sanctum of management, and why did he want to see the business editor immediately? This was fairly irregular. Editors dealt with the fourteenth floor, not section editors. Journalists only went there for press conferences when company results were announced.

When Deans arrived, he could see that Grant was furious. Just what was happening on that editorial floor; who was running the place? Grant was jabbing angrily at an article in that day's business section headed 'AWA Sues Deloittes'.

Deans felt like he was being physically kicked around the office. He was not used to this sort of treatment. But as Grant shouted on, it all started to fall into place. Grant was a partner at Deloittes. He was apparently co-receiver with Des Nicholl, although he hadn't been a regular visitor to the Broadway building.

In fact, as far as anyone could recall, he hadn't been there before—until he turned up that morning white with anger. The thrust of the article was wrong, Grant claimed. The story by Anne Lampe, a senior business writer, stated that Amalgamated Wireless Australasia (AWA) was suing its auditor Deloittes for being negligent in the 1986 audits 'by not bringing to the attention of AWA management and board that certain foreign exchange transactions had blown out alarmingly in magnitude and were of a speculative and unauthorised nature'.

AWA had dropped $50 million on foreign exchange losses in 1986. It was still a high-profile business story at that time. And Lampe had pointed out that this was the first major negligence claim against an auditor since the 1987 stockmarket crash.

Grant demanded that the article be corrected. This case was so minor that Deloitte had not even bothered to file a defence, and in any case a judge had already thrown it out of a lower court two years before, he said. This was outrageous journalism. There was a hearing next month to have it struck out of the Supreme Court.

Deans was shocked. How could Anne Lampe get it so badly wrong? It would have to be corrected straight away. This was extremely embarrassing.

Anne Lampe could hardly believe what Deans was telling her. This meant her research had been inadequate and her contacts had lied. She had court documents, but obviously she only had half the story. She called Deloitte lawyer Warren Madgwick as Jim Grant had instructed. He repeated the information—AWA had failed to make a case, so no defence had been filed and in any case a judge had struck out the claim in the common law division two years ago. When the directions hearing came up on the commercial list of the Supreme Court next month the amended damages claim, if it was returned to the common law division, would again be defeated.

Lampe wrote a new story, correcting that day's error. The next day the story ran prominently in the *Herald*'s business pages. It was real cringe material for the section. No one likes to have to print corrections of this magnitude. It was headed 'Deloitte Moves to Strike Claim'.

But Alan Deans' and Anne Lampe's embarrassment turned to anger very rapidly that morning. Their phones ran hot with lawyers from the other side and Lampe's original contact. Lengthy court transcripts clogged the fax machine. The facts were indisputable. Deloitte had lodged a defence—and here was a copy of it, dated 2 February 1989 and signed by Warren Madgwick. The judge had not struck out the claim. He had said, 'I decline the defendant's motion to strike out the statement of claim. In lieu I grant leave to the plaintiff [AWA] to amend his statement of claim ...' The *Herald* had published an assessment of the legal action which was defamatory to the other side.

Alan Deans rang Jim Grant. 'Our story this morning is incorrect. The information you gave us was wrong.' Grant laughed and retorted that at least the balance had been restored from the previous day's damaging article. Deans was livid. The *Herald* had been exposed to a defamation action by the interference of its own co-receiver.

The article the next day was headed 'Claim Not Struck Out' and Anne Lampe wrote a tough first paragraph. 'A solicitor for accounting firm, Deloitte Ross Tohmatsu, Mr Warren Madgwick, has admitted to two major inaccuracies in his comments to the

Herald yesterday concerning AWA Ltd's $50 million negligence suit against Deloitte.'

As other journalists became aware of what had occurred the anger level rose. This was no different to an interventionist proprietor. How many other stories are going to go into the newspaper because the receiver wants them in? What happened to editorial independence? The Fairfaxes would never have allowed such blatant and misguided interference. But mixed with the anger was a certain level of glee. When the House Committee of the AJA (Australian Journalists Association) held its routine weekly meeting over the lunch hour, the importance of Grant's actions became apparent.

This was a perfect example of why a charter of editorial independence was needed while the company was in receivership. And once the receiver had signed it, it would be hard for any new owner to repudiate it when he took over control of the newspapers.

Grant had handed to the journalists on a platter the perfect basis for a renewed plea for an editorial charter. This was worth making a stand on. A full meeting of journalists was called and a strong motion passed calling for a signed charter.

Nicholl was to be given forty-eight hours to reply, or industrial action would be taken. Nicholl refused. No charter would be signed. It was outside a receiver's brief to undertake such contracts—he would leave himself open to legal action by creditors because such a contract could be seen to have an impact on the value of the asset.

The journalists wouldn't budge and a full twenty-four hour strike went ahead. There was national television coverage of journalists accusing the Fairfax receiver of editorial interference.

Nicholl and Grant were grim-faced as they fronted the Industrial Commission the next morning. They were on the back foot. At the judge's urging, the AJA and the receiver entered into negotiations.

The outcome was a memorandum of agreement incorporating the main elements of the editorial charter. Nicholl also undertook to inform all serious bidders for Fairfax of the AJA's demand that a charter be signed and to request that the bidders meet with AJA representatives before a sale took place.

Mark Burrows was furious. This sort of situation was exactly what he had hoped to avoid. The receivers had slipped up badly. It emphasised the whole management vacuum at Fairfax. A decision had to be made either way soon on the appointment of an interim chief executive.

. . .

Chris Anderson was blunt. Seated opposite Burrows and Nicholl, he outlined his list of demands. If the banks wanted him to go back to Broadway, it would be on his terms only.

In recent months Anderson had been in demand as Jamison and Independent attempted to interrogate those who could give them a feel for Fairfax. Both bidders had canvassed his views on joining their groups as they prepared their offers for the media group. So this approach from Burrows was another option. However, going back to Broadway to run the company during the receivership was a risky business.

A new owner might quickly dispense with his services, leaving him with the unenviable record of leaving the same job twice in controversial circumstances. There would be conditions. He knew he was the favoured candidate, so he pushed hard.

Anderson, in his mid-forties with his olive skin and sleek, black hair, can affect an ice-cold demeanour when the occasion demands. He reeled off his first condition.

Nicholl would have to vacate the fourteenth floor at Broadway immediately. Anderson had no intention of reporting to Nicholl sitting in some other office in the same building. Nicholl could either visit occasionally, or Anderson would come to Deloitte's office.

Nicholl sat quietly and did not respond. Burrows glanced at Peter Breese, the large, grey-bearded man sitting next to him. Breese raised his eyebrows, and then they both eased back in their chairs, as if to push themselves out of the way in a tight situation.

The bluntness of Anderson's demands shocked them: Anderson was demanding to his face that Nicholl pack his bags. Nicholl would go, with not even a few weeks to assist Anderson to settle in.

After all, as receiver he was legally responsible for the operation of the Group. Anderson continued, stating that he wanted to deal with the banks directly, not through Nicholl. He would only return if he received a decent twelve-month contract. He also wanted a full indemnity, not just for what he did during the receivership, but for when he was at Fairfax previously. The spiel finished; the room was suddenly silent.

The demands left both Burrows and Nicholl speechless. There was not much else that could be said, Burrows mused. Thanking Anderson for his time, Burrows stood up and escorted him back to the foyer.

The banks were as unimpressed as Burrows with Anderson's demands. The demand that Nicholl vacate the premises was not such a bad idea in principle. However, it was unreasonable to expect him to leave immediately, without giving him the opportunity to discover where things were up to regarding the receivership. The request for a contract rankled the bank executives in particular.

Anderson had done quite well out of Fairfax in the last twelve months. When he resigned the previous August, he walked away with a $2 million plus payout, including superannuation. There was a strong view that this was more than enough, and the demand for a lucrative contract was taking it a step too far. The banks believed they were offering Anderson a good deal anyway.

In all probability Anderson would be retained as the chief executive when the company was sold—both Jamison and Independent liked him and they were the two obvious bidders so far.

Burrows heard back after the next meeting of the bank steering committee—Anderson's demands were unreasonable. The only one other name mentioned as a possible candidate was Trevor Kennedy. Burrows knew from their telephone conversation before the receivership that Kennedy was interested. Also Turnbull's last-ditch plan put to Burrows on that frantic final weekend in December 1990 had included Kennedy as chief executive. On the surface Kennedy's credentials looked exceptional as a long-term Packer employee.

But the lengthy connection with Packer was a serious problem; Kennedy would be seen by many as Packer's Trojan Horse and he was worried about how the staff would react—he didn't want a repeat of the Jim Grant episode.

● ● ●

Since Burrows knew that he must conduct an auction to get as many bids up as possible, he couldn't do anything that caused a potential bidder to believe the sale process was a charade either.

Thus Kennedy was too dangerous. After some further debate, the banks decided that the best option was to appoint a management committee to run Fairfax, utilising existing management, or what was left of it.

The following week Nicholl summoned the editors and company senior executives and announced that he was going to form the committee.

Greg Taylor was the obvious choice for chairman. Peter Gaunt, the general manager of Broadway, was given the job of running the New South Wales operations. The finance director, Andrew Hogendijk, and John Alexander were also appointed.

● ● ●

The O'Reilly camp knew that the first presentation was crucial. If they could convince John Fairfax that their team had the necessary financial and management skills to run the Fairfax Group, he might decide to join their consortium.

All the key Independent people sat around the table. Cameron O'Reilly—Tony's son—John Reynolds, the chief executive of Australian Provincial Newspapers (APN, Independent's Australian operation), and Rowan Ross and Peter Hunt from BT formed the nucleus of the contingent.

While these four were primarily responsible for the carriage of the Fairfax bid, it was management consultant Chris Tipler who spoke the most at this meeting.

John and his adviser Brian Wilson, a corporate adviser with investment bank Schroders Australia, listened intently as Tipler forcefully argued a case that there was a lot wrong with Fairfax. Many of the operations were just not generating the sort of profits possible. Non-core operations should either be improved or possibly sold. Printing labour costs were too high, and much of the Broadway presses were obsolete. Editorial expenses should be less too.

● ● ●

Although Tipler had no formal position at either Independent or APN, his views had a lot of clout in the Irish camp. He is one of an informal group of Australians who O'Reilly uses constantly as sounding boards for his business ideas. Kevin Luscombe, a Melbourne advertising executive is another and Peter Cosgrove, the Irish-born boutique publisher based in Sydney is another. Tipler, an executive with Melbourne firm the Collins Hill Group, had been retained after Independent bought APN in 1988. A management consultant, his analysis of the sleepy Brisbane-based APN was a major factor in the subsequent shake-up.

APN had been a successful regional publisher, but Tipler and Independent considered it too bureaucratic. Years of staid, benevolent management had left it over-staffed. It delivered steady profits to its shareholders, so there had been no complaints.

When Independent arrived, there was no time for such a management structure. It needed to improve the cash flow of the business to lower the borrowings utilised for the takeover.

This was classic post-takeover stuff, and hundreds of Australian companies experienced the same thing during the 1980s. When Independent was making the acquisition, it gave the standard, well rehearsed line that there would be no job losses. Once Independent secured control, the clean-out began.

Staff numbers and overheads were slashed, and a more aggressive approach was taken to secure advertising revenue. Since the shake-up in financial terms was considered a success, Independent was confident it could transplant the management style to Fairfax.

Tipler's credentials due to his work at APN made him the ideal person for this preliminary sales job. The spiel from the Independent people sounded fine, but as the meeting progressed, it was time to consider John Fairfax's own commercial interests.

John talked about his own plans for his regional publishing empire and the *Newcastle Herald* was an asset that he had been keen to buy for some time.

If the newspaper could be sold to him, presuming Independent's offer for Fairfax was successful, he was more likely to be interested in participating in the consortium.

The Independent camp now knew where they stood; it was up

to them to consider in the next few weeks if they were willing to part with the newspaper in return for John's support.

■ ■ ■

Securing the support of an influential name like John Fairfax was only one aspect of the plans being hatched for the Fairfax purchase. From the outset O'Reilly's men knew that Canberra was an important part of the equation in the Fairfax sale given that they were foreigners. Well aware of the twenty per cent foreign ownership limit on television and the furore over Maxwell's bid for the *Age*, Independent quickly decided on the level of foreign ownership likely to be allowed in Fairfax.

Even without going anywhere near Canberra, a level of twenty per cent or perhaps as high as forty per cent was considered the likely limit. To many foreigners, this sort of limit was a negative, since it was hardly enough to warrant the effort.

Lazard Freres discovered this in no uncertain terms when it scoured the world for Warwick six months earlier. Although O'Reilly publicly stated that Australia should allow 100 per cent—if it was good enough for Rupert Murdoch to buy UK newspapers, then Australia should also allow foreign owners—he was pragmatic.

Indeed, when he worked it through, it was really a plus for his Independent group. O'Reilly realised that the likely foreign shareholding limit would dramatically lower the number of foreign competitors in the bidding process.

If the Federal Government allowed 100 per cent, major world groups would devour Fairfax, and his smaller Independent group wouldn't have a chance. Clearly the politicians were going to be important in the debate on what level of foreign ownership should be allowed. And after Maxwell, a 'good' and 'bad' foreigner would be an issue.

O'Reilly may have been well-known and liked by the Irish contingent in the Labor Party, but he wasn't going to take any chances. He ordered his team to make sure he was in the 'good' foreigner category.

So Cameron and Hunt got this underway by early March. A list of the forty or so important people in Canberra was drawn up, and the first visit made. Cameron, Reynolds and Hunt flew to Adelaide and walked into the electoral office of Chris Schacht, the talkative, influential senator in the Labor Party's centre left faction.

Discussing the likely level of foreign ownership, the three men danced around the issue of the possible top limit, and asked about the prospects of thirty per cent or thirty-five per cent. Schacht didn't waste too much breath about his faction's likely response.

'If anyone tries to get more than twenty per cent of Fairfax there will be a blue in Caucus,' he said.

■   ■   ■

Leaning back in his chair, Schacht was amused when the three men looked startled. Returning to Sydney, Schacht's comments combined with the response to feelers put out over the past few weeks convinced them twenty was actually a very good number.

In tandem with the survey of the political landscape, the other crucial issue was the need to establish Independent's credibility with institutional investors.

Faced with the strong prospect of a twenty per cent limit on foreign ownership, Independent would need to find about eighty per cent of the cash for an offer from the institutions. While Burrows was working on the main information memorandum on Fairfax, the Independent team had decided that they just could not wait.

An information memorandum would obviously contain strict confidentiality clauses, and this would impede their campaign to secure institutional support. The best option was for Independent to pull together its own document on Fairfax, describing why the Irish had the best credentials to secure the crucial institutional support.

Corrigan's advantage of already having some influential institutions as shareholders was a problem they had to overcome. Rowan Ross, the experienced senior BT adviser and Hunt knew that they must introduce Independent to Australian fund managers who probably had never heard of the media group.

The other task would be to convince Jamison's shareholders that Independent was a better proposition to manage Fairfax. As far as they were concerned, Corrigan didn't compare at all well with Independent because he had no experience in newspapers.

At the very least, Corrigan would need to get a chief executive with strong credentials to show that Jamison could actually run Fairfax—even Jamison's shareholders would want that.

Throughout March Independent frantically pulled together a proposal on Fairfax to be circulated to the institutions. There was no time to waste, since they wanted everything ready to make a big splash when O'Reilly arrived in late April. He was the ace card, and they needed to be ready to play it skilfully.

■   ■   ■

Mark Burrows and Jeff White were bemused. The two gentlemen from Melbourne were serious. They really thought that they could buy Fairfax. Burrows recalled Beerworth discussing 'Dad's Army from Melbourne' but thought that they were just on the periphery, not to be taken seriously.

They were determined to enter the process, however, and had come to find out what they had to do.

'What is your corporate structure?' Burrows asked Rob McKay with a sceptical look on his face.

'We don't have one at present,' McKay replied. 'It is less formal than that at this stage,' he added as an afterthought.

'But you have got to have a company,' Burrows said incredulously.

'You must have funds committed. We can't let you have confidential financial information without some indication that you have the substance to complete the purchase.'

Burrows didn't know it, but McKay and Harley were getting well prepared. They were an odd couple in the context of Burrows' world, however.

You don't have to ask Tom Harley whether he has studied at Oxford. He carries it with him. Tall and wiry with cropped, curly, black hair and wire-framed glasses, Harley has perfectly rounded vowels, yet a disarming, friendly manner. At thirty-five he had still managed to retain the lankiness of youth and an 'end-of-term' style of enthusiasm, despite the ever-present pipe. Harley is a keen supporter of the 'wet' faction of the Liberal Party in Victoria, with an academic view of what Liberalism should mean in Australia.

McKay is a much more reserved character—rather like a nineteenth-century British gentleman of independent means. He has wavy, greying hair, clear skin and bright eyes and has impeccable social graces.

Both men have a sharp intelligence but lack the macho exterior, so much a part of the Sydney business ethos. The two became friends in London in the early 1980s while McKay was managing director of publisher Macmillan and Harley was completing his post-graduate degree in politics at Oxford.

Ironically Harley and Warwick Fairfax were acquainted at university in England. Harley found young Warwick painfully shy. Just by saying hello to him, Harley had felt he was burdening Warwick with the huge social dilemma of how to reply. They had dinner together once or twice, but had little in common.

Now Harley and McKay were angling to form the basis of a bidding consortium called Australian Independent Newspapers (AIN). Its genesis went back four years to 1987. At that time the Herald and Weekly Times (HWT) group had just been taken over by Rupert Murdoch in the early summer.

Fairfax had ended up extracting the booby prize from the HWT fallout. It bought Melbourne television station HSV7, which it couldn't keep because of the recently introduced rules on cross-media ownership. But it was worse than that. Before Fairfax managed to sell HSV7 it practically destroyed the channel's value.

Fairfax managed to alienate a huge swag of Melbourne viewers in their bumbling attempts to create a proper Seven network (with their existing Seven stations in Sydney and Brisbane), replacing some of the locally produced programmes with those sent from Sydney. Ratings plummeted. Fairfax looked like a bunch of dunces.

Holmes a Court was in the background. He had played the HWT takeover like a violin, emerging with the very profitable *West Australian* newspaper group. Now in mid-1987 he was stalking Fairfax.

Harley knew Robert Holmes a Court well. He had wrestled with him in another corporate battle—the BHP takeover play. Harley, as a young Treasury executive, was part of BHP's takeover defence team—what they called the BHP bunker.

That four-year-long takeover play for Australia's biggest company had reached an uneasy truce by mid-1987—Holmes a Court still had over twenty per cent of BHP and a seat on the board but had agreed not to alter his position without prior consultation.

He was to move out almost completely a few months after the October stockmarket crash later that year. For now Holmes a Court, another British-style gentleman, was a hero, if a somewhat unlikeable one, of the Australian takeover scene.

Tom Harley was only just thirty in 1987. He loved newspapers, contributing the occasional book review to the *Age*. And he was a friend of the then editor of the *Age*, Creighton Burns. They frequently discussed the vulnerable Fairfax corporate situation, idly speculating what would happen to the *Age* and David Syme if Fairfax came into play. Harley had no doubt that something would happen to destabilise the Group. Once Holmes a Court fixed his gaze on a company, life was never quite the same again.

Harley had an appetite for corporate intrigue. And Burns, who had worked for the *Age* for twenty-three years, becoming editor in 1981, had a close knowledge of the dynamics of David Syme.

Harley's and Burns' conversations proved to be much more prescient a few months later in August 1987, when Warwick Fairfax made his takeover bid for the Fairfax Group. Part of his method for financing the takeover was to float David Syme on the stock exchange. The two friends came up with an idea.

If David Syme was to be floated or up for sale, why couldn't Harley and Burns become players? It was an idea that captured their and McKay's imagination. They began speaking to business contacts about the possibility of raising funds.

When Maxwell expressed interest in the *Age*, which caused an outcry among educated Melburnians, Harley and McKay were in the fray. They too would bid for David Syme. Burns, since he was still editor of the *Age*, had to step away from his friends at this stage.

They retained Macquarie Bank as advisers and began discussions with Fairfax management. The effort was fruitless, however. The price Warwick wanted was too high, and the Fairfax management decided to take the junk bond route to solve their financing problems.

Harley and McKay kept a watching brief on Fairfax through 1989. Macquarie Bank, however, did not stay on as advisers. As Warwick sank into even deeper trouble, Johnson was called upon to help. Capel Court stepped in to represent the Melbourne team.

About mid-1990, when receivership was looking a possibility, Harley and McKay again approached Fairfax management with an equity injection proposal—$400 million in return for a good chunk of the equity. It was the year of the insulting offer. They wanted their equity to rank above all other in the event of collapse.

When Beerworth joined the Fairfax board, Harley and McKay were still keen to be involved in some way. Beerworth dubbed them 'Dad's Army' because they were so pleasant and genuine but, by inference, a little naive. The Oxford image dogged them; it was hard for Sydney operators to take them seriously.

Harley and McKay were determined. They could see receivership looming. They began to look around for extra team members. First they wanted a credible chairman, someone who was an experienced non-executive director and who had a business track record which would impress the large institutions like AMP and National Mutual.

It was important too that the chairman be publicly acceptable—McKay wanted to avoid the glitz of the 1980s. Jim Leslie seemed to them to be the perfect candidate. He had been chairman of Qantas from 1981 to 1989, a director of groups such as National Mutual and Capel Court, and Chancellor of Deakin University.

McKay and Leslie knew each other. They were both on the board of the International Cultural Corporation. Leslie was enthusiastic when approached. He, like McKay and Harley, thought it was important that the Fairfax newspapers remain in Australian hands.

Shortly after Leslie joined, Fairfax had gone into receivership. During January the AIN team realised that it would be crucial to attract someone to the team who had newspaper experience.

Creighton Burns suggested John D'Arcy. An earthy Queenslander with thirty-four years in newspapers behind him, D'Arcy was an old HWT hand. He had been chief executive of the group for almost two years when Rupert Murdoch took it over in 1987. Murdoch didn't seek D'Arcy's resignation when he arrived at HWT; instead he made him chairman of the company and gave him a seat on the News Corporation board.

D'Arcy retired from the board in 1988 but remained a consultant to News Corporation. He was keen to be involved with Harley and McKay, but not until his News Corporation term expired on 30 June 1991. D'Arcy doesn't suffer from an Oxford image. He is the quintessential Queenslander with a dry wit, an earthy turn of phrase and an abhorrence for anything he would classify as 'bullshit'. He is a straight shooter who knows more about running a newspaper company than just about any other executive in Australia. He was sixty-one and he had worked in newspapers for most of his life.

As they returned to Melbourne after their meeting with Burrows, Harley and McKay realised they would have to form a corporate structure and show that they had access to substantial funds before Burrows would have anything to do with them. Little did Burrows know how much work had been done the previous year.

In 1990 Harley had spoken to Sir James Balderstone, the former chief executive of BHP and the first Melbourne-based chairman of AMP. Sir James put Harley in touch with the AMP's Sydney investment division. It was a weighty introduction.

In February McKay and Harley began approaching potential investors. The responses were promising; the idea of an institutional consortium appealed to many small funds management executives. The approaches were well-timed, since Independent had not progressed very far.

Boasting impeccable connections in the Melbourne business community, Harley and McKay approached several company superannuation funds, including CSR, ICI, BHP and Shell. They also approached Commonwealth Funds Management—which controls the funds of Federal public servants—and ANZ Funds Management, Rothschild Australia and Wardley Australia. The Australian Industry Development Corporation was also approached and was sympathetic to their plans. Each of these institutions signed a letter of support for AIN indicating their level of interest in investing in a Fairfax bid and undertook not to allow their funds to be considered as part of any other bid. The undertaking was valid until 1 July 1991. The letters were only indicative. They did not actually commit the institutions to the investment. As Harley and McKay called on the small funds, the pitch wasn't just about the need to protect Fairfax for Australians. They pointed out that an institutional group could probably pick up Fairfax cheaply. It was Corrigan's line, except neither men had Australia's largest funds backing them.

The plans ran into a hitch in the middle of these approaches. Their adviser Capel Court was a member of the National Mutual Royal Bank group, which was sold to the ANZ. AIN needed a new adviser, and discussions were held with Macquarie Bank. Since Mark Johnson had finished his Fairfax brief rather abruptly, he was again available to work on Fairfax. He quickly agreed to allow the bank's Melbourne corporate advisory team to assist AIN. Johnson and Macquarie were back on the Fairfax trail again, although this time it was more of a charity situation—only small fees would be charged. Macquarie Bank would then be paid a success fee.

Impeccable Melbourne connections are very useful and so is an adviser of the calibre of Mark Johnson of Macquarie Bank, but Harley and McKay were up against some of the world's best. On his way to Australia in his personal jet was Tony O'Reilly, nominated US chief executive officer of the year in 1990, racehorse owner, collector of political friendships across the globe, personal friend of Treasurer Paul Keating and the founder of the Ireland Fund.

· CHAPTER SIX ·

A TOUCH OF THE BLARNEY

AT TONY O'Reilly's fiftieth birthday party in Kilcullen, Ireland, in 1986, his son Cameron told the 500 guests 'You might be surprised that Valery Giscard d'Estaing and Ronald Reagan are not here. There's a very simple reason for that—they weren't asked.'

■ ■ ■

In Ireland O'Reilly has been a national identity since his teenage years. He has been a high achiever in two arenas—Rugby Union and business. In both he has made it into the international league.

He is best known in world business circles as the dynamic chief executive who revived food conglomerate, H J Heinz & Co.

To a different group of people he is the good-looking former Rugby Union international. In 1955 at the age of nineteen, he was the dashing 6 foot 2 inch winger who played in ten games on a tour of South Africa. His try scoring exploits filled the sports pages of the newspapers in Ireland, beginning a long career in international rugby.

As well as playing football, O'Reilly completed a law degree at University College in Dublin. When he finished, however, he decided that a career as a lawyer did not offer the same sort of financial opportunities and rewards that business could return.

With a good CV and years of cultivation of older businessmen in the rugby fraternity, he had no trouble securing a position as an assistant to the chairman of general merchant company Suttons.

O'Reilly didn't dally there for long either. By twenty-five he was head of the Irish Dairy Board and launching Kerrygold butter on the world market—a marketing triumph. A few years later the next rung up the ladder was the top job at the Irish Sugar Company.

It was here that his business and marketing nous attracted the attention of Heinz, while he was forging a partnership between Heinz' UK offshoot and the sugar company's subsidiary Erin Foods. Heinz' UK operations were sluggish, and O'Reilly was offered the top post in 1969. He took to the job of improving profit with gusto, impressing the Heinz executives in Pittsburgh. Nine years later he was their chief executive. It was an extraordinary appointment—he was neither a member of the Heinz family nor an American.

The ambition that drove such an astounding career grew out of an unusual childhood and, friends say, the insecurity it brought with it. O'Reilly was the son of a Dublin public servant, who didn't marry O'Reilly's mother until 1973, after his first wife had died. He told the *Wall Street Journal* in April 1992: 'We are all prisoners of our childhood.'

While he climbed the career ladder, O'Reilly maintained a keen interest in rugby—and this unfortunately led to an international comeback at the age of thirty-four in 1970.

His mind might have conjured up visions of youthful exuberance on the field, taking a pass on the fingertips, sprinting eighty metres and evading fifteen defenders to score under the posts. Sadly eighteen-hour days and years spent frequenting expensive restaurants and cocktail parties had loosened the muscles and reduced the lung capacity.

The comeback experience has become one of the oft-repeated anecdotes of his life. The Irish were playing England, and were being beaten badly. According to O'Reilly, as he lay on the ground shaken after being crushed by the marauding English forwards, he heard an Irish fan, who was unimpressed with O'Reilly's trappings of wealth, yell at the English team, urging them to kick him.

'And while you're at it, give him one for his chauffeur as well.'

When he took over the top job at Heinz, the group was not living up to its potential in terms of profits. O'Reilly, however, improved its performance with a tough line on production costs throughout the world and a zeal for marketing.

In 1980 Heinz was returning a poor margin of gross sales to profit of 8.2 per cent. By the end of the 1990 financial year, Heinz had nearly doubled this to 15.1 per cent. Shareholders were rewarded handsomely as the company's worth rose from US$900 million to over US$8 billion.

In the cut and thrust of the US market, such a feat didn't go unnoticed. In 1990 the *Chief Executive Officers* business magazine chose him as the number one chief executive in the USA.

His remuneration has also grown with the success of Heinz, and his personal wealth took a great leap in 1991—thanks to cashing in some options over Heinz shares granted during the early 1980s he received US$75 million including salary. This package was the second highest in the USA during the previous six years. Only entertainment group Time Warner's chief executive pipped O'Reilly with a US$75 million package in 1990.

His position as chief executive of a major world food conglomerate with some 3000 products has ensured O'Reilly a smooth entrée into the world of international business and politics.

He has collected some important directorships. These include the prestigious *Washington Post* and the New York Stock Exchange. He also holds the position of chairman of BT International, the Wall Street investment bank and also sits on the advisory committee to Harvard Business School. Connections are something O'Reilly is not short of.

Since he has been chief executive of Heinz, O'Reilly has assembled an impressive coterie of contacts, including former US Secretary of State Henry Kissinger; US President George Bush; Zimbabwe President Robert Mugabe; and Teddy Kennedy.

In Ireland he has even contemplated a political career and was offered the position of agricultural minister when in his late twenties. But the lure of the business world and the influence it brought were too strong. O'Reilly turned it down—his world is far more international than that of an Irish government minister.

O'Reilly jets between countries to meetings with businessmen and politicians in the Heinz Gruman-3 aeroplane. He obviously enjoys the role.

'There is a geopolitical quality to it—dealing with Mugabe, going to see de Klerk, meeting with Mandela. I find it very stimulating,' he once said in an interview.

Living in the USA for so long might have dulled the Irish accent, but O'Reilly remains a fervent supporter of his homeland. He founded the Ireland Fund in 1976, with a charter to foster the 'trinity of peace, culture and charity' within Ireland. It is non-political, non-sectarian and totally opposed to the use of violence in a country where religious warfare is virtually the only international coverage the country receives.

. . .

O'Reilly has all the trappings of success. His net worth is estimated at between US$250 million and US$300 million. He owns an impressive eighteenth-century manor, Castlemartin, south-west of Dublin, a mansion once owned by The Rolling Stones. It boasts a full sized rugby field, stud and pool.

O'Reilly also has his own business empire, which took shape as he climbed the corporate ladder at Heinz. It began in 1971 when he helped set up an Irish investment company, Fitzwilton. This venture was extraordinarily successful in its early years. He turned his US$80 000 investment into US$3 million within three years. Unfortunately since then the company has had a chequered history.

His next public company venture was in the early 1980s when he was involved in the formation of Atlantic Oil, an oil industry hopeful in the North Sea. The oil business is high risk, and although Atlantic found a pool of oil in 1983, the hiss of water and mud through a half-inch choke of an oil rig has been the most frequent sound since.

Apart from extensive property holdings, O'Reilly's other major investment was made in 1990 when he formed part of a consortium that secured a twenty-nine per cent shareholding in Waterford Wedgwood, the famous but struggling crystal and china company.

The media has attracted O'Reilly ever since his teenage days when he would send letters off to Irish Nationalist newspapers. His interest was indulged in 1973 when in a business coup he secured control of Independent Newspapers PLC, Ireland's largest publisher, whose titles include the *Irish Independent*, *Evening Herald*, *Irish Star*, *Sunday Independent* and *Sunday World*.

He orchestrated a deal to seize control and hence end the grip of the wealthy Murphy family, which had let the business run down. O'Reilly outlayed $2.3 million for 100 per cent of the voting shares, although they only represented four per cent of the total shares on issue. O'Reilly then put up an amazing proposal to make all the shares hold voting rights, provided he received a swag of bonus shares which then gave him a twenty-eight per cent voting shareholding.

These transactions delivered him control of the majority of Ireland's newspapers.

The Independent group has not stood still. It expanded into cable television in Ireland and diversified into regional and suburban newspapers and magazines in England. Outdoor advertising businesses were acquired in France and Mexico. There is also the Australian arm.

O'Reilly has always maintained close connections with Australia, despite spending most of his adult life criss-crossing the Atlantic between Pittsburgh and Dublin.

On a rugby tour to Australia in 1959 with the British Lions O'Reilly met Susan Cameron, the daughter of a wealthy family from Sydney's eastern suburbs. They married in 1962. They have since divorced—an event which his Irish newspapers declined to report—but the union, twenty-six years later, provided Independent with a foothold in the Australian media through the deal to buy Australian Provincial Newspapers (APN) from Rupert Murdoch.

In late 1986, when Murdoch took over the Herald and Weekly Times (HWT) group, the deal did not all go his way. He secured the Melbourne *Herald* and *Sun* and a monopoly of the morning newspaper markets in Adelaide and Brisbane. But there had to be divestments too.

One of those necessary, after the intervention of the Trade Practices Commission, was a forty-nine per cent shareholding in APN, which went to O'Reilly. He had begun spending more time in Australia since 1984, when he bought a share in Buspack—an outdoor advertising business, specialising in advertisements on the sides of buses. It was jointly owned by Peter Cosgrove, a bright young Irishman whose family is close to O'Reilly's.

On a trip to Australia in late 1987 to preside over the launch of the Ireland Fund in Australia, O'Reilly expressed publicly his interest in joining the Australian media club. Merchant bank Hambros Australia, acting for Murdoch on the sale, contacted O'Reilly and asked if he was interested in purchasing Murdoch's shareholding. He was. Australia's foreign investment laws posed a serious problem, however. Independent was unable to hold more than a 14.99 per cent share of APN without obtaining Foreign Investment Review Board (FIRB) approval. There was no chance that approval for 100 per cent would be allowed under the Labor Government's policy on foreign ownership of newspapers.

The lawyers and corporate advisers produced a scheme to overcome what appeared insurmountable obstacles. Because O'Reilly's children carried Australian passports, it was decided to use their status to comply with Australia's investment laws. An elaborate structure was set up that involved eighty-five per cent of APN being controlled by a trust. The sole beneficiaries are his six children.

It was cheeky, and O'Reilly knew that he would have to lobby in Canberra to ensure the scheme got through. When it came to Australian Federal politics, he had a powerful connection— Treasurer Paul Keating—whom he had known since the early 1970s. The Ireland Fund had also brought him into contact with the Irish contingent of the Australian Labor Party.

He had also been awarded an Order of Australia for his promotion of Irish–Australian relations. The thought of O'Reilly entering the media in Australia, albeit a provincial newspaper chain, was greeted warmly.

With Canberra on side, a takeover offer was made for the other fifty-one per cent of APN. There were no difficulties anticipated as Murdoch was keen to sell to O'Reilly. But there was one hitch.

John B Fairfax was also interested in APN and so was Associated Newspapers, which held a shareholding in Northern Star Holdings, the media group then based in the northern New South Wales town of Lismore. There were discussions about forming a joint venture to counter-bid.

This idea was good in theory until News Corporation was approached. Murdoch's Australian executives were blunt. It was too late for any counter-offers—even at a higher price.

APN was a good acquisition. But a regional newspaper chain like APN was not enough for O'Reilly. He joined the crowd watching and waiting for the opportunities Warwick Fairfax's troubles would eventually present.

Gradually O'Reilly became mesmerised with Fairfax as he saw the likely opportunities for securing either individual assets—the *Newcastle Herald* or the *Illawarra Mercury* would fit well with APN—or perhaps the whole Group.

* * *

Since Independent's interest in Fairfax was made public the day after the receivership, O'Reilly had been kept informed about the progress of the bid through seemingly endless conference telephone calls.

Liam Healy, the taciturn, elderly, grey-haired chief executive of Independent handled the offer process on a day-to-day basis. But by late April it was time for O'Reilly to come to Australia and press his case as a credible media proprietor.

O'Reilly was a major positive for the deal—his urbane, charming presence was considered an advantage that should be exploited to its fullest. Just before Anzac Day, he cruised into Australia aboard the Heinz jet, one of the perks of being a chief executive of a major multi-national food corporation.

* * *

John Reynolds led the presentation to the institutions, since he was the man who would be running Fairfax if the offer was successful. O'Reilly explained that his involvement with Heinz would limit his input in Fairfax, then outlined his philosophy about newspapers, stressing his commitment to editorial independence and fairness and balance in newspaper editorial content.

O'Reilly might have downplayed his future involvement, but the fund managers present were left under no illusions that they should look at Independent in the same vein as Heinz—his presence would ensure Fairfax delivered the same sort of profit growth as the baked bean and baby food conglomerate.

* * *

O'Reilly's strategy required a visit to Mark Burrows. Burrows was going to be a key part of the equation, and O'Reilly wanted to meet the auctioneer.

He was well-briefed on Burrows by Rowan Ross of BT before he arrived at Baring Brothers' Macquarie Place offices. Despite being on opposite sides of transactions many times, Ross and Burrows maintained a good relationship. The two met socially quite often, and Burrows never seemed to mind if it was Ross who picked up a job he missed out on.

O'Reilly turned on his charm with Burrows, Breese and White. The jokes flowed freely in his Irish–American accent. Burrows found him charming. On this occasion O'Reilly was keen to glean any first hand information he could about the progress of the sale.

The meeting, however, came at an awkward time for Burrows, since BT and Corrs, Independent's lawyers, were arguing over the terms of the confidentiality agreements that he wanted the prospective buyers to sign. The document was very tough, and drew an angry response from Independent, AIN and the other interested parties. Burrows wanted to keep tight control over the flow of information.

He didn't want bidders talking to each other, picking holes in the financial information exchanged between them or, more importantly, the institutions. Hence the document banned any bidder talking with institutions without the approval of Burrows.

There were also strict conditions regarding the bondholders— prospective bidders were forbidden from contacting them. This task would be handled exclusively by the banks through Baring Brothers and Morgan Stanley. The strategy was still the same— cut Turnbull out of the whole deal.

Burrow's pitch to O'Reilly was simple—he explained that once Independent signed the information memorandum, it would be able to proceed in the sales process. When it came to the likely length of the sales process, Burrows was cagey and O'Reilly was left uncertain whether it would be six weeks or six months before offers went in.

* * *

Neville Miles was methodically running through his latest plan to squeeze into a role in the Fairfax sale process.

The other brokers had mostly given up, but not this eager South African. As John Fairfax listened, nodding occasionally, Neville gave this one his best shot.

'The bondholders will be crucial to the strategy, since they can hijack the whole process,' he explained.

While Miles spoke John knew he had to ask *the* question. Miles' argument on the strategic value of the bondholders seemed reasonable, but was he speaking with authority ? It was okay to be sitting here offering Malcolm Turnbull as the carrot, but could he actually deliver?

'So do you have the bondholders tied up?' John asked. Miles was dreading this inevitable question. It had hung like a sword over this meeting.

'No, not at this stage,' Miles replied. 'Though if you were willing to become the cornerstone shareholder in a consortium, then I'm sure Malcolm and the bondholders would be interested.'

Returning to his office, John later discussed the idea with Brian Wilson. There didn't seem to be anything fatal about doing a deal with the bondholders, although the involvement of Turnbull was a factor to be considered. It was extremely hard to divorce Turnbull from Packer's camp.

The main issue was still the extent of involvement. John wasn't really interested in being a cornerstone shareholder, despite his emotional interest in the fate of Fairfax. The matter was left hanging until John's secretary buzzed him a few days later to say that Turnbull was on the telephone.

'Hello, John. How are you?' Turnbull asked, his manner familiar as if they were great friends.

As Turnbull spoke it became obvious that Miles had been speaking with him. Miles must have indicated that his talks with John were very promising. Now John twigged to the game. *He* was actually the carrot, not the bondholders.

Miles had spoken to Turnbull—whom he hadn't met before— and hinted strongly that John was keen on the consortium idea. It was a commendable try by Miles to generate a role—John's carpet at his Pitt Street office was showing signs of wear from the Fairfax approaches—but this latest one wasn't good enough.

As the conversation turned to a discussion of the sales process, Turnbull launched into a diatribe against Burrows.

'He refuses to even acknowledge me if he runs into me in the street,' Turnbull lamented, much to John's amusement.

A few days later John enjoyed another good chuckle when he began reading a fax that Ords sent him suggesting ways to move forward. The document was addressed 'Dear Malcolm'!

The next letter from Miles was a stronger one, carefully worded but urging John to make an early decision or risk missing the bondholders.

By now John was rapidly losing interest in Ord's ideas.

■   ■   ■

The John B Fairfax development was the only good news that Ezzes got from Turnbull when he arrived from the USA. It seemed like all the doors were still being slammed in Turnbull's face. The latest plans to use the bondholders as a crucial ingredient in a consortium were getting nowhere.

A few weeks before Ezzes' arrival Turnbull had telephoned Corrigan to run through his ideas before arranging a meeting. Corrigan gave Turnbull a good hearing. The broad strategic plan—the same outlined to Packer—had some merit in theory, except Corrigan had advice that the litigation was not as horrific as Turnbull would lead him to believe.

Also a forty-odd per cent stake in Fairfax that Turnbull indicated the bondholders would accept for their debentures seemed rather high. In fact Corrigan wondered whether it was an offer being made that he had to refuse.

As he considered what Turnbull was putting up, he also knew that Burrows preferred that no one should deal with the bondholders. Since Burrows was running the sale process, Corrigan felt if he started negotiations with Turnbull, Burrows might excommunicate him. He decided to put Turnbull's plans in his drawer to sit for a while.

After updating Ezzes about the talks with Corrigan, Turnbull explained that they would now do the rounds of the major institutions with the broad outline of a bondholder consortium.

Over the next few days they visited AMP and National Mutual, who were handed a six-page letter seeking support for a Turnbull & Partners underwritten consortium. The letter explained how the debenture holders had a very real economic claim on Fairfax, and that the bonds had strategic value demonstrated by the legal action against the banks.

Turnbull argued that the potential bidders could choose to by-pass the Fairfax corporate structure and bondholders, but he said this would cost at least $50 million in stamp duties and mean the buyer missed out on $250 million or more in tax losses.

Therefore, because of this cost, Turnbull claimed it was not possible to effect a sale or reconstruction of Fairfax without the debenture holders' involvement. It was a familiar theme and involved the bondholders swapping their debentures for some shares in Fairfax. But given the potential FIRB problems for the bondholders, they were happy to take non-voting shares and have no management control.

Under the Turnbull valuation, Fairfax—assuming no stamp duty and retaining the tax losses—was worth about $1 billion. The consortium offer would be $850 million cash for Fairfax, comprising $600 million of debt and $250 million in equity provided by new shareholders who would own 62.5 per cent of the company.

The bondholders would exchange their debt for shares and hold a 37.5 per cent stake in Fairfax. Under the heading 'Cornerstone Corporate Participation and Management' for the consortium, the letter cryptically stated that this would be discussed later.

The letter did drop a broad hint about Turnbull's hopes of involving Packer. Turnbull said that apart from Consolidated Press Holdings, in Australia there was no possible purchaser of Fairfax that had the financial resources to acquire the assets entirely for its own account.

'CPH is, however, committed to its investment in Nine Network Australia Ltd and is therefore limited to owning no more than 14.9 per cent of Fairfax equity.'

The reaction from the institutions was polite, but did not inspire a lot of hope in Ezzes. Turnbull and Ezzes then paid a visit to BT to see whether there was any interest from O'Reilly's Independent. They met Ross and Hunt, and Ezzes repeated his well-rehearsed line of the previous few days: someone was going to to buy these assets at some stage and the bondholders had some leverage because of the legal action against the banks.

Ezzes detected scepticism, and concern about the involvement of Turnbull due to the Packer connection. Later Ezzes began to have his own misgivings about the Packer issue. He telephoned Hunt to suggest another idea.

'I will handle the negotiations. It does not have to go through Malcolm, and Malcolm does not need to be told any details,' he suggested.

The approach was communicated to O'Reilly, together with BT's reservations about dealing with Turnbull. There was one more door to be shut in Ezzes face before he returned to the USA and Turnbull headed for the USA and then Europe.

Burrows was still refusing to give Turnbull or Ezzes anything, but they had been able to arrange a meeting with Nicholl. Agitated, Turnbull demanded a copy of the information memorandum. Nicholl refused.

There was one matter in particular to raise with Nicholl, and one which Ezzes was most unhappy about. Ever since Burrows sought professional advice from Morgan Stanley on the tactics needed to deal with the bondholders, the US investment bank had been criticising Turnbull's role.

'Did you appoint Morgan Stanley and ask it not to deal with Malcolm but the bondholders individually?' he asked Nicholl. 'If you think that you can divide and conquer you are wrong. Life doesn't work that way in the USA.'

Nicholl demurred on a response. When Turnbull flew out on Anzac Day for his mother's funeral in the USA, there was little interest from any of the public bidders. However, Turnbull detected that Packer was warmer to the bondholder consortium idea.

Packer, with Kennedy still pushing hard on Turnbull's behalf, was a little bit more interested in Turnbull's plans and there was another development. Turnbull had been talking with Packer about how he was going to cast his net wider and mentioned the name Conrad Black. This prompted a quick response from Packer. He told Turnbull not to speak to Black—he had already spoken about Fairfax to Black months before at a cocktail party in London.

*   *   *

Turnbull sat in his room in the Hotel Goldener Hirsch in Salzburg, Austria, listening to O'Reilly express scepticism about the value of the litigation against the banks.

Turnbull had missed O'Reilly in Australia and this was the first chance to talk about the bondholders. It was a lengthy telephone conversation with O'Reilly in Dublin.

'I can tell you, Malcolm, in the USA, even with all the detailed discovery process they have available, it is very hard to sustain cases in the junk bond market. It would be even more difficult under Australian law,' O'Reilly said. 'It seems like a case of *caveat emptor*,' he added.

Turnbull disagreed and explained the uncertainty of litigation. Turnbull thought O'Reilly sounded interested.

'If you line up with us, we can't be beaten,' he enthused.

However, Turnbull was unaware of just how strong BT had been in its recommendation that the consortium shouldn't deal with him. O'Reilly also had his own views on the Packer bogey. Knowing Turnbull's close, long-term relationship with Packer, he felt that all things being equal, Turnbull would be with his old friend.

At the end of the conversation O'Reilly said someone would get back to Turnbull. The holiday in Austria after his rushed trip to the USA was not enough to keep Fairfax off Turnbull's mind. The next day he fumed over John Fairfax and Ord Minnett.

His telephone conversation with Rob Mactier, an accountant who had joined Ord Minnett to get into the world of corporate advisory work and who was now working with Neville in the Fairfax pitches, was unsatisfactory. Turnbull had gleaned that John wasn't really interested in doing anything with Ords. Staring at the screen of his lap-top computer, he bashed out a one-page fax to Miles about the latest gossip. If John wasn't interested enough, he needed to know now.

'It is not appropriate for us to enter into discussions with Ords and reach a conclusion on a structure which Ords would presumably endeavour to sell to others,' he wrote.

'In brief, I am a little puzzled in the absence of John, what Ord's role is. I trust this is not offensive, but just as you need to know if we are serious (which we are), we need to know the same from you also.

'I have been keenly looking forward to working with both John and yourselves and have little doubt that with our forces combined we would win, but we do need to know what John's level of interest is.'

When he read the fax, and knowing John was not interested, Miles had no option but to cool things with Turnbull. He sent a fax explaining the position. On 8 May Turnbull responded with another fax to Miles.

'You might tell John he is missing the opportunity of a lifetime. If he did take a leading role in this deal, which clearly he will not, he would make more money than when Wokka bought him out.'

. . .

One person who didn't mind seeing O'Reilly leave Australia in the Heinz jet in early May was Corrigan. O'Reilly had been pitching at his Jamison shareholders to back Independent, and he was aware that Peter Hunt was suggesting to institutions that Jamison didn't have the management capabilities to match Independent.

In recent weeks Anderson was spending a lot more time at Jamison's office. He had quickly run out of options for a return to Broadway in his endeavour to back the winner. Burrows had not taken their discussions any further after the talk with Nicholl in March.

The talks with his acquaintances Tony O'Reilly and Cameron O'Reilly had also fallen through. O'Reilly had been keen to hire Anderson on some capacity—he had known him for many years. Anderson's wife Gai came from the same district as O'Reilly in Ireland. As Warwick lurched from crisis to crisis, the two men had been in contact and met occasionally in either Ireland or Australia.

Just before receivership Anderson spoke at length about Fairfax to Cameron. So when it came to working out who would be chief executive if Independent secured Fairfax, Anderson was obviously considered. Plenty of time was devoted early on to decide if Anderson was the right man.

He certainly possessed the editorial skills and was widely respected for the revival of the *Herald*, taking over the job commenced by Vic Carroll. Not everyone in the Independent camp agreed, however—feedback from within Fairfax suggested ill-feeling towards Anderson because he favoured the *Herald* over the *Age* or the *Australian Financial Review*.

There were doubters too about his tenure of top management positions. He had been in management for less than three years. Did he have the right skills on the financial side? In his defence, they were three extremely tough years that few experienced managers would ever need to face. The bulk of this time was taken up by the refinancing issue and trying to hold the Group together with chief executive Peter King.

By any measure this was successful in operating terms before the heavy interest expense swamped profits.

Independent had Reynolds as the other candidate, someone who had run a metropolitan newspaper in Perth for Robert Holmes a Court and was doing a solid job at APN. What Reynolds lacked in editorial experience, he more than made up for on the financial side of operations.

O'Reilly became frustrated when Anderson would not make up his mind. He confided to others that Anderson was being too non-committal on what Independent considered a good offer. He believed that Anderson was being cagey, over political, and was unwilling to commit himself because he wanted to make sure he was an executive in the winning consortium. It was understandable considering the circumstances of the previous three years.

To O'Reilly, however, it was a snub, an insult to Independent's chances. Finally Independent formed the view that they needed to present a chief executive designate to the institutions in their strategy documents and they were sick of waiting for Anderson. Reynolds was named as the chief executive if Independent won Fairfax.

This left Anderson out in the cold—unless he joined up with Jamison. During the past six months Anderson and Corrigan had met numerous times at his office in the Qantas Centre, discussing Fairfax and other media opportunities for the so-called vulture fund. So there was little surprise when Corrigan confirmed in early May that Anderson was Jamison's chief executive designate for Fairfax.

*   *   *

Anderson's appointment was a boost for Corrigan—Jamison could now fight back at Independent's barbs. He had someone with newspaper experience to improve the management credibility of his bid.

Anderson alone, however, was not enough and as May wore on Corrigan found himself deflecting more barbs that Jamison was just a vulture fund and an unsuitable owner of Fairfax. The critics were saying that Jamison was keen only to pick up Fairfax cheaply, slash costs and then sell it in a few years time to the highest bidder.

It was hard to refute, considering this is what Corrigan himself said of the strategy for Jamison when it was set up. The connection with AFP was also becoming a drawback in political circles. There was no love lost in Canberra for AFP, considering its executives' close friendships with John Elliott.

As a recent president of the Liberal Party and undisguised aspirant to walk into Federal politics and become Prime Minister of a Liberal government, Elliott was intensely disliked in Labor Party circles.

AFP's elaborate tax schemes were also a contentious issue, particularly in the left wing of the Labor Party.

Apart from the barbs, Corrigan's whole strategy of buying Fairfax cheaply and quickly just wasn't working. It had been crucial to Corrigan's plan that the institutions commit themselves quickly to Jamison, to avert the bidding war that Burrows was anxious to start.

As the months dragged on Corrigan was becoming increasingly anxious about how slowly the sale process was proceeding. Despite the merits of his strategy, none of his shareholders had yet committed themselves to a Jamison offer for Fairfax.

Leigh Hall at AMP had made it clear to his investment committee that AMP had an obligation to look at all the alternative proposals before committing itself. And that meant giving the other bidders time. Since none of Corrigan's institutional shareholders had told him that he shouldn't continue to spend his time concentrating on Fairfax, he took this as passive reassurance. But he was nervous.

The waters were now becoming muddy. Independent had time to crank up an offer, AIN was still doing the rounds of institutions and the other groups examining Fairfax had not not given up. As each week wore on, Jamison was rapidly slipping back in the field.

∎ ∎ ∎

Returning to Australia, Turnbull was keen to find out if O'Reilly was interested in the bondholders. Of course Packer was a possibility, but it would be better if there was another bidder to improve Turnbull's bargaining position with Packer.

Within minutes of his first conversation with Rowan Ross, however, Turnbull knew that O'Reilly had declined his offer to participate in a consortium offer. As he thought about the response during the afternoon, he decided that he would telephone O'Reilly in Pittsburgh late that evening.

Catching O'Reilly early in the morning, he had a simple message.

'I think you have just cost yourself Fairfax,' he said in an angry tone of voice.

∎ ∎ ∎

It was late in the evening, and Miles was irritated when the telephone rang.

'Hello, Neville. It's Malcolm here. I've got some great news,' Turnbull babbled, unable to disguise his delight.

Miles replied that sounded good, but it was Turnbull's next comments that were unexpected.

'Kerry has said he will be a shareholder in a consortium. If Kerry is in, then Conrad Black will go in.'

This development came as a complete surprise to Miles—in any discussion on Packer's interest in Fairfax, Turnbull maintained Packer was an unlikely participant.

According to Turnbull, however, Packer and Black had obviously been talking again, and Packer had invited Black to go jointly for Fairfax, with the Canadian as the core shareholder.

Turnbull was elated; he was certain that he was on the verge of producing a commercial and personal coup.

∎ ∎ ∎

What a team! Packer as a shareholder and Trevor Kennedy as chief executive.

Turnbull was determined to become a director himself at the second attempt. The pre-receivership plan on the eve of Warwick's collapse might have failed, but this time around he had a bargaining chip as the representative of the bondholders.

A board seat would enhance his status in the business community. There would also be the vindication of his treatment by Burrows and the banks. Burrows thought he was so clever shutting Turnbull out—now he would suffer the ignominy of Turnbull having a say on the restructuring.

Of course, the very basis of the deal would also deliver his bondholder clients an as yet undetermined payment. Then there were the fees—multi-million dollar fees for Turnbull's firm.

Finishing off the conversation, Turnbull excitedly said that there was something in it for Ords, since he was inviting them to be the underwriters of the consortium.

The Ord Minnett name would give the consortium credibility among the institutions. Turnbull told Miles they would have to act quickly and the two men agreed to meet the next morning to begin work on a proposal.

Sitting in Ord's offices in Grosvenor Place, the Harry Seidler-designed building full of stockbrokers and merchant banks, Turnbull and O'Connor handed over pages of detailed financial models on Fairfax. Miles and Rob Mactier also had boxes of material on Fairfax.

There was no shortage of information—dozens of financial documents on Fairfax had been circulating through merchant banks and stockbrokers for months.

. . .

Trevor Kennedy, who was dealing with the Tourang plan on behalf of Consolidated Press while Packer was in London, was sick of waiting in the twenty-fifth floor reception area of Ord Minnett. He had come down to discuss this consortium, and now the secretary couldn't find anyone! Kennedy was blunt.

'Where the hell are they?' he demanded when the secretary returned.

The woman nervously said she was still looking. Trevor wasn't prepared to wait and stormed off to the lifts, heading back to the Consolidated Press offices several blocks away in Park Street.

Meanwhile up on the thirty-second floor Turnbull, Mactier,

Miles and O'Connor were waiting for Kennedy. Finally the secretary, tears in her eyes, came into the conference room and explained what had happened. Shaking his head, Turnbull remarked that it was typical Kennedy behaviour.

After waiting ten minutes Turnbull telephoned Consolidated Press and listened to an angry Kennedy on the speaker phone. Kennedy blasted everyone for wasting his important time.

'Settle down, Trevor,' Turnbull replied with a wry smile.

●　　●　　●

The final document outlining the basis of the Tourang consortium was finished by Thursday, 23 May. The thrust of the proposal was clear, and Turnbull and Ords were making sure there was no room for error or disputes later about their roles.

Ords and Turnbull & Partners entered into an exclusive agreement to form the consortium—it would then invite Black and Packer to become shareholders.

In turn the bondholders would give exclusive support to it, cancelling their legal action against Fairfax and the banks if the consortium was accepted by the banks. This would pre-empt any other offer and leave the institutions no option but to back what the consortium believed would obviously be the winning offer. They also thought the banks would have no choice either, even if this meant an offer lower than the $1.25 billion bank debt. Armed with the proposal, Turnbull planned to convince Black and Packer that the opening bid should value Fairfax at around $900 million, plus the implied value of the debenture holders equity.

Black and Packer would each take a fifteen per cent shareholding, putting up $67.5 million each. Both Consolidated Press and Black's Telegraph would also receive 100 million options, exercisable at $1.00 each in 1993, with this cash to be used for capital expenditure. Ords would then underwrite the raising of $165 million from institutions. About $600 million of bank debt would remain in Fairfax after a re-financing.

The financial data completed, there was just one more issue that would need to be raised with Black and Packer. The fees. Of course Turnbull was already on a retainer and a success fee from the bondholders. Turnbull had fought hard for his fee structure—

the bondholders needed someone who didn't care whom he upset. Such loyalty has a price.

As far as Turnbull was concerned, this work on a consortium was different, an extra to his efforts as the bondholders' financial representative. Turnbull had no trouble convincing himself that an extra fee was justified. When the fees were being discussed with Miles, there were no qualms, since it was due to the offer of Turnbull that Ords was now set to become involved in the biggest corporate event of the year.

Turnbull and Miles discussed suitable fees. In the end a figure of $6 million was considered appropriate to put in the proposal as the initial ask from Black and Packer. Both men knew that Packer was not known for being generous in his fees to advisers, and they expected Black would be no different.

So it was decided that thirty per cent of the fee would be rebated to Black and Packer, and the rest split between Ords and Turnbull, reaping them $2.1 million each. Since Turnbull was adamant that the banks would be forced to accept his consortium proposals quickly, it was going to be a nice extra fee for probably three months' work. This Fairfax saga was becoming a financial windfall.

* * *

'I have to go to bed now. My milo will be getting a really thick skin on it.' The crowd roared as the pyjama-clad, young Warwick (comedian Jonathon Biggins) crept out of the room—the magnificent new dining-room of the State Parliament House in Sydney's Macquarie Street.

The Friends of Fairfax fund-raiser was raging. Three hundred people including journalists, stockbrokers, investment bankers and public relations executives had paid $75 a head on 17 May to listen to Patrick Cook, Phil Scott and Shirley Purvis mercilessly send up the Fairfaxes and the *Herald*. Leo Schofield was master of ceremonies.

David Marr, journalist and author of a biography of Patrick White, helped conduct the charity auction. For anyone involved in the Fairfax deal it was the place to be and be seen. It also served as a public launch of the Friends of Fairfax lobby group.

This was set up in January, after lengthy and heated meetings of all Broadway journalists, as an offshoot of the AJA's Broadway branch.

Its role was to fight against any further concentration of print media ownership and to protect the editorial independence of the Fairfax newspapers. It was pushing for a charter of editorial independence to be a condition of any sale agreement. The Friends of Fairfax had seemed a natural progression from the Media in Peril conference, which concerned journalists had held at the Sydney Opera House just three weeks before the Fairfax Group was placed in receivership. This had packed the Opera Theatre to capacity and attracted a number of passionate speakers, including author Thomas Keneally, playwright David Williamson and broadcasters Quentin Dempster and Paul Murphy. Establishing a lobby group was all very well, but the journalists realised that they needed money—for printing and advertising and travelling—if they were going to get their point of view across on how crucial it was to get the right new owner for the Fairfax newspapers. Raising money is not a strong point for most journalists. Early efforts at selling T-shirts and requesting donations had been unsuccessful.

A huge function with invitations to the right people, including the highly paid financial services industry, was the only way to go. It had taken months to organise, but it was worthwhile—it was a gala event.

Chris Corrigan and Malcolm Turnbull with wife Lucy were seated at the one table, much to the hilarity and gratitude of the television camera crew. Rowan Ross and Peter Hunt from BT were there; Mark Hodge from Beerworth & Partners; Cass O'Connor from Turnbull & Partners; Colin Winter; Mark Johnson; and Rob Mactier.

Alongside them were dozens of Sydney's angriest journalists and writers, those who had fought hard, spoken publicly, organised and attended rallies designed to ensure that Australia's print media didn't become more concentrated than it was already. They weren't all Fairfax employees.

There were Paul Murphy, Marian Wilkinson, Richard Ackland, Andrew Olle, Quentin Dempster, David Marr and Robin

Williams from the ABC. Also playwright David Williamson; writers Kristin Williamson and Richard Neville, journalist Brian Toohey, barristers Virginia Bell and Henric Nicholas, and writer and commentator James McClelland.

It was an impressive turn-up. It earned the Friends of Fairfax a welcome $25 000 and was one of the sharpest comedy shows of 1991. The laughs began with Cook and Scott in 'What is going to happen next':

> When you see a business die out
> Because some turkey's tried a buyout
> And the whole concern collapses in a heap
> And you wonder if your purity will earn you job security
> While others sell their by lines on the cheap
> We will all crawl to Murdoch when we go
> We'll all go together when we go . . .

As the night wore on the dining-room rang with voices singing Warwick's Anthem composed by Patrick Cook in 1987 (to the tune of the Nazi song from Cabaret) and revised slightly as events unfolded:

> The building on Broadway will have to come down
> I'm founding a new dynasty
> The noses around me will all be brown
> The prayers will be held at three
> O Harvard, dear Harvard, your favourite spunk
> Has learned that no lunches are free
> That bonds between brothers should all be junk
> The Herald belongs to me
> O, Mother, dear Mother, don't take it so hard
> I've cut the umbilical cord
> You'll always be welcome on Burke's Backyard
> But not on the Fairfax board
> And Mother, dear Mother, I know you'll be pleased
> I climbed over James and John B
> Who cares that my assets have all been seized
> The Herald belongs to me
> O Father, dear Father I can't tell a lie
> I've cut down the family tree
> The rest of the clan can eat shit and die

The Herald belongs
The Herald belongs
The Herald belongs to me.

* * *

The sale of the Fairfax newspaper empire might have been the most serious media event of the decade, but on 17 May it was all laughs. The dinner was a tremendous morale booster for the Sydney-based journalists. But most importantly it provided a war chest to fight against any further concentration of press ownership. Essentially that meant making sure Kerry Packer and Rupert Murdoch stayed away from Fairfax.

If the journalists had known that Malcolm Turnbull was on the edge of the deal of a lifetime, to be sealed in London on a fortnight from Monday, their laughs would have taken on a very hollow ring. And he might not have left the function unscathed.

CHAPTER SEVEN

THE SAVOY: TOURANG IS BORN

WHEN KERRY Packer heads off to England each year for the English summer polo season, he holds court at the grand old establishment Savoy Hotel off the Strand in London.

Like to a feudal baron, executives of his Consolidated Press come to meet their master for the annual management strategy session in May, allowing Australia's richest man to mix business and pleasure.

Packer's suite of rooms at the Savoy is impressive, even for those accustomed to grandeur. On the first floor of the hotel and overlooking the Thames embankment, the suite has meeting rooms, bedrooms and sitting-rooms. The large dining-room is attended by Packer's own staff, its furnishings supplemented by a few pieces from the family collection. It is a princely office.

Polo has been Packer's passion in the last few years, which has meant that more time is spent at his manor outside London. But the city and the Savoy have remained his base. Close to the casinos, the cricket and Wimbledon, Packer has on occasions spent months at a time in London. The Savoy Hotel was the obvious choice of venue when Packer summoned his appointed partners to determine if it were possible to form a consortium to bid for Fairfax.

* * *

Having arrived in Heathrow before breakfast, Turnbull, Mactier and Miles decided to liven up with an invigorating jog around the streets of London. Even corporate tyros like Turnbull need exercise. The three were jet-lagged after the long flight from Australia. Any thought of a restful sleep on board had disappeared when the aircraft lost altitude rapidly somewhere over the Middle East, prompting oxygen masks to be released to panic-stricken passengers. The bondholders could have lost their feared adviser before he got anywhere near a success fee!

The three set off, pounding the pavement. After a while Turnbull stopped and, puffing, pointed out a church. In short sentences he explained the building's historical significance to his jogging companions.

A few minutes later Turnbull—a noted rubberneck—again stopped to point out another building. At first Mactier and Miles thought Turnbull was an English history whiz—until he did it again and again. The penny dropped. They decided that the red-faced Turnbull was stopping only to catch his breath.

The trio certainly looked out of place when they trudged through the foyer of the Savoy Hotel that Sunday morning dressed in running shorts and T-shirts. It was hardly the attire for the crusty old Savoy.

■   ■   ■

When Brian Powers arrived at the Savoy Hotel later in the day, there was a message from Packer's secretary to telephone Malcolm Turnbull, also a guest at the hotel. The message was a surprise.

Powers had come to London at the behest of Kerry Packer and thought Conrad Black was the only other person he was meeting. Puzzled, he wondered what Turnbull was doing in London. It was not a name that Powers particularly wanted to hear.

Although he had only joined Hellman & Friedman in April, Powers' first briefing on the investment group's progress on Fairfax included uncomplimentary references to Turnbull. There was still deep-seated animosity over Hellman & Friedman's experience with Nine Network. Turnbull had been acting as an adviser to Packer, and Hellman & Friedman remained angry about Turnbull's tactics during the transaction.

Powers thought the request to speak with Turnbull before he had met with Packer was odd. Turnbull's name had not been mentioned in his telephone discussions with Packer the previous week.

This visit to discuss a possible consortium to bid for Fairfax had been arranged hurriedly and was the result of calling on an old and influential connection to assist in giving Hellman & Friedman an entrée into the Fairfax deal.

Since Fairfax went into receivership, all Hellman & Friedman's talks with prospective partners had got nowhere. The discussions between Mark Carnegie and Cameron O'Reilly proved fruitless; the Irish didn't want extra foreign equity and were confident they could secure the necessary institutional support.

Burrows was still keeping Warren Hellman informed about Fairfax and had now been speaking to Powers. A few weeks earlier Burrows was strongly hinting that Hellman & Friedman should contemplate joining the AIN consortium. However, Powers had another idea. He wondered what Packer was up to, figuring there was little point in taking on Australia's richest and perhaps most politically influential man on his home turf.

Rather than telephoning Packer directly, Powers opted to do the next best thing. He contacted Jim Wolfensohn, the expatriate Australian financier and Powers' former boss. Powers had worked at James D Wolfensohn, the boutique Wall Street corporate advisory firm, before moving to San Francisco.

Wolfensohn's impressive list of clients has for many years included Packer. Wolfensohn has been one of Packer's most trusted advisers for two decades and Packer rarely makes a major business decision without Wolfensohn's counsel. Wolfensohn sits on the boards of Packer's Bahamas-based companies and was a key person behind Packer's privatisation of Consolidated Press in 1983.

Wolfensohn is, however, much more than an adviser to Consolidated Press. He is undoubtedly the most successful Australian on Wall Street. His fee income is estimated at US$75 million a year, his partners include Paul Volcker, former chairman of the Federal Reserve and Lord N M Rothschild. He served as chairman of Carnegie Hall for twelve years, is chairman and chief executive of the John F Kennedy Centre for the Performing Arts in Washington and is on the board of the Metropolitan Opera. His advice is valued by Rupert Murdoch, Sir James Goldsmith, and a long list of US blue-chip corporations which comprise his client base.

Wolfensohn and Packer also socialise together. Saul Steinberg, a Wall Street financier, tells of an Alaskan fishing trip that he, Packer and Wolfensohn took in 1986. Steinberg recounts how Packer challenged Wolfensohn to cast his line a certain distance. Wolfensohn accepted the challenge. 'Kerry said, "If you can do it in three tries, I'll pay for the whole trip for everybody." So we measured the distance very officially and Jim tried a first time— twenty feet. He tried a second time and got within three or four feet. And, by God, on the third try, Jim did it—sixty feet three inches. And Kerry Packer paid for the trip.'[1]

Wolfensohn is also a friend of Warren Hellman. The two men were class mates at Harvard in the late 1950s. There was another Australian there that year—Rod Carnegie. He shared a room at Harvard with Wolfensohn, and this enduring friendship had led to Carnegie's son, Mark, the young, Geelong Grammar- and Oxford-educated financial adviser, assisting Hellman & Friedman in the pursuit of Fairfax.

Powers was keen to be involved in Fairfax and contacted Wolfensohn to find out what he knew about Packer's position. Wolfensohn said he would be seeing Packer in London in early May and would make enquiries. Aware that Packer would be limited to 14.99 per cent in any bid for Fairfax, Powers wanted to know if Packer was interested in a consortium bid. If he was, then that was the consortium that the energetic Powers wanted Hellman & Friedman to be part of. Two weeks later in mid-May Wolfensohn telephoned Powers with the fascinating news that Packer was considering a consortium involving Conrad Black. Packer was also prepared to talk to Hellman & Friedman about providing some cash for the offer.

Powers was delighted—the business network had produced an entrée to Packer. Powers had met Packer a few years earlier when he was with Wolfensohn, so he wasn't a total stranger when he telephoned Packer in London.

■   ■   ■

Packer suggested Powers come to London for the meeting with Black. They had quite a lengthy conversation and Packer was

---

[1] The *Good Weekend*, 28 March 1987

very keen to find out what Powers' plans were at Hellman &
Friedman. He clearly respected Powers' abilities.

A few days later Powers was contacted again and told to be in
London for a meeting on Monday, 3 June. As he left San Francisco
he ranked the chances of a successful deal at about ten to one.
These odds seemed infinitely better than anything else available.

●   ●   ●

Powers was on the verge of making a flying start with his new
employer if Hellman & Friedman joined a consortium involving
Conrad Black and Kerry Packer. It was thanks to the years
working for Wolfensohn or in close association with him. Indeed
Powers' climb through the ranks of corporate advisers and his
contact with the rich and powerful in international business is
largely owed to working with Wolfensohn.

After graduating from Yale University and The University of
Virginia law school, Powers set his sights on a career on Wall
Street, lured by the vision of working on billion-dollar transactions. He completed two years with a Wall Street law firm and
then joined Wolfensohn, broadening his skills from law to corporate advice.

In the mid-1980s Powers, a tall, fast-talking man, spent a large
amount of his time in Hong Kong advising a particular client,
Jardine Matheson. Jardine is the exotic and unwieldy conglomerate founded in 1832 by two Scottish traders—some say pirates—
in what was then known as the Far East.

Jardine's massive Asian interests cover trading, property and
financial services. In Australia the group's businesses include
supermarket chain Franklins and Pizza Hut restaurants. But
Jardine is perhaps best known as the trading house fictionalised in
novelist James Clavell's *Taipan* and *Noble House*.

In 1986 Powers left Wolfensohn to become a strategist at
Jardine at a time when the group was going through a major
examination of its corporate structure and operations. There was
a legion of corporate advisers and stockbrokers in the frenzied
atmosphere of the booming sharemarket in Hong Kong putting
up proposals to split up the corporate structure, and these inevitably ended up on Powers' desk.

Under his supervision Jardine underwent a major restructuring, splitting up operations into new divisions and listing them on the sharemarket. It was a huge assignment and Powers, who borders on being hyperactive, worked incredibly hard to effect the complex re-organisation.

In a hectic two years Jardine split Dairy Farmers and hotel group Mandarin Oriental out of property group Hong Kong Land. Powers also oversaw a proposed expansion of Jardine into US financial services when it bought a twenty per cent stake in Wall Street firm Bear Sterns. The move was badly timed, just days before the October 1987 sharemarket crash. Bear Sterns' share price crashed to US$12, well below the US$23 a share takeover offer, and the bid was called off. Bear Sterns sued Jardine for reneging on the deal.

Powers' achievements in the Jardine restructuring were rewarded in a way that shocked many in the British and Chinese business community in the Colony. In March 1988 he was appointed chief executive of Jardine, succeeding Simon Keswick, a descendant of one of the two founders of the empire.

The thirty-eight-year-old Powers became the first non-English head of Jardine, effectively 'the Taipan' (Big Boss) of the conglomerate. The appointment lasted only five months when Powers announced his sudden resignation citing the ill-health of his wife.

The rumour mill in Hong Kong worked overtime to find other reasons for the departure as gossip of palace coups swirled around financial circles. Powers returned to the USA and rejoined Wolfensohn's firm.

■　■　■

While Turnbull, Mactier and Miles jogged around the streets of London, Steve Ezzes was arriving at Heathrow. He had flown in from New York on three days' notice. Turnbull had rung him on Thursday. He was ecstatic. Packer had agreed to be part of the consortium and he was bringing in Conrad Black. Could Ezzes get to London for the meetings on Monday?

Ezzes was the only bondholder Turnbull contacted regarding the London meeting. Drexels was not told by either Turnbull, its financial adviser, or Ezzes, the co-chairman of the bondholder committee, about the talks. But there were complications at the decimated junk bond group. Atanasio had just left Drexels to set up his own financial consultancy. Doug McClure of Drexel New York, who had worked on Fairfax with Atanasio, was not as familiar with the deal.

When Ezzes arrived at the Savoy he contacted Turnbull, who sternly told him of the presence of Hellman & Friedman for the first time. Turnbull was clearly miffed that Packer hadn't told him earlier of this other potential investor.

The proposal that Turnbull and Miles had put together didn't include Hellman & Friedman, and Turnbull couldn't see the benefit in letting the US group come in. As far as Turnbull was concerned, they only brought cash to the deal, and there would be no shortage of that from institutions in Australia for a bid for Fairfax.

However, since Packer had delivered Turnbull an edict to see Powers, he wasn't going to argue. Later in the evening Powers came to Turnbull's suite and listened while he outlined the plans for the consortium based on an exclusive agreement with the junk bondholders.

Powers thought Turnbull's plans reasonable and logical. The conversation ambled along until Powers mentioned to Turnbull that he might be interested in the chief executive's position at Fairfax. This comment amazed Turnbull.

His close friend Kennedy was the obvious choice. Powers had no management experience in media and Turnbull, suppressing his anger at the suggestion, informed Powers that the position was for someone with media expertise.

Perhaps Powers should think about a position at Consolidated Press to replace Kennedy? When Powers left, Turnbull was even more unhappy about Hellman & Friedman's presence in the consortium negotiations.

*   *   *

On a cloudy Monday morning just before 10 am the nucleus of the Tourang consortium gathered in a meeting room in Packer's suite.

Half an hour earlier Powers had enjoyed a private meeting with Packer to explain to him the investment philosophy of Hellman & Friedman. Powers stressed that the firm's reputation was based on conservative, non-entrepreneurial activities.

As Powers was leaving Packer formally raised the possibility of a job—if this consortium didn't work out, why didn't Powers come across and work for him? What Powers didn't know was that shortly before he arrived in Packer's suite, Malcolm Turnbull had paid a quick visit. He was anxious about the conversation the previous night. Turnbull suggested to Packer that perhaps Powers could replace Kennedy at Consolidated Press.

As Packer raised the Consolidated Press job, it wasn't something Powers was going to rule out immediately. Powers deferred the issue by saying he would think about it. He imagined the response from his family to another move after just settling in San Francisco. He was also keen to put his skills into Hellman & Friedman's investment plans—the philosophy of the firm, similar to Wolfensohn's, appealed to him.

At 10 am the meeting began. Powers, Turnbull, Ezzes, Miles, O'Connor and Mactier angled for places at the table. Packer's large frame dominated.

With everyone seated, Packer and Turnbull engaged in light-hearted banter as Turnbull introduced his team. Black wasn't there—Packer announced that he wouldn't be joining negotiations until 3 pm.

Turnbull then took control of proceedings, confidently running through the plans contained in the document that had been faxed to Packer nine days before. Packer nodded occasionally, periodically barking sharp questions at Turnbull.

It was not difficult for Turnbull to field queries on the proposal; he had spent so long mulling it over in his mind during the last few months that he knew it as well as he would a brief when he was a barrister.

Cass O'Connor then gave a rundown on the valuation of the Fairfax Group. Packer was getting agitated. He was taking a tough line on how much the junk bonds were worth, with continual interjections. He questioned Turnbull and Ezzes sharply on why the bondholders—unsecured creditors under Australian law —should get $150 million if Fairfax was only worth $800 million to $900 million. Packer was starting his valuation of the bond-holders' package at zero!

Turnbull explained the strategic value of the bonds and how their exclusivity agreement was a key plank of the plans. With their exclusive support, Tourang would be unbeatable—these were the sort of words that Packer liked to hear. Still he was uncompromising. It was clear that his problem was not with the substance of Turnbull's argument; it was the cost of the support.

Bluntly Packer said he was only prepared to pay $50 million, not $150 million. He would not be swayed from this number.

With a stand-off, the meeting broke up for lunch and they assembled in the dining-room of the Packer suite, presided over by the butler. Discussions would resume when Conrad Black arrived.

•   •   •

Black, a tall, large man with narrow eyes, effects a stately presence. On this occasion it was also a quiet and thoughtful one. He listened intently as first Packer and then Turnbull outlined the plans and the discussion to date.

When Black broke his silence, his comment stunned Turnbull.

'Malcolm, if you don't mind my saying so, don't you have a problem representing the bondholders and receiving a fee from Ords for the consortium concept?'

Turnbull sputtered as the others broke out in loud laughter, the loudest coming from Powers' direction.

'No, of course not,' he replied indignantly. 'I am quite capable of doing both. Steve Ezzes is here. He is the chairman of the bondholders. He has no problem with it.'

The subject was dropped and the wicked smile gradually left Black's face.

The broad parameters of the shareholdings were discussed. The Telegraph would take a twenty per cent interest, and Packer's Consolidated Press would stick to 14.99 per cent. Hellman & Friedman would take another fifteen per cent.

The issue of how much foreign equity would be allowed was discussed. Neither Turnbull nor Packer could see any problems with the Government allowing thirty-five to forty per cent, although it was mentioned by Turnbull that the issue would be sensitive. The politics were also going to be important, due to the presence of Packer.

The issue of media cross-ownership would be raised, so it would be necessary to ensure that there could be no question about any Packer control of the consortium. Independent directors would be sought for the board, and it would be made quite clear that Black was leading the consortium and that Packer was nothing more than a passive shareholder, complying with the laws on cross-ownership.

With Packer's influence in Canberra—particularly the powerful New South Wales right-wing faction—and Turnbull's own professed lobbying skills, Government approval didn't seem like an insurmountable hurdle.

The conversation swung around to the issue of how much the bondholders should receive. After Turnbull repeated his arguments on why the bondholders were crucial to the whole transaction, Black demurred on Packer's hard-line valuation of the bonds.

Black suggested that a $100 million price tag seemed fairer. This was still $50 million short of Turnbull's asking price. Even at $150 million it only meant thirty cents in the dollar for the bondholders who had outlaid $450 million on the junk bonds less than two years before.

The discussion was becoming heated as Turnbull tried to stand his ground on price. Packer now had an ally in Black, and they were both pushing for the maximum of $100 million.

Turnbull, exasperated, again went through the argument about the benefit of the exclusivity agreement. Why couldn't they see the enormous benefits? There could not be any other winner than Tourang. Packer was stubborn and was also clearly enjoying the debate with Turnbull.

To the others in the room, the money seemed only one side of it—having the upper hand in the debate was also important. Finally Turnbull laid down the ultimatum—it was $150 million or nothing. But Ezzes interjected.

'Let's go and talk about this first, Malcolm,' he said hurriedly.

Turnbull, O'Connor and Ezzes retreated to the dining-room. Ezzes was stern with Turnbull.

'I am not walking out of here with nothing. Let us offer to settle for $125 million.'[2]

---

[2] Turnbull insists that Ezzes was in fact prepared to agree to $100 million and that Ezzes only suggested at this point that they ask for a 'sweetener' of some options.

Turnbull warned he was prepared to walk out on this one. He finally demurred, however, but queried who was going to ask.

Ezzes replied quickly and sarcastically. 'I would ask, but I am paying you to ask.'

Returning to the room, Turnbull said the bondholders would accept $125 million or they were leaving. Powers and Black agreed to Turnbull's compromise immediately.

Packer smiled and then acquiesced to his partners' decision — the broad parameters of the consortium were now agreed. There was one more issue that had been on Packer's mind, however. The bondholders would need to have a representative on the board.

'I want to be on the board,' Turnbull said bluntly.

A seat on the Fairfax board would be a suitable prize for his efforts — and a prestigious and influential position for someone who had pursued Fairfax for so long. There wasn't any opposition to the suggestion — to the others it didn't seem like a really important issue. As the meeting wound up, Black announced that his lawyer Dan Colson would be handling future negotiations.

Black then invited Turnbull, Ezzes and the team to a 'getting-to-know-you' meeting at his office at the Daily Telegraph PLC headquarters the following day.

* * *

Conrad Black, in a dinner suit and clutching a glass of red wine, stood beaming outside Lord Jacob Rothschild's mansion in the heart of Mayfair. It was well after midnight and a few months after the Savoy meeting.

'Look, everybody loves me!' he exclaimed to a journalist as he saw off the last of the guests who had paid homage to the relatively new entrant to media barony at his annual Hollinger dinner.

Hollinger Inc. is Black's listed Canadian holding company. The gathering epitomised the circles in which Conrad Black now mixed, a testament to the power and prestige that his media business success had delivered him.

His heroine Margaret Thatcher — whom he once described as the only true revolutionary in British history — mingled with the other guests, friends and acquaintances.

Packer's friend and business partner in huge takeovers, Sir

James Goldsmith, was a guest, along with Richard Pearle, a former Assistant Secretary of State to Ronald Reagan; Paul Volcker, former US Federal Reserve boss; and Zbigniew Brezinski, former National Security Adviser to ex-US President Jimmy Carter. There was even royalty, represented by Princess Alexandra and husband Angus Ogilvy.

If Conrad Black owned an international manufacturing business with identical revenues and geographical spread to that of his Hollinger group, the chance of boasting the names that grace his board of directors and international advisory boards would be very slim.

However, an invitation for a directorship of a company owned by a successful media proprietor—especially a staunch conservative—has a certain allure, reflected by the high-profile, successful businessmen and politicians who have befriended Black.

Black's directors are definitely of the conservative persuasion, a political stance that he embraces with a passion. Hollinger's advisory board, set up in the autumn of 1990, includes former US Secretary of State Henry Kissinger and former head of the US Federal Reserve Paul Volcker.

Black's rapid entry into the UK's powerful business circles was facilitated by the presence of Lord Carrington, the UK politician who was Secretary-General of NATO between 1984–88; Lord Hanson, the chairman of sprawling conglomerate Hanson PLC; and Lord Rothschild, chairman of banking dynasty J Rothschild Holdings PLC.

Black's acquisition in 1985 of the Telegraph, publisher of the conservative newspapers the *Daily Telegraph* and the *Sunday Telegraph*, brought with it prestige.

The Telegraph board includes Sir James Goldsmith; Sir Evelyn de Rothschild, chairman of N M Rothschild and Sons Ltd; and Sir Martin Jacomb, deputy chairman of Barclays Bank PLC.

Black also included a number of peers on his board: Viscount Camrose, Lord Hartwell, Lord King of Wartnaby (who is also the chairman of British Airways) and Lord Rawlinson of Ewell.

Black's zeal for right-wing politics meant that he had two heroes during the 1980s—Reagan and Thatcher. Black was a staunch supporter of Reagan's economic and new world order formula. Margaret Thatcher's attack on unions and the welfare system and her push for privatisation found solid support from Black.

His historic hero is Napoleon and a portrait of the Emperor and paintings of military battles adorn his London office. The Canadian is unabashed about his political stance, although he bristles at the label of extreme right-winger. If he is, he once argued, then so are the voters who elected Margaret Thatcher and Ronald Reagan.

Black is precise about his political allegiance, maintaining that his:

> ... conservatism is based on respect for the fact that in a sophisticated society the incentive system is the only basis on which an economy can properly function.
>
> Obviously, in any sophisticated society, the system has to temper its economic Darwinism with a reasonable safety net for those who don't succeed in that environment. But the safety net ought not become a hammerlock. The whole process of taking money from people who have earned it and giving it to people who have not earned it, no matter how deserving they may be, is one that the state should enter into with great caution. Beyond a certain point it becomes an essentially corrupt system where the property—income being defined as property—of the productive elements of society is confiscated and redistributed in exchange for votes. My interest is not in short-changing the needy. My interest is in not removing the incentive for those who are the producers and creators of jobs. That is a matter of economic justice as well as expediency.[3]

Support for conservative policies has been a trade mark of Black's newspaper group, particularly the small newspapers in the USA and Canada, which formed the backbone of his media interests until the purchase of the *Daily Telegraph* and the *Jerusalem Post* in Israel. Into the 1990s Black has continued the expansion of the small rural and regional titles. The regional publishing group is run by David Radler, the Toronto-based Hollinger executive, who has no qualms about pursuing a political agenda. 'One of the reasons their conservative owners let us buy them,' he believes:

> is that they feel more comfortable selling to us than to someone else.
>
> We now own seven papers in Mississippi and I know we got the *Meridian Star* over two higher bids strictly because we're so

---

[3] The *Bulletin*, 23 July 1991

conservative. Our ideological reputation has been a real plus for us.

We gear the products to the people who read it—and we're good at it. We give the people what they want. I don't try to determine what's good for them—and that's the difference— because many publishers put in all that liberal nonsense and then wonder why circulation has dropped.[4]

The Telegraph group ran conservative papers before Black arrived, and the tradition has been maintained. Black vigorously denies he is an interfering, meddling Fleet Street proprietor, but he certainly makes sure his editors are under no illusions about where he stands on particular issues.

Black often writes to his newspapers expressing his views, dissenting from the views expressed in the articles appearing in the editorial pages. One of the most notable disputes on matters of editorial content occurred in 1986 when the *Daily Telegraph* criticised the US bombing of Tripoli. Black made it clear to the editor Max Hastings that his newspaper was not going to take a stance that gave comfort to Colonel Gaddafi or weakened the UK–US alliance.

Black has always publicly professed full support for the principles of editorial independence and denies he has ever instructed or directed his editors to pursue a political agenda. He espouses non-interventionist principles, but once made a telling remark that indicates the potential for a proprietor to ensure there is limited grounds for dissent on issues. After acquiring the Telegraph, he commented: 'I have felt all along that the best available course was to engage people with whom I was in general sympathy ideologically and philosophically, and vice versa, knowing that there would be differences from time to time.'

■ ■ ■

Unlike the three Australian media families—Fairfax, Packer and Murdoch—Black was not born into a newspaper and magazine business. His family wealth, however, gave him an excellent start

---

[4] *Maclean's*, a Canadian weekly magazine, 3 February 1991

in life. There was no struggle out of poverty to be a successful man; Black has only ever known comfort.

Black's father George was a successful businessman who founded a brewery and later became chairman of E P Taylor's Canadian breweries when he sold his operations into the larger company.

Profiles of Conrad Black usually recount his interest in money from an early age—the purchase of a single share in General Motors Corporation and washing dollar bills. He was later expelled from an expensive private school for stealing copies of exam papers and selling them to other students.

While at university studying civil law and history, Black and two friends bought a small, loss-making Quebec newspaper. After some savage cost-cutting, the venture proved successful. The purchase was the start of a chain of similar papers in Quebec and Vancouver. After university Black completed a 700-page book on Maurice Duplessis, a former Premier of Quebec, and assisted in developing the newspaper chain.

In 1978 he turned his focus solely to a business career and chose Argus Corporation, a conglomerate with assets of over $4 billion, as his target. There was an element of revenge in the choice of Argus, since Black's father was once a significant shareholder but had lost out in a power struggle with the board.

Black and his partners seized control of the group, replacing the two widows of former company executives in the process. The widows had effectively controlled Argus since the death of their husbands. Black appeared to enjoy the jousting of a major take-over move as much as he did his great love for war games and military history.

In commercial terms it was a clever victory, since Argus was secured with an outlay of only $30 million, and it suddenly put Black in the position of running a large, diverse group. It had delivered him control of farm equipment producer Massey-Ferguson; of thirty per cent of supermarket group Dominion Stores; fifty per cent of Standard Broadcasting; and Hollinger Mines.

Black approached his new group with gusto, spending the next two years in cost-cutting, staff retrenchments and engineering the merger of various group companies, the first being Argus, which merged with Hollinger Mines.

Black became chairman of Massey-Ferguson and vowed he would return the struggling group to profits, undertaking the closure of loss-making activities. The task proved more difficult than he anticipated and he gave it away before succeeding, quitting as chairman in 1980—observers claimed at the time that he had lost interest in the project.

Expanding the newspaper chain was a strategic goal and included a $100 million offer for F P Publications, the publisher of eight titles including the *Toronto Globe* and the *Mail*. This bid failed, partly because the staff encouraged a counter-bidder, Lord Thomson.

The machinations at Argus prompted criticism in some quarters in Canada. There were grumblings that minority share-holders in the group were not faring as well as Black's private company Ravelston Corporation, which was at the top of the corporate tree.

Publicly listed vehicles like Dominion Stores—which was finally split up and the stores sold to German interests—were left lumbered with underperforming businesses from elsewhere in the group.

Black's critics, both business and political, ensured an incident involving a superannuation fund attracted widespread publicity. About $60 million was transferred out of the Dominion Stores pension fund into a Black private company after being authorised by the pension commission of Ontario. The removal of the funds prompted litigation by one of the unions whose members were members of the fund, and there was an outcry against Black.

A politician Bob Rae attacked Black repeatedly over the matter, claiming under parliamentary privilege that Black was stealing from widows and orphans. Rae also labelled Black a 'symbol of bloated capitalism at its worst'. There was an inquiry by the Ontario Securities Commission, whose findings vindicated Black's actions: he was totally exonerated since he had complied with the law.

• • •

In 1985 Black turned forty and was already a very wealthy man, keen to acquire more substantial newspapers. The opportunity to purchase a holding in the Telegraph presented itself. The newspapers, the *Daily* and *Sunday Telegraph*s, were run down and losing money. The Berry family, which controlled the group, had shown little inclination to take the hard decisions necessary to revive it.

Black entered into negotiations and struck a deal involving the payment of £10 million for a fourteen per cent holding plus an option to buy the rest of their holding. The holding was important but not as critical as the rest of the agreement. Black had the right to purchase any further shares that the Berry family sold—effectively they were trapped into eventually giving him control.

There was some later consternation among Berry family members. The John Fairfax Group was also on the lookout for offshore expansion at that time and some members of the family contemplated a belated rival proposal. However, the option agreement had been carefully drafted by Dan Colson and left no chance of Fairfax or the Berrys overturning the initial agreement without litigation which they would almost certainly lose.

The Canadian focused his energies on the *Daily Telegraph* and undertook a major overhaul. The defeat of the UK print unions on Fleet Street by Rupert Murdoch allowed Black to follow suit, slashing non-newsprint production costs and moving the newspapers out of Fleet Street. Management was shaken up as Black moved new people into the top management positions.

He appointed Andrew Knight, a former editor of the *Economist*, as chief executive and Knight continued the rationalisation. He left after three years, not very popular with Black but somewhat richer thanks to a generous option scheme. Knight is now an executive with Murdoch's News Corporation.

Within five years total staff numbers at the Telegraph were slashed from 5000 to 1000, the bulk of this from the production area. The Telegraph returned to profitability, and rival newspaper group executives labelled the initial purchase as one of the shrewdest ever achieved on Fleet Street. Black eventually bought out the remainder of the Berry family's holding to own eighty-five per cent of the newspaper company.

Black's next international foray was into Israel, where he bought the struggling *Jerusalem Post* in 1989 for about US$16 million. The newspaper was a fierce critic of the Government, and for this reason, it was claimed, many advertisers shied away from it.

Black didn't waste any time remedying what he considered were the faults of the newspaper. He sacked the editor and appointed new directors. The new regime adopted a more sympathetic approach to the Government. The advertisers returned, and the newspaper returned to profitability.

By the time Black was agreeing to participate in a consortium to bid for Fairfax, his bid to build a chain of small US newspapers had made his the US's thirtieth largest media group.

Black's corporate structure is messy. His private company Ravelston Corporation holds fifty per cent of the publicly listed Canadian flagship Hollinger, which has assets of about Can$1.4 billion and annual profits of about Can$130 million.

In turn Hollinger holds the investment in the Telegraph. Black's expansion has resulted in the group carrying a sizable amount of borrowings in Hollinger. He is highly geared and the group is vulnerable to economic downturns. The Canadian company is reliant on strong dividends from the Telegraph to assist debt repayment and continue the healthy dividends that are shunted upstream to Ravelston, Black's private company.

* * *

Conrad Black joining forces with Kerry Packer in many ways represented a complete mismatch. Packer's pursuits outside the business world are certainly not scholarly or intellectual. In his youth he wielded a mean cricket bat and he plays a good round of golf. In his leisure time it is more likely that he will be found on a polo pony or in front of a television in a darkened room watching cricket or having a bet on the horses.

Black encourages the image of an intellectual whose business success is just one facet of a broad persona. Black is bilingual, speaking fluent French. Apart from the biography of Duplessis, Black is an obsessive expert on history. He regales people with his knowledge of nineteenth-century prime ministers, adding to his repertoire of obscure facts of famous battles.

He also likes war games and is a voracious reader. He has large libraries in Toronto and London with thousands of books. Some have interpreted this bent to propagate his intellectual prowess as vanity—a successful businessman whose life purpose has been to accumulate wealth but who also craves recognition for his other pursuits.

Aside from the worthy and the intellectual, however, Black is known among close associates for his irreverence and wicked sense of humour. Friends say he can be scathing about certain British lords and barons, targeting with sarcastic delight their foibles and relating embarrassing incidents in their family history.

One constant thread in Black's life has been his bitter resentment of what he claims is unfair criticism of his business career and political views. Black's ability to deliver impressive invective against his critics is legendary—he labelled Canadian politician, Bob Rae the 'symbol of swinish, socialist demagoguery', and dismissed the late Fleet Street press baron Robert Maxwell as 'buffoonish and demagogic'.

Journalists have not escaped his barbs: 'In my experience the working press are a very dangerous group. There is a terrible incidence of alcohol and drug abuse.'

• • •

In his office at the Daily Telegraph, Black was a charming host to Turnbull and the team. He listened intently as Turnbull pursued his favourite theme of the potential cost-savings at Fairfax. The Group was heavily overstaffed. He knew how to make it leaner. Turnbull was convinced he should be on the Fairfax board if Tourang won so that he could contribute to these matters.

Later in the day Dan Colson had his first clash with Turnbull. Colson wanted to make it clear from the beginning who held the power in this transaction. It was going to be the people who put up the money to buy Fairfax—not those who were trying to extricate themselves from a bad investment decision.

Turnbull and Steve Ezzes were discovering how tough dealing with the Hollinger group could be. Colson was dismissive about Turnbull's documentation. He then expressed amazement at the size of the payment to the bondholders. It was too high. The debate raged again.

Colson is a formidable and stubborn lawyer. He attended university with Black and later joined Canadian legal firm Stikeman, Elliott and handled Black's private work. In 1985 he was the lawyer who drafted the tight agreement with the Berry family. He ended up living in London and continued working on the restructuring and financing of the *Daily Telegraph* after the acquisition.

With the full authority of Black, Colson didn't take kindly to Turnbull's attitude. For over an hour the two men sparred as Colson suggested strongly that the bondholder payment should be reduced.

Turnbull was angry—who the hell did this guy think he was, trying to re-negotiate a deal that Packer, Black and Turnbull had shook hands on? It was also frustrating for Ezzes who had been through it all before.

In the end Colson left Turnbull and Ezzes in no doubt that he considered them lucky to get the $125 million. If Turnbull claimed a victory it was short-lived. Colson let Turnbull know who was boss when it came to drafting the agreements on the formation of the consortium.

Turnbull had spent hours producing a draft document in his suite at the Savoy the night before, assisted by his former Australian legal partner Bruce McWilliam, who was living in London. When Turnbull handed his work across to the Canadian lawyer, Colson's response was cool and cutting.

'Well, thanks a lot. But you are not running this transaction. I will draft the documents,' Colson said.

As Turnbull left, the comment about who was running the transaction stuck in his mind and he complained to Ezzes about it as they walked down the street.

• • •

With a proposal to give the bondholders $125 million Turnbull and Ezzes returned to New York to meet the other bondholders and present their triumph. Both men were excited—they believed they had struck an excellent deal and could hardly wait to receive the compliments from their colleagues.

The following day they sat opposite McClure and representatives of the other bondholders in the offices of a law firm in the Pan Am building in mid-town Manhattan.

Within minutes of beginning a summation of events to explain how the deal was done, Turnbull and Ezzes found that compliments were not flowing as they had expected. McClure was absolutely furious. Why was it that Drexels was the largest bondholder and it hadn't even been told of these high-level meetings in London? If Steve Ezzes could be invited, why hadn't McClure or other major bondholders been informed at the very least? Now he and the other bondholders were being presented with a *fait accompli*. They could change nothing.

Turnbull handed around term sheets setting out the parameters of the exclusivity agreement. He was giving the bondholders only days to sign it. It was a case of take it or leave it; if you don't like it, bad luck.

McClure seethed. Why weren't these documents couriered to them earlier to give them some chance to frame a few sensible questions and provide the basis for informed debate? This was just too much.

The bondholders' representatives talked through the deal exhaustively for five hours. Turnbull was at his persuasive best, his manner ranging from polite and understanding to angry and sarcastic as he tried to cope with this unexpected opposition. By the end of the day McClure and the others realised that in the view of Turnbull and Ezzes, they didn't have much choice.

Turnbull forcefully argued that he had tried all other options for eight months—Jamison, Independent, John B Fairfax—and it was either the $125 million or be at the mercy of Burrows and the banks. This deal or nothing.

As McClure walked back to Drexel's headquarters in Broad Street in the centre of New York's financial district, he knew what his decision would have to be despite his reservations.

The Fairfax matter was one of Drexel's 'large trouble situations', as they had become known. Large trouble situations had dominated McClure's life for two years now. It was not pleasant or stimulating work. It was depressing.

So was being in bankruptcy. Drexels was a shadow of the firm it had been during its glory days in the mid- to late 1980s. Then the fees had rolled in as Milken and his team funded the takeover frenzy on Wall Street.

It seemed that fund managers—the once conservative custodians of widows' and orphans' money—couldn't resist a Milken deal. With the US economy booming, there were few failures as rising asset and share values ensured that takeovers and the subsequent asset sales worked.

A new breed of aggressive corporate raiders gobbled up the funds Milken's high-yielding bonds provided. Carl Icahn, who swallowed up the airline TWA, oilman T. Boone Pickens, and Sir James Goldsmith (Kerry Packer partnered him in some audacious deals like the $28 billion takeover bid for UK tobacco giant British American Tobacco, BAT) used Drexels.

Milken became a hero and an incredibly rich one until the Securities and Exchange Commission began to investigate his deals.[5]

By mid-1991 Drexels was a hated name in America; the takeover boom it had fuelled was blamed for much of the USA's economic malaise. Milken was in jail as the regulators fought over the seizure of his wealth.

The Drexel offices had become tatty. The entrance doors through which McClure walked had signs drawn in red Textacolour on butcher's paper taped to the glass pronouncing 'Pull' or 'Mail Office This Way'. The bright green carpet squares were dirty. The reproduction antique furniture was stacked in small meeting rooms. It was a depressing environment. For McClure it also didn't help having people like Turnbull treating him with such obvious disdain. Despite this McClure would agree to the exclusivity agreement with Tourang—it seemed like the bondholders' best chance.

■   ■   ■

In Sydney John Fairfax felt it was time to make his choice Independent had been harassing him to let it know if he would support its offer.

Sitting quietly in the Macquarie Bank conference room, John knew that this was the final proposal he would listen to. The matter had dragged on now for six months and was distracting him from his mainstream business.

---

[5] *The Predators' Ball*, Connie Bruck, Information Australia Group Pty Ltd, 1988

Robert McKay, in well-rounded vowels, was explaining the management philosophy of AIN after outlining the good level of support it had received from institutions. Nodding occasionally, John thought that AIN had come a long way since that first tentative, and somewhat secretive approach to him in January.

McKay, Harley and Johnson were able to give a good rundown about the advantage of AIN being the all-Australian bidder, offering the banks a sale to institutions and investors with no foreign investment or cross-media law problems. John supported AIN's plan to use existing management and its intention to install Greg Taylor as the chief executive of the Group.

Johnson's claim that AIN had already received good institutional support was also encouraging. The presentation over John returned to his office. He decided that he would confirm his decision the next day with adviser Brian Wilson.

Running through the options, there were three candidates to consider—Jamison, Independent and AIN. As John and Wilson mulled over the pros and cons, the name Kerry Packer was raised. There had been no sign of the big man so far, but neither Wilson nor John were convinced he would not show up at some stage.

Packer could not possibly let Fairfax be sold without trying to have some involvement. John knew of the rivalry as well as anyone else. But where was Packer?

Both were aware of the speculation that he would possibly sell out of Nine Network and bid for Fairfax alone—the endless talk in financial and political circles was depressing Nine Network's share price.

They agreed that if Packer sold out of the network, it was unlikely he could be stopped from buying Fairfax—he certainly had the financial and political clout to do so. But a sale seemed extremely unlikely. Packer's membership of a consortium could not be ruled out. Turnbull's cryptic answers when they spoke a few weeks ago indicated there was smoke from Packer's direction.

In making a decision the two thought there were three criteria to consider: personal compatibility, commercial benefits to John and, most importantly, the possibility of winning.

Jamison was quickly ruled out; the talks earlier in the year had been stilted. John had misgivings about the connection with AFP, and the fund seemed likely to be just too entrepreneurial.

Since the first serious meeting with Corrigan in mid-February John had not been comfortable with the vulture fund. However, Corrigan had been sounded out about the possibility of selling the *Newcastle Herald* and he had no real opposition to divesting the newspaper if Jamison was successful. On the prospects of winning, Jamison seemed to have a good chance provided its shareholders stuck together.

John liked the AIN people and their ideas for Fairfax. In terms of compatibility they scored a one. They were his type of people— conservative and dour. There was nothing entrepreneurial; they were blue chip.

While Harley and McKay were not well-known, Johnson as an adviser and proposed director had a lot of kudos. He boasts an impressive career in corporate advisory work on many of Australia's largest transactions, plus directorships including Australian Gas Light Co. and Pioneer International.

John D'Arcy's media experience was excellent, although the Fairfaxes and the old guard at the Herald and Weekly Times (HWT) had a chequered past.

The AIN board would be well-suited to discharge the commercial and societal obligations of running the Fairfax newspapers.

John was confident that if he supported them, he would also be able to fulfil his objective of picking up the Newcastle newspaper. But there was one major problem with AIN. He didn't think AIN had much hope of winning. And if they didn't win, his commercial objective stood to fail.

Of course Harley and McKay had secured some support from institutions, but from none of the major ones. A dozen or so second-tier institutions were not enough to raise the $400 million-plus required to secure Fairfax.

This brought the conversation around to Independent. John had found O'Reilly, whom he had taken to calling 'The Doctor', personable when they had dinner in late April. John was interested to know if there were any surprises in O'Reilly's closet and asked a friend to make a few discreet enquiries.

In commercial terms there were a few misgivings. APN was a competitor to Rural Press in the regional publishing market.

There were not many areas of direct competition, but what would happen if APN and Rural Press both wanted to acquire a newspaper in another state for instance?

John also had misgivings about Independent's proposal, which discussed the possibility of a joint printing venture with Rupert Murdoch in Sydney. He thought the suggestion that O'Reilly could be too close to Murdoch was a negative, especially regarding what had happened between Murdoch and O'Reilly with APN back in 1988.

John had no love for Murdoch despite his belief that media proprietors should maintain friendly not hostile competition.

Independent was extremely sensitive to criticism in its April proposal to institutions about deals with Murdoch. So in early June, in a nine-page update of its proposals, it revised its stance to state that following further investigation a joint venture facility with News Corporation was now considered unlikely.

Independent was going to say just about anything to further its offer and minimise any potential criticisms.

For John the other sticking point was his fear that O'Reilly was prone to massaging the Labor Party's ideas for Fairfax just a little too closely. However, the feeling that O'Reilly could be too political wasn't strong enough to be the reason John wouldn't support Independent.

On the positive side Independent was prepared to sell him the *Newcastle Herald* for $32 million. Clearly John believed that if he joined Independent's consortium, it would be strengthened and was likely to assist it to secure institutional support.

John decided that Independent had a good chance of winning. With a core shareholder already willing to put up probably $100 million, it was a good start to raising further funds. John was confident that if he backed O'Reilly it would assist the consortium in wooing the support of AMP.

When everything was added up, O'Reilly scored twos in the three categories. O'Reilly appeared the best chance at this stage in the absence of a Packer move. The next morning John thought he would make one last appointment with Leigh Hall to get some more intelligence on what the institutions planned to do before making a final decision.

Sitting in Hall's office on Thursday morning, overlooking the ferries scuttling across the Harbour, Hall quietly told John that AMP had not yet made up its mind. However, one option that AMP wouldn't mind was if Jamison and Independent joined forces.

This confirmed what John had heard elsewhere. On the Melbourne group Hall said that AMP's media analyst Alex Hagop wasn't convinced that AIN had the management skills or newspaper experience to run Fairfax.

Hall mentioned that he would be meeting with McKay and Harley the next day for a short presentation and added that Sir James Balderstone had asked him to give the AIN people a good hearing before a final decision was made.

John was not surprised about Sir James' request to give AIN a decent hearing. A few weeks earlier John had discussed Fairfax with the chairman of AMP. Balderstone seemed more interested in the fate of the *Age* than the *Herald* or the rest of the Group.

In the afternoon McKay rang John again, asking if John had made a decision. As McKay spoke, John wondered why he didn't mention that he was going to see AMP the next day. This annoyed John a little, even though it was unimportant as he had arranged to telephone Hall the following day before he made up his mind to learn of AMP's impression.

When John rang Hall late the next morning, Hall said he was going overseas for a few weeks and that AMP might make a decision on 30 June. The Melbourne group seemed pleasant, Hall assured John, but indicated that AIN wasn't exactly what AMP was looking for. AIN's management seemed weak and had not yet finished its financial models or profit forecasts.

When John hung up, Hall's comment stuck in his mind: 'They are not what AMP is looking for.' If AIN was unlikely to receive the support of AMP, John reasoned that he should give the O'Reilly bid a nudge by lending the Fairfax name to its offer.

If he backed Independent, John might shift the odds more in its favour in securing institutional and general support for its bid. John rang Wilson to bring him up to date on what Hall had said. He then told Wilson that he felt Independent was the one to support.

In the afternoon Wilson telephoned Hunt to say that, subject to tying up some loose ends, John and members of the Sir Vincent

Fairfax family were prepared to support Independent through the family company Marinya Media Pty Ltd. In financial terms the investment would be minimal. John would put up about $10 million, which would only give a token shareholding.

However, the good will of attracting John's support could not be measured in financial terms and the prospect of securing AMP were dramatically improved. Just with so many other capital raisings in Australia, once other institutions thought AMP was in, they nearly always followed.

* * *

Robert McKay travelled directly from Tullamarine Airport to his country property Clunie, about one-and-a-half hours from Melbourne. It had been an exhausting day. The AMP presentation had been a little disappointing, but it was still early days.

At 10 pm the phone rang. It was John Fairfax. He had made up his mind. McKay waited as John went slowly through the preliminaries. The anticipation was nearly killing him. Then came the letdown. 'I have decided to lend my support to Independent.' McKay was devastated. This was the biggest blow AIN had suffered to date. He had thought that John's support was almost a certainty.

McKay rang Tom Harley immediately and again several times over the weekend. By Sunday night the depression had lifted. 'We are not going to be beaten by that,' McKay told Harley. 'We can win this one ... We will go out now and get all the institutions.' His resolve was stiffened.

* * *

Within a fortnight John Fairfax was wondering whether he had made the right decision. On 18 June when he turned to the business pages of the *Herald* he received a surprise. There was an article on Independent's proposed appointment of Australian Airlines chairman Ted Harris as a director of Fairfax if its offer was successful.

John was stunned. To discover who could be a potential fellow director in the pages of a newspaper was odd—no one from Independent had ever mentioned anything about Harris in this capacity. John was offended by the lack of protocol or etiquette.

There was a different reaction in the Independent camp. Harris was considered an incredible coup because of his impeccable political connections and insights into Canberra.

Ted Harris likes playing down his political and business connections—especially his friendship with Bob Hawke. Independent had no such misgivings—they had grabbed a direct line to the then Prime Minister.

Harris began his working life as a sports commentator and rose through the ranks at the Macquarie radio network to become assistant to the managing director. Through this position Harris met William Walkley, the chairman of Ampol, the Australian oil company.

Harris convinced Ampol to sponsor the popular Jack Davey radio show as part of its marketing drive. Walkley became a mentor, and in 1954 the young Harris joined Ampol. In the early years he kept up some of his commentating activities, broadcasting tennis and also the 1956 Olympics in Melbourne. Harris also persuaded Walkley to put his name on the Australian Journalists Association (AJA) annual awards for excellence.

Over the next sixteen years Harris climbed the ranks at Ampol to become managing director of Ampol Petroleum in 1971. In 1977 he was appointed managing director of the whole group. Board positions were taken outside Ampol as Harris mixed in business and political circles.

Between 1974 and 1977 Harris was appointed a commissioner of the ABC by the Whitlam Government. In his days at Ampol in the early 1970s Harris came across an aggressive, young and badly dressed president of the ACTU Robert J Hawke. Initially the two men didn't get on well on the employer-versus-union battlefield.

This antagonism finally gave way to a good friendship. Both men love sport, and Harris isn't an affected businessman with an ideological hatred for Labor. He has a strong nationalistic ethos, which tied in well with the running of an oil company whose marketing pitch is its Australian ownership.

The two men had another close friend in common by the late 1970s—Peter Abeles, the chief executive of transport group TNT.

Ampol joined TNT in 1979 in acquiring sizable parcels of shares in Ansett Transport Industries, a raid that became the catalyst for the eventual takeover of the airline by TNT and News Corporation.

When the Hawke Labor Government came to power in 1983 Harris, who played tennis regularly with Hawke until age wearied the body, popped up as chairman of the interim committee of the Australian Sports Commission. He was considered a possible head of the ABC in 1986 before the appointment of David Hill.

In 1987 Harris was appointed chairman of the government-owned Australian Airlines. This brought him into constant contact with the then aviation minister Kim Beazley, who was of course also Minister for Communications.

Such credentials were excellent for O'Reilly's purposes. Harris publicly downplays his friendship with Hawke, stating when he picked up a Companion of the Order of Australia in 1989 that he only spoke to Hawke about six times a year. If Harris could enhance Independent's offer in six telephone calls, that would be more than enough.

Harris wasn't the only person lined up to give Independent assistance in Canberra. The Irish retained Arthur Fitzgerald who is a man with excellent connections on both sides of the political spectrum. Fitzgerald is even more publicity shy than Harris, which belies his influence.

Short, balding and with a cheery smile, the seventy-two-year-old Fitzgerald is better known on Sydney racetracks. Since 1984 he has been a committee member of the Australian Jockey Club, a venue that Bob Hawke frequents. Another racetrack follower is Lionel Bowen, the former Deputy Prime Minister. Fitzgerald is also well known in charity circles and for his work on the board of St Vincent's Private Hospital.

A barrister by training, Fitzgerald worked in Canberra as a public servant for eighteen years until 1956, working as a private secretary to both Liberal and Labor ministers. He then joined Caltex and spent thirty years there, the last five as a director, retiring in 1985. During his long career in politics and business, Fitzgerald built up an impressive list of acquaintances. John Reynolds commented to outsiders that Fitzgerald could get either the Prime Minister or the Leader of the Opposition on the telephone within fifteen minutes. He was appointed to the board of the Australian National Gallery in 1988 and received an Australia Medal in the same year

Independent came across Fitzgerald through his friendship with BT chairman David Hoare, also no stranger in Canberra. Hoare is a director of the Telecommunications Interim Board, OTC Ltd and is on the Australian Securities Commission's Corporations and Securities Panel. BT does a lot of government work, bringing Hoare and Rowan Ross into contact with ministers. Hoare is close to Attorney-General Michael Duffy. He is also a driving force behind the board of St Vincent's Private Hospital, where he often sees Fitzgerald.

Even though Independent was confident that it would have no problems securing a twenty per cent shareholding in Fairfax, there wasn't any point in sitting back. O'Reilly wanted to make quite sure Canberra was a strong not lukewarm supporter.

* * *

While Packer was finally playing his hand in his bid to gain a crucial shareholding in his family's historic enemy, the two highest profile Fairfax bidders were beginning to tear each other apart.

To Independent—and adviser Peter Hunt in particular—Chris Corrigan was becoming a serious problem. All the efforts Independent had put into the roadshow and wooing of institutions had not produced the level of support it had expected. A good hearing by AMP, National Mutual and others was fine, except that they were still shareholders in Jamison.

Time and time again Independent was confronted by a perception among many of the smaller institutions that Jamison could expect the support of its major shareholders, and on this basis it was best to wait and see what happened. Also there was no need to commit to O'Reilly, since there had been little activity on the sale process.

These were points that Peter Hunt didn't have any problems explaining to his clients at Independent. What was making him angry were the barbs about Independent's management ability compared with Jamison. While the transformation of APN was impressive in terms of profit, the sceptics were pointing out that running a group of regional newspapers would be vastly different to managing a major media group like Fairfax.

APN's annual revenue was heading towards $130 million; Fairfax's was around $800 million. Fairfax employed around 5600; APN employed only 1200. Regional newspapers in Australia are crammed full of advertisements, with editorial space (except in rare cases) securing only thirty per cent of the space per page compared with fifty to seventy per cent in many pages of metropolitan newspapers. APN's revenue is derived from mainly local advertising, not multi-million dollar national accounts. The editorial content is also localised, and journalist salaries are considerably less than their metropolitan counterparts. There are no pages devoted to international news boasting dozens of stories bought from newspapers around the world, nor do the regional papers have to bear the cost of posting correspondents around the globe. APN's products often have the advantage of holding monopoly positions in their towns.

Fairfax on the other hand is always in competition with Murdoch's newspapers in Sydney and Melbourne. Although the documents sent to institutions put forward a good argument about the merits of Independent as a media group, there were perceived to be plenty of holes.

Independent's margin of earnings before interest and tax to sales, a popular yardstick on performance, was not great. Hovering around ten per cent, it was less than half the twenty-three per cent achieved by Fairfax management. The Irish group made about eighty per cent of its revenue from newspapers, but the Australian offshoot APN contributed just thirty per cent of this amount.

Independent's plans to delay a public float of about twenty or thirty per cent of Fairfax for two or three years was also a problem for some institutions. They wanted an earlier float to give them a readily accessible market for their shares.

Hunt felt confident he could overcome each of these problems. But it would be much easier if Independent could be perceived without doubt as the best candidate. He was certain that Independent was far better than Corrigan and his group.

Hunt convinced his client that a tougher line on Jamison was required. There were no problems on this score with O'Reilly, who was preparing to fight hard on this particular front.

At Independent's annual meeting in May 1991, O'Reilly labelled Corrigan as 'an intelligent and able financial engineer' who unfortunately lacked Independent's management expertise.

The appointment of Chris Anderson as proposed managing director of Fairfax had given the company some much needed clout on the management front. This really rankled the Irish, considering Anderson had been sought by Independent. Here was Anderson reappearing and boosting the credentials of Independent's main rival. Jamison had to be stopped.

This was an important commercial transaction with large fees and reputations riding on the outcome and it was time to dig into the bag of dirty tricks. Hunt contacted institutions arguing that Reynolds would be a better chief executive and by implication cast grave doubts on Anderson's abilities.

The whispering campaign had begun and the attack was broadened to capitalise on the disquiet about Jamison's connection with the entrepreneurial AFP group.

The BT advisers then stepped up the campaign by putting its case down on paper. They compiled a dossier comparing Independent with Jamison and distributed it among institutions. It was a particularly nasty document, comparing the qualifications and track records of chairmen Tony O'Reilly of Independent and Peter Scanlon at Jamison; chief executives Liam Healy (Independent) and Chris Corrigan (Jamison); and proposed managing directors John Reynolds (Independent) and Chris Anderson (Jamison).

It would not be difficult for an objective reporter to compare O'Reilly's career very favourably with Peter Scanlon's. This assessment, however, was most unfair. There was no mention of Scanlon's achievements, for example, his time at Heinz and his directorship of Elders through its early growth phase. Nor did his role in the takeovers of Elder Smith and Carlton & United Breweries rate a mention. Instead it credited Scanlon with only poor decisions, noting that he was primarily responsible for AFP's investment in Harlin, which had to be written down by $100 million, and had had no previous newspaper experience. The pattern was continued throughout the dossier.

Corrigan received little credit for his tremendous achievement in getting BT Australia off the ground. Instead the dossier compared how much bigger BT was today than when Corrigan left in 1985 and claimed that he had left his position as regional director for Asia due to management differences.

The most scathing treatment of all, however, was reserved for Chris Anderson. He was compared with John Reynolds and every dirty trick was used. For example, Reynolds' CV began in 1990 and went backwards, but only to 1975. Anderson's started in 1965 when he left university and became a cadet journalist and continued to the present. With their CVs presented in adjacent columns, a first glance showed Reynolds as a chief executive and Anderson as a journalist.

The comparison managed to make Reynolds' period working in the media in Western Australia and his three years as managing director of the *West Australian* and TVW look much more impressive than Anderson's role running Fairfax, a group several times the size.

The dossier pointed out that Anderson had been chief executive only briefly, but neglected to mention that he had been a director and general manager for three years. It credited Anderson with the junk bond raising; accused him of having a potential conflict in his fiduciary duty to shareholders because he promoted a re-capitalisation of Fairfax that involved shares for management and employees on favourable terms; and noted that he had planned to join News Corporation shortly after Warwick's takeover, taking a swag of senior journalists with him.

The most stinging barbs about Anderson were left to last under the heading 'Generally'. Anderson was:

- chief executive for only ten days before resigning in August 1990 with a $2.2 million termination payment;
- regarded as strongly favouring the *Herald* against the *Age* and *Australian Financial Review* and being highly political by nature;
- rejected by INP (Independent) as a proposed chief executive of Fairfax

It concluded that there was no evidence that Anderson had the management expertise and capacity to improve efficiency at Broadway.

Jamison wasn't shy in replying. Corrigan in an interview in the

Herald and the *Age*'s Saturday *Good Weekend* magazine made one damning comment on the suave O'Reilly: 'You've seen those pictures of him getting off the Heinz Lear jet in wraparound sunglasses holding open the door of the limousine. That's not Fairfax.'

■　■　■

The brawl horrified executives and board members of institutions. It was too public and too personal. Leigh Hall, a senior executive at AMP, couldn't believe what was happening. He had already suggested to Corrigan and Hunt that the two groups should join, rather than run separate bids.

However, this petty corporate warfare was now making the AMP team think twice about whether they wanted to be associated with such knock-'em-down and drag-'em-out brawls.

Independent had also upset some of AMP's board of directors by approaching them directly to seek support for their offer. For a large, conservative group such as AMP this was most improper. The Irish lost a lot of support by attempting their Canberra-style lobbying tactics on AMP board members.

The smear campaign was extremely dangerous for Jamison. It had still not convinced any of its shareholders to commit themselves. Corrigan himself was now beginning to have doubts about the amount of time and energy he had spent focusing on Fairfax with no results. It was over six months since the receivership and there was no sign of a sale, not even an indication of when offers would close.

He knew his original strategy of forcing a quick sale at perhaps $1 billion had failed—other bidders were now involved. He had lost the advantage.

Corrigan was hooked on Fairfax, however. He also wanted to show his shareholders that Jamison was capable of pulling off a large deal.

While the battlefield was being defined in the central business districts of Sydney, Melbourne, London and New York, the corporate players were ignoring the political backlash that had been gaining momentum for seven months among journalists, politicians and newspaper readers. The Media in Peril Conference held at the Sydney Opera Theatre on 19 November 1990, had tapped a genuine community fear of increasing concentration of media ownership in Australia. Rupert Murdoch already controlled sixty-five per cent of newspaper circulation in Australia. Now the country's quality newspapers were up for grabs. In Melbourne the State Government had established an inquiry into the ownership of the print media in mid-1990 and the union movement had voiced its concern with the Trades Hall Council, voting in November to oppose further concentration of the print media.

This was only the beginning, however. The sale of Fairfax would not be just a business transaction. The fate of Australia's quality newspapers was far too important to be left to businessmen to decide.

CHAPTER EIGHT

THE POLITICS OF PRINT

WARD O'NEILL was rushing to complete his illustration for Saturday's *Herald*. It was 6.30 pm on Friday evening, 14 June 1991. This was really pushing the deadline—the drawing was usually finished by 5 pm.

Alan Ramsey's political column on the op ed page (the page opposite the letters to the editor and the editorials) was a show-case for O'Neill's artwork. It was his spot in the newspaper, the envy of other artists.

It had been a particularly busy week, and O'Neill was finding it a struggle. A bearded, dark-haired forty-year-old with a fair complexion and a quiet, warm manner, O'Neill was chairman of the Friends of Fairfax. As he worked with his fine ink pen on Bob Hawke's wrinkles, he reflected with satisfaction that at last a plan of action was taking shape.

The past few days had been packed with meetings, faxes and long-distance phone calls. There was a lot more to be done. The money that had been raised in May at the Friends of Fairfax dinner could now be put to a useful purpose. The drawing had to come first, however. It was a caricature of Hawke—barnstorming.

This had been the most momentous fortnight in Australian politics since the Hawke Government came to power in 1983. A disenchanted Paul Keating, upset that Hawke was not honour-ing a two-year-old agreement to step down in his favour, had challenged Bob Hawke for the post.

The date was 3 June, the same day that Kerry Packer and

Conrad Black met at the Savoy Hotel in London. Keating lost the challenge and the former Treasurer and Deputy Prime Minister found himself banished to the backbenches. What Hawke once described as the 'greatest political partnership in the country's history' had been ripped apart forever.

Keating's supporters were devastated. But they certainly weren't beaten. Even as Hawke claimed the party remained unified, the Keating camp was reassessing its campaign. Time was on its side.

In his column Alan Ramsey revealed to readers how Hawke and Keating, now political foes, had coincidentally chosen the same Port Douglas resort hotel to spend a few days the following week. Their stay overlapped by one night. They did not speak to one another.

That the two most senior Labor Party politicians had chosen to stay in a swish hotel in one of Australia's classiest resorts in far north Queensland to recover from a leadership joust was perhaps an indication of how far the Labor Party had moved from its traditional working-class base.

The traditions of the party, however, were particularly relevant and being re-lived in 1991. It was the one-hundredth anniversary of the party's foundation. The Centenary Labor Party conference was coming up in Hobart, Tasmania, in ten days' time. It was this conference that was exercising Ward O'Neill's mind.

The subject of Ramsey's column that week underlined how charged the atmosphere would be at the Hobart conference. It was a perfect time to tug at the ideological heartstrings of the party apparatchiks; make them change the Labor Party platform on the media to ensure diversity; get them to push for a royal commission into the ownership of the print media; and push for changes to the broadcasting legislation to plug the loopholes governing cross-ownership of television and newspapers.

Such conferences presented the opportunity for the rank-and-file of the Labor Party to have their say. With instability in the leadership, the issue of media ownership was more likely to gain a sympathetic hearing.

The Friends of Fairfax and the Age Independence Committee (AIC) each decided to target the conference to get across their message to the Government. The *Age* journalists planned to run a large advertisement in the Saturday *Age* the day before the conference began, outlining the issues and through endorsements revealing how many key community leaders supported their cause. It would be like a re-run of the Save the *Age* advertisements that had been so successful in 1988.

The Friends of Fairfax decided that, rather than duplicate the *Age* advertisement in the *Herald*, they would spend their funds on a full explanatory kit that set out the issues. This kit would be given to every delegate at the Labor Party conference. It would contain pie charts and graphs on ownership and essays on freedom of speech.

The basic message both groups wanted to convey was that the Fairfax papers were important to Australia. The press in this country was already too concentrated. Any further concentration, or prospect of further concentration, could not be good.

The journalists would have had cause to be a lot more nervous if they had known of the Savoy Hotel gathering in London the previous week. The Fairfax bidder they feared most, Kerry Packer, had already shaken hands on an excellent consortium. The rumours about Packer's interest in Fairfax had been circulating for well over a year. In the last month they had reached fever pitch. Kerry Packer already accounted for forty-nine per cent of the circulation of Australian magazines, and his television network reached fifty-two per cent of the population.

If Packer managed to exercise control over the Fairfax Group, the Australian media would be dominated by Packer and Murdoch.

In terms of focusing attention on the media concentration issue, an amazing article appeared on 4 June in the *Independent Monthly*. The *Independent* is a newspaper published jointly by Max Suich, the former editorial executive of Fairfax, and John B Fairfax.

Suich wrote an article entitled 'The News Bros'. It alleged that Kerry Packer and Rupert Murdoch had a game plan between them to carve up the Australian print media. Suich's evidence for such a game plan was compelling—a contemporaneous memorandum of an April meeting between Kerry Packer, Malcolm Turnbull and two merchant bankers, Mike Tilley and Will Jephcott from Lloyds Corporate Advisory Services. Tilley was the author of the memo, which he had penned immediately after the meeting at Packer's Park Street headquarters.

The memo somehow ended up in Suich's hands. Tilley's client was Bell Group, the financially crippled Alan Bond company, which owned a majority stake in the Perth morning newspaper, the *West Australian*. Packer had offered to buy out the newspaper, but his bid was considered too low. Packer was trying to persuade Tilley otherwise.

Tilley's six-page memo contained a bombshell. Packer told Tilley that Murdoch had been in his office the previous afternoon. According to the memo Packer said 'that he and Mr Murdoch had developed a plan for the newspaper industry in Australia which he described as a "game plan" and that under that game plan there was no room for the *West Australian* to be owned by anybody else or operated successfully in the face of the onslaught that would be forthcoming [from the Murdoch competitor, the *Sunday Times*, in Perth]'.

Those concerned about media concentration were horrified by the message in Tilley's memo and what it meant for the print media nationally. The Friends of Fairfax Committee decided to capitalise on the publicity that the Max Suich story generated and force Murdoch and News Corporation into a corner. They drew up an advertisement urging readers to fight the Packer–Murdoch game plan and planned to try and place the advertisement in a showcase position, page three, in Murdoch's the *Weekend Australian*. If the *Australian* refused to run the advertisement, it would be a key example of how views could be squashed by a limited number of media proprietors under the alleged game plan.

When the draft wording was read to him over the telephone, the *Australian* advertising salesman whistled and said, 'Whoa! This is going to be fun.' He was wrong. After vetting by top News Ltd management, the advertisement was allowed to run. The sting was that it cost the Friends of Fairfax $7000—more than a quarter of its entire budget—and it went straight into Murdoch's revenue. The plan had backfired.

The advertisement on 8 June read: 'FIGHT THE PACKER GAME PLAN. Kerry Packer and Rupert Murdoch will control ninety per cent of Australia's newspapers and magazines if Kerry

Packer buys the Fairfax Group. Who will be watching the watchers and their mates? Would you like anyone to have that much power? Don't let the Fairfax newspapers—the *Sydney Morning Herald*, the *Age*, the *Australian Financial Review*, the *Sunday Age* and the *Sun–Herald*—be swallowed up. We urge you to write to your local member urgently and demand a royal commission into media ownership in Australia.'

The advertisement's failure to be blocked by News Ltd management and prohibitive cost made Ward O'Neill and Alan Kennedy, also on the Friends of Fairfax Committee, realise that a more cohesive strategy had to be developed. Tom Burton, the *Herald*'s communications writer in Canberra, suggested that the Friends of Fairfax employ a lobbyist to help with strategy. A more sophisticated approach was needed. Other community and business interest groups utilised lobbyists; why not journalists?

Burton suggested Anne Davies, the Sydney director of the Communications Law Centre (CLC). The CLC is the acknowledged specialist public interest group on government media policy. It is affiliated with The University of New South Wales and funded by The Law Foundation of New South Wales and the Victorian Law Foundation. Paul Chadwick, author and commentator, is the Melbourne director; Anne Davies, a lawyer and former *Financial Review* journalist, is the Sydney director.

In her early thirties, Davies is blonde, slim and beautifully groomed and knows her way around the corridors of Parliament House in Canberra after three years working in the newspaper's bureau. Her enthusiasm for media policy is infectious and her appointment as a consultant was perfect for the Friends of Fairfax. The timing couldn't have been better.

Burton had been chatting recently with Davies about an Australian Broadcasting Tribunal case, reported in the first week of June, which had pointed to glaring gaps in broadcasting laws. One of the options Davies was looking at to plug these gaps and effect changes in the legislation was to push for an amendment to the Labor Party platform to be debated at the Hobart Conference.

She was already conferring with John Saunderson on how to draft the amendments. Saunderson was a Labor conference delegate and a former member of parliament who had chaired the Transport and Communications Committee. He knew as much about media policy as anybody and had excellent connections on the left of the party.

The Friends of Fairfax also wanted to push for changes to the Labor media policies. It made sense to co-ordinate the effort. The issue that Davies was most concerned about was the operation of the cross-media ownership laws. There were doubts whether the cross-media ownership regulations worked, and those doubts arose from a case involving none other than Kerry Packer.

The Kimshaw case provided a classic example of Packer's efforts to try a scheme to retain control of both a television station and radio station in the one city—*prima facie* a breach of the Broadcasting Act. Packer ended up owning Sydney radio station 2UE after he bought back Nine Network from Alan Bond.

Packer's lawyers made an application to the Australian Broadcasting Tribunal (ABT) to restructure 2UE in order to reduce Packer's shareholding to less than fifteen per cent to avoid breaching the cross-media laws. The first proposal, however, left Nine Network with ninety-nine per cent of the profits and was rejected. So Packer and his lawyers proposed a new structure using a shelf company called Kimshaw. Once again the lawyers attempted to separate ownership of 2UE from control, reducing Packer's stake to below fifteen per cent but delivering him ninety-nine per cent of the station's dividends. The scheme, it was maintained, wasn't a device to retain control; it separated ownership from control. The ABT decided to hold a public inquiry.

While this was going on, there was an interesting sidelight. There were media reports that Packer—who supposedly had nothing to do with 2UE—had ordered the sacking of former Test cricketer Rod Marsh from the station's commentary team. Marsh told the ABT he didn't want to comment, and the 2UE management told the ABT it was responsible for the decision to sack Marsh.

In the end the ABT didn't need to delve into how much control Packer would have exercised at 2UE and whether the proposed structure was valid. The station was sold. The ABT could see problems arising from the situation, however. Was it necessary for an inquiry into whether there was de facto control in such schemes—after the event?

In the Kimshaw report the ABT was scathing about the

structure used. Its judgement was strongly worded: '... whether or not the Kimshaw structure is legally effective, it has served its purpose of allowing continued ownership of 2UE by interests associated with Mr Packer in circumstances where a flagrant breach of the ownership and control limits would otherwise have occurred. In the event that such structures are employed, there appears to be no quick cheap way for testing for actual control. This may be an area for consideration in any review of broadcasting legislation.'

Davies had written to Transport and Communications Minister Kim Beazley, pointing to the deficiencies in the Broadcasting Act that allowed a structure such as Kimshaw to slip through the cross-media ownership provisions. She suggested that the cross-media laws be applied to associates as well and pointed to the associates definition in the Companies Code and the Income Tax Act as possible models.

The Communications Law Centre had also been urging the establishment of an inquiry into the ownership of the print media for over three years. It seemed to make sense that it should join with the Friends of Fairfax to push for an inquiry motion supported by the Hobart Labor conference.

Paul Chadwick in Melbourne and Chris Warren of the Australian Journalists Association (AJA) had almost succeeded in getting a media inquiry going in August 1989. They had made a joint push through the Labor Caucus' Transport and Communications Committee. John Langmore and Chris Schacht, two key members of the committee, had also pushed hard and the Communications Minister at the time, Ralph Willis, was sympathetic.

But it was nine months before an election and was not the time to upset media moguls. Willis agreed to support such an inquiry after the election. As is the way with politics, Willis did not score the communications portfolio in the next government. His successor, Kim Beazley did not share Willis' enthusiasm.

John Langmore and Chris Schacht kept the message alive, however. Schacht spoke at the Media in Peril conference at the Sydney Opera House in November 1990. He pushed for an inquiry there. And Langmore introduced a private members bill calling for an inquiry in March 1991.

There had been a strong push in Victoria too. The State Labor Government had set up a working party in mid-1990 to report on ownership and control of the print media. The report, released in January 1991, recommended a major public inquiry into all aspects of print media ownership. In December the Victorian media unions had called for a Royal Commission into print and the Victorian Trades Hall Council was actively lending its support. So by June, in the lead up to the Labor Party conference, Schacht and Langmore had plenty of ammunition to fire at Beazley.

They all but turned him around. Beazley said if the issue was pushed successfully at the conference, he would accept it as an issue on which he would act. He also had Hawke's approval. Hawke felt keenly the lack of editorial support from the Murdoch and Packer publications in the Keating leadership challenge—he held no candle for the media giants now. Without Keating at the Hobart conference the chance of pushing through a motion on an inquiry were greatly increased. Keating had always been diametrically opposed to a media inquiry.

Davies gave three key pieces of advice at her first meeting with the Friends of Fairfax representatives on Thursday, 13 June—prepare a kit that would explain what the Friends of Fairfax represented and clearly set out the statistics of media concentration in Australia with simple graphs and a number of scenarios showing what would happen if Packer, Murdoch, O'Reilly or Corrigan gained control of Fairfax.

Second, Davies recommended that someone—not a Fairfax journalist—represent the Friends of Fairfax and launch the information kit. Third, that the committee prepare the proposed set of amendments to the Labor Party platform and the broadcasting legislation.

The next step was to lobby conference delegates to ensure the amendments were passed. The Communications Law Centre was retained to prepare the kit and assist with the lobbying and Davies and John Saunderson began drafting possible amendments to the Labor Party platform.

Ward O'Neill had irons in the fire too. He had been chatting over the past few weeks to his friend Andrew Casey, a former industrial writer on the *Herald* and now communications adviser to Martin Ferguson of the Australian Council of Trade Unions (ACTU), the key umbrella union body in the country.

From Casey, O'Neill was able to glean that Ferguson had taken a keen interest in the media issue. It was possible that Ferguson might agree to write to all conference delegates the week before the conference, outlining the issue and giving his support to the fight against further media concentration. O'Neill knew that there was a difference of opinion between Bill Kelty, the Secretary of the ACTU, and Ferguson on this issue, which could cause difficulties if Ferguson took a public stance.

A draft letter was faxed to Casey for his views. O'Neill's fears were confirmed. Ferguson was opposed to the letter. It called for a Royal Commission into print media ownership, and Ferguson thought this wouldn't achieve anything. He was also concerned that the letter was too confrontational in its attack on the Packer–Murdoch game plan. This could cause problems with Kelty, who was aligned with Paul Keating and the New South Wales right.

O'Neill refused to water down the letter. He believed Murdoch and Packer posed a real threat to the Fairfax papers and a specific threat to people's jobs.

'Andrew, we can't pretend to be what we're not. They want these papers and we don't want them to have them,' O'Neill told Casey.

O'Neill knew this would remain a sticking point. No one wanted to personalise the debate. But the fact was that if Packer was involved in an offer for Fairfax, it could possibly increase the concentration of media ownership in this country, either now or in the future. No other likely bidder fell into that category.

Casey tried to placate O'Neill and suggested Simon Lloyd, the president of the Fairfax Broadway branch of the AJA, arrange an appointment with Ferguson in Sydney early the next week. Perhaps a discussion would help. In the meantime Ferguson was happy to lend his name to the *Age* advertisement on the Saturday.

●   ●   ●

On Friday night, 21 June, there was a superbly timed function being held in the dining-room of the elegant Park Hyatt Hotel on the shores of Lake Burley Griffin in Canberra. The irreverent tones of Patrick Cook and Phil Scott rang out once again.

'O, Father, dear Father, I can't tell a lie/I've cut down the family tree ...'

Helping them along were two hundred journalists, politicians, political staffers and lobbyists bellowing out 'The *Herald* belongs to me'.

It was the eve of the Labor Party conference. The last gathering before most of them made the pilgrimage to Hobart. The Friends of Fairfax and the Age Independence Committee had combined their efforts for this one. It was expensive holding a fund-raiser at the Park Hyatt and it didn't raise a lot of funds. In public relations terms, however, it was a spectacular success.

This time the O'Reilly team had booked a whole table.

■ ■ ■

The AIC was much better organised than the Friends of Fairfax. There were two reasons for this. They had had the dry run with the Save the *Age* Committee in 1988 when Robert Maxwell was bidding for the newspaper. Second, they had the backing of their editors and a cohesion that Fairfax's Broadway headquarters could only dream of. The *Age*, although there was a separate Sunday edition, was essentially one newspaper.

Broadway published three newspapers but had, until recently, published five. The Fairfax culture meant that these three news-papers—the *Herald*, the *Sun–Herald* and the *Australian Financial Review*—were fiercely competitive with one another.

The early meetings in January to establish the Friends of Fairfax had on two occasions finished rather like a Middle East peace conference with vitriolic shouting matches between *Review* and *Herald* staff. So the joint body that grew out of this process was fragile. Distrust lurked beneath the surface.

At the *Age* only the internal politics common to any working environment had to be accommodated. The AIC had the support of editors too; the Friends of Fairfax was only reluctantly acknowl-edged at Broadway. John Alexander, editor-in-chief of the *Herald*, was at times openly scornful of the 'bunch of losers' who made up the Friends of Fairfax Committee.

There was another important difference with the *Age*. It had the wider support of its community. Melbourne and Victoria rallied to Save the *Age* in 1988 and were ready to do it again. These people had an extraordinary affection for the *Age*. The residents of Sydney, on the other hand, had a much more equivocal relationship with their quality morning newspaper. While the *Age* could rally to its support present and former state premiers, union leaders, Anglican archbishops and knighted businessmen, Broadway could rely only on support from authors, playwrights and ABC presenters.

■   ■   ■

David Wilson is brusque and hard-nosed. He is a journalist who has earned his reputation as an investigator, working with author–journalist Bob Bottom, specialising in organised crime. He has written books on the *Age* tapes (the police tapped telephone conversations that led to the trial of High Court judge Lionel Murphy in the 1980s). Wilson, now in his late thirties, is associate editor of the *Age*.

A chain-smoker and an uncompromising boss, Wilson is a fervent believer in the need for an independent press and, above all, an independent *Age*. He was also chairman of the Age Independence Committee. His vice chairs were editorial writer and restaurant critic Claude Forell and state political roundsman Robyn Dixon. They were superb organisers.

They correctly tapped the Melburnian's love of the *Age* and tapped too a fount of funds that allowed them in 1988 to spend almost $30 000 on advertising to mobilise readers. The same tactic was used again and again to good effect. In the Saturday *Age* of 22 June they ran an advertisement that took the entire side of an *Age* broadsheet page. Headed 'Under Threat', it showed the mastheads of the five Fairfax papers.

These papers, readers were told, 'are likely to be sold to the highest bidder and could end up in the hands of an interventionist proprietor with conflicting non-media business interests. The cherished editorial qualities and characteristics of these newspapers may be lost forever.

'The traditional forums for debate and discussion, explanation and exposure, comment and communication are in danger.

'We believe that it is essential that your newspapers remain free from manipulation, free from outside interests and free from interference.

'We believe that it is in the interests of all Australians that the level of newspaper ownership in Australia be as diverse as possible.'

The list of signatories was extraordinary. It included Martin Ferguson; Sir Rupert Hamer, former Liberal Premier of Victoria; Joan Kirner, Premier of Victoria; Gerry Hand, Federal Minister for Immigration; Michael Eassón, President of the New South Wales Labor Council; Bill Kelty, Secretary of the ACTU; Bruce Ruxton, former head of the Returned Services League; David Williamson, playwright; Archdeacon Alan Nicholls; and many others.

In fine print at the bottom was the line 'Donations are welcome'. They poured in.

That same afternoon Jim McClelland, veteran politician, former Labor minister in the Whitlam Government, judge and media commentator, launched the Friends of Fairfax information kit in the lobby of the Herald Building in Broadway. It was essentially a media event and it worked. Each of the television networks gave the story a run in their Saturday evening news bulletins.

With the dinner in Canberra on Friday night, the advertisement in the *Age* on Saturday morning and the launch of the information kit on the Saturday evening news, momentum was beginning to gather. At least that is what the journalists hoped.

．　．　．

Simon Lloyd stepped out of the taxi and walked into the Wrest Point casino hotel in Hobart. This was new territory for Lloyd, a thirty-two-year-old Englishman and banking editor of the *Australian Financial Review*. He had never been to a Labor Party conference and to top it all off he didn't have a bed for the night.

Lloyd had taken on the presidency of the Fairfax House Committee of the AJA in January. Out of the 'Middle East War' that had erupted between the *Financial Review* and the *Herald* in the attempt to form the Friends of Fairfax lobby group, Lloyd had emerged as a peacemaker. He was the agreed candidate by all papers as the president of the newly constituted union House Committee.

Part of the peace settlement had been that the union would be kept apart from the Friends of Fairfax. Concentration of media ownership, it was felt, was not an industrial issue. It was not about jobs, but about diversity of opinion in a democracy. And, more importantly, it could alienate potential supporters if it was linked with the union movement.

The analogy was presented—if TNT wanted to take over Brambles, there would be more public support for the Friends of Brambles than for the Brambles division of the Transport Workers Union. So Lloyd should not have been a Friends of Fairfax lobbyist under the strict definition. But the Labor Party conference was different. Union affiliation was a big plus here. And the AJA was throwing its weight behind the cause. They had agreed to contribute to the Hobart lobbying costs.

Alan Kennedy had to pull out of the Hobart trip at the last moment because his father was critically ill. That left Lloyd in the lobby of the Wrest Point casino alone and without a bed. It had been too late to snare a booking. Anyway the Friends of Fairfax was trying to do this cheaply.

The meeting with Martin Ferguson earlier in the day had been unsatisfying. Ferguson was a soul mate, yet reluctant to give public endorsement. He had given the amateur lobbyist a few tips, however: stay away from the New South Wales right—it was a lost cause; don't waste time with the left—it was already in the bag; target Chris Schacht and the centre left—they were crucial.

■　■　■

Lloyd and Anne Davies, due to arrive in Hobart later that evening, had a difficult task ahead of them. The antipathy between the Labor Party and the Fairfax press is the stuff that legends are made of.

Take this Tarzan version of media politics: 'It's a jungle out there and I'm a tiger. Where do you shoot a tiger? Between the eyes, that's where. Well, they missed; they only wounded me.'

This was Paul Keating in 1986, commenting on a *National Times* article canvassing Keating's friendship with businessman Warren Anderson.

Then there was this comment: 'I've hurt you more than you've hurt me.' This was Keating again to a Fairfax executive after the new cross-media ownership laws were introduced in late 1986. The comment came from a board minute by editorial executive Max Suich in early 1987, reporting on a five-hour meeting with Keating, then Federal Treasurer:

... Keating says his motives for getting involved in the Herald and Weekly Times takeover were a desire to see the [Melbourne] *Herald* broken up and a desire to hurt Fairfax ... The Treasurer is a product of the New South Wales right wing of the ALP and his conversation is littered with threats, references to getting even, doing deals and assisting 'our crowd' in business, the press and within the ALP.

He is very blunt about the fact that the New South Wales right are 'deal makers' and that they provide favours to 'our crowd' in return for favours given.

He also has very strong feelings about old money or establishment money, which he describes as dead money stultifying the economy, and he sees great advantages in new money—in which he includes Murdoch and Packer—being given opportunities to knock off old money. This I guess is the last glimmer of the class warrior ... Unless some deal can be made to the Treasurer's advantage (and he acknowledges that Fairfax does not do 'deals') I think the venom will remain, although the meeting did allow him to let off steam.

Keating's sensitivities reflected his intimate knowledge of the historical power of Australia's media proprietors. Since the Labor Party's formation it has generally come off second best with the media moguls.

Murdoch's father Sir Keith Murdoch was seen as anti-Labor in the 1930s when he was working his way into control of the HWT group. Alongside him during that period was the Fairfax newspapers, staunch supporters of the conservatives.

During Sir Frank Packer's reign, the *Daily Telegraph* was his vehicle for unwavering support for the Liberal–Country Party coalition during the 1950s and 1960s.

Since the 1970s the media proprietors have been more eclectic. Murdoch bought the *Daily* and *Sunday Telegraph* from Packer in 1972 and has followed his father's tradition of meddling in politics, but not always on the same side. In 1972 he gave support to Whitlam's Government but in 1975 turned ferociously against it.

His direct intervention through editorials and slanted political coverage against Labor prompted industrial action and left a bitter feeling in the Labor Party rank and file.

However, in the late 1970s and into the 1980s the Labor Party gradually regained general support from the Murdoch newspapers and Kerry Packer was not seen as the arch political conservative that his father had been.

Key party figures knew that antagonising media proprietors was useless if Labor was to return to power federally. In fact the odd favour didn't go astray.

The Fairfaxes, however, had tended to eschew the dealings with Labor governments that Packer and Murdoch embraced. One example was the Lotto licence granted amid controversy by the New South Wales Wran Labor Government in 1979 to a consortium including Murdoch and Packer.

The Fairfaxes had been invited to participate in the lucrative Lotto licence by government go-between Franco Belgiorno Nettis, but had declined.

To the New South Wales branch of the Labor Party, the *Herald* was historically the organ of the conservatives. The *Herald* had never printed an election editorial in favour of Labor in a New South Wales state election. In 1976 when the Labor Party was poised to return from the electoral wilderness under Neville Wran, the *Herald* editorialised that Wran was 'Whitlam writ small', waving the socialist bogey at the electorate.

Just a year after the sacking of the Whitlam Government and with the astute Wran trying to distance himself from the Federal Government debacles of the previous two years, this was a heinous political insult. If that was not enough, the *Herald* had more.

The election day editorial ran on the front page of the *Herald* and it referred to the Liberal Party as 'a party with a long record of honest government'. This was patently untrue—as the Fairfax papers were to claim, quite conclusively, a few years later as they investigated the entrenchment of corruption in politics and the police force under New South Wales Premier Robin Askin in the 1960s and 1970s.

Alongside the conservative tones of the *Herald* arose the impertinent digging of the *National Times*. During the first half of the 1980s the *National Times*, largely under the editorship of Brian Toohey, had printed story after story that severely embarrassed the Labor Party and its friends.

In 1983 Sir Peter Abeles, one of Bob Hawke's closest confidants, came under scrutiny in an article by Marian Wilkinson, entitled 'TNT's Brush with the Mafia' in which she outlined Abeles' dealings with known mafia members when establishing his trucking business in the USA. Part of her material for the article came from court evidence and documentation provided in a US legal case over the payment of two consultants.

In 1984 Rex Jackson, Minister for Corrective Services in Wran's cabinet, resigned his ministry after questions put to him by Wilkinson showed conclusively that he had misled Parliament. Wilkinson was investigating the early release scheme for prisoners. Jackson was later convicted of receiving money to secure early release for prisoners.

In 1984 Kerry Packer was under the microscope too. Again Marian Wilkinson wrote a profile of Packer, partly based on evidence gathered by the Costigan Royal Commission. Later in 1984 the *National Times* printed extracts from the Costigan Commission's forty-seven confidential references to the National Crime Authority, the most spectacular of which was the Goanna accusations.

In that year too the *National Times* and the *Age* published extracts from telephone taps by police, which led to the trial of High Court judge and Labor Party hero Lionel Murphy. In 1986 two articles were written canvassing the relationship between businessman Warren Anderson and Paul Keating, and an assessment of Anderson's business interests.

It was all too much for the Labor Party. Hawke made his feelings clear at a two-hour meeting with Max Suich in September 1986. He said that he could not be persuaded that attacks on him, Keating, Wran and their friends, Sir Peter Abeles, Warren Anderson and Kerry Packer, were not motivated by a desire to destroy the most effective politicians in the Labor Party.

It is tempting to conclude that if it wasn't for the busybodies on the *National Times*, Fairfax and the Labor Government would have got on like a house on fire. But that doesn't bear scrutiny. The *National Times*' investigations deepened the rift, but the Fairfaxes, at least in Sydney, represented conservative politics. The old money of the Fairfax dynasty was the antithesis of everything the Labor Party purported to stand for.

Perhaps most important of all, the Fairfax culture that developed under James Fairfax's chairmanship in the 1980s meant that editorial policy was difficult to manipulate. The Fairfax board kept out—there was little point in complaining to a board member and expecting him to do something about it. A church and state division was becoming entrenched.

This was frustrating for any politician, particularly when the newspapers in question included the country's two premier quality broadsheets and the national finance daily. Some political scientists could conclude that this was the price of free speech and a vigorous democracy.

This was not the view of the right wing of the New South Wales Labor Party, however. It bleated Fairfax conspiracy and complained about unfair investigation of its friends. Journalists, in turn, tended to ask if there is nothing to hide, why be so concerned?

But in late 1986 it was the Labor Party's turn to laugh and watch Fairfax squirm with the change in media laws and the HWT takeover.

The HWT takeover was a great humiliation for the Fairfax company. The takeover transformed Murdoch's Australian print media interests from third in the nation with relatively poor quality titles to number one with over sixty per cent of the circulation of major metropolitan dailies, forty-five per cent of magazine circulation and virtual monopolies in Adelaide and Brisbane. It was a huge swing in media power.

The success of the HWT takeover had its genesis, as Keating admits, in the new cross-media ownership regulations introduced by Keating on 25 November 1986. Murdoch and Packer had prior warning of the change. They were personally briefed by Keating—Murdoch twice, once at the International Monetary Fund conference in October and again in Canberra closer to the announcement. This allowed Packer and Murdoch to plot strategies ahead of their competitors, the HWT and Fairfax, who had not been briefed formally, although a Seven Network executive was given some indication.

HWT had been ruled out, Keating told Suich in his five-hour chat, because of a campaign run by the Melbourne *Herald* against the assets test and rules concerning lump sum superannuation. Fairfax had missed out because of attacks in its publications on Keating, his friend Warren Anderson, Prime Minister Hawke, Kerry Packer and Sir Peter Abeles.

The new cross-media ownership laws represented a major change to ownership of media in Australia. Until 1986 television proprietors were limited to owning two television stations. This had its inequities—an owner who had television stations in say Wagga and Tamworth, reaching a small percentage of the nation's population, was subject to the same restrictions as an owner who had stations in Sydney and Melbourne.

From an industry point of view, the policy prevented networking, which had the potential to bring with it valuable economies of scale. The situation in early 1986 was that Packer and Murdoch each had television stations in Sydney and Melbourne. Their two stations reached forty-three per cent of the population. Fairfax had a station in Sydney and one in Brisbane, reaching thirty-one per cent of the population. HWT had stations in Melbourne and Adelaide reaching 27.5 per cent of the population.

The policy was set for change under the Labor Government. Prime Minister Hawke took a personal interest in it. He wanted to make the new limit thirty-three per cent (so that an owner could have as many stations as he wished as long as his audience reach didn't exceed thirty-three per cent of the population) but he also wanted to allow Murdoch and Packer to keep their forty-three per cent.

Under normal grandfather clauses, which work to protect existing situations and ensure that the legislation is not unfairly retrospective, that forty-three per cent concession would disappear once the stations were sold to another party. Hawke wished to take this one step further, however. He wanted to allow Packer and Murdoch to sell that advantage on. Communications Minister Michael Duffy objected.

Duffy wanted a limit of forty-three per cent for all. The policy was deadlocked until Paul Keating stepped in with a new solution—a total media policy, which would greatly increase the limits on television audience reach but at the same time apply limits to cross-ownership of television, radio and newspapers in any one market. Keating claimed at the time that media owners could be prince of print or queen of screen, but not both.

Grandfather clauses would apply to existing owners. Murdoch's reaction when Keating pre-briefed him on the new laws was that he would jump in and acquire the HWT before the laws were introduced to give himself the advantage of grandfather provisions. As it turned out he did not do this, but his bid for the HWT came just eight days later on 3 December.

The new cross-media ownership laws offered a tremendous advantage to the Packer and Murdoch camps. The two-station limit was broken and it made their existing television stations with forty-three per cent of reach immensely valuable as the cornerstones of national networks. They each sold out to entrepreneurs within months—Packer to Alan Bond and Murdoch to Frank Lowy. Their profit was around $1 billion tax free.

Fairfax fumbled the HWT takeover badly. It ended up paying $350 million for HSV7 in Melbourne, a station it could not own as well as the *Age* under the new cross-media laws. It eventually sold its three Channel 7s (Melbourne, Brisbane and Sydney) later that year to Christopher Skase's Qintex for $638 million.

So the HWT group disappeared and Fairfax was nobbled, missing out on expanding its newspaper interests. This wasn't all due to changes in cross-media ownership. Management contributed with some stupid decisions, caused to some extent by the dithering of the Fairfax family. The result was clear. Fairfax had been placed at a significant strategic disadvantage.

The right wing of the Labor Party, in particular Paul Keating, appeared to be delighted. When Warwick took over Fairfax later that year and crippled the company with debt, he took it even further. He managed to destroy Fairfax far more effectively than any cross-media ownership laws could.

Now the Friends of Fairfax and the AIC felt it was their role to ensure that at least the Group's editorial integrity remained intact and that it would be difficult for the nation's print media to ever fall under the control of just two men, known for their strong interventionist approach to operating newspapers.

*　*　*

Anne Davies and Simon Lloyd were waiting anxiously in the Wrest Point casino hotel coffee lounge. It was 7 am on the morning of Tuesday, 25 June. They had only a day and a half to lobby before the debate on media policy got under way. There were 104 delegates. How were they going to get their attention?

The amendments that Davies and John Saunderson had drafted had five elements. The first was support for charters of editorial independence. The charters gained extra power by being included in newspaper companies' articles of association.

The second aimed to ensure that the Government use all of its powers, including the Trade Practices Act and Foreign Takeovers Act, to stop further concentration of media ownership. The third supported a Royal Commission into print media ownership.

The fourth proposed that the cross-media ownership rules be strengthened to stop de facto control being achieved through associates. And finally, as an interim measure, it was suggested that the Trade Practices Act be amended to stop future purchase or merger of magazine or newspaper titles, which would cause an owner to increase their ownership to more than 33.3 per cent of national circulation.

They were major requests. But Davies and the Friends of Fairfax saw it as an ambit claim—negotiable at the conference. The thirty-three per cent didn't signify anything in particular; it was more a tactic. If you placed a numerical limit on it, Davies reasoned, the tendency would be to argue about the number rather than the concept. This proposed cap on newspaper ownership would not be retrospective.

For example, Murdoch would not have to divest any papers. He simply couldn't buy any more.

Even at this early hour the tables in the coffee shop were filling up with earnest-looking party members and hangers on. There were many heads close together. It would be like this until midnight, and for the next three days. The coffee shop was a hot bed of political activity. Lloyd felt like he was on Mars—a banking writer dropped cold into the most intense political environment in the country. He was particularly shocked by the informality of it all.

In the twelve hours he had been here (spending the night on *Age* journalist, Glenda Korporaal's couch) Lloyd had taken several lift rides with ministers and brushed the Prime Minister in the lobby. It was wall-to-wall Labor Party. Everyone who mattered was here.

Everyone except Paul Keating, who probably mattered more than anybody but who, out of politeness, had decided to take his new backbencher status seriously. Even a political naif like Lloyd knew that this was a big plus for the Friends of Fairfax's efforts. Davies filled Lloyd in on the logistics. The best place to catch people was in the long galley-like lobby outside the convention centre auditorium, in which all the debates were taking place.

The lobby was lined on one side with doors into the auditorium and on the other with floor-to-ceiling windows overlooking the Derwent River. The bright sunlight pouring in all day did little for the early 1970s cinema-style carpet and the airport departure lounge furniture. This was to be their working turf for the next thirty-six hours.

The best tactic, Lloyd and Davies decided, was to work separately for a few hours and speak to as many centre left delegates as possible. Saunderson arrived at last with some disappointing news. He couldn't get the numbers for a Royal Commission into print media ownership, but a parliamentary inquiry was still a possibility.

Saunderson had been in Hobart since Saturday. The weekend before the conference is arguably the most critical period in the whole process. Cabinet ministers are always there to finalise agendas. The days are packed with factional meetings, discussions on proposed policy amendments and lobbying for support.

The print media amendments were not part of the formal amendments before the conference. They did not fit the usual procedure whereby draft policies are worked out by each of the policy committees (there is one for each ministry), then assembled by the national office to be circulated to the state offices for suggested amendments before the conference. Saunderson, however, had placed the print media amendments before the left faction meeting on Sunday and they had agreed to support them.

It was Monday night before Saunderson could get time with Beazley. They met in Beazley's room at Wrest Point. Beazley was totally opposed to a Royal Commission, but agreed to take a proposal for a parliamentary inquiry to senior ministers. A parliamentary inquiry was more controllable and less expensive than a Royal Commission.

Beazley would not consider the thirty-three per cent ownership cap either—this was something which could be raised before an inquiry; why pre-empt its findings? Saunderson's good news was that he was confident they would have the support for a tougher associates clause in the Broadcasting Act, and probably charters of editorial independence. This wasn't the assessment Davies and Lloyd were hoping for, but at least they now had limits within which to work.

Saunderson disappeared to redraft the amendments while Lloyd and Davies continued their lobbying efforts.

■　■　■

Lloyd strolled through the casino—the quickest way from the hotel's reception area and coffee shop to the convention centre. It was about 9 am. Walking straight towards him was Kim Beazley. Here goes, thought Lloyd.

'Mr Beazley, I am Simon Lloyd from the Friends of Fairfax. I would like to speak with you for a few minutes about concentration of media ownership.'

Beazley's hands fluttered as he dismissed Lloyd, muttering 'no time' as he strode on.

This is not going to be easy, Lloyd thought. In the lobby he intercepted Peter Cook, Minister for Industrial Relations. He made slightly better progress with Cook, who listened politely but was clearly disinterested. As Lloyd wound up his spiel prematurely, Cook said, 'What a bastard of a job you've got.'

But the next two ministers, Neil Blewett and John Button, treated the issue seriously. Lloyd felt he had swayed them. The lobby was emptying. Now for the auditorium. Lloyd positioned himself just behind Michael Easson, Secretary of the New South Wales Labor Council. Easson was a surprise as he was deeply interested in the fourth estate. Lloyd left certain they could count on Easson's support.

During the lunch break, Davies and Lloyd distributed the kits through the auditorium. It was covered with the Friends of Fairfax literature. 'It looks as if we have the resources and clout of a National Farmers Federation lobby,' Davies chuckled.

It was shortly afterwards that they snatched Beazley's attention for five minutes in the lobby. Davies did the talking. Beazley was dismissive. He clearly felt they were exaggerating the dangers of media concentration with the Fairfax purchase. He did listen, however, and so did his adviser Patrick Walters.

By the early afternoon Saunderson had extraordinary news. He slipped into a chair beside Davies who was listening to a debate in the auditorium and wondering who she could collar next.

'It's going to be all right. I've got the right to second it.' Davies was flabbergasted.

Beazley had given it the nod. He had spoken to Graham Richardson, Michael Duffy, John Button and Hawke's staff. It would get through.

Davies and Lloyd still continued the lobbying with everyone they could waylay, however. Davies felt the antipathy of the right towards Fairfax would raise its head before the amendments were debated. Saunderson seemed overconfident.

On Wednesday afternoon the media debate began. Davies and Saunderson were sitting towards the back of the auditorium. Just a few seats away was Chris Anderson, in Hobart to do a little lobbying of his own for Jamison. The votes were being counted on the print media inquiry proposal.

'Will it get through? I can't stand it,' Davies moaned. Saunderson was laconic.

'There is nothing to worry about. I stitched it up twenty-four hours ago.'

With cross-factional support, the amendments sailed through. That day Prime Minister Hawke announced that the print media inquiry would indeed go ahead. It would begin in the August sitting of Parliament and complete its hearing by the end of the year.

It was a huge boost for the AIC and the Friends of Fairfax. At least the issue of media concentration would be debated—and in a national forum with maximum publicity—while the auction for the Fairfax Group was taking place.

But the most critical change of all to the platform was overlooked in the media coverage the next day—the suggestion for tighter associates clauses in the cross-media ownership laws.

The Tourang team was on track to walk right into the middle of a political nightmare.

CHAPTER NINE

THE LAUNCH OF TOURANG

NEVILLE MILES was ashen-faced when he walked into the Turnbull & Partners boardroom. As he and Brian Powers walked across town on this cold and cloudy Friday on 28 June he had been subjected to ten minutes of abuse from Powers about the original junk bond proposal penned in May by Miles and Turnbull. It was the document that formed the basis of the agreement to establish the bidding consortium.

Powers claimed they had been cheated. The basis of the junk bondholders' argument was that their bonds had value because it would be so costly for the banks to sell Fairfax without their approval. The banks would be forced to sell the assets out of the Group rather than sell the company structure. This meant an extra $55 million in stamp duty and foregoing available tax losses of $250 million.

Turnbull, Cass O'Connor and Geoff Levy, the South African-born partner of Freehills working on the consortium bid, were already waiting, seated around the boardroom table.

Powers' opening line was gruff. 'I think we have a problem here. We have taken some advice on the stamp duty and it is $20 million less than we expected.'

Turnbull jumped in. 'So you mean the deal is off?'

'No,' said Powers, 'but we are not happy with the numbers.'

The idea of overpaying a group of junk bondholders advised by Turnbull didn't appeal to Powers—especially so given Turnbull's behaviour during these negotiations on the exclusivity agreement.

Powers was still fuming over a sarcastic fax from Turnbull sent to him in San Francisco two weeks before. It related to comments that Mark Carnegie, the Australian-based adviser to Hellman & Friedman, had made to Miles in a meeting at Ord Minnett. It read:

13 June 1991

Dear Brian

There was a bit of a kerfuffle at Ords today when your Mark Carnegie called in to tell Ords that:

(a) Hellman & Friedman were acting for both Packer and Black, and that Hellman & Friedman would be responsible for giving Ords instructions on behalf of the consortium and that

(b) Packer wanted you (Brian Powers) to be chief executive officer at Fairfax.

As to (a), could you tell Mr Carnegie (whose father very recently tried to undermine my position with the bondholders) that the bondholders have the largest single economic interest in the consortium and that no instructions can be given on behalf of the consortium unless they were agreed by the consortium which includes us.

As to (b), it isn't very helpful that those matters are discussed with Ords, who are now anxious that the CEO matter be resolved. Instead, I thought the CEO job Kerry Packer had his eye on for you was CEO of CPH, not Fairfax.

On the representation matter, I don't think it is for Hellman & Friedman to act for Packer and Black, particularly since we are going to be telling people that Black and Hellman & Friedman are acting independently of Packer.

I would suggest that everyone represent themselves.

Malcolm Turnbull

Against this background Powers was in no mood for a meeting with Turnbull. Miles was also anxious. He was worried about Powers' hints that he might sue Ords.

'We believe you have overstated the economic leverage of the bondholders,' Powers said emphatically. 'We want to reconsider the $125 million figure.'

Turnbull couldn't believe this—the deal was done and now Powers was trying to re-trade. Turnbull had spent the last three weeks, with many sleepless nights in conference calls, coaxing the bondholders to agree to the deal. Now this.

'Look, we already have a deal and we agreed on a price. We have an oral agreement.'

Sitting back in his chair, Powers sneered at Turnbull. 'Come on, Malcolm, you know there is no such thing as an oral agreement. There is no deal done until it is signed.'

The atmosphere in the room was poisonous. Powers' attitude infuriated Turnbull.

Powers brought up Lady Mary Fairfax's annuity, another issue that figured in the comparison of a share or asset sale. 'We have looked at the annuity and the net present value is $67 million.'

O'Connor was shocked. 'My God, they've actually worked out when she is going to die!' she thought.

Turnbull, however, was adamant. Jumping to his feet, he walked over to a white board, grabbed a felt pen and began scrawling an explanation of the benefits of the bondholders' litigation and why there was a good case against the banks. 'Look at this,' he almost shouted, jabbing at his figures on the board.

Levy interjected, throwing in questions about the difficulties of proving a case for the bondholders under the Trade Practices Act on false and misleading conduct. With Turnbull's temper rising, Levy was quite enjoying stoking the flames. Then Powers spoke up again, needling, saying he still couldn't see the value of the litigation. Powers can be a daunting opponent. Tall, wiry, direct, he speaks with the confidence of one who knows he has the solution.

Turning away from the board, Turnbull pointed his pen at Powers. He was sick of this American's tough, half-arsed negotiation tactics. 'Either you do the deal at the $125 million, or you drop dead.'

Powers laughed. 'Oh, come on, Malcolm. Stop all this macho shit. Sit down. You are embarrassing yourself.'

Turnbull strode across to open the door. 'If you want to re-trade, get out of this office.'

'Don't be silly, come back,' Powers said.

There were shocked looks around the table as Turnbull walked back, picked up a pile of papers and threw them down. They slid across the shiny surface of the boardroom table.

Turnbull clenched an upturned fist. 'I will destroy you. You will never do a deal in this town,' he bellowed.[1] O'Connor leaned forward and put her hands over her head.

Turnbull glanced at his watch, realised he was running late for a court case, and stormed out of the office. The others were silent for a few seconds, before Powers stood up and collected his papers.

■　■　■

Heading back to Freehills, Powers couldn't believe Turnbull's explosion. He had never seen anything like it in his business career. Certainly people get heated in meetings—Powers was no exception—but Turnbull was something else. He had heard of Turnbull's reputation for temper tantrums and now he had experienced it first hand.

The worrying thing, though, was Turnbull's presence on the board of the bidding company. This was not set in stone— originally Turnbull was to have been the representative of the bondholders on the board, but Freehills was worried about being too specific about Turnbull's role.

On 17 June Freehills had sent a memo stating that board positions might be a real issue with the Foreign Investment Review Board (FIRB). It was deemed prudent, therefore, not to be too clear on the roles of board members. Two days later, in a letter to the bondholders discussing the progress of the negotiations on the exclusivity agreement, Turnbull discussed this issue:

... It was originally proposed that the bondholders would have a representative in myself. The foreign ownership situation probably requires that we are not specific about any foreign representation, including Black and Hellman.

So it is proposed that we simply establish the board with myself on it. There is a risk that the day after completion the

---

[1] Turnbull denies he used these words. He maintains that he said: 'If you want to do business in Australia, you've got to be prepared to be bound by your word.'

other shareholders will throw me off the board, but I think that is highly improbable.

On Monday, 1 July Colson and Powers met with Kerry Packer at his Park Street offices. It was awkward, but Turnbull's behaviour had to be raised. This meeting, one of the first of many intimate chats between this threesome, was being held to discuss progress on the formation of the consortium. Colson and Packer were shocked at Powers' account of the previous Friday's meeting.

Packer agreed that Colson should write to Turnbull and attempt to pull him into line. No one wanted Turnbull causing problems. He wasn't a shareholder and would have to learn to settle down. The transaction was going to be tough enough without additional internal problems.

The next day, 2 July, Turnbull received a tough letter from Colson saying that he had been asked to relay some points from the talks:

... We would like any further discussion of Hellman & Friedman's participation in the consortium to cease immediately.

We are satisfied with the proposed revised agreement in regard to Hellman & Friedman's participation and see no point in discussing this matter any further with you.

In the same vein, we do not wish to be subjected to any further threats by you of litigation or other unspecified action against the original shareholders, their representatives or advisers.

And we would be obliged if you, your partners or other members of your firm would refrain from communicating with any government official, media or other third parties in Australia or elsewhere concerning the project unless specifically requested to do so by one of the original shareholders.

I trust you appreciate that the above points are being made in the hope that we can concentrate our respective energies and efforts in a more positive manner, which will ultimately lead to the successful conclusion of this project.

Turnbull wasn't pleased. Powers had started the whole argument and now the American had run to Packer, telling tales about 'naughty Malcolm'. Turnbull planned to speak to Packer and explain; Powers had overstepped the mark.

●　　●　　●

Over the next few days Turnbull's energies were concentrated on finetuning the bondholder agreement in lengthy discussions with Levy. Preparations were being escalated for the announcement of the consortium.

By now Freehills had obtained a shelf company called Tourang to become the bidding vehicle for Fairfax. Until now the consortium's plans had been conducted under the code name 'Project Falcon', reflecting the bold plans to swoop and grab Fairfax.

Details of the financial commitments of the partners were finalised. Levy's prime concern, however, was to make sure the bondholder agreement was extremely tight. The Tourang consortium would only have an advantage in any dealings with the bondholders if the agreement couldn't be breached. The bondholders had to be controlled, be unable to even contemplate a higher offer. The $125 million seemed a good price now for the bondholders, but there was no point in taking any risks should the value of Fairfax rise before the sale was completed.

The clause was tough, banning any of the parties from directly or indirectly making, participating in, or otherwise being interested in any other offer for the shares or assets of Fairfax or in any proposal for the reconstruction or acquisition of Fairfax.

If the expiry date was reached without the offer being accepted, the parties were required to negotiate in good faith to continue the agreement for as long as there was a reasonable prospect of the offer being accepted. This was provided that the extension would not continue for a period of more than thirty days after the expiry date without the approval of the bondholders.

The key words in the clause were 'reasonable prospect'—a good, arguable clause that Levy was happy with since it would probably allow a lot longer than thirty days.

Another clause gave the shareholders the right to call the bonds at any time prior to the expiry date or the extended expiry date for the $125 million. The settlement date of this call option would be on completion of the purchase of Fairfax.

Elsewhere in the agreement there was a clause that Hellman & Friedman was forced to accept reluctantly. Although Tourang was confident that there would be no foreign ownership problems if it stuck below forty per cent, Turnbull made sure that his bondholders ranked ahead of Hellman & Friedman if the shareholdings had to be restructured. If the foreign ownership level came down, Hellman & Friedman was required to reduce its holding before the bondholders. It was a nice victory for Turnbull.

One other clause stated that the balance of Tourang's capital would consist of not more than $700 million of bank debt. This was designed to ensure the capital structure of Tourang, if it succeeded in securing Fairfax, was suitable.

As his firm was a party to the deed and had the authority to accept the offer on behalf of the bondholders, Turnbull made sure he was intimately involved in the agreement process.

When he saw the final version, Powers was confident that the agreement would hold together. Despite the recent fight he grudgingly gave Turnbull credit for what he had done with the bondholders. Turnbull had achieved a unique situation with Fairfax as junk bondholders rarely came together in agreements like this. It had been a zoo in the USA since the collapse of the junk bond market and many bondholders were suing everyone and anyone. At least Malcolm had brought this group together for six months.

• • •

Turnbull paid little attention to Colson's fax warning him against any approaches to politicians. Turnbull was well-connected in political circles. His long association with Packer, who had in recent years developed close connections with the New South Wales right wing of the Labor Party, and his partnership with Neville Wran, one of the Labor Party's most successful politicians, ensured his entrée into Federal political circles. What did Colson know about Australian politics?

To test the waters on foreign ownership Turnbull decided it would be a useful exercise to go to Canberra. He arranged a lunch with Graham Richardson, a cabinet minister and the most important powerbroker in the Labor Party.

As godfather of the New South Wales right wing, Richardson's power was unrivalled.[2] He made and destroyed Labor Party

---

[2] Graham Richardson resigned from Cabinet on 18 May 1992 amidst controversy over assistance given to his cousin by marriage, Greg Symonds, who was facing fraud charges in the Marshall Islands in relation to the operation of a business migration scheme.

leaders and ministers and was at the forefront of the push that replaced Bill Hayden with Hawke, who went on in 1983 to win the Federal election. Just six weeks earlier on 3 June, Richardson had suffered a rare defeat when the campaign to replace Hawke with Keating failed.

In the 1980s Richardson associated closely with Packer and other key businessmen such as construction giant John Roberts of Multiplex and stockbroker Rene Rivkin. He had come a long way in the Party since his humble background. The son of an official in the Postal Workers Union now dined in trendy Sydney restaurants with people like Kennedy and Rivkin.

The Fairfax sale intrigued Richardson and he was keen that the owner should be one who was more amenable to the cause of Labor election victories.

Turnbull spoke to Richardson who agreed to bring along to lunch Communications and Transport Minister Kim Beazley on Monday, 16 July. Turnbull decided he would take his client Ezzes down for the lunch. It would be useful for Ezzes to hear things first hand and anyway, Turnbull and Ezzes had become close friends through this exhaustive process.

* * *

Ezzes had returned to Australia for the final discussions over the exclusivity agreement and had spent the past few days with the Tourang team at the Ord Minnett offices. The atmosphere was buoyant as the announcement date for Tourang approached —everyone was confident that Tourang was unbeatable and would snatch Fairfax within weeks. Trevor Kennedy was buzzing around, keen to give Fairfax the shake-up he had dreamed about for years.

Arriving in Canberra, Turnbull and Ezzes caught a cab to the restaurant where Richardson had suggested they dine. Ezzes was amazed—they were meeting Richardson and Beazley in a cheap Italian restaurant, La Dolce Vita. This would never happen with cabinet ministers in Washington.

'Don't you guys have bodyguards?' Ezzes asked an amused Beazley as the minister plonked his large frame in his chair.

Over lunch Turnbull explained why Tourang should be acceptable to the Government. On Packer's involvement he was emphatic that Packer was complying with both the spirit and letter of the law if he took a shareholding in Fairfax below fifteen per cent.

There would be independent directors, he explained—former Governor-General Sir Zelman Cowen and former New South Wales Chief Justice Sir Laurence Street. He stressed, however, that Black would be the driving force behind the consortium.

Beazley and Richardson listened; the consortium wasn't new to them. Packer's political adviser Peter Barron, who was close to the New South Wales right wing and one-time adviser to Hawke, was a constant emissary to Canberra and he had told Beazley of the Tourang consortium several weeks earlier. Barron kept a close watch on broadcasting industry regulation, lobbying for Packer's commercial interests. Packer despises regulation of any sort— an ironic attitude, given his family's wealth has been built on a licence awarded by the Government—and the files at the Australian Broadcasting Tribunal (ABT) are full of stern, often sarcastic letters from Barron.

Turnbull finished his spiel. It was obvious that he was fishing for information on Beazley's thoughts. To his questions on the cross-media issue, Beazley replied with his standard line: 'I am in the process of taking advice on the capacity of the ABT, in the context of the Fairfax transaction, to uphold the cross-media laws.' The issue was being discussed by his department and the Attorney-General's department. His advice was that the powers were adequate and, anyway, there was major work being put into a total overhaul of broadcasting regulation. This view of the cross-media laws wasn't, however, shared by Peter Westerway, the chairman of the ABT.

Regardless of the advice from his department, Beazley knew that any consortium involving Packer was a political nightmare. If Packer complied with the existing black letter law, there wasn't anything he could do. Given the political sensitivity, however, if the ABT felt that it needed additional powers to make sure there was no breach of the cross-media laws, he knew he would be under pressure to accede. The motions passed at the Hobart Conference recommending a tightening of associates clauses in the broadcasting legislation were strong indications of what was to come if he failed to act.

As the lunch ended Beazley invited Turnbull and Ezzes back to his office where he arranged a meeting with John Kerin, the new Treasurer appointed to replace Keating. Kerin's demeanour surprised Ezzes. He is very serious and somewhat humble.

Kerin admitted that he had no idea what a junk bond was. He rested a large leather notebook on his knee and took copious notes in fountain pen. His aide was dressed very casually in slacks and a pullover. This certainly wasn't Washington.

Turnbull and Ezzes pushed a simple line: don't change the law for one situation—it will impact on future foreign investment in this country. Both Kerin and Beazley seemed amenable.

* * *

Walking into the foyer at Baring Brothers on Tuesday morning, 16 July, Powers felt he owed this chat to Burrows.

Tourang was to be announced to the public that afternoon and Burrows had been helpful to Hellman & Friedman, even if his suggestion to look at AIN hadn't been considered a good idea.

Powers knew that Burrows and Turnbull didn't get on, each claiming the other was unbalanced. The friction was a potential problem in the sale negotiations and Powers felt he should be the one to tell Burrows and allay fears of Turnbull's involvement in the sale process. Powers had a suspicion that Turnbull would not be able to resist gloating over how he had outsmarted Burrows. Diplomacy not confrontation was needed here.

In a conference room Powers quickly outlined some of the details of the Tourang bid to be announced later that day. It was not a complete shock to Burrows. Packer had told the ANZ Bank in May that he would be a player in the Fairfax sale process. Burrows was also aware that Packer and Black were joining forces. While in London late the previous week investigating whether Pearsons remained interested in Fairfax, he had heard the rumours about Packer and also Black's plans to come to Australia. He had spent a day in London, then jumped on a plane to return before Black's arrival. What Burrows didn't know was exactly what Turnbull had been up to.

Powers ran through the shareholders and explained about the exclusive agreement with the bondholders. Burrows seemed nonplussed but was unable to coax more detail from Powers. Instead he was told that Powers had done him a favour; that Burrows and the banks would have had to deal with the junk bondholders at some stage.

'Tourang has done it for you,' he said.

The consortium would put the lid on the risk that individual bondholders might launch separate court actions—at least for six months—and ensured that there would be no scope for the bondholders to force a higher price for the bonds. The price was locked in—the bondholders were accepting their $450 million worth of bonds was only worth $125 million now. Powers concluded by telling Burrows that Tourang would be announced in a few hours. Burrows was immensely impressed by Powers. Powers has the uncanny knack of making business discussions sound like a chapter from a management school text. It is there, it is written, this is the way you do it, we are not trying to outsmart anyone, this is the way sensible people conduct transactions. It was a technique that Burrows felt comfortable with. Emotional wrangles were not his forte, nor his preferred method of doing business. The only sign that Powers gives of tension is a slight speech impediment and he sprinkles 'you know' (pronounced 'ya gnaw' in his US accent) liberally through his conversation when the going gets tough.

After escorting Powers out of the office Burrows called in Breese and White to pass on the news. He was delighted. He had a third bidder for his auction.

As they discussed the implications Breese struck a good point on the impact of any exclusivity agreement. If the bondholders were worth $125 million, then repayment of the full bank debt was assured. Theoretically the bonds were worth nothing until the banks had been repaid. The banks were adamant that they didn't need to take a haircut on their loans and, effectively, Tourang was guaranteeing the bank debt would be met, even if it tried to bid low in the first instance. As long as the junk bondholders were tied up with Tourang, the other bidders would now have to compete seriously on price. They would also need to top the bank debt. Burrows agreed with him.

. . .

Trevor Kennedy began one of his last working days in the Packer family empire. He had been looking forward to this for over a year now. He was tired of working under Packer and with Kerry contemplating some major changes at Consolidated Press they could do with a fresh chief executive. He and Packer had agreed back in 1990 that Kennedy would leave within two years—before his fiftieth birthday in June 1992.

Packer's empire had a few problems. He was facing a huge $200 million provision for a write-down on a property investment in Perth, Westralia Square, a venture with Paul Keating's close friend Warren Anderson. Then there were other festering sores like Muswellbrook Mining—Packer's foray into coal and the exploration for rich gold deposits in old volcanos in tropical Pacific Rim islands. The mining company was an absolute disaster—Packer had effectively lost over $100 million on it.

Kennedy had always maintained he would retire at fifty in order to enjoy the wealth he had amassed working for Packer. He also talked about writing an autobiography and kept a diary for this purpose. There was plenty of material. Working for Packer was a heady ride—money, political connections, and larrikin activities when Packer and his mates partied hard.

He was prepared, however, to postpone early retirement for Packer and Black. It was a once-in-a-lifetime opportunity. Instead of worrying about gold mining, property, engineering and chemicals, at the Fairfax Group he would be concerned with newspapers, magazines and little else. The job he was going to— chief executive of Fairfax—was arguably the best media position in the country. Kennedy would be powerful in his own right; no longer just Kerry Packer's loyal servant. Returning to Fairfax—if Tourang won—would also be rather like going home. Kennedy had worked at Fairfax in his twenties and it was where he had first made his mark in journalism as the inaugural editor of the *National Times*.

For today, however, he had to face the inevitable uncertainty at Consolidated Press. He looked at the memo Kerry Packer had sent to staff from London. Headed 'Strictly Private and Confidential', it read:

Trevor Kennedy has resigned as managing director of the group. I am personally very sad at this event but Trevor has chosen to pursue an opportunity as chief executive of a group which will try to acquire the Fairfax newspapers. As a result, he is severing his connections with this company.

Trevor has made an outstanding contribution to this company—over nearly twenty years of service. He leaves with my goodwill and good wishes—as I'm sure he does yours.

It continued in typical Packer fashion: 'However, our disappointment at this event should not interfere with the smooth and efficient running of the business . . .'

News of Kennedy's impending departure had leaked in the previous few days. It was actually included in an article set to run in that week's *Bulletin* magazine. Kennedy was anxious to ensure that Tourang received some good publicity, given its potential problems of Packer and foreign ownership.

This publicity wasn't hard when Packer's media interests could be used to push the message. Kennedy arranged with the editor of the *Bulletin* for an interview with Conrad Black to be the cover story for Wednesday, 17 July, coinciding with Black's arrival in Sydney.

The story was entitled 'How I Would Run Fairfax'. Black took the opportunity to answer one of the vexing questions likely to be asked about Tourang—the appearance of Kennedy as the proposed Fairfax chief executive and Packer's involvement. Journalist Bruce Stannard quoted Black as saying:

Kerry's involvement arose out of me seeking to hire Trevor Kennedy as the prospective managing director of the Fairfax Group, were we to gain control of it.

Since I knew Kerry, I thought this would be a gross breach of protocol if I did not ask him in advance. When I did, he said he would not stand in the way of any man's career, but if I did go ahead he would like a piece of the deal. I agreed.

Black's account of these events was curious. At the Savoy Hotel meetings in London on 3 June, the chief executive's position had not been decided upon and Kennedy was not actually interviewed by Black for the Fairfax job until 18 June.

The *Bulletin* cover was a perfect opportunity for Black to answer any criticisms ahead of time and in a sympathetic medium. The Stannard article was gentle.

It began with Black's comment: 'I hope that my arrival [in Australia] will dispel the notion that I have cloven feet and pointy ears.'

Stannard wrote: 'Although Black has strong personal political views, he declares himself "absolutely in favour of editorial independence"—one of the main issues flung from the Fairfax barricades in Sydney.' Stannard editorialised to push the case, raising fears that hadn't even been expressed yet. Black was unknown in Australia; Stannard made it sound like he was and already controversial: 'Although there is little evidence to support it, another of the great fears expressed by Fairfax journalists is the belief that Black would be an interventionist proprietor'.

The *Bulletin* article also gave Black the opportunity to answer any suggestion that he was acting on behalf of Packer:

The facts are that, under the framework now under consideration, Kerry will be very much a minority shareholder.

He will be a shareholder at the kind of level that normally gets you a free lunch and a tour of the plant. Kerry is not going to be controlling anything in that company and he is certainly not going to be muzzling journalists.

He stepped into Blackspeak:

I realise that there is this fear in some circles that any association between Kerry and me is some saturnine, diabolical, Machiavellian conspiracy conceived by him and in which I am playing merely a cameo role.

I have my detractors, but not even the most rabid among them have ever accused me of being a front for anyone. I am certainly not a front for Kerry Packer.

These rebuttals were a little premature. The Fairfax journalists were not even fully aware Black was a player until the day the magazine hit the streets—they had not had the opportunity to claim a Packer conspiracy.

Pitched a little like the arrival of the conquering hero, Kennedy organised a media blitz for Black's arrival partly to ease the heat on Packer. Powers was surprised at the media campaign, but was happy to stay in the background, keeping Hellman & Friedman's involvement very low profile.

It was not his style to take the running in any case. Nor did he want too much attention drawn to the foreign aspects of the bid. There was obviously no need to have two heads out there competing for media attention—particularly two North American heads.

* * *

There was an air of suppressed excitement on the newsroom floor of the *Herald*. It is a huge expanse of open-plan office space, littered with computer screens, grey-blue desks and pink filing cabinets. The first news of the Tourang bid came through the fax machine from Neville Miles' office.

On that Tuesday afternoon, 16 July, huddles of journalists, heads together, discussed the details of the Tourang bid. They had been living with this bidding process for eight months now, since before Christmas. The jargon of junk bonds and receiverships and bank bill rollovers flowed easily.

An Australian Journalists Association (AJA) meeting of all journalists, artists and photographers in the Broadway headquarters was set down for 4 pm. Television news editors rang throughout the day for interviews with Alan Kennedy, spokesperson for the Friends of Fairfax, and asked permission to bring cameras to the union meeting.

But there was serious division in the House Committee over what style of motion, if any, should be put to the meeting. This blew up at a lunchtime gathering.

The Friends of Fairfax line was the one it had warned about in Hobart. The Tourang bid represented serious concerns on two fronts—it would effectively add to concentration of media ownership because, it believed, the prime influence on the bid was Kerry Packer. He had a planned fifteen per cent of the equity in Fairfax, and he had two close associates, Malcolm Turnbull and Trevor Kennedy, proposed for the board of Fairfax, with one of them, Kennedy, its chief executive officer.

In addition all attempts to have meetings with Packer or his representatives on issues of editorial independence and the editorial charter had been ignored. Now was the time to object to the Tourang bid. If it was left a day or a week, the perception of the politicians and the institutional investors would be that the Fairfax staff accepted the situation or at worst were equivocal.

Not all Fairfax staff agreed with this line, however. Some wanted to wait until more information was obtained and the significance of the bid assessed. The House Committee meeting was heated and nasty and there wasn't unanimity on the wording of a motion nor the timing of any objection.

The *Herald* representatives carried the vote. There were mutterings of Stalinism. A motion would be put to the meeting of the full house that pronounced the Tourang bid as totally unacceptable. It read:

The full house of the Fairfax Group Broadway finds that the Conrad Black–Kerry Packer consortium would be totally unacceptable as the new owner of the Fairfax Group.

The consortium would be effectively controlled by Mr Packer and, as such, a successful bid would constitute a breach of cross-media ownership legislation and a dangerous increase in concentration of the print media.

It would lead to the unacceptable situation where ninety per cent of Australia's metropolitan newspapers and magazines would be under the control of two men—Kerry Packer and Rupert Murdoch.

Alan Kennedy and Ward O'Neill were nervous as they walked past the television cameras and into the packed auditorium on the seventh floor of the Herald Building. It was a strong turn up of about 300 at the meeting and the presence of cameras added to the tense atmosphere. A defeat of the motion would virtually kill the support base for the Friends of Fairfax.

The debate was equivocal at first, with some journalists pointing to the potential transfer opportunities with Black's Daily Telegraph Group in London. But it was veteran journalist Peter Bowers who saved the day. He gave a stirring speech on the importance of an independent media climaxing with an emotional plea: 'Do you know what it will take to change the prime minister of this country if Kerry Packer gets hold of Fairfax? One phone call; that's what it will take. From Kerry Packer to Rupert

Murdoch or vice versa. You might say, well we can still vote at election day. You can go along and cast your vote if you like, but it isn't going to do you much good.'

Bowers drove home the point that it was the journalists who knew what editorial interference meant. If the journalists didn't take a stance against it, against the prospect of two men virtually controlling the media in Australia, then how could you expect anyone else to?

Bowers was a hard act to follow and no one tried. The motion was put and carried unanimously. Bowers felt very strongly about an independent Fairfax and he carried a lot of weight with journalists. The Friends of Fairfax lived on.

At sixty-two Bowers had retired from journalism more than once after a distinguished career as a political reporter and columnist. Now he reported sport, the rural scene, whatever took his fancy. Bowers rarely speaks without emotion. Nicknamed 'Daffy' for his eccentric personality, he is nevertheless revered as an astute judge of the political wind. His access to Federal politicians is almost unrivalled. His passionate support was a big boost for the Friends of Fairfax.

The *Herald* had carried an interview with John B Fairfax written by Bowers the day before the Tourang bid was announced. In discussing why he supported the O'Reilly bid for Fairfax, John told Bowers:

The main factors for even looking or listening to any of these approaches we have had have been specifically about the future of the country, because there is a responsibility to see these papers ... go into the right hands.

I don't think that aspect can be overemphasised. It's very important for this nation and the democratic processes that there is a healthy and competitive press which has the right interests and, I suppose to some degree, the traditional Fairfax interests at heart.

Bowers had worked for Fairfax for more than thirty years. He couldn't have put it better himself.

The divided house at Fairfax's Broadway headquarters was not mirrored at the *Age*. David Wilson decided against a full house meeting of staff, instead issuing a short statement concentrating on Packer's failure to reply to letters asking him to endorse a charter of editorial independence and on Black's record as an interventionist proprietor at the *Jerusalem Post*. 'It was a paper with similar editorial values to the *Age*. Within six months of Mr Black acquiring it, both of the newspaper's co-editors had resigned, as has the managing editor and twenty-five other senior editors and long time reporters,' Wilson said.

• • •

In Canberra the response to the Tourang bid was mooted that day. Kennedy had already organised meetings for Conrad Black with Kerin, Hawke and Beazley for Thursday. The politicians were holding their fire—at least for the time being.

On Wednesday morning, 17 July, a jet-lagged Conrad Black walked out of Sydney's International Air Terminal and into a waiting limousine. It was his first visit to Australia, and Sydney had turned on a magnificent sun-drenched winter's day. Black was whisked straight to Ords where one floor was devoted to the Tourang blitz. Black's face on the *Bulletin* cover was plastered over every news-stand in town. His arrival was top of the news bulletins on radio stations across the country. Most Australians had never heard of him before—and in all likelihood weren't interested.

When he was finally doorstopped by a group of journalists in the Ords foyer he reeled off his prepared line on the link up with Packer. As far as Black was concerned, political hurdles were not a concern:

I don't think we have a great political problem. I know and accept that there are many in this country who would wish reassurances on that point, but I know in fact that we are not foul of any legitimate political considerations that have been raised.

This is not a Packer takeover, this is not a foreign takeover, it's not some conspiratorial coalition to subvert the independence of the press, or to muzzle anyone's objective reporting in your papers.

When questioned on whether O'Reilly was his main rival, Black laughed. 'He's a great man ... he's the world's greatest leprechaun and a very capable industrialist. Doctor! I mean I could call myself Dr Black but I don't.'

His joke wasn't that well-known—O'Reilly likes to call himself Dr O'Reilly due to his marketing degree—and in the USA he is known as Mr O'Reilly.

Ending the impromptu interview, Black was asked how he would like to be seen.

'As the samaritanly philanthropist that I am. I'm just here to help you, you know that.'

The next day, Powers asked Black: 'Conrad, did you really say that?'

'Yes, I suppose I did get a bit carried away,' Black replied with an irreverent grin.

. . .

In Canberra the scene was no longer so sanguine. Hawke weighed in with comments designed to dampen the euphoria of the Tourang team. The Prime Minister told journalists: 'As far as Mr Packer's concerned, let me make this point quite clear. Mr Packer, if he's a bidder, will have to satisfy the law.'

And on foreign ownership: 'You've got Mr Black, you've got a US merchant bank, and then there's whatever they're proposing about the junk bondholders. We'll have to consider all of these things and then we as a government will make a decision as to what we think is appropriate as to the degree of overseas ownership.'

Hawke's attitude was less than comforting for the Tourang team. The sands had shifted in Canberra politics, at least for the time being. While Paul Keating was on the backbench sniping at the Prime Minister for his job, the clout of the New South Wales right wing was very limited.

Trevor Kennedy and Peter Barron had been left in charge of the Canberra lobbying and it was becoming apparent to the other team members that their luncheon connections were very firmly in the Keating rather than the Hawke camp. Hawke saw Laurie Oakes of Packer's Nine Network as leading the media pack against him, and for Paul Keating, in the leadership stoush. He was bitter about it.

In Kim Beazley's office there was more bad news for Tourang

that Wednesday, 17 July. The announcement of their bid had uncovered a letter from Peter Westerway, who was worried about the Kimshaw case—the attempts by Packer to get around broadcasting legislation on the ownership of 2UE.

Westerway faxed a very strong letter to Beazley warning that there were major deficiencies in the law. Westerway suggested that the Broadcasting Act be changed to adopt the very wide associates test used in the Income Tax Act. This could mean that although Packer's Consolidated Press could own less than fifteen per cent of Fairfax—the maximum allowed under the cross-media rules—it could still be in breach of the broadcasting legislation if it could be shown that it in fact controlled the newspaper company through an associated person.

Westerway also asked that the ABT be given powers to allow it to demand provisional clearance of any transaction which, if completed, could lead to a contravention of the Broadcasting Act.

Beazley decided to release Westerway's letter to prove that any changes to the broadcasting legislation were in response to previous concerns, in particular the Kimshaw debacle, and not simply in response to the Tourang consortium's bid for Fairfax.

* * *

Black and Kennedy arrived in Canberra the next morning to a media blitz. The trip was well-organised by Kennedy, and Black had almost an hour with Hawke and Treasurer John Kerin. The conversation was polite and restrained.

Black was charming. He had been well-briefed on Hawke's passions and spoke at length on Israeli politics—Hawke claimed some knowledge of them, while Black claimed some influence over them with his ownership of the *Jerusalem Post*.

Hawke and Kerin gave away nothing on foreign investment policy. They listened while Black and Kennedy explained the agreement with the bondholders and what Tourang hoped to achieve. Black emerged from the meeting to tell the waiting media that he was sure Hawke would apply 'reasonable criteria' on the Fairfax bid.

Kennedy had lined Beazley up for lunch and this is where the royal visit dipped into the realm of the absurd. A media contingent worthy of the Princess of Wales followed the white limousine to the Carousel Restaurant on Canberra's Red Hill.

The Carousel has pleasant views over the lakes and dried winter grass of the nation's capital. That also means that it has plenty of glass windows to take advantage of the view.

As Beazley tucked into his baby barramundi topped with a coulis of tomato sauce and Black picked at his avocado salad with crudités, journalists and news teams peered through the windows, reading the menu, taking photographs and generally making the foursome (Kennedy and Beazley's adviser Patrick Walters were also present) feel uncomfortably like freaks at a country show.

Beazley was enthralled by Black. An avid reader of military history, he found Black an enthusiastic conversationalist and wonderful company, despite the drawbacks of the lunchtime audience. They discussed Abraham Lincoln and the Civil War at length over their Chardonnay.

Beazley had already made his mind up on the broadcasting law, however. It had to be changed—the Government had to quell any anger in the left wing of the party that the laws were not being upheld. Of course if Packer went through the hoops untouched, he was clean.

Beazley told Black that he did not want to change the rules of the game. All he would do was make sure that the existing rules were capable of being implemented.

Following the lunch, Beazley took the opportunity to tell journalists what he had told Black. He told the news teams: 'I pointed out that if the control and ownership provisions are incapable of being upheld as far as the ABT is concerned, then they will be rendered capable.'

In fact Beazley had been even more blunt with Black over lunch.

'It is the fellow sitting next to you who will be the problem,' he said, referring obliquely to the proposed stricter associates test, which could bring Kennedy in as a factor in assessing Packer's level of control over Fairfax.

Black nodded and paused. Then he turned to Kennedy.

'Okay, Trevor, you're sacked.' Everyone at the table laughed.

· CHAPTER TEN ·

THE PACKER
FACTOR

THE DEPTH of the public's concern about Packer's involvement caught Black, Powers and Colson by surprise. They had been warned the consortium would be controversial but they hadn't understood why. They couldn't comprehend the mythology that surrounded Packer in his home country. Why did his presence in a media deal arouse such emotion? Why were his newspaper caricatures so off-putting, so grotesque? What was it about Packer and Fairfax that stirred such depth of feeling? As businessmen who thrive on the adrenalin of multi-million dollar transactions, issues like media concentration and whether a handful of people dominate the major source of information and ideas in a society, and whether that is good for democracy, don't engender much sympathy. If the law allows it, you can buy whatever you like.

All three men were at a major disadvantage as the storm erupted about Packer—they hadn't been living in Australia for the past two decades. If they had, part of the intangible equipment that makes up a native would include knowledge of Packer's father Sir Frank Packer and the rivalry with the Fairfax family; of Kerry Packer's impatience with regulators and bureaucracies, demonstrated by his dealings with and bullying of the ABT; of his audacious but brilliantly innovative World Series Cricket— sparked by a fit of pique over the lack of access for his television cameras to Test cricket; or of the bulldozing and re-designing of the Australian Golf Club for the Australian Open—a sporting event televised on his own Nine Network until he withdrew his support when the tournament returned to Melbourne.

Most of all the foreigners in Tourang knew little about Costigan and the *National Times*. It is impossible to understand Packer and his feelings toward Fairfax without understanding first the fallout from the Costigan Royal Commission.

Frank Costigan is a Melbourne barrister, a QC who, in 1980, was appointed by Prime Minister Malcolm Fraser to conduct a Royal Commission into the Ship Painters and Dockers Union. Ironically the appointment was sparked by revelations in an article in Kerry Packer's own *Bulletin* magazine.

Costigan helped uncover a huge tax avoidance racket, involving schemes known as Bottom of the Harbour, which relied on 'straw men' such as members of the painters and dockers union to become directors of dumped companies.

The companies were left with no assets but with sizable amounts of tax owing. There were over 600 charges arising from the Royal Commission, and vast areas of investigation were undertaken. It was the first time that computer systems had been used on such a large scale to uncover criminal patterns of behaviour and trace the money trails of organised crime in Australia.

When Bob Hawke came to power in 1983 he sang Costigan's praises. His enthusiasm cooled rapidly, however. Attorney-General Gareth Evans was the first to voice the Government's displeasure with claims that Costigan was too 'gung ho'. By June 1984 Hawke was demanding that the Costigan Commission be wound up.

In 1983 and 1984 the path of the Costigan Commission investigators had crossed that of Kerry Packer. Costigan's inquiries had led in 1983 to the uncovering of what he believed to be a large Queensland drug-distributing ring connected with members of the dockers union in Brisbane.

The commission then tried to discover how the network was financed. They used computers to scrutinise at random thousands of Brisbane banking transactions. One series of transactions that caught their eye involved $225 000 in cash being withdrawn from a Brisbane branch of the Westpac bank.

That money finished up with Kerry Packer as an unsecured loan from Queensland property developer Brian Ray. Costigan also discovered that Ray and an associate Ian Beames had been involved with promoting a tax avoidance scheme involving film financing.

They had managed to gain access to $1 million to fund this scheme from a company in Singapore. The commission eventually called Packer to give evidence. Initially he agreed to voluntarily give evidence.

He then changed his mind, however, and fought Costigan through the Federal Court, claiming that Costigan's questions of him were outside his terms of reference. This attracted the media and linked Packer publicly for the first time with Costigan's investigations.

Eventually Packer gave in and testified. Packer told the Costigan Commission in evidence that he had nothing to do with funding the film tax scheme. The cash loan from Brian Ray, he said, followed a telephone conversation in February 1980.

Packer claimed he told Ray: "'I lost too much at the races" or whatever it was. He said, "Do you want some money?" I said, "Yes, have you got any?" He said, "Yes, I have got a bit." I said, "Have you got any to spare?" He said, "I certainly have.'"

Packer told the commission that he wanted the money in cash because 'I like cash. I have a squirrel mentality. I like to keep money in cash. It is by no means the most cash I have ever had in my life.'

■ ■ ■

The publicity on the Federal Court challenge was acutely embarrassing for Packer. Not only was it featured on the national news but the *National Times* ran a five-page feature by investigative reporter Marian Wilkinson in August 1984 titled 'Kerry Packer and the Costigan Commission', canvassing in detail the issues being pursued by the Commission.

That wasn't the end of the matter, however. Prime Minister Hawke decided abruptly in mid-1984 to wind up the Costigan Commission. It was to complete its investigations and report by 31 October of that year and hand outstanding matters for investigation and prosecution to the newly established National Crime Authority.

Costigan prepared an eleven-volume report (five of which were released publicly) and passed on forty-two references to the National Crime Authority.

Brian Toohey, then editor of the *National Times* and a master of the monstrous leak, got hold of a copy of the references and ran extracts in the paper.

The most fascinating of the references he codenamed Goanna (changed from Costigan's codename, which Toohey thought might have identified Packer because of the publicised evidence he had given to the Costigan Commission).

Packer was later completely cleared by the Attorney-General of suggestion of any offences but back in September 1984 the identity of the Goanna became a national guessing game. 'Packer is the Goanna' appeared as graffiti at Sydney's Central Railway Station.

Eventually Packer released a 5000-word statement identifying himself as the Goanna and attacking in detail each of the Costigan allegations and suspicions.

Packer was livid and he blamed in part his competitors Fairfax. He said in his statement:

The allegations published about me in a recent edition of the National Times are, without exception, completely false.

Their publication had been but another step in a malicious and disgusting campaign of vilification by my commercial rivals. In developing these allegations the Royal Commission into the Ship Painters and Dockers Union has conducted itself grossly unjustly and improperly.

The person who stood beside Packer, who fought almost as hard as Packer himself and who had a large hand in preparing Packer's well argued and meticulously researched 5000-word defence, was Malcolm Turnbull.

Packer was very grateful. It was a low point in his life and Turnbull had come fiercely to his defence.

So the publication of the Costigan references drove a wedge between Packer and the Fairfaxes. But there were other issues too.

■　■　■

The Packers and the Fairfaxes had been competitors since 1923 when Kerry Packer's grandfather Robert Clyde Packer launched the *Daily Guardian* newspaper in Sydney in competition with the *Herald*.

For most of the next seventy years the Fairfaxes were the patricians on the hill; the Packers were the hands-on proprietors, fighting in the market place.

Time and again the Fairfaxes beat the Packers to important acquisitions. They beat them on Associated Newspapers in 1953, giving the Fairfaxes the *Sun* and the *Sunday Sun* and an important edge in printing facilities and technology. They also beat them to the *Newcastle Herald* and to the *Canberra Times*.

In newspapers, the *Daily Telegraph*, established by Sir Frank in the 1930s, was up there every morning against the *Herald* competing for readers and advertisers until the sale to Murdoch in 1972. On Sundays it was the *Sunday Telegraph* versus the *Sun–Herald*.

The families were head-to-head in magazines too, with the Fairfaxes having *Woman's Day*, the Packers *Women's Weekly*; the Fairfaxes *Cosmopolitan* and the Packers *Cleo*, and so on. This was the case until 1988 when, thanks to Warwick's takeover bid for the Group, Packer managed to snaffle up most of the Fairfax magazines.

In television also the Fairfaxes and the Packers held for over a decade the only two commercial television licences in Sydney, ATN7 and TCN9.

Packer's nature is extremely competitive. It was highly unlikely that he would ever walk away from nearly seven decades of inter-family rivalry, particularly when the opportunity finally presented itself to place his foot very firmly on the Fairfax family neck.

An example of Packer's enthusiastic approach to good competition was the AT&T Pro Am Golf Tournament held at Pebble Beach, California, in February 1992. Packer and his partner Greg Norman, the White Shark, stormed home to victory, with Packer on a sixteen-stroke handicap.

What few of the spectators realised was that Packer could have won by an even greater margin. He firmly requested that his handicap be reduced from the twenty awarded by the Pebble Beach tournament organisers (to allow for the degree of difficulty of the course) to his usual sixteen. He didn't want the organisers embarrassing themselves when he won by a landslide, he told staggered luncheon guests back home in Australia.

A strong supporter of self-regulation, Packer's clashes with the ABT in its early days are legendary. In one celebrated episode in 1980 he spent a good deal of the first hearing on the Fairfax's licence for Channel Seven standing in the doorway at the back of the room, as one journalist reported 'a giant and solitary figure bearing a fixed gaze down on Bruce Gyngell' (Packer's former employee and the first chairman of the ABT).

At TCN9's hearings Packer rose at the outset and said he would be answering all questions as he could not subject his executives to the process. The hearings were a debacle and were marred by public interest groups being ejected from the room by Federal Police.

Packer has proven himself to be a far better businessmen than either of his predecessors in the media dynasty—his grandfather Robert Clyde Packer and his father Sir Frank Packer. He took charge of the company in 1974 at the age of thirty-six on the death of his father. In 1983 he took the group private in a controversial $150 million deal. He increased the family's holding from forty-four per cent of Conspress to 100 per cent and within ten years was being touted as Australia's first billionaire.

In the 1980s the totally private Conspress branched out into a plethora of other interests including coal mining. But the business that made Kerry Packer a billionaire was television. He sold his Nine Network to Alan Bond for $1 billion in 1987 and spent the money well. He bought a coupon insert business—coupons in newspapers that give discounts if taken to shopping chains—in the USA called Valassis Inc.

Packer also purchased Chemplex, a chemical manufacturer, and made a daring takeover for manufacturing group Australian National Industries. He sold his holding within three years for a handsome profit.

After spending his proceeds from the sale to Bond wisely, he then capitalised on Bond's collapse by re-purchasing control of the network for about $200 million in a complex transaction.

As Packer himself quipped: 'You only get one Alan Bond in a lifetime and I've had mine.'

By the time Packer decided on a partnership with Black to ensure at least an investment in his historic rival Fairfax, he was unquestionably the richest man in Australia.

However, Packer is not the conventional billionaire—he has ample time for his other passions. He is now a fanatic about polo, spending millions of dollars developing his polo complexes in Australia, Argentina and England. His other passion remains gambling—in casinos, at the racetrack (where he has been dubbed Mr Millions) and on the foreign exchange markets, trading currency.

He attracts criticism for being a low taxpayer. His companies make extensive use of overseas tax havens and paid tax at around ten cents in the dollar for much of the 1980s—compared with a statutory rate of thirty-nine cents in the dollar.

Packer lives extravagantly, with homes in England, at Bellevue Hill and Palm Beach in Sydney, and Ellerston near Scone in the New South Wales countryside. He has narrowly escaped death with a heart attack in 1990 while playing polo when he was clinically dead for nearly ten minutes.

Most notably, by 1991 Packer had established a formidable reputation as one who took 'no nonsense from anybody'. He was an awesome opponent in the bid for Fairfax—even if his share of the consortium was limited to 14.9 per cent.

Despite Tourang's best efforts to argue that Packer was a mere passive shareholder and Black was firmly in control, Kennedy gave a clear insight into why Packer was there in an interview in the *Herald* on 26 July: 'There is no downside in the thing. It gives him a strategic foothold if he wants to go further later on, and in the meantime he can probably make a good turn if we are at all successful.'

There were plenty of possibilities. Packer didn't want to sell Nine Network to buy Fairfax right now. In the future, however, things could change. Smart investors make sure they cover the options. If Packer ever decided to sell out of Nine Network, he could find Black a seller of his holding if the Canadian tired of being limited by foreign investment laws.

There was also Hellman & Friedman. An investment fund like this doesn't hold investments forever. The fund has a long-term philosophy and said it would hold the Fairfax investment for ten years. But this doesn't mean a well-priced takeover offer wouldn't be accepted if directors recommended it.

Tourang gave Packer co-shareholders he could trust, people he could deal with. Australia was his home territory—and he was in the best syndicate for his own long-term commercial interests.

• • •

The Packer factor was one very sticky problem for Tourang, but there was another personality problem too—the Turnbull factor. Everyone was worried about the relationship—or lack of it— between Turnbull and Burrows. Tourang felt the coup with the bondholders would upset Burrows, ruining his precious auction process. He would have to be treated gently and this would mean underplaying Turnbull's role in the transaction. Freehills had another idea to make things easier. What about retaining David Gonski, the former Freehill lawyer now running his own business, Wentworth & Associates in the same building as Freehills?

The next afternoon Gonski walked into the reception area of the Ritz Carlton Hotel and asked rather tentatively for Conrad Black's suite. Black had asked Gonski to join the Tourang team of advisers. Black said he wanted someone who was good at structuring deals and Gonski was a genius at this. Gonski, who is in his mid-thirties, also had a long and detailed, if not totally successful, association with media group takeovers. He was involved in shopping centre king Frank Lowy's unsuccessful foray into media through the purchase of Ten Network from Murdoch. He assisted Murdoch on structures and strategy on the Herald & Weekly Times (HWT) takeover in return for an entrée to the deals. Lowy's Northern Star bought a number of newspapers from Murdoch, including the Brisbane *Sun* and the Adelaide *News*, helping the media mogul around his Trade Practices problems. Lowy then held the newspapers for six months before on-selling them to former Murdoch executives.

Northern Star then picked up Murdoch's two television stations, making them the cornerstone of a new Ten Network. This was where the disaster set in. Expertise in shopping centres doesn't necessarily translate to television. Lowy's Westfield dropped many millions on the deal before selling out. Ten Network was eventually placed in receivership.

Gonski gets on extremely well with Burrows. The two men speak frequently, often on a day-to-day basis. He was one of the 'seniors' in the closely knit takeover advisory network. Burrows,

Ross at Bankers Trust, Johnson at Macquarie Bank and Gonski were part of an informal clique, widely acknowledged as the best in their field.

Malcolm Turnbull, on the other hand, was very clearly not one of the old boys. Sydney is a small town when it comes to the corporate advisory world—they tend to mix in the same circles, among the lawyers and accountants who handle the major transactions. Friendships form, and names often pop up in the same places.

Gonski is the chairman of Film Australia along with Burrows who is deputy chairman. One of the board members is Christina Kennedy, Trevor Kennedy's wife.

When Gonski met with Black he was impressed; it was one of the most memorable meetings of his life. It was scheduled to last thirty minutes but lasted three hours. By the time Gonski left, he was on the Tourang team and Tourang had a conduit to Burrows.

The next task for Tourang was the round of institutional presentations, following the path already well-worn by Independent and AIN. Powers wanted the presentation to be impressive but was disappointed when Kennedy didn't seem overly interested in running through the numbers for the institutions. Kennedy wanted to give the broad-brush approach, leaving the details for the accountants. Powers felt since Kennedy was the man nominated to be chief executive, and someone who was supposedly the best media executive in Australia, his approach should be very detailed.

By the time Black and the Tourang team—including Turnbull —fronted the large group of institutions the following Monday, Kennedy didn't take a front-line role. Powers handled the financial details.

Institutions were told that Tourang intended to bid $1 billion for Fairfax, a valuation consisting of $400 million cash and debt of $600 million. The bondholders would be credited with the $125 million of new debentures. Effectively Tourang was expecting the banks to take a $300 million loss on their loans.

When it came to exactly how Tourang would significantly boost Fairfax's performance to ensure a handsome return to institutional investors, the document was vague. Tourang stated that it couldn't quantify the improvements to be made due to the input of the strategic shareholders until it undertook full due diligence.

One contentious point for the institutions was that Tourang didn't plan to re-list Fairfax on the sharemarket for up to two years, but this would allow Tourang to achieve higher profitability for Fairfax through 'enhanced management'.

With the rounds of the politicians and institutions out of the way, Black left the country. In just six days he could leave knowing one thing for certain. His high-profile partner in the consortium was a potential obstacle to winning, regardless of the merits of the exclusivity agreement.

Black was honest when pressed on ABC Radio's AM programme about whether he would contemplate dropping Packer if the heat became too intense:

> If the hypothesis is 'If that was the only way to get our bid accepted, would I consider it?', I suppose, in honesty, I would have to say, yes, I would consider it.
>
> It would be an unfair treatment of [Mr Packer], an unnecessary treatment of him and certainly something I would do with great reluctance.

The comment was not unexpected; Black was angry that he was being seen as a Packer stooge, a cardboard man just there to make up the numbers. Black had relentlessly pursued the creation of his own empire by himself. This partnership with a rich man he didn't know very well was an unusual one for him. Two strong-willed people; a potentially volatile situation.

* * *

The announcement of Tourang was not a total surprise to Independent. O'Reilly had always believed that Packer would show his face at some stage. As Cameron O'Reilly discussed the implications with Rowan Ross and Peter Hunt, they agreed it was best that he was out of the woodwork. They could see the target now.

The worrying thing was Turnbull and his exclusivity agreement. Just what did it mean for the other bidders? A series of meetings and telephone conversations with Baring Brothers didn't elicit much joy. It was obvious Burrows was in the dark also.

There was some resentment about what had happened. Indeed Burrows had told Independent to ignore the bondholders when

Turnbull had approached them. Burrows had been adamant that they were not relevant to the process and shouldn't be dealt with. It was Burrows' job to do that, not Independent's. Now there was this mysterious agreement. It was all very well for Burrows to maintain that the bondholders were not important, arguing that there was the alternative of selling the assets out of Fairfax if the exclusivity agreement became a problem.

Independent knew that an asset sale would mean they couldn't access the Fairfax tax losses. Also a sale out of the corporate structure would be very messy.

However, when Ross, Hunt and Cameron met with the Baring Brothers executives and the bankers, including Rupert Thomas and Jake Williams, they left after two hours feeling better about the issue. The message of the meeting was presented concisely by Williams.

'The bondholder agreement is worth diddly squat,' he said emphatically. It was clear the banks weren't going to accept a haircut. Independent should just continue putting its offer together.

This was a familiar chorus as Baring Brothers sought to hose down the worries that Tourang was the only viable bidder now. When Mark Johnson met with Burrows he received the same spiel. Luckily for Burrows, his persuasive skills paid off with both Independent and AIN.

Burrows had avoided a potential disaster. If Independent or AIN believed that they couldn't compete with Tourang, he would find himself with only one bidder. And it was a bidder Burrows knew was talking an offer of, at best, $1 billion knowing there were two other bidders. If they dropped out, the price offered could fall. Suddenly the Tourang offer could end up as $900 million or even less.

Burrows needed an auction and would do everything necessary to ensure that he had more than one bidder.

■   ■   ■

'We've got to do something, mate,' Peter Bowers said to Alan Kennedy as he paced up and down the newsroom floor.

'We've got to get to Hawkie and put a stop to it. We can't let it happen. If we don't do something, mate, no other bugger will.'

The prospect of Murdoch and Packer controlling over ninety per cent of the Australian metropolitan print media between them (and that is how Bowers saw it developing if Tourang won) was unacceptable.

Ever since the Tourang bid had been announced and the Australian public had been treated to television images of Conrad Black lunching with ministers and meeting with the Prime Minister, Bowers knew that Canberra had to be hit.

Kennedy agreed. He and David Wilson from the Age Independence Committee had discussed the possibility of a delegation to Canberra. Bowers promised to fix a meeting with the Prime Minister.

And he went two better. He lined up the Treasurer John Kerin and Communications Minister Kim Beazley as well.

Bowers' decades in the press gallery were paying off. The date set was 26 July and it was to be a joint meeting—the three ministers and delegates from the Age Independence Committee and Friends of Fairfax. The journalists gathered in Canberra the night before at the Park Hyatt to discuss strategy.

They were joined by Canberra-based journalists from both papers, including Tom Burton, the *Herald*'s communications writer.

'Leave me until last, fellas. I am going to pitch the emotional plea to the bastards. This is too important to get wrong,' Bowers told the gathering.

In Hawke's office the next day the Prime Minister, in shirt sleeves between Kerin and Beazley, was showing some impatience with the journalists' set piece.

David Wilson was stressing the importance of editorial independence and the role of an editorial charter. Hawke sat side-on to the central table. He sat hunched up, almost in a foetal position, his classic posture in such private negotiating sessions. He interrupted Wilson abruptly. 'Are you saying Packer is poison at any price?'

There was silence. Bowers, sitting at the opposite end of the table to Wilson, who was on Hawke's left, was tense. He was thinking: 'For Christ's sake, David, get it right! Get it right, son!'

After what seemed like two full minutes, Wilson nodded. 'Yes.'

Bowers breathed a sigh of relief. 'Yes,' came in unison from around the table.

The ice was broken and the conversation flowed. Claude Forell expanded on the virtues of the AIN group. He mentioned John D'Arcy. Hawke jumped in again.

'Well, he'd be independent, wouldn't he?' Without waiting for an answer, Hawke turned to Beazley: 'Not fucking much.'

It was the first indication that AIN, the all-Australian, pure vanilla bidder had a problem. Hawke hated D'Arcy from his HWT days. The Melbourne *Herald* had led a sustained campaign against the Hawke Government's assets test on pensions in 1985. It was considered to be electorally damaging to Labor.

Also Labor bears a grudge. It wasn't good enough for D'Arcy to claim that he was management and didn't control editorial policy or that he didn't even come to Melbourne and the HWT until later in 1985 (he had still been in Brisbane at Queensland Press).

No, D'Arcy was tarred by the HWT brush, and that was that.

Finally, as conversation was dying, it was Bowers' turn. He addressed his words directly to the Prime Minister.

'We all have a terrible responsibility, Prime Minister,' he began. 'We get just one shot at this, just one shot and that's it. That's it for today, for the rest of this century and well into the twenty-first century.

'We want future generations of Australians in the second half of the twenty-first century to look back and say: "The government of the day got it right. The Prime Minister of the day got it right. And thank God he did."'

Hawke listened. Bowers gained heart.

'And by the way, Prime Minister, if you are looking for a chairman of the print media inquiry, can I be so bold as to suggest Barney Cooney?'

Hawke laughed. 'Thanks, that's terrific Peter. That's fucked Barney Cooney.'

As the journalists rose to leave, Kim Beazley spoke to Ward O'Neill and Alan Kennedy. 'Don't worry about the associates tests [in the Broadcasting Act]. We will check them out right down to their BVDs. Who pays for their kids to go to school, the lot.'

Kerin walked up to Bowers. 'Peter, I didn't know that you were such an emotional bastard.'

'Well, John, this is a matter to get emotional about,' Bowers replied.

The journalists had been promised fifteen minutes. They were in there for an hour and ten minutes. They had done well. The two ministers and their advisers stayed on with the Prime Minister a few minutes longer. The consensus was that the views expressed were pretty much what the three men also thought privately. Packer and Murdoch had enough of the media— although saying that publicly would be very stupid. No one wanted to antagonise the media proprietors.

On foreign investment Hawke and Kerin felt that the journalists—or at least the Friends of Fairfax group—were a bit too tolerant on foreign investment. They were prepared to accept up to fifty per cent if it meant less concentration of ownership.

Hawke knew that Caucus wouldn't wear that. Twenty per cent was the limit for television. While they might be able to squeeze another few per cent or so for print media, that would probably be the maximum.

．　．　．

Colin Winter was choking with rage. He had been working on the junk bondholders' litigation for seven months now, and this was the most despicable of dirty tricks. It was 5.30 pm on Wednesday, 31 July. If the journalist from the *Herald*, Jeni Porter, didn't ring back by 6 pm, that was it, he was going for an injunction.

Winter had been fretting about the possibility of this occurring for over two weeks now. Ever since he found that two-line letter from legal firm Blake Dawson Waldron in his in-tray on 12 July.

Attached to it was a four-page fax. Winter had thought: 'What the hell is that?' and then the enormity of what had occurred began to sink in. He recognised the fax as one he had sent to Duker & Barrett, the lawyers for Resolution Trust Corporation (RTC), three days previously. It was a letter of advice.

At that stage the RTC had all but decided to join the litigation. The RTC represented three failed savings and loans, which accounted for about $61.7 million worth of bonds. Winter and Turnbull were keen to have them involved because then they could genuinely say they had all the bondholders in the litigation—in fact, they would have had about ninety-eight per cent of them with only Heytesbury and one or two tiny ones holding out.

Also it would have been the first time in history that the US Government had sued a US bank. Winter felt this would really put the heat on Citibank. It would also send a message to Tourang and Burrows—if the US Government was prepared to join the litigation half way through, then it showed the integrity of the litigation.

The credibility factor of the RTC joining in was high. Winter had worded this letter of advice very carefully. He was in the very early stages of the legal discovery process, he didn't know how much more was coming, and he had not yet clarified in his own mind how they would pitch their argument.

Winter wanted to be careful not to encourage the RTC into litigation. The last paragraph of the letter was the most important. It gave a number of caveats on the advice, saying that the particular section of the Trade Practices Act was a difficult one to apply and noted the early stages of discovery. He had then stuck his neck out and said at the very least the bondholders' case was highly arguable and he recommended that it was worth going forward into litigation.

This was an important letter—it was the last one that you would want to drop into the hands of competitors. But that is exactly what happened. The fax operator at Phillips Fox had inadvertently picked up this letter with another fax he was sending to Blake Dawson Waldron and sent the lot. The tough security procedures of fax registers and the like were rendered useless by one simple human error.

Winter had been meticulous in his introduction of a security system on the faxes. Only certain people could send faxes, various boxes had to be ticked off by the operator and numbers were carefully programmed into the machine. It was so tight it bordered on a worrying case of paranoia.

Blake's were representing the banks in the junk bond litigation and that they had inadvertently received a copy of the RTC letter was a disaster. Winter was furious that it had taken three days for the fax to be returned. It had been sent by mistake on 9 July and arrived back in Winter's in-tray on 12 July having been sent by ordinary post the previous day.

The relationship between the two sets of lawyers had already been acrimonious. The few times they had met in Sydney court rooms there had been enormous tension. There had been nasty jokes in elevators and howls of laughter—the sort of schoolboy humour that the legal fraternity is very good at if the situation demands. This misdirected fax was the last straw.

Winter attempted to contact the Blake lawyers by phone, but calls were not returned. So he sent off a sharp letter saying he was seriously concerned by the delay in returning the fax and at the very least he would like clarification of who had seen the letter.

He wanted undertakings given that all copies would be returned with a full list of who had seen it and an undertaking that it wouldn't be shown to anyone else. Winter received a two-line letter from Blakes in reply—we are not responsible for your mistakes and we don't propose to be interrogated.

He decided not to press the issue further—it would only serve to draw attention to the incident. A few days later, however, he began receiving phone calls from a journalist from the *Australian Financial Review*. He had heard about the misdirected fax but had not seen it. He heard it contained negative legal advice. The bondholders' case was weak. Winter managed to convince the journalist not to write anything on the issue for the moment.

Then the call had come from Jeni Porter. Winter asked her for an undertaking that she would not write about the fax but she would not give it until she had spoken to her editor. Winter told her that if he had no response by 6 pm (in thirty minutes time) he would seek a court injunction.

When Porter didn't call back Winter frantically dictated the necessary papers in forty minutes. He screamed at his staff who were searching for legal precedents: 'I want to stop reference to the existence of this letter, not just the contents. It can be done; show me why it can't be done.'

Winter and his counsel Bruce McClintock were seeking an injunction outside of court hours. They were allocated a judge— but the judge wasn't in his chambers. They had to travel to Justice Philip Powell's house at St Ives—a good forty minutes drive from the central business district.

Powell granted Winter's request—one of the stiffest injunctions the Fairfax lawyers had ever encountered. It did indeed stop reference to the existence of the letter, its contents and the mishandling. Winter rang through the injunction by car phone from outside Powell's house. The *Herald* did not print any reference to the legal advice and the lawyers decided not to defend it when it came up for hearing in the court a few days later.

But Winter didn't succeed in muzzling the press completely—columnist Bryan Frith in the *Australian* printed a lengthy column on the injunction and the lead up to it. The game was heating up.

In the same column Frith gave a long account of sections of the Broadcasting Act that could trap Packer on de facto control through associates—Trevor Kennedy and Malcolm Turnbull. If there was de facto control, this would breach the cross-media ownership rules. It could sink the Tourang bid.

∎ ∎ ∎

Miles was happy. He had chosen a good venue. The Rockpool is one of Sydney's premier restaurants under chef Neil Perry. A stylish, modern, predominantly seafood restaurant with a comprehensive wine list, it was the right sort of place to go. With prices for entrées around sixteen dollars and main courses around twenty-five, it was a favourite haunt of bankers, lawyers and corporate executives.

The dinner was going well. Tourang would be wise to present an offer that could take the banks out clean and it would be smart to present an alternative finance package. Miles was eager to make sure that Ord's role was not just underwriting the Tourang offer. It would be great if Ord's parent, Westpac, grabbed some fees from replacing ANZ and Citibank as bankers to Fairfax.

So he had arranged this dinner with Iain Thompson, a senior Westpac executive in corporate lending. It was an introduction to Powers and Matt Barger of Hellman & Friedman, a preliminary get-to-know-each-other session.

As Thompson and Powers chose a bottle of red off the menu—the most expensive one Miles noted nervously, knowing he would be putting the bill into Trevor Kennedy for approval—Barger looked across the room and saw a face he recognised.

It was George Roberts from Kohlberg Kravis & Roberts (KKR). When Barger told the others Miles joked that Tourang might have some formidable competition for Fairfax. He was just about right. Roberts was in Australia casting his acquisitive eye over some of Australia's list of corporate carcasses.

There was the Adsteam group—in particular its prize asset, retailer Woolworths. Or Foster's Brewing Group, with major shareholder John Elliott's 37.8 per cent shareholding possibly up for sale. This was a good global business of the kind KKR was always on the lookout for.

Roberts would probably not have been recognised by more than a handful of people in The Rockpool but his firm was. He was a high flyer.

KKR is famous as the leveraged buyout fund that, along with Drexels, fanned the fires of takeover mania on Wall Street in the 1980s, culminating in KKR's US$25 billion takeover of tobacco and food group RJR Nabisco in November 1988. It was the biggest takeover in US history, a fitting epitaph as the US economy lurched into recession and the bubble burst.

During the 1980s KKR was awash with readily available funds from financial institutions and had Drexels on stand-by for a huge junk bond issue. KKR, which had been doing leveraged buyouts in the 1970s, quietly became a colossus, gobbling up dozens of large companies. It then sent in the young, aggressive financial engineers to knock the business into what it deemed shape and float it back to the public or sell it on.

Underperforming divisions would be sold, staff numbers slashed and stringent cost controls and debt repayment schedules imposed. This had a dual purpose—retire the large bank and junk bond borrowings from the purchase and leave KKR and its investors lucrative profits. The men at KKR and their associates were the new rich—they travelled the world first class and the invitations flowed to the charity cocktail parties. They discovered art and culture.

Fairfax was the sort of company that the hungry crowd from KKR preyed on—a distressed sale of a business with excellent titles—or brand names to the financial engineers. The word that Roberts was in Australia quickly swept the financial community, however, KKR was well aware of Fairfax since Baring Brothers had made contact with the firm already.

When White was in the US two weeks before, trawling for potential Fairfax buyers, he had visited both Time–Warner and KKR. At the leveraged buyout group he met Ned Gilhunty, an associate director of the group in San Francisco.

Gilhunty was very interested in knowing about Fairfax although he was worried about the foreign ownership issue. KKR liked controlling stakes and if the Federal Government was going to restrict a major foreign shareholder to less than forty per cent, KKR was probably not interested.

The two agreed to stay in touch and Gilhunty was left with some financial data on Fairfax. When White returned to Australia, KKR was pencilled in as a potential bidder or member of a syndicate.

CHAPTER ELEVEN

A DASH TO
IRELAND

IT WAS a tradition. Every Bank Holiday long weekend, the first weekend in August, Rowan Ross headed for the ski fields. This year the snow was fantastic.

Ross wasn't going to make it this year, however, and reluctantly cancelled his booking at the last minute. Instead of heading towards Goulburn on the freeway, he was sitting on a Qantas jumbo on his way to London and then Ireland.

A few seats away sat Chris Corrigan and Jamison employee David Vaux. None of them relished the task they had been given. From being locked in a slanging match over the respective capabilities of each group, they were now virtually ordered by Australia's major institutions to do the unthinkable: merge and jointly pursue Fairfax.

Ever since Tourang had been announced the fund managers had pushed even harder for Independent and Jamison to merge. It would make everything so much easier. AMP was annoyed at both groups; the petty fighting, the direct approaches to board members and the disgraceful dossier had ruined much of the good will toward them.

Even Bankers Trust Australia's funds management had a dilemma—the corporate advisory division was advising O'Reilly and the funds management arm was a shareholder in Jamison.

A merger made sense to the institutions, even if the egos of the respective sides found it distasteful. Ultimately the cash for both groups' purchase of Fairfax came from the same source—the institutions. A merger would solve the problem of deciding between the two and would also provide stronger competition for the formidable Tourang consortium.

Corrigan was disappointed. He now realised that his whole Fairfax strategy was in tatters. The slow sales process had ruined his goal of an early, cheap offer. It was now the beginning of August; no commitments had been made by his shareholders and this demand that he consider merging with the O'Reilly team demonstrated their lack of commitment to the bid and the philosophy behind it.

Despite his disappointment, he was obliged to make this trip to Ireland and meet with Tony O'Reilly as requested. He wasn't optimistic about the outcome.

Arriving in London, Corrigan and Vaux spent Saturday night relaxing at the Capital, a cosy boutique hotel in Basil Street.

Ross continued on to County Cork in Ireland to make sure O'Reilly was well-briefed when his guests arrived the next day. Instead of suffering sore muscles from skiing, Ross now found himself experiencing a bad case of jet lag. There wasn't much positive news: Independent didn't have significant institutional support and its offer was floundering in the most important arena—the commercial one.

O'Reilly welcomed Ross to his country home, Shorecliffe House in Glandor, West Cork—a lovely, rambling old home, not grand but big enough to accommodate several guests. O'Reilly's fiancée, Greek–American shipping heiress Chryss Goulandris was there too. O'Reilly and she were due to marry in six weeks.

Corrigan and Vaux arrived at Shorecliffe House on a misty Sunday morning. With the rain pouring down outside the four men gathered in the sitting-room to broach the possibility of a merger. The discussions were not easy. There was none of the natural affinity that exists if two parties have come to the table willingly to consumate a merger. Both sides knew, even if it remained unsaid, that they were only there because they were forced to be there.

O'Reilly was not too concerned about Jamison. He believed Corrigan knew little about newspapers and felt sure that Corrigan's shareholders would eventually coerce him into a merger.

On a personal level he soon realised that Corrigan was sharp despite his measured and often slow responses to questions. He obviously possessed an excellent grasp of investment fundamentals.

Corrigan was reserved as he listened to O'Reilly espouse his views on Fairfax and the changes required. Corrigan felt uncomfortable—he was in a strange country discussing an idea that he knew in his heart he didn't want. He also believed that O'Reilly's confidence was misplaced. A dose of the blarney. Corrigan had something that O'Reilly didn't—Australia's major institutions were behind Jamison, even if their non-committal attitude had put him in O'Reilly's sitting-room, thousands of kilometres from Australia. And those institutions owned the money that O'Reilly needed to remain a bidder for Fairfax.

As he listened Corrigan thought O'Reilly was putting a lot less effort into the newspaper management side of the deal than Jamison. O'Reilly seemed to see it more as a corporate play, Corrigan reflected—he was buying it at the right time and looking for a good valuable shareholding when he eventually re-floated Fairfax to the public.

Jamison, Corrigan believed, had done much more thinking about what needed to be done to the newspapers than the Irish team.

When it got down to the vexing issue of who was the dominant partner, O'Reilly made it very clear that Independent would be in control and would retain the commercial management of Fairfax. Reynolds must be the chief executive, not Chris Anderson. O'Reilly would be happy, however, if Anderson was given a position of editorial control of Fairfax's newspapers.

As far as board seats went, O'Reilly was not negotiable. He was to be the deputy chairman. Independent would stick to its plan of a twenty per cent shareholding and Jamison could only hold the same level of shareholding in Fairfax. The remaining funds would come from other institutions.

Corrigan nodded, more to let O'Reilly know he had heard the ideas than agreed to them. Corrigan could see potential problems down the track if each side had a twenty per cent stake. How could any disputes be sensibly resolved? The meeting broke up late in the afternoon and the conversation turned to other matters.

The next morning Healy arrived early from Dublin and discussions resumed. There was no real momentum to the negotiations, however. Both sides were procrastinating and by the latter stages of the meeting it was clear that the idea didn't seem feasible.

Corrigan couldn't see any future in joining an O'Reilly bid where he would have little management input. O'Reilly felt that Independent still had an excellent chance on their own without Jamison, aware from the briefing Ross had given him that Corrigan's shareholders didn't seem likely to support him. If that were the case, why not wait until Jamison was ruled out completely and then pick up its shareholders?

Tourang was surely going to find political problems, and Independent could be the white knight who saved Fairfax from Packer's grasp. By the time the meeting ended, all both sides would agree on was that they would keep in touch. In the afternoon Healy, Corrigan and Vaux set off in one of O'Reilly's Bentleys for the long drive to Dublin. It took almost six hours, and it rained all the way.

In Dublin they went straight to Independent's newspaper headquarters for meetings with each of the editors and a tour of the plant. It was clear to Corrigan that while these editors worked well in Dublin, there would be little transferability of talent with Fairfax. O'Reilly's papers in Dublin were the middle to down-market range, he thought. It was not the Fairfax market.

That night Corrigan and Voux stayed at O'Reilly's manor, about an hour outside of Dublin. It was 2 am, they were very tired and they sensed this trip was a failure. Neither side could offer the other anything. They were incompatible—even if combining would see a stronger offer.

* * *

The AIN group pressed on. They had none of the publicity or gloss of the other bids but they worked doggedly toward their major presentations to the institutions.

Tourang was a setback as was John B Fairfax's backing of O'Reilly. But at the meetings with McKay and Harley there had never been any suggestion of pulling out. If anything the setbacks seemed to have hardened their resolve to win the support of the major institutions.

Macquarie Bank had managed to secure a copy of the O'Reilly consortium's presentation to the institutions from a friendly institution. It was a slick, well-presented document. But McKeon and Kent felt Independent's figures looked rubbery. They got to work on economic models and projections, financial structures and the means for putting across their corporate governance philosophy to the institutions.

Harley, meanwhile, approached the managing director of David Syme Greg Taylor and asked if he would be the chief executive if AIN won Fairfax. AIN needed management credibility and Taylor was the ideal person. Craggy-face, chain-smoking, sixty-year-old Taylor had worked for the *Age* for over forty years, joining as a cadet straight from Hobart High School. He had a three-year stint as editor of the newspaper in the late 1970s, but for the past decade has worked in administration where he has a reputation for being a hands-on operator and a cautious manager. Harley also wanted Taylor's assistance in outlining a workable management plan for their bid. Then came the crunch. Would Taylor mind if Harley told the institutions that he was to be CEO of Fairfax?

A few days later Taylor agreed on all points. He was also willing, for the larger institutions, to attend presentations.

By late July the Macquarie Bank team was close to completing the formal presentation. It was a ninety-six page document setting out the history of Fairfax, an analysis of the Australian advertising market, economic projections and their effect on advertising revenues, and AIN's plans.

AIN outlined its ideas for profit enhancing initiatives, targeting what it deemed were weaknesses like sub-standard work practices, under-developed group strengths, existence of 'baronies' and unrealised marketing potential. The document set out AIN's vision: 'Reinforce John Fairfax Group as the most efficient, high-quality and innovative newspaper group in Australia.'

Under AIN's direction title accountability would be introduced—for each product a general manager would be employed who would be responsible to the chief executive for the overall performance of the publication.

Institutions were to be asked to subscribe $450 million. AIN also requested that they supply letters of commitment and to make public that commitment, to assist AIN in dealings with Baring Brothers. All equity holders were to be granted the same rights of participation. AIN would be floated on the stock exchange within twelve months to ensure maximum liquidity for the investment.

In the meantime Macquarie Bank would provide a secondary market in the stock. The document placed particular emphasis on the all-Australian nature of the bid and support for editorial independence. The price AIN proposed to offer was nominally $1.325 billion. However, the structure of the bid didn't allow for the banks getting out clean at $1.25 billion.

AIN proposed to give the banks soft equity: $325 million of convertible shares that were only repaid if certain profit forecasts were met. Because of the structure of these shares, AIN argued that the banks could effectively disguise taking a loss on their loans. In reality, though, AIN were forcing the banks to take a $325 million haircut on their loans on day one. All the academic jargon didn't disguise this fact. AIN was actually planning to offer the banks a minimum of $1 billion.

AIN knew that O'Reilly was due to make a visit to Australia in mid-August for another round of the institutions. It was crucial, therefore, that AIN should get in first and tie up the institutions with firm commitments before O'Reilly brought in his Irish charm. Happy with the document, AIN hurriedly conducted talks with its twelve core backers—a dry run to pick up any flaws in the presentation or suggestions for improvements before the major institutions and secondary institutions were approached. This was progressing well until AIN struck a snag.

Burrows discovered that AIN was set on conducting a road-show of the major institutions and he insisted on reviewing AIN's presentation documents. When he came to the section entitled 'Price and Capital Structure' he was furious—the price AIN was planning to tout to the institutions was really only $1 billion!

These guys from Melbourne were going to ruin his seven-month efforts—so far unsuccessful—to get the perceptions of Fairfax's value over the bank debt level.

There were heated conversations for an entire week before

Burrows agreed to a compromise. He would allow the presentations to go ahead if every document had a sticker on it stating that the offer did not conform with Burrows' guidelines—Baring Brothers expected the full bank debt to be repaid.

With this sorted out, McKeon confirmed that the presentation to AMP would take place on Thursday, 8 August. McKeon didn't know it but this was to be the day that Chris Corrigan arrived back in Sydney from his trip to Ireland.

* * *

For weeks Ward O'Neill and Alan Kennedy had been trying to get a meeting with the investment managers of the large institutions on behalf of the Friends of Fairfax.

Finally AMP relented. The delegation was refused a meeting with Leigh Hall but another was arranged with the investment team in charge of the Fairfax purchase—Paul Edmondson, Alex Hagop and Mark Jackson.

On the morning of 8 August the Friends of Fairfax representatives walked into AMP's headquarters at Circular Quay. Kennedy and O'Neill were joined by Lloyd and Colleen Ryan. The AMP delegation directed the conversation firmly to the Fairfax sale and sat poker-faced while the journalists made their pleas.

Ward O'Neill made the opening statement, stressing that the Friends of Fairfax was not a fringe group of lefties but had been created by a vote of all Australian Journalist Association members at Broadway; that all policies were approved by full meetings and that their only brief was the maintenance of editorial independence and the prevention of further concentration of media ownership.

Ryan outlined the statistics of present media ownership levels and the Friends of Fairfax position on Tourang—it had the potential to be influenced by the Packer organisation and that was unacceptable.

Edmondson from AMP asked for an assessment of each of the bidders. Kennedy had been frightened of this. There was no consensus at Broadway about the best owner—he would be lynched if he took a firm position.

'We have no brief to do that. We are about editorial inde-

Chris Corrigan flew to Ireland to hold secret merger discussions with Tony O'Reilly as his bid floundered in August 1991. (John Fairfax Group)

Kerry Packer's failure to defend Kennedy and Turnbull in their fight with Colson and Powers left his two associates embittered as the Australian Broadcasting Tribunal contemplated an inquiry into Tourang. (John Fairfax Group)

Chris Anderson demanded that Fairfax reciever Des Nicholl vacate Fairfax's Broadway premises as a condition of his return as interim cheif executive. His stand shocked ANZ and Citibank executives. (John Fairfax Group)

Leigh Hall, the powerful AMP investment division manager, became angry at the public bickering between Jamison and Independent. (John Fairfax Group)

Peter Breese (right) and *Jeff White* (below), the two Baring Brothers Burrows executives, worked out the flick pass option to deliver the bondholders to either AIN or Independent if Tourang was forced to withdraw. (Lorrie Graham)

Australian Broadcasting Tribunal chairman *Peter Westaway* **read Kennedy's recollection notes on a plane to Canberra. The next morning he announced an inquiry into Tourang.**
(John Fairfax Group)

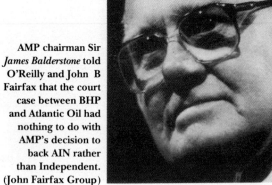

AMP chairman Sir *James Balderstone* **told O'Reilly and John B Fairfax that the court case between BHP and Atlantic Oil had nothing to do with AMP's decision to back AIN rather than Independent.**
(John Fairfax Group)

John Langmore offered the only dissenting voice when Treasurer Willis canvassed key MPs on allowing the restructured Tourang to buy Fairfax. He labelled Black a capital C consevative. (John Fairfax Group)

John Kerin's final act before he was sacked as Treasurer by Prime Minister Hawke was to reject the Tourang offer. (John Fairfax Group)

The unwanted AIN offer sent to Baring Brothers in August 1991 prompted a heated argument between Burrows and Macquarie Bank corporate advisory executives *Simon McKeon* (right) and *Wayne Kent.*

Chris Schacht couldn't believe John Langmore's Caucas mistake in September 1991: 'You've opened the door right up for Kerry Packer,' he yelled at Langmore.

Independent thought *John B Fairfax's* support for its offer would deliver AMP. He confronted Sir James Balderstone over AMP's decision to support AIN. (John Fairfax Group)

Rowen Ross of Bankers Trust Australia met with Mark Johnson in early December 1991 to put forward O'Reilly's request for a merger with AIN, which embraced Independent's terms, including removing John D'Arcy from the board. (John Fairfax)

The extraordinary alliance between *Malcolm Fraser* (left) and *Gough Whitlam* against media concentration escalated the backlash against Kerry Packer's involvement in Tourang. (John Fairfax Group)

At a fiery Sunday morning meeting at the Regent Hotel on 13 October 1991 *Dan Colsen* outlined to Kennedy why the former Consolidated Press chief executive wasn't showing the skills to run Fairfax. (John Fairfax Group)

Trevor Kennedy was deserted by Kerry Packer after twenty years' loyal service. His colourful recollection notes about his involvement in Tourang forced Packer to quit Tourang. (John Fairfax Group)

The AIN directors (left to right) *Rob McKay*, *Mark Johnson*, *John D'Arcy* and *Tom Harley* considered Burrows' request to merge with Tourang. (John Fairfax Group)

Bill Beerworth was ambushed by the bondholders in Los Angeles while he tried desperately to save Warwick Fairfax as the banks closed in. (John Fairfax Group)

Brian Powers' problems with Turnbull began when they met at the Savoy Hotel in London in May 1991. By November he considered it worth taking the ten per cent chance of losing the deal by dumping Turnbull. He said there was a point when one's personal feelings needed to override winning a deal. (John Fairfax Group)

John Singleton (left) telephoned Prime Minister *Bob Hawke* to urge that Tourang's restructured foreign investment proposal not be rejected. (John Fairfax Group)

Lady Mary Fairfax's squabbles with Warwick over her annuity and entitlements were a factor in bank executives' scepticism about mother and son agreeing to accept retaining only a token shareholding in the media group. (John Fairfax Group)

Warwick Fairfax's blind ambition to acquire Fairfax in 1987 and
his subsequent inability to face up to his financial crisis prompted
the banks to put John Fairfax Group into receivership.
(John Fairfax Group)

Dan Colson's meeting with Malcolm Turnbull in Sydney's Botanic Gardens added a bizarre dimension to their feud. This Bill Leak cartoon includes some of the other key participants in Australia's most controversial takeover (clockwise from left: Neville Miles, Kerry Packer, Geoff Levy, Stephen Chipkin, Bob Hawke, John Kerin, Brian Powers, Dan Colson, Malcolm Turnbull).

Tony O'Reilly's bid for ownership of Fairfax became an obsession. His group waged a relentless campaign to destroy Tourang and commenced a court action when he lost. (John Fairfax Group)

Canadian *Conrad Black* slammed Treasurer John Kerin's decision to reject Tourang as 'sleazy, venal and despicable'. (John Fairfax Group)

Mark Burrows, Australia's leading corporate advisor delicately conducted the auction to recoup the bank's $1.25 billion in loans. His firm received a $18.6 million fee for its efforts. (John Fairfax Group)

Malcolm Turnbull's damaging letter alleging Tourang was trying to remove an excessively independent director (himself) from its board was sent to the Australian Broadcasting Tribunal. (John Fairfax Group)

When *Kim Beasley* (centre) suggested over lunch to *Conrad Black* (right) that *Trevor Kennedy* was a potential problem, Black turned to Kennedy and said: 'Okay, Trevor, you're sacked.'
(John Fairfax Group)

The two Ord Minnett Securities executives *Neville Miles* (left) and *Rob Mactier* were caught in the cross-fire as Turnbull fought with Colson and Powers.

pendence and media concentration. Otherwise the Broadway journalists don't want to show a preference,' Kennedy said.

Edmondson persisted. 'What about AIN? Any objections?'

'No, they are almost too good to be true,' Kennedy replied.

'But they've got no experience in newspapers,' Edmondson snapped.

'Well, they've got John D'Arcy and Greg Taylor,' Ryan pointed out.

The conversation shifted abruptly to the O'Reilly team. 'They're very experienced in newspapers,' Edmondson said.

'Well, we don't have any objections to them either,' Kennedy said. 'They have said they will sign the editorial charter and on concentration issues they only have regional papers at present.'

After an hour the Friends of Fairfax team left confident that the approach had been worth it. The AMP team had made it clear that their preference would be for O'Reilly to merge with either Jamison or AIN. The name Tourang did not seem to be an option.

*   *   *

Bleary-eyed, McKeon and Kent walked into Macquarie's Sydney office after the plane trip from Melbourne and the crawl in a taxi through peak-hour traffic.

Neither had slept since the previous night. They had spent twenty-four hours straight refining the documentation. AMP was the first stop in a roadshow planned to cover sixteen institutions over the next week.

But they had a surprise for the fund managers. They wanted the institutions to commit themselves within the week. AIN intended to place an offer with Baring Brothers on 23 August, the day expressions of interest closed.

When Hall arrived at the conference room at Macquarie Bank that afternoon he was not expecting a great deal from the AIN presentation—their pitch and plans had been so thin nine weeks before. However, D'Arcy and Taylor were welcome additions to the team; Hall was well-aware of D'Arcy's esteemed reputation and respected him as a good manager.

A team of four from AMP made the journey from Circular

Quay—Hall and the investment team members who had seen the journalists earlier that day.

The AIN delegation was much larger—Johnson, McKeon, Kent, Harley, McKay, Leslie and D'Arcy. Taylor also honoured his pledge to AIN and made the trip from Melbourne.

Everyone from AIN knew that this meeting was crucial. If they could convince AMP to reject Jamison and Independent, they could confidently expect to secure the support first of the other major institutions and then the smaller ones.

When it comes to investment in Australia, there is often a sheep mentality among fund managers—if AMP or National Mutual back something the others tend to follow. As the two-hour presentation drew to a close, there was an air of excitement in the room.

D'Arcy and Leslie performed well, adlibbing their way through the slide show, throwing in comments where they saw fit. Taylor gave a solid outline of the management structure and Johnson led the discussion about the bid proposal.

Hall was impressed—he couldn't believe how AIN had advanced in the last few weeks. Catching Johnson's eye, he called him aside and told him his impressions. The presentation had changed his view of AIN.

When the AMP delegation left Johnson could hardly wait to convey Hall's comments to his colleagues. It was the morale booster they needed.

Over the next few days AIN pushed through presentation after presentation, notching up sixteen visits. Each one seemed better than the last—they could now anticipate questions and had honed their responses. They had it finely tuned.

*   *   *

Today was Monday, 12 August, and Hall knew that a Fairfax decision would be made on Wednesday. The AIN group was pushing for a decision. There was a board investment committee meeting scheduled—a group chaired by Sir James Balderstone—and Hall knew he must have a briefing paper ready nominating the bid favoured by the investment division.

He didn't need reminding that the decision on who AMP backed was an important one; he had been at the coal face of investment decisions for years. Hall had become a well-known figure in business circles during the 1980s. He had led a new push for AMP as Australia's largest investor to be more outspoken about corporate practices and to be openly critical about the antics of certain entrepreneurs.

Alan Bond had threatened to sue Hall during the Perth entrepreneur's bid to grab control of Robert Holmes a Court's Bell Resources. Hall had stood his ground. He has a formidable intellect but little of the arrogance that often accompanies it.

A quiet, polite man in his forties, Hall was feeling the weight of the Fairfax decision keenly. There was a tremendous level of community interest, not to mention the political debate about Tourang. It was crucial that AMP make a rational and defensible decision.

The three-man investment team headed by Edmondson was now leaning toward AIN. The price was right—a cheap entry into Fairfax for the institutions—and the presentation professional. The management structure looked good even if Taylor and the existing management remained.

Both Independent and Tourang were arguing that Fairfax was badly run; an interesting concept considering the impressive margins and profits achieved before the onset of the recession.

AMP was also attracted by AIN's plan to lock in the majority of the institutions and pitch a well-priced offer that would probably avoid a bidding duel.

When it came to making the decision, the public bickering between O'Reilly and Jamison was an important factor. Hall knew that AMP should steer clear of this type of public spectacle.

Tourang, on the other hand, was not really an option. The media concentration issue made it political dynamite. Also Kerry Packer and AMP have not been traditional allies. AMP is establishment, something Packer is not. The feeling is mutual—Packer refers to AMP as the enemy.

In the end the professionalism of the AIN presentation, the inclusion of John D'Arcy, and the all-Australian nature of the bid swung the balance for AMP.

Hall asked Edmondson for his decision. It was AIN. Hall agreed and so did the board investment committee.

Before he told AIN the good news Hall thought as a gesture of friendship he should warn Rowan Ross of the direction in which AMP was headed. They know each other well and sit together on the board of the Securities Institute of Australia.

Ross had returned from Ireland the previous week and reported to Hall on the rather ambivalent nature of the discussions there.

On Tuesday afternoon he telephoned Ross and gave him a strong hint that AIN had won over O'Reilly for AMP's support. Ross was shocked.

Several hours before John B Fairfax himself had a brush with the AMP management. Attending a function at the Sydney Town Hall he ran into AMP managing director Ian Salmon and, keen to find out AMP's thinking on the Fairfax sale, John decided there was nothing to lose by asking.

'You may not want to do this, but could we have three minutes on Fairfax?' he asked.

Salmon replied that he was leaving shortly and they could talk in a taxi. Cruising down George Street, Salmon gave John a strong hint that AMP would decide in favour of AIN. John's heart sank—he had backed the wrong horse.

Back in his office John called Ross. Added to Hall's oblique conversation earlier, Ross knew what had happened. He telephoned Hall back and desperately tried to argue Independent's case in a bid to convince him to reverse the decision. It was no use. Johnson received the call from AMP the next morning—they had got the backing of Australia's largest investor.

The ecstatic AIN team begged a few hours' delay on the announcement while it conferred with National Mutual. A joint announcement of the country's two largest investors would be a tremendous boost. They knew National Mutual had liked the presentation made on Monday and National Mutual chief executive Gil Hoskins was attracted by the all-Australian bid.

Hoskins was happy to approve his investment team's decision. Board members were contacted and National Mutual was in. It agreed to AIN's request for a joint announcement.

Later that day faxes were sent to media outlets as Harley, McKay and Kent sat in Johnson's office supervising the press release. Johnson sent out for French champagne and they toasted their staggering success in plastic cups.

The next morning the Macquarie Bank fax machines were swamped with written commitments from large and small institutions around the country. The sheep were desperately making sure they were in the pen.

There was a depressed atmosphere at BT as Ross and Hunt tried to fathom what to do next. Their client O'Reilly had been out-manoeuvred by the two Melbourne blokes with briefcases labelled no-hopers. John B Fairfax had been deserted by his father's old company.

Chris Corrigan was blunt when a journalist asked him what AMP's and National Mutual's decision meant.

'We are fucked.'

■   ■   ■

During the soul-searching in the Independent camp for reasons the two major institutions had backed AIN, conspiracy theories were seized upon. It was a deal by the close-knit Melbourne establishment—the Collins Street crowd.

An intriguing explanation was offered for the horrible setback. Balderstone must dislike O'Reilly because of a court battle when he was at BHP. Perhaps the investment committee had been overruled; Balderstone had intervened and the real preferences of the investment division were interfered with by the board.

In the early 1980s when O'Reilly's Atlantic Oil was searching the icy, windswept North Sea for oil, BHP's London office had entered into talks about farming-in to some of Atlantic's acreage. Later BHP pulled out and didn't pay some money Atlantic claimed was due. There was then a lengthy dispute over the terms of the agreement and O'Reilly resorted to the courts to sort it out. It was an amazing decision—an obscure Irish company that struck more mud than oil suing The Big Australian.

There was litigation in the British courts and BHP won.

This was the reason Sir James would intervene to crush Independent's bid for Fairfax.

John B was in his Pitt Street office on Friday morning when the receptionist announced the arrival of Sir James Balderstone. John knew Balderstone well. His father Sir Vincent had been chairman of Stanbroke Pastoral Company for the seventeen years that Jim

Balderstone, as he then was, had been managing director. John remembered holidays with Balderstone and his father on Stanbroke's vast Queensland properties.

Balderstone still visited his father, now quite frail, at Darling Point every few months. For John AMP's decision was a betrayal. They had left him out on a limb. AMP's relationship with the Fairfaxes was severed.

John waited for the right opportunity to express his anger at AMP's decision and then dropped the scorpion. Had Balderstone influenced AMP's decision because O'Reilly was too entrepreneurial and had dared sue BHP?

Balderstone was astounded. The Irish Sea litigation had nothing to do with the decision. He was emphatic that AMP had made the right decision in backing AIN. But had John made the right decision in backing the O'Reilly team?

∎ ∎ ∎

McKay was holding a party. With the institutions falling in behind AMP and National Mutual, he had decided it was time to ask the AIN team to celebrate at his large country home Clunie at Romsey about one hour north of Melbourne. The property is much more than a hobby farm. It has a full-time manager and about 1500 acres farmed. The two-storey, white homestead is set among picturesque, rolling hills like an English country manor that has been picked up and transplanted in Victoria. There are lines of black gumboots, and horses and lambs. There is a tennis court and swimming pool. Inside it is English country decor— paintings on the walls of a fox hunt, open fire places, raw silk wallpaper and contrasting blinds. McKay, his wife Sarah—a member of the Melbourne Baillieu family—and their three children stay at the property as often as possible. Robert McKay is a descendant of Hugh Victor McKay who invented the Sunshine Harvester in 1885, one of the first stripper harvesters in the world. By 1904 he was the largest manufacturing exporter in the Commonwealth. He was a fierce anti-unionist whose plants figured in landmark disputes. When he died in 1926 he left an estate worth £1.4 million.

The AIN team had been spending long hours on the Fairfax deal—late into the night and on weekends. It was obsessive, and their spouses, friends and families were feeling the pressure.

The transaction was important for Macquarie Bank—it was really a charity deal as it wasn't charging normal fees. Neither was the legal firm Arthur Robinson Hedderwick. Many others supporting AIN were giving their time for free; the Fairfax sale was about principles, not a chance to generate some fee income. This created a strong *esprit de corps* and the party atmosphere at the barbecue demonstrated this.

The key AIN people were there. Harley, McKeon, Kent, Creighton Burns and D'Arcy. AIN's lawyer Colin Galbraith, and Greg Taylor brought their wives. The mood was buoyant.

Tourang was a tough competitor but it had enormous problems with foreign investment and broadcasting regulations and, most importantly, public perception. AIN had most of Australia's institutions behind it. It supported the editorial independence of the Fairfax publications. How could it lose?

* * *

Arriving at work on Monday morning, 19 August, Burrows was looking forward to the deadline on Friday. It was time to get this sale moving more quickly.

Burrows had finally overcome the problem of Turnbull gaining access to confidential financial information through his participation in Tourang—each member of the Tourang team would have to sign the confidentiality agreement individually. Turnbull would not be invited into the process.[1] Burrows had also won on strategy with the Tourang consortium. He felt it essential that each of the serious bidders acknowledge that the receiver intended to cover the bank debt in any sale price.

Brian Powers was most reluctant to agree to this in writing but finally did so after much haggling. Burrows received a letter that he could show to the banks to calm their nerves. Powers wrote: 'We are working towards seeking to fully recognise the bank debt.' It was hardly a firm undertaking considering Tourang was contemplating an offer of about $1 billion minus the $125 million for the bondholders. It kept Burrows happy, however.

---

[1] Turnbull claims there was only temporary hesitation on the receiver's behalf to give him access to confidential financial information due to fear of litigation, but ultimately Turnbull received the same financial information as all parties involved with Tourang.

To Burrows the letter meant something. At least Tourang recognised that this wasn't a bargain basement sale. Baring Brothers had all the key players signed up—O'Reilly's Independent Newspapers, AIN from Melbourne, Tourang and Corrigan's Jamison—although the latter was now considered out of the game following AIN's coup with the institutions. Even AMP and National Mutual were signed up.

In the last few weeks White and Breese had organised the due diligence process for Independent, Tourang and AIN. This is the process where potential buyers are able to scrutinise closely the company's operations and its finances to make an informed valuation. There were many critical issues other than hard cash in a sale of this magnitude. There were complex tax issues, questions on loan documentation and examination of the option of selling the assets out of the Fairfax corporate shell if the bondholder issue became serious. No one at Baring Brothers or the banks had any idea of the contents of the exclusivity agreement of course and still maintained that it wouldn't be an issue in the sale process. Bidders had to structure their offers without consideration of the bondholders' rights. Theoretically this was to be handled by Burrows and the banks.

There was plenty of tyre-kicking going on. Black sent out his production expert Alan Rawcliffe to examine Fairfax, to get a feel of the likely level of capital expenditure required on printing presses in the future. If Tourang was going to achieve its plans of slashing production labour, it needed to know the cost of introducing new technology. Ernst & Young began working on the financial due diligence. It was all humming along nicely as the deadline approached.

■　　■　　■

On Thursday Kerry Packer walked into Baring Brothers' offices. There were some worried smiles from Fairfax executives. This meeting was to discuss Fairfax management plans and financial data. Packer wasn't going to take a back seat in the process.

Packer's presence dominated the room and a nervous group of executives—Greg Taylor, Peter Gaunt and Gerry Austin, the group financial accountant—were sitting around the table with the Baring Brothers team. Packer listened as Austin ran through the financial data before asking a question.

'How much money does Fairfax make each year?'

From the other end of the room Austin began to give a complex explanation. He wasn't sure what figure Packer wanted. Did he mean earnings before interest, tax and depreciation?

Frustrated, Packer gave an abrupt reply.

'Look, just how much fucking money do you put in the bank at the end of the year?'

During an informal discussion on the price the Group was likely to fetch, Packer made it clear that Tourang was not going to pay a huge price—they couldn't afford to because of the extra investment that would be required at Broadway for new printing presses, etc when they moved in.

The numbers being discussed were already too high, Packer growled. The laconic Peter Breese suggested that if that was the case, then why was Packer so interested in being part of Tourang? Packer smiled before answering.

'This isn't about money. It's about ego.'

∎   ∎   ∎

Jeff White was adamant. 'We don't want your bid. It's too early. Don't give it to us.'

Simon McKeon was equally stubborn when he answered, his voice coming out of the speaker phone: 'I am going to send it anyway.'

'Well, if it comes in over the fax, there's not much I can do about it,' White replied.

This was not what White needed on the day that final expressions of interest closed. Didn't these Melbourne people understand it was not the date for final offers! AIN, however, was playing the card its members had discussed with the institutions. It wanted to force the pace—put in an offer and try to persuade Burrows to decide immediately.

Angry at McKeon's attitude, White stood by the fax as the pages containing the AIN offer came through. Grabbing it page by page, he came to the crucial line: AIN would pay $1.325 billion for Fairfax. White examined the unwanted offer and quickly realised it wasn't a straight figure. The offer included $300 million of soft equity—in effect AIN wanted the banks to take a haircut of over $300 million on their loans. That is, the banks were required to convert one-quarter of their loans to a form of equity which would be repaid to the banks as the health of the company improved.

The equity component of the bid was $450 million in cash from the institutions and the bank debt would be reduced to $575 million.

There were other limitations—there was a cap on the interest rate payable on the debt, which varied from year to year. And under certain circumstances, the interest could be capitalised (added to the loan instead of paid on time). For the banks it was not an attractive offer. Certainly not one they wanted to accept simply to cut the auction process short. White left the pages in his office and headed home. It could wait until Monday.

. . .

When Burrows, Breese and White sat down on Monday to review the expressions of interest received, they found it difficult to concentrate on anything but this crazy tactic of AIN's. What was more surprising to Burrows was that AIN didn't seem to realise that no offer was going to be accepted before the end of August. The AIN team was obviously unaware of one crucial factor.

In 1991 when Beerworth hired Lazard Freres, the US investment bank, to search for a large foreign equity investor for Fairfax, there was some interesting fine print in the retainer agreement—extraordinary even by Wall Street standards.

There was one particular clause that could turn out to be very expensive. Under the terms of the agreement Fairfax was required to pay Lazards up to US$20 million if an offer for Fairfax was accepted.

The Lazard agreement was simple: if John Fairfax Group terminates this agreement then all success-based fees remain payable and continue to accrue as if Lazards remained adviser to the company until 31 August 1991.

There was a cap on this amount of US$20 million. In Wall Street parlance this was a 'kill fee'—a way of making sure the adviser wasn't dispensed with without payment for work that might be useful to a board of directors. When Burrows told the banks about it, they had been shocked.

It was a sizable incentive to drag out the sale process —why give the firm that was unable to find a foreign equity participant for Warwick a huge fee? There was a certain irony in the attitude—the ANZ Bank and Citibank received enormous fees from Warwick's reign at Broadway. But that was different—Warwick was gone and the banks were paying the receivership fees. There was an important distinction that only bankers would understand.

Burrows was surprised that AIN continued to persist with its plan for a take-it-or-leave it bid with a 31 August deadline. Surely Mark Johnson was aware of the terms of the Lazard agreement from his days as adviser to Warwick Fairfax?

There were no surprise contenders from the expressions of interest. The field was narrow—Tourang, AIN, Independent and the option of a public float. This last alternative was still on the agenda and Peter Thomas, the energetic chief executive of stockbroking firm CS First Boston, put in a letter explaining that the firm was interested in working on a float proposal.

Burrows already had Melbourne firm J B Were & Son on the payroll giving advice on the float option. But Thomas' interest was most welcome. There were also a few loonies who responded to the advertisements in Australian and overseas newspapers. There was one fellow from Port Macquarie who insisted on using a pseudonym.

A Mr Iqbal Khan of London who claimed to represent a group of Lebanese investors wanted to be part of the process. Baring Brothers told Mr Khan that they would need to know more about his clients if they were to hand over reams of confidential information on Fairfax. Mr Khan replied that he wanted to know more about Fairfax before he would reveal the identity of his clients. It was a stalemate and he never wrote back.

There was no other interest from overseas newspaper groups. Baring Brothers had made sure that the major groups were well-aware of Fairfax. The expected tight restriction on foreign ownership was a major deterrent, however, plus the pressure as the recession bit into earnings in the UK and the USA.

Brierley Investments had also gone cold on the deal. It was much too high-profile and politicised. This wasn't the sort of thing that the Brierley team of raiders liked. When they dealt with governments in New Zealand it was done a lot more quietly—the team didn't like banner headlines.

In the end KKR decided that it wasn't interested in Fairfax either. White spoke to Gilhunty who conveyed the news. There was some solace, though. KKR ran through the Fairfax numbers and concluded that Fairfax was worth at least the bank debt of $1.25 billion. It was very heartening that the world's most feared leveraged buyout group gave Fairfax the value Baring Brothers wanted.

∎ ∎ ∎

Over the following few days the exchanges between Baring Brothers and AIN were farcical. McKeon and Kent couldn't understand how Burrows could say the offer was outside the bidding process.

'Just what is the bidding process, Mark?' Kent asked tersely in one speaker phone conversation, sitting with McKeon in their Melbourne office.

'The process is the process,' Burrows angrily replied, 'and your offer is outside the process.'

'But Mark, how do we know what we can and can't do if you don't tell us what is required by the process?' McKeon chipped in.

Exasperated with Burrows' attitude, McKay, Leslie and the two advisers went to Sydney and joined Johnson for a meeting with Burrows, White and Breese. The debate raged again. It was a real catch 22. Burrows kept to his line about the offer being outside the process and made the prickly comment that he had come out of a Brambles board meeting for this discussion.

Heading back to Melbourne, AIN convened a board meeting to work out what to do. Advice was sought about the legal position of making an offer for a company in receivership. The advice was that an offer could be made at any time; AIN wasn't wrong in trying to make an offer.

In the next conversation Burrows remained angry and firm on the situation. Either AIN withdraw the bid or it would be publicly rejected. Against its better judgement the AIN board decided to withdraw the offer. It made sure, however, that executives at the ANZ were told the offer had been made.

Burrows was running the process—whatever it might be—and the AIN team decided that they had antagonised him enough by refusing to withdraw the offer for those few days. Some of the elation in pulling in Australia's largest institutions to support the offer faded. Financial clout wasn't everything. Kerry Packer and Conrad Black had the support of the bondholders. Also Tony O'Reilly's enthusiasm for the deal wasn't dead yet. The Irishman was preparing to sup at the highest table in the land.

CHAPTER TWELVE

COURTING CANBERRA

TONY O'REILLY had everyone laughing deep belly laughs. He is good at this—telling jokes, talking about horse racing. He makes wonderful company.

They were standing by the open fire in the Brown Room—the sitting-room just to the right of the entrance hall at The Lodge, the Prime Minister's residence. Although two days before the beginning of Spring, it was still cold in Canberra.

Bob Hawke had taken O'Reilly upstairs to meet his wife Hazel before joining the others for a pre-dinner drink. It was the first time Hawke and O'Reilly had met and they clearly liked each other.

They joined the organiser of the dinner Graham Richardson, Col Parkes, Hawke's political adviser, and Ted Harris. Even if Harris did nothing else to assist the Independent cause, this dinner was more than enough. It was the perfect example of networking: who better for O'Reilly to bring to The Lodge than Harris, a close friend of Hawke's?

As they ate the rack of lamb, knives rasping on the plates, O'Reilly briefly outlined his plans for Fairfax. He didn't need any favours from the Government. He could live with a twenty per cent limit on foreign ownership; it was all he could afford. Hawke commented that this was just as well because twenty per cent was likely to be the limit.

He couldn't make any promises on editorial policy, O'Reilly said, apart from ensuring that the Labor Party would be treated fairly. Considering the Labor Party's hatred of the Fairfax press this was as good as supporting the party.

Hawke, a non-alcoholic drink in his hand, nodded as O'Reilly spoke. They were words he was satisfied with—his favoured candidate was Independent and meeting O'Reilly only reinforced his view. Packer had enough media—Hawke didn't want Tourang to succeed.

Having finished the last drops of the Lakes Folly red and white wines, they crossed the hallway back into the Brown Room for port and coffee. It was an early night for O'Reilly and Harris. At 10.30 pm they called for their limousine and returned to Canberra's Park Hyatt, the national capital's best hotel.

Richardson and Parkes stayed at The Lodge. There were more important matters on their minds than the ownership of a newspaper chain. Hawke's job was under a cloud. Richardson began to talk about Keating's challenge for the leadership and the future of the party under Hawke.

For O'Reilly, however, the dinner was a major success. From that night he had the Prime Minister firmly on his side.

■　■　■

O'Reilly's *bonhomie* at The Lodge was not a true indication of his mood on this August trip to Australia. He arrived in the country just a few days after AMP, National Mutual and nigh on every other institution in Australia had publicised their backing of AIN. He was devastated about this setback; worried and angry about the progress of his offer.

Sitting in his suite at the Ritz Carlton Hotel, Ross and Hunt tried to give him answers on what had gone wrong. Reynolds and Cameron O'Reilly listened. The flood of institutions that were backing AIN now that AMP and National Mutual had given their support made matters worse. The bottom line was that without substantial institutional support O'Reilly wouldn't have the money to mount a credible offer for Fairfax.

O'Reilly had been convinced that he would secure at least AMP's support. It was a major reason he had wanted to bring John B Fairfax onto his team. In the Independent scheme John was supposed to deliver AMP.

Even the irksome suggestions by Leigh Hall of an Independent and Jamison merger had been followed up to appease AMP. Not one of the Independent group could understand what had gone wrong. They had no grasp that the public fighting with Jamison and approaches to AMP board members were major tactical blunders.

In explaining AMP's decision, the North Sea oil row with BHP and a magnification of Sir James Balderstone's influence seemed a much easier way to account for what went wrong.

The Irishman was obsessed with Fairfax but realised it was slipping away. He still didn't think that AIN had any chance against Packer; he, however, did because of the careful efforts to woo the politicians and present himself as the only acceptable proprietor of Fairfax. He ran through the options and decided he had to be pragmatic. If AIN had the money, perhaps they should be approached about the possibility of a merger.

On Friday, 30 August O'Reilly waited for Jim Leslie and Rob McKay at the Hyatt on Collins. He had come to Melbourne to visit both politicians and institutions. This meeting, however, was more important. O'Reilly had known Leslie since the early 1980s when Leslie was chairman of Mobil Oil in Australia and O'Reilly was on the US board. This fact allowed for a more relaxed meeting than might have been expected.

The purpose of the meeting remained unspoken: O'Reilly needed AIN's money. This didn't deter him from acting like he was calling the shots—he was the successful media baron and business tycoon and the two men sitting opposite him were neither. O'Reilly declared that if the two groups were to combine, Independent must have a twenty per cent stake. It was a figure that McKay wasn't keen on and he countered by suggesting that a 14.9 per cent shareholding would mean a combined offer that didn't require Foreign Investment Review Board approval.

O'Reilly disagreed on AIN's management ideas as well, however. AIN would tolerate neither management fees to Independent nor agreements on asset sales like the one O'Reilly had struck with John B Fairfax.

The meeting became tense over board structure. O'Reilly suggested that Reynolds was the logical choice as chief executive.

It was something that neither Leslie nor McKay was prepared to wear. The best they could offer was Reynolds as deputy chief executive to Greg Taylor.

The talks began to break down. As when O'Reilly met Corrigan, neither side was prepared to compromise. Each believed they had the advantages; egos would not allow any serious pursuit of a merger. There was no sense of urgency or the realisation of imminent failure that would normally set the scene for a business partnership. There was still time with no deadline date yet set for final bids. Fear of failure wasn't an overriding concern at this stage.

Shaking hands, Leslie told O'Reilly it was likely they would be proceeding with separate bids. They agreed, however, to stay in touch in case it was mutually beneficial to link up further down the track. At least contact had been firmly established. It was O'Reilly's only consolation—he still didn't have the cash.

* * *

The next morning Tony O'Reilly walked up the steps to the front gate of Trahlee, the mansion in Bellevue Hill owned by Mark Burrows. It is a magnificent Leslie Wilkinson-designed home with a marble entrance hall featuring a sweeping, forged iron staircase. It is situated just off Fairfax Road. To add to the irony, it is the former home of Hanne Fairfax, Sir Warwick's second wife. (He divorced Hanne to marry Mary and Hanne moved into Trahlee.)

O'Reilly had come along for this one-on-one chat specifically to pick up as much intelligence on the Fairfax deal as he could before he left Australia.

They were sitting on two pale green sofas in the sitting-room when Burrows' daughter Sasha came into the room to say hello. Burrows introduced her, saying that she was home for the weekend from Frensham, the exclusive girls boarding school at Mittagong. O'Reilly laughed and, to the amazement of Burrows, began to sing the school song. He knew it through his former wife Susan and hadn't forgotten it.

They finally settled down to discuss Fairfax. O'Reilly was concerned about his offer; he was depressed about the lack of institutional support; and he was seething about the Balderstone matter.

'How can we get the money for our bid?' he asked Burrows.

Burrows was prepared to be helpful. The last thing he needed was Independent dropping out of the bidding. He suggested that O'Reilly secure a large stockbroking firm as an underwriter for a substantial slice of his bid. That way the equity funds from the institutions did not need to be firmly committed before a final offer was made. The stockbroker would take on that risk—presumably banking on the expectation that the institutions would buy into Fairfax regardless of who the winning bidder was. Burrows suggested that J B Were would be a good underwriter.

O'Reilly told Burrows that he was very confident on the political side of the transaction. In his view there was no way that Packer would ever be allowed to buy Fairfax. The politicians would never allow it. He suggested that the only minister backing Packer was Richardson.

Burrows listened carefully—he could see the passion O'Reilly felt for Fairfax. He could also see the Irishman's exasperation that he wasn't winning hands down.

．　．　．

Kim Beazley had endured this bureaucratic infighting for weeks. His officers in the Department of Communications didn't want any more changes to the Broadcasting Act. It was a nightmare already, they claimed. They had been working hard on the draft of a new Broadcasting Services Bill and it was almost complete. If they had to turn around now and amend the old legislation, it would take all the policy drive away from the important new legislation. In the Department's opinion Peter Westerway and the Australian Broadcasting Tribunal (ABT) were being obstructive. The old Act didn't need amending to enforce the cross-media ownership rules; it could already catch control through associates. The necessary powers were already there, the bureaucrats maintained. It was a cat fight and Beazley hated it.

Peter Westerway continued to insist that the Act was not strong enough. The ABT needed overt powers to investigate a transaction before it actually occurred. If an investigation was done after the transaction and it was found that it did, in fact, contravene the Act, the ABT was left in an impossible situation. Surely

Beazley could see that? It would be very hard to reverse a transaction—the old management would have already been sacked and the direction of the company changed.

The officers from the department argued that the ABT already had the right to seek an injunction under the Act to prevent a transaction from taking place. Westerway thought this debatable.

In any case, if they had sought an injunction the party involved would take them straight to the Federal Court to test the law. Instead of a detailed inquiry by Tribunal members the process would be obstructed and the inquiry would effectively take place in a Federal Court environment.

Beazley relented. He would prepare to amend the Act so that the Broadcasting Tribunal could undertake extensive inquiries before a transaction. This inquiry could be triggered by the existence of associates. For example, if associates of the holder of a television licence were to be connected with a newspaper in the same area, an inquiry could be undertaken to assess whether this would give control of the newspaper to that licence holder— hence leaving him in control of a television station and a newspaper in the one area, in clear breach of cross-media ownership regulations.

The definition of associate was very broad but it served only to trigger an inquiry. Once an investigation was under way it was the old and narrower definition of an associate already in the Broadcasting Act that would be used to assess control. Control could only exist if the association continued; a past association was relevant only to trigger an inquiry not to prove control.

It was an important tool for Westerway. It gave him the indisputable power to ask probing questions of parties associated with a transaction well before the transaction took place. The answers to those questions had to be presented within seven days, or even sooner if required, rather than the twenty-one days allowed for replies under the old legislation. Westerway was pleased with the changes to the Act.

But they didn't earn Beazley any friends in the anti-Packer lobby. The Friends of Fairfax Committee was bitterly disappointed. It was imperative that the new definition of associates be actually used in the inquiry, not simply to trigger it. It felt that Beazley had misled them, promising one thing and delivering another.

Beazley was angry. He had allowed changes to the legislation and now he was still being criticised. His view was that there was nothing untoward about Packer having a passive 14.9 per cent investment in Fairfax. It was within the Act and it was a smart move for Packer to make given his position in the electronic media and his magazines. He didn't believe Packer would be silly enough to try and get around the cross-media rules.

The new associates definition would probably trigger an investigation and perhaps an inquiry but he was sure that Tourang would come through unscathed. Beazley was sticking to his guns—the existing legislation would not be changed to target any individual or group; it was simply to be made more workable for the ABT. The goal posts would not be moved.

* * *

Tom Harley was furious when he telephoned Rob McKay early on Wednesday, 11 September. He repeated Beazley's comment to himself as the telephone rang—'Uptown Melbourne Establishment'. Beazley had referred to AIN in this derogatory manner at a Caucus meeting the night before. It was all over the early morning news bulletins.

Harley had felt sick when he heard it. For the past few days the feedback from Canberra had been bad despite the visits on 3 September to see politicians—including Beazley, Attorney-General Michael Duffy and Opposition Leader John Hewson.

AIN was being portrayed as a syndicate of rich Melbourne Liberal Party members working from the Melbourne Club. Harley couldn't believe it and McKay agreed it smacked of dirty tricks. Here was a local trying to secure Fairfax—and in doing so keep it out of foreign hands—and the Labor ministers were dismissing it as unsuitable. To Harley it was stupid, tribal behaviour.

Certainly Harley was a member of the Liberal Party. But AIN wouldn't have got as far as it had without strong support from Labor Party members and sections of the trade union movement. This attempt to write off the syndicate as being backed by big business and intrinsically against the Labor Party was absurd.

It was also ironic that this came from politicians whose business 'mates' included the disgraced Laurie Connell and the failing Alan Bond. The Labor Government seemed attracted to the fast money boys. And this was a government that had once boasted a strong stand against foreign ownership of key assets as an important plank in its ideology. It was now backing foreigners and in the process assisting Kerry Packer to secure a foothold in Fairfax.

The Beazley comment came on top of Hawke's character assassination of John D'Arcy in the meeting with the Friends of Fairfax and the Age Independence Committee (AIC) six weeks earlier. Harley had urged D'Arcy to send off a letter refuting Hawke's argument about the assets test campaign.

Once again, it was a supreme irony. AIN, which as part of its plans promoted editorial independence, faced a Prime Minister who was hostile to its bid because D'Arcy as chief executive of the Herald and Weekly Times (HWT) hadn't interfered in editorial matters.

Not only was John D'Arcy copping it from Hawke, Jim Leslie was also being singled out for criticism over his performance as chairman of Qantas. Beazley's office was the source of this as far as AIN could work out.

■　■　■

Chris Schacht was embarrassed about the 'Uptown Melbourne Establishment' leak from the previous night's Caucus committee meeting. But it was done now. He had to press on.

Earlier in the week John Langmore had approached Schacht with a motion to go before the Transport and Communications Committee which would effectively limit any foreign interest in a newspaper company to twenty per cent. Langmore reasoned that it was important to establish the ground rules before the Fairfax transaction was completed. Caucus should have an input.

Schacht agreed. If Langmore moved the motion, Schacht would second it.

Langmore spoke in favour of his motion at the committee meeting the previous night. There were good grounds for supporting Australian ownership, he argued. Australians can better identify what is in the national interest and there is more likely to be conflicts of interest with foreigners—it could influence the reporting of global events. We wouldn't necessarily get the Australian perspective. There are limits on foreign ownership of the electronic media, he said, and these should be extended to all forms of media.

Schacht spoke next. Twenty per cent was a reasonable limit and it was fair for the Government to indicate the maximum limit now to allow future bids to be restructured accordingly.

Kim Beazley was the only minister who was a member of the Transport and Communications Committee. He reacted strongly to the Langmore motion. It did not come within Beazley's portfolio but he had strong views on foreign investment. When it came to newspapers, the rules should be as liberal as possible, he argued. The electronic media was different; it was a finite resource. There were barriers to access. This was not the case with newspapers. In any case the Murdoch group had a high foreign ownership level—rules could not be made for one party and not for another. Beazley couldn't see why Black should be persecuted.

The chances were that a motion like this on foreign investment could knock all the bidders out of the running. AIN would be the only one left standing.

'Why should we do any favours for an uptown Melbourne establishment mob?'

The Caucus committee members listened to his pleas but weren't convinced. Gary Punch, a member of the New South Wales right wing of the Labor Party, intervened at that point. It was getting late. This was an important decision. It needed a lot more debate. Could it be deferred until Thursday evening, two days away? The committee members agreed.

■ ■ ■

At 8.30 pm on Thursday evening, members of the Transport and Communications Committee traipsed along the pink carpets of the Senate corridors once again and into committee room 3.

It was a large turnout—twenty-one members out of a possible twenty-eight compared with just fourteen at the Tuesday meeting. Schacht looked around the room and counted the various factions—the vote was safe. It would be twelve to nine. The left faction had met on the issue and would vote for it and the centre left had had informal discussions. They were locked in. The nine members of the right would vote against it.

He could see Beazley was all fired up, ready for a strong debate. The atmosphere in the room was tense. This issue was important to those on the left of the Labor Party. Letters were read out from the AIC and from Martin Ferguson of the ACTU. Both argued for the twenty per cent limit on foreign ownership. Langmore moved the motion again and Schacht seconded it.

Then Beazley began. The motion was too restrictive. It referred to a twenty per cent limit on foreign interests. This might rule out all sorts of sophisticated financial instruments that were really just loans from foreign banks. The motion should refer to foreign ownership, not foreign interests. It should be just voting equity, not non-voting equity.

Schacht jumped to his feet. 'If you don't make it twenty per cent all up, then you are making a decision to favour the Tourang bid over all others. They have got the financial resources, they have got the bondholders, they could give them non-voting equity. It will be all over red rover.'

Langmore spoke next. He is a polite, thoughtful man who has a deep dislike of confrontation. Perhaps Beazley was right, perhaps they were being financially naive. Langmore thought that Schacht was being alarmist. Beazley's suggestion was really no different to what Langmore was suggesting. The word interest could be changed to ownership, he said.

Beazley leant across the table and snapped: 'I'll accept that.'

Gary Punch took the cue and immediately moved an amendment to change foreign interest to foreign ownership.

Schacht groaned. This was a shambles. 'Do you know what you are doing?' he yelled across the table at Langmore.

All those hours spent together working out the motion to restrict foreign ownership to a total of twenty per cent and now Langmore was ruining everything. They knew they had the numbers to override Beazley. It was so simple—the left and the centre left could ram their motion through twelve–nine.

Just one motion, one vote and it was through. A decision that would sail through the full Caucus and tie the Government's hands on the whole issue. Schacht sat there shaking his head. There was only one last chance.

Under the rules he could put up the original motion as an amendment. If the left and the centre left backed it, he could overrule Punch's motion. He read out the motion.

'All those in favour?' chairman Neil O'Keefe said. Schacht looked around the room, sighing when the hands went up. He counted to five and that was it.

'All those against?' He watched the hands go up quickly. He didn't really need to count them. His amendment motion was defeated sixteen to five.

He sat forward and looked at Langmore. 'You don't realise what you've done. You've opened the door right up for Kerry Packer.'

The left faction had followed Langmore to a man. Schacht spat his words out to Jeanette McHugh, a member of the left faction who had voted with Langmore.

'For Christ's sake, Jeanette. Langmore doesn't realise what he is doing.' He then walked over to Langmore. His words were chilling. 'You wait until I tell the rest of the Labor Party what you have done. The left will burn you alive!'

Schacht walked out of the committee meeting and vented his spleen to the press. The next morning Chris Schacht was on page three of the *Herald*: 'There is no doubt it has advantaged the foreign bidders, particularly Conrad Black. I was very disappointed that most members of the left voted in the end to allow open ended foreign ownership.'

Four days later, on Monday morning, Langmore was ready to repent. He still believed the amended motion would have the desired effect of limiting foreign ownership to twenty per cent but he was happy to put up a new, carefully worded motion before the full Caucus to clarify the situation. He would get lawyers to draft it; this time it would be right. The next meeting was almost a month away in October.

• • •

For the AIN team the Caucus Committee decision was a disaster. And to think that they had been celebrating only three weeks earlier! Their reasoning had been faultless—if they had almost all the Australian institutions tied up and foreign equity, voting and non-voting, was limited to twenty per cent, then they had a good chance of winning Fairfax.

Now that foreign interest was virtually unlimited, if non-voting equity was included, their chances of pulling off this takeover by the sheer weight of available funds was diminished considerably. Somewhere along the line they had played the wrong card.

That card was a political one; Harley and McKay had virtually ignored Canberra. On the face of it AIN never felt the need to pay homage to Canberra to the extent that Tourang and O'Reilly had. AIN had no cross-media ownership or Trade Practice Commission worries nor any need for foreign equity. But the Caucus Committee decision had demonstrated that they were wrong. Canberra did matter.

AIN needed someone to push its case in the capital—the problem was, who?

After discussing the matter with supporters, John Saunderson, who had helped push the print media amendments to the Labor Party platform through the Hobart Conference in June, was considered the best choice. Harley made the approach.

On the weekend of the ACTU congress in Melbourne Harley fronted at the conference and asked Saunderson to have a cup of coffee with him. Saunderson accepted the AIN commission with alacrity. At the first meeting with both Harley and McKay he urged them to go to Canberra themselves and talk to Caucus members. He suggested that AIN relaunch its bid with press conferences in Sydney and Canberra and that it nominate a particular spokesperson, probably Rob McKay. But, Saunderson added, McKay would have to get rid of his half spectacles when he was interviewed for television. It made him look like Kerry Packer: arrogant.

'But I can't see without them,' McKay protested.

'Too bad, they've got to go,' was Saunderson's advice. McKay and Harley would also have to stop wearing striped shirts—it was bad for their image.

'Do you want us in boiler suits and clogs?' Harley joked.

'It would be an improvement,' was Saunderson's laconic reply.

As well as retaining a lobbyist, AIN decided that it needed a broader base for its board. Harley approached Michael Easson, the secretary of the Labor Council of New South Wales with an offer of a board seat if AIN was successful.

Then, better late than never, Harley, McKay and Mark Johnson prepared to travel to Canberra for some serious lobbying.

* * *

Peter Hunt was excited when he told John Reynolds that the ABT had agreed to meet and hear Independent's case on the cross-media laws. It was going to be another chance for a free kick at Tourang at a time when the pressure was obviously growing for an ABT inquiry.

For weeks Hunt had been trying to keep up the pressure. He was in constant contact with Anne Davies at the Communications Law Centre, canvassing what was happening on the new associates rules under the Broadcasting Act and her assessment on where the ABT members stood.

Hunt also had legal opinions on the status of Kennedy and Turnbull in relation to Packer and was keen to promote them to ABT chief Peter Westerway. He even sent them to Hawke's office. Hunt knew that the more trouble he could cause Tourang, the better would be the chances of Independent.

Westerway's decision to agree to meet Independent was in many ways odd since the Irish clearly had no cross-media problems. However, Westerway justified his agreement on the basis of the ABT's need to be fully informed before the new amendments were introduced.

On Tuesday, 17 September the Independent contingent— Liam Healy, Hunt and Ted Harris—headed off in taxis across the Harbour Bridge to the ABT's North Sydney office. Hunt pressed his case against Tourang.

* * *

Tourang's legal representatives from Freehills made the same journey, carrying folders of information clarifying the position of Turnbull and Kennedy. The ABT was given a clear brief on why, even under the proposed amendments, neither could be considered in any way associates of Kerry Packer.

Westerway was acutely aware of the growing political pressure for an inquiry into Tourang. Both Hawke and Beazley's staff were clearly worried that, if there wasn't an inquiry, Hawke's Government would be seen to be doing favours; another deal for a media mate.

Beazley was stumbling over the whole Fairfax matter. He was still on the back foot over the Transport and Communications Committee decision with criticism growing that his support of the non-voting equity was seeking to assist Packer.

On ABC's 'Lateline' programme on Thursday 19 September Beazley denied that he was trying to favour one bidder and argued that it was important to keep the bidding process competitive.

Mark Burrows couldn't have put it better himself.

. . .

Bob Hawke was taking a very keen interest in the Fairfax auction. On the Wednesday of that week, 18 September, he decided to do a bit of his own intelligence gathering. He asked Mark Burrows over to Kirribilli House for lunch. It was very informal—lunch was to be held on the verandah overlooking Sydney Harbour and joining them was a former Oxford University colleague of Hawke's, now an English policeman and holidaying in Australia.

But the meal was delayed while they watched a little television. Graham Richardson was on 'Midday Show with Ray Martin' on Nine Network, telling viewers that there wasn't going to be another leadership challenge by Paul Keating.

Burrows brought Hawke up to date on the technicalities of the bidding process. But Hawke added a bit of his own intelligence— Tourang wouldn't get up with Packer involved—Caucus wouldn't stand for it.

. . .

Stephen Loosley glared across the table at Tom Harley.

'In 150 years the *Herald* has never written an editorial in favour of the ALP in New South Wales.'

Mark Johnson, sitting next to Harley, could feel the venom in Loosley's statement. If he had had any doubts about how strongly entrenched the anti-Fairfax feeling was within the New South Wales right wing of the Labor Party, they had been dispelled in just one sentence. There was a shocked silence while Harley collected his thoughts. The atmosphere was almost eerie, the depth of the emotion underlying Loosley's statement having an even greater impact during the ensuing lull.

The AIN team had come to Canberra to meet the politicians just as Saunderson had suggested. He had organised a meeting room and an invitation had been issued to all parliamentarians—anyone who wanted to meet the members of the AIN team could come along. Only six had bothered to turn up.

Stephen Loosley, the Federal President of the Labor Party and a key member of the New South Wales right wing, was one of them. Harley was taken aback by the anger implicit in Loosley's comment. Is this guy serious, he wondered and couldn't resist answering back.

'Well, I'll disregard the first part of your comment because, as you know better than I, the ALP has only been in existence for 100 years.

'But I'll tell you now, we are not in the business of giving editors instructions. It will be up to the editors to make the decisions on editorials.'

He went on: 'The *Age* has supported the Victorian Labor Party in editorials in every State election since 1976, so you can't say that paper is against Labor.'

Loosley didn't look convinced. He got up and left the room, leaving an uneasy feeling. This is ridiculous, Harley thought. What is the point of dealing with politicians with their minds already set on Fairfax? If Fairfax was the devil, AIN was clearly the next worse thing in the eyes of many of these Labor Party politicians.

For Rob McKay, Loosely introduced a new element into the equation—blind hatred.

The trip to Canberra was a waste of time for AIN. The Liberal Party was useless and Hewson was trying his hardest to stay out of the debate. There were too many politicians too scared of upsetting Packer.

On the plane back to Melbourne Harley and McKay reviewed the trip and agreed it would be counter-productive to try any more serious lobbying in Canberra. Hawke, Beazley and Richardson had their preferences for the winning bidder, and it certainly wasn't AIN.

All the indications pointed to the Irish and Tourang peddling misinformation against AIN to improve their own chances. Harley knew Turnbull was lobbying against AIN—he had even gone on radio and dished out some vitriol against the consortium. There was little chance of winning on the political front and from now on AIN would concentrate on making sure it had the best commercial offer for Fairfax. It would leave Tourang and Independent to slug it out in Canberra.

■ ■ ■

Trevor Kennedy was concerned about the political opposition to Tourang. He was blunt with Colson and Powers—they shouldn't be associating so closely with Packer. If they were all independent members of the consortium then they should be seen that way. It wasn't good that Colson and Powers were spending so much time with Packer, dining at his Bellevue Hill home and the like.

Packer seemed to be spending more time with Colson and Powers and less with Turnbull and Kennedy. They were uncomfortable about it.

Colson's attitude was unpleasant too. He was seizing every opportunity to put Kennedy down. He seemed to resent Kennedy's relationship with Conrad Black and hated Kennedy's tendency to treat him as a lackey, a hired gun, rather than a key member of the team. The atmosphere in meetings was becoming increasingly tense. Tourang was not a happy team.

■ ■ ■

Langmore and Schacht were immediately suspicious. They were ready to put a new motion on foreign ownership of the print media to the full Caucus meeting on Tuesday evening, 8 October, but Beazley was pleading with them to delay it. The matter really should be considered first by Caucus committee.

Foreign ownership came under the Treasurer's portfolio and he wasn't a member of the Transport and Communications Committee. The matter, therefore, should be considered by a joint committee meeting—the Economic Committee and the Transport and Communications Committee. This could take place on Thursday and it could be followed by a special meeting of the full Caucus to consider the matter.

This sounded reasonable, but both men remained wary; they

had been misled on this whole issue too much already and it was becoming an embarrassment.

They knew there was a full Cabinet meeting on Wednesday and could see a potential hitch if they agreed to Beazley's request. The newspaper foreign ownership matter could be raised and a motion put to Cabinet. If that happened, ministers would be bound by the vote on the motion when the matter came before Caucus on Thursday.

Schacht was straightforward with Beazley. 'We are not going to fall for the trick of deferral so you can lock up Cabinet in the meantime.'

Beazley was assuring. 'No, no, I won't do that. It's too sensitive.'

* * *

For Hellman & Friedman this Caucus decision could potentially be the end of the road. If Caucus went for the strict limit the investment group would end up with a maximum of only five per cent of Fairfax. Nearly twelve months of effort for five lousy per cent.

Powers was angry about the whole political process. The conflicting signals about what the joint committee would do were starting to exasperate him; there was too much shifting.

For weeks Powers had been dubious about the wisdom of Tourang's main conduits to Canberra. Kennedy had professed to be great mates with senior politicians like Beazley, Richardson and even Hawke but so far he had called the whole political debate wrongly. Then there was Peter Barron's alleged contacts.

Once again the product wasn't living up to expectations. Both Packer and Colson had been very supportive of Hellman & Friedman's potential problems. Given the tension developing with Kennedy and Turnbull, however, he knew that they couldn't care less if Brian Powers wasn't around.

Mark Carnegie had been following the events in Canberra closely and for weeks had been pointing out to Powers the difference between the facts and the perceptions coming from Tourang's Canberra 'experts'. Finally Powers was persuaded that they needed their own lobbyist in Canberra to provide intelligence and open a few doors to see politicians. Carnegie recommended Terry Cutler, a lobbyist well-connected in the Labor Party and with particular expertise in communications.

On Wednesday, 9 October Powers set out for Canberra to walk the corridors of Parliament House, visiting as many politicians as Cutler could gain him access to. He saw Beazley, Kerin, Button and Schacht and an enormous amount of effort went into briefing Neil O'Keefe and Ric Charlesworth, the chairmen of the Transport and Communications and Economics Committees respectively.

His message was short and direct. Don't change foreign investment policy for one transaction. Very few countries in the world place a limit on foreign investment in the print media.

And what about the existing situation? News Corporation was more than twenty per cent foreign owned since Murdoch became a US citizen. APN, O'Reilly's provincial newspaper group, was essentially foreign owned. Australia will be a laughing stock.

Powers didn't stop at the politicians; he spoke to financial commentators as well. That Wednesday night Mark Westfield of the *Herald* and Bryan Frith of the *Australian* wrote their columns for the next day's newspaper on the same topic—don't change the foreign investment rules for one transaction.

■　　■　　■

Mark Burrows spent Wednesday in Canberra too. The last thing Burrows needed was a strict twenty per cent foreign ownership limit. None of the bidders were putting offers up anywhere near the $1.25 billion he required to get the banks out clean. It was vital to keep as many players in the game as possible if he had any chance of achieving a suitable result. It had been hard enough coaxing AIN and O'Reilly to stay in the race after the bondholder exclusivity agreement; another setback was just not on.

Carefully Burrows timed his visit to be the last person Kerin saw before he went into the Cabinet meeting that afternoon. He put his argument to Kerin forcefully. He emphasised the importance for the Treasurer to retain the discretion on foreign investment policy and not hand it over to Caucus. He stressed the need for non-voting equity. What was the problem, he asked. Hundreds of Australian companies listed on the sharemarket have passive offshore institutional shareholders who don't exercise any control.

Burrows also warned Kerin of the dangers of a strict twenty per cent decision. It wouldn't just cruel the Tourang bid. O'Reilly might also have trouble staying in the race unless he was allowed additional foreign equity. How could O'Reilly accommodate the junk bondholders if he took up the entire allocation of available foreign equity? After all O'Reilly said he wanted twenty per cent.

Burrows was dismissive of AIN—he told Kerin the group was just bottom-feeding. They had tied the institutions up on the promise of a cheap price. If the AIN offer was to be taken up, the banks would not be paid back in full; nor would the 2800 unsecured creditors in Fairfax. It would have a serious impact on the economy.

The float proposal being put together by stockbroker CS First Boston was also in jeopardy, Burrows told Kerin. Boston was owned by an overseas bank and it wouldn't be able to underwrite a public float if the strict twenty per cent limit was adopted.

The message was clear and Kerin was worried.

As Burrows walked out of Kerin's office and along the corridor he bumped into Brian Powers and Terry Cutler leaving Kim Beazley's office.

●　　●　　●

The banks of bright fluorescent lights in the Cabinet room disguised the fact that it was nearly 2.50 am on Thursday morning. This tortuous Cabinet meeting had gone on for nearly ten hours.

The last item was being debated and it would be all over in a matter of minutes. Outside Parliament House in the chilly spring air dozens of white cars waited for the ministers and their staff to whisk them home.

Beazley had already scored an important victory that night, winning support—after a knockback a few months earlier—for proposals to facilitate the speed in which pay television was introduced in Australia.

There was one more victory planned and this time it was Kerin's. Among his pile of papers and folders he had seventeen sheets of paper on which were typed two neat paragraphs. He pulled them out and passed them around the table. It was an alternative resolution to be put before tomorrow's full Caucus meeting on foreign ownership of the print media.

As they read it some ministers frowned, realising the implications not only of the content but the impropriety of bringing it up unannounced at the end of a marathon meeting. Ministers began asking questions and John Kerin leapt into a strong defence.

He argued that it was for Cabinet to determine foreign investment policy, not Caucus. What's more, Kerin said, he must have the issue sorted out now. He was in possession of confidential commercial information, which he could not disclose, on how the resolution would assist each bidder, including AIN.

Kerin also explained why he didn't want to be restricted in his discretion. As it was up to him to determine whether a proposal with foreign equity was acceptable, he wanted to do so unfettered.

Kerin was rebuked strongly by Gerry Hand, the left-wing minister from Victoria and Robert Ray, Minister for Defence and fellow Victorian. Why was Kerin trying to lock up Cabinet and so thwart the special Caucus meeting discussing a very sensitive matter?

John Button joined the opposition, but it soon became quite clear that there wasn't enough support to block it. There was no vote taken. The discussion petered out and the ministers trudged out of the room at 3.20 am.

* * *

It was a huge turnout for a joint committee meeting the next day—thirty-eight attended. The right had been working hard, Langmore thought; everybody was wheeled in. It was one of the biggest turnouts he had ever seen for a meeting of this type.

Kerin addressed the meeting very seriously. He explained that the receiver has a statutory obligation to get the maximum return for the creditors. It would not be in the nation's interest for the Government to be taking an approach that would place impediments in the receiver's way.

Chris Schacht interrupted. 'It is not the Government's role to assist the banks in recouping their money. If the ANZ is stupid enough to lend \$2 billion to Warwick Fairfax without even meeting him, then they deserve to be in trouble.'

It was senseless to pre-empt the print media inquiry, Beazley argued. Caucus would have an opportunity to discuss the matter after the report of the inquiry. A decision of this nature might restrict the bidding process leaving only one bidder. It could even rule out a float because it was a foreign underwriter. It was best to wait until the receiver had made his decision and then the matter could go back to Caucus.

The minister's motion was put to the meeting. It was a tied vote. Three members of the right, including Ralph Willis, had wandered in at the last minute for support. Then Langmore's motion was put—it was a tied vote again.

There was only one more scene in this policy-making debacle to be played out. That evening Caucus re-convened for the special meeting to discuss the issue. The night before word had circulated about the Cabinet discussion and the efforts of the right wing of the party at the joint committee meeting. There were bitter feelings among Caucus members that Kerin had even raised the issue in Cabinet. Nevertheless Schacht and Langmore were confident that they had the numbers to push through their resolution. With the left and centre left voting as a block, they thought they could manage it.

General discussions continued for over an hour before Beazley and Kerin's resolution was put up for debate. Kerin appeared to be pushing the resolution as one that had already been accepted by Cabinet. Chairperson Carol Jakobsen was asked if Cabinet ministers were bound to support the resolution and she looked around bewildered as some ministers yelled out that they were.

Richardson, Kerin, and Beazley led the push, yelling: 'Yes, yes, yes' to Caucus members.

Schacht was outraged. He accused Beazley of reneging on his word.

'No, I told you that there wasn't going to be a firm Cabinet decision on it,' Beazley shouted back.

Amid the confusion Jakobsen put the motion to the Caucus. The hands went up. Some Cabinet ministers abstained, refusing to co-operate; John Button and Gerry Hand were not prepared to accede to this example of politics at its worst. Other ministers, however, who were strongly opposed felt obliged to support it, knowing the potential penalty within the Labor Party for breaching Cabinet solidarity.

Jakobsen read out the result. The troika's ambush was passed by forty-six to forty-one.

Afterwards as Caucus members broke into huddles outside the room, confusion remained. No one was certain whether Cabinet members were bound by the decision. If they weren't, the vote had been a fraud. Seventeen votes had been effectively locked into supporting the resolution because of ministers bound by Cabinet solidarity; only a handful of the ministers would have voted for it had they been free to choose. The Schacht–Langmore motion for a strict twenty per cent limit would then have been debated and adopted.

Over the weekend there was widespread discontent about the outcome, but the motion stood. Schacht and Langmore had been duped again.

Brian Powers and Mark Burrows earned full marks for political lobbying.

CHAPTER THIRTEEN

GOODBYE TREVOR

TREVOR KENNEDY stormed out of the vast marble foyer of the Ernst & Young building just as the taxi pulled up. It was nearly 11.30 am on Saturday morning, 12 October, and Colson and Powers were three hours late. These were the same two men who had complained that Kennedy's attendance at due diligence meetings was poor and now they hadn't even bothered to show up on time. He wouldn't have been surprised if they had been at Packer's place.

'This is a fucking great time to turn up to an 8.30 meeting,' Kennedy barked. Nonplussed Colson and Powers stood there as he continued his diatribe, his face reddening with fury while he pointed out the inconsistencies in the argument that he wasn't pulling his weight. He refused to wait any longer. 'I've got a game of tennis on.'

He turned and walked to his BMW parked across the street.

Colson and Powers looked at each other. They didn't need to speak. Who did this guy think he was? Their bid for Fairfax was due in on Tuesday and he was intending to spend Saturday playing tennis?

To them it was another typical Kennedy performance, revealing his arrogance and tendency to bully. In this instance Kennedy's personality traits cut no favour.

■ ■ ■

Over dinner Kennedy's name kept cropping up. It couldn't be ignored any longer; a crisis point had been reached. They felt they could no longer work with this man.

For weeks the doubts about Kennedy's performance had been building up. Colson was fast forming the conclusion that Kennedy would not be the kind of Fairfax chief executive they wanted.

Colson and Powers considered the problems. Kennedy's broadbrush attitude to the institutional presentations in July still irritated them; in their view Kennedy had not immersed himself in the details of financial analysis. Initially they had dismissed this—maybe they were being unduly pedantic, considering Kennedy was still extricating himself from Consolidated Press and had launched straight into another demanding job.

As they went over August and September, however, their case against Kennedy grew. Colson lamented that Kennedy was showing little personal involvement in the due diligence work on Fairfax—it seemed to them that he had failed to apply himself to the arduous task of pulling Fairfax apart to find out how it worked. Kennedy's own view, however, was that he was already spending up to twelve hours a day on due diligence and he had far greater knowledge about Fairfax than Colson and Powers anyway.

There also developed a dispute between Colson and Kennedy over the Fairfax newsprint agreement. Colson was annoyed because Kennedy's analysis of the agreement fell far short of what Colson had expected. Kennedy on the other hand considered the work he had done was all that was necessary.

Powers' views mirrored Colson's. It annoyed Powers how Kennedy had told him that he could sack 300 people at Fairfax without difficulty. According to Powers, Kennedy was very light on detail when questioned which 300 jobs would be lost.[1]

Alan Rawcliffe, a production executive from the Telegraph, had come to Australia in August to help with the due diligence examination of Fairfax and had commented that Kennedy wasn't a production man. This worried Colson. In a few years' time Fairfax's Broadway operations faced heavy capital expenditure on new printing equipment and colour presses. The company

---

[1] Kennedy disputes that he was asked to elaborate or that he was expected to. He estimated a percentage of possible staff reduction only. He says Tourang had no information in the due diligence to identify particular employees for retrenchment.

needed someone with production knowledge to handle the $200 million-plus project.[2]

On the finance side there were gaps too. Kennedy did not share their preoccupation with compiling the fine detail of the business plan. In the end Colson did it himself. He was the one who spent days and nights—and every weekend—cooped up in air-conditioned offices.

Colson's resentment grew. Kennedy is the only person on the payroll and the proposed chief executive, he thought. What the hell am I doing all this work for? Coupled with doubts about Kennedy's abilities to run Fairfax effectively were the concerns over the ABT.

The furore over Kennedy's relationship with Packer was a problem, particularly in the light of the new associates test. If the ABT came across other evidence that indicated Packer might be exercising control, the Packer–Kennedy association might be a factor in the decision to hold an inquiry. It could jeopardise the whole deal. A lengthy ABT inquiry could ruin Tourang's whole strategy. Even worse, it could throw Packer's involvement into grave danger.

Neither Colson nor Powers wanted that. They were becoming fond of Packer—the long dinners at his house and hours spent plotting Tourang's strategy had made them close.

Even putting aside Kennedy's attitude on the Tourang offer, Colson considered Kennedy's appearance at the Print Media Inquiry had been a disaster—Colson was disappointed with Kennedy's chatty, off-the-cuff answers the previous week. Also many of Kennedy's answers about the level of foreign ownership Tourang would hold in Fairfax were confused. He had great difficulty in explaining how Tourang planned to limit its voting equity in Fairfax to twenty per cent and the meaning of convertible debentures.

Many of his answers were also laced with comments such as 'as far as I am aware'. Colson couldn't believe that Kennedy wasn't

---

[2] Kennedy, however, thought it was understood he was not a production man; indeed his extensive background in editorial/journalism was well-known. As far as he was concerned the strategy was that the Daily Telegraph would look after the production aspects.

better prepared for his appearance. The last thing Tourang needed was to hand over ammunition to the politicians.

To make matters worse Kennedy had admitted that Packer was an interventionist proprietor and on occasions ordered articles to appear in his magazines. Kennedy also seemed to resent the fact that he was excluded from certain meetings, a problem he shared with Turnbull, and that he was often treated more as an employee than a partner. Being excluded from meetings with Packer seemed to particularly upset him. But as far as Colson was concerned, this was Kennedy's problem—he wasn't a principal in the deal.

After reviewing Kennedy's perceived problems, Colson and Powers decided it was time to sort Kennedy out. They had little confidence in him and something had to be done.

Kennedy hadn't signed his employment contract yet. It had been agreed that he would be paid $500 000 a year plus $150 000 in expenses. The contract terms were to be three years and he would receive 10 million free options to subscribe for shares in Fairfax.

Doubts arose now whether Kennedy was worth such a lucrative package. The two men agreed they would have to see some changes—Kennedy must convince them he had the ability to do the job.

■　■　■

The odds were stacked against Kennedy. It was at least two against one. This was highly dangerous. The politics of business consortiums in emotionally charged transactions are always difficult, but this one was getting out of control. These three successful and ambitious businessmen had been thrown into the same corporate cage thanks to a billion-dollar takeover. It was not working out at all and Kennedy felt vulnerable.

Having been managing director of Consolidated Press, Kennedy was used to giving orders. He had done it for years as he directed the business interests of Australia's richest man. No one, except Kerry Packer, kicked Trevor Kennedy around.

Brian Powers had been the Taipan as head of Jardines in Hong Kong. He knew what power was and how to use it. He expected, and usually received, respect. Dan Colson was no novice to large commercial transactions either.

The three men came from very different corporate cultures. Colson and Powers compounded the differences because they were working in a strange environment. They were away from their families in a hotel in the middle of the central business district of a city they didn't particularly like. Kennedy was in familiar territory, however. He knew Fairfax well: he had worked there and it had been his major competitor for the last twenty years. He didn't need to do the cramming that Colson did to understand the market. Kennedy also had his social life to lead—he was not focused on the one business transaction.

Their personalities were very different too. Kennedy was expansive, sociable and very Australian. He suddenly found himself hard up against a Diet Coke brigade with calculators. Colson and Powers didn't drink coffee, nor much alcohol—only crates of Diet Coke. Kennedy placed much more emphasis on the social side of doing business. For him, in Australia, it had worked well until now.

When they arrived in Australia Colson and Powers had thought that Trev and 'Kerro'—Kennedy's nickname for Packer—were such good friends that it would be unwise to question Kennedy's credentials as a chief executive. So they were particularly careful when broaching their discontent about Kennedy's performance with Packer. They had raised the matter the previous week, as they threw a ball to each other around Packer's office—one of Packer's pastimes as he sits talking to those he knows. Packer, however, was lukewarm in his defence of his long-time right-hand man.

• • •

'Do you think he will get violent? Colson joked to Powers.

Kennedy was due to arrive in Colson's suite at the Regent Hotel at any minute. He had rung up to see what was happening for the day. It was Sunday morning.

'We'd like you to come in for a talk,' Colson said, and Kennedy had agreed, even though it would mean he would miss lunch at the home of Sam Chisholm, former boss of Packer's Nine Network.

Quickly Powers outlined the major problems to be raised and Colson scrawled them down on a piece of paper.

Powers believed that the discussion could be a constructive exercise to establish where both sides stood. It was not an execution. Kennedy would, however, have to accept a revised employment contract. Powers wondered how he would react, especially after the performance the previous morning.

'Perhaps he will start throwing punches,' Colson said, fidgeting as he tried to ease his nervousness.

Powers laughed as Colson jokingly picked up a heavy ashtray, then a letter opener and a pair of scissors and hid them in a cupboard.

There was a knock on the door. Inviting Kennedy in with a smile, Colson barely gave him time to sit down before his expression changed. He picked up the piece of paper and explained abruptly that there were problems that needed to be sorted out.

Then began the tough analysis of Kennedy's performance over the past three months. Kennedy listened as the Canadian lawyer reeled off his shortcomings and mistakes. The overseas trips, particularly his trips to the UK and Indonesia; his failure to become more involved in the valuations of Fairfax and the newsprint contract; his lack of skill in the production area; and his performance at the Print Media Inquiry made a strong case against him.

Colson dropped the bombshell. Before Tourang was prepared to give Kennedy a long contract, they needed to see more evidence that he was the right man for the job. It would be best if Kennedy took some financial risks, Colson said, if there was some incentive built into the contract. Kennedy should not expect lucrative financial rewards without first showing he could handle the position of chief executive.

This was too much for Kennedy. He had enjoyed the reputation as the most respected media executive in Australia and now he had to endure this assault on his ego, this questioning of his capabilities by two foreigners who had never worked in the industry.

Kennedy was furious. He argued vehemently that the trip to the UK was to finish off some Consolidated Press business. And Indonesia! He was part of a delegation to meet Indonesian President Suharto as a member of the Australia–Indonesia Institute. What employer could deny leave for that?

On his performance during due diligence he was blunt: 'I have been getting out there seeing advertisers and editors to get a feel for the business.' Raising his chin, he then launched the attack:

'What have *you* brought to the transaction?'

'At least I sit down until 8 pm [in meetings],' Colson replied with a snort.

Bristling, Kennedy turned on Colson: 'You're a mediocre lawyer.'

'You're a mediocre media executive,' Colson retorted.

Kennedy said that he wasn't going to listen any more. This arrogance astounded him. He could not tolerate another second of this personal assault. And to have the insults delivered by Colson made the situation even more unbearable. To Kennedy, Colson was a boring man who simply did the bidding of his master Conrad Black. He had come to despise Colson. Crimson-faced with anger, Kennedy stood up abruptly. He headed for the door and closed it firmly behind him.

* * *

Driving home across the Harbour Bridge to his waterfront home in Kirribilli, Kennedy thought long and hard about the disagreement with Colson and Powers. This job, which had looked so attractive, now had major drawbacks.

The demand that the employment contract be renegotiated was serious. How he wished he had signed it earlier when he had had the chance. He had been remiss and now regretted it.

Kennedy began to doubt whether he should accept the new terms for his employment. Colson and Powers were always going to be demanding, hassling him from overseas and watching his every move. The three would never get on.

There was also Packer to consider. For some reason he wasn't acting like an ally either. After all those years of loyalty, Packer was now deserting him. Powers and Colson were Packer's new mates. He knew of their visits over the past few months to Packer's Bellevue Hill estate for dinner; how Packer would insist on driving them back to their hotel. Kennedy wouldn't have been surprised if they'd been at Packer's the previous morning while he was waiting with the accountants. It was all very chummy.

His fears about being a chief executive in a consortium involving Packer were confirmed. Legally Packer could not be seen to have any involvement or influence at Fairfax if Tourang won, but there would be problems; he knew Packer too well.

The row with Colson and Powers compounded his fears, despite the fact that in the future they would only be in Australia for board meetings. As he ran through the issues, Kennedy knew that he must make a quick decision. It was only two days until the final bids for Fairfax went in.

He weighed his misgivings against the fact that the post as Fairfax's chief executive was one he had desperately wanted. To get this far and then drop out seemed crazy. He decided he would press ahead.

．　　．　　．

At 5 pm the next day Kennedy and his lawyer John Landerer walked into the reception area at Freehills and were escorted into Geoff Levy's office for a meeting with Colson. They were to run through the contract again. Kennedy intended to sign.

Within minutes he realised there were major problems: the terms were very different. There was no three-year contract—Tourang was only prepared to give him one for twelve months—and there was a six-month notice period.

Kennedy couldn't believe it—he had only six months' security of employment. The share options were much less attractive too—he would have to wait twelve months before he received any. They had reneged and changed the contract again. He left the room to find Powers.

'Yet again you have done the wrong thing,' he said sharply when he found him in the Tourang room.

Powers, on the back foot, was conciliatory: 'It's okay, we will change it back.'

Kennedy marched back into Levy's office saying with a sneer that he had sorted out the 'mistake'. Landerer and Levy were then spectators to a heated argument that ensued between Colson and Kennedy. The depth of the animosity between them made rational negotiation impossible. They could barely look at each other.

During a brief lull in the dispute, Landerer signalled to Kennedy to step outside briefly.

'Are you really sure you want to go ahead?' Landerer asked.

'Let's get out of here,' Kennedy replied.

Ten minutes later Colson and Levy, sick of waiting, came looking for them. There was no one there.

■ ■ ■

Kennedy decided it wasn't worth it. The prospect of a contract for six months was the last straw. In two days his employment contract had gone from three years to six months. It was unacceptable and he felt betrayed by the Canadian and American.

Kennedy was also bitter about Packer's involvement. He suspected that Packer was behind this fight somehow. The thought of Packer conspiring with Colson and Powers hurt.

Perhaps Packer had concluded that Kennedy would no longer be influenced by him if Tourang was successful. Being free from Packer suddenly appealed to him—he would be his own boss with his own power base.

Kennedy decided he would quit. The only obligation he felt was to telephone Black and tell him. The two men had got on well and as he dialled the telephone number Kennedy knew he would regret missing the opportunity to work with the Canadian media baron.

Black was gentle. He said he could give a thirty-minute dissertation on the reasons Kennedy shouldn't quit, how things would settle down. But Kennedy had made up his mind; he couldn't work with Powers or Colson.

The next morning Kennedy headed off to Park Street to tell Packer. As they spoke, any hopes that Packer would support him disappeared.

'You can stop this if you want too,' Kennedy said sharply.

Packer declined to be drawn into it. However, he did claim that he wasn't behind the manoeuvres to force Kennedy's hand.

'Losing your temper with Colson was a sign of immaturity,' Packer said.

Kennedy ran through the grievances that had been presented as examples of his lack of performance. Despite dubbing the whole thing a kangaroo court, Packer said he couldn't do anything.

'They are determined to get rid of you.'

Colson and Powers were contacted by Packer's secretary and half an hour later arrived down at Park Street. A calm Kennedy announced that he was resigning. The only thing to be sorted out was the terms of the resignation and he wanted that done quickly—he intended to call a press conference and explain what had happened. Packer, Colson and Powers were shocked. They couldn't allow that to happen.

An angry Kennedy on the loose would be a disaster for Tourang; he could not be allowed to ruin the deal. It was going to be enough of a public relations disaster losing the man they had touted to the institutions as Australia's best media executive without Kennedy fanning the flames. Already there were enough people looking for excuses to destroy the consortium.

They decided that in return for a severance payment of $500 000, a strict termination agreement would have to be signed. There was still the spectre of an ABT inquiry and Tourang wanted to make sure that Kennedy was circumspect about his knowledge of Tourang.

Colson called Levy and asked the lawyer to work out the termination agreement. But there was one more flank to be covered.

Powers rang Mark Burrows to ask if David Gonski could see him immediately; Gonski was to be the emissary to ensure that Kennedy's departure would not affect the Tourang bid being lodged that afternoon.

'That doesn't make any difference,' Burrows said, despite his surprise at the sudden exit of Kennedy. 'All the banks want is their money back.'

* * *

Kennedy retreated to Turnbull's office. Turnbull was shocked at the dumping of his friend. He and Kennedy had been working on this deal long before the birth of Tourang when Turnbull put up his plan for the bondholders to swap their debt for shares. Kennedy was to be the chief executive then and Turnbull couldn't believe Tourang would force him out now.

The episode fuelled his own resentment against Colson and Powers. Suppressing his anger temporarily Turnbull spent the next few hours arguing with Levy over the wording of the termination agreement.

Kennedy would receive his $500 000 with an immediate $100 000 payment plus another $400 000 in an escrow account. The terms were tough. Kennedy was not to disclose information about the affairs of Tourang and was required to return all information he had acquired during his employment by Tourang. He was not permitted to do anything that could reasonably be regarded as hindering Tourang's bid nor make any statements to the ABT unless those statements were vetted by Freehills.

A directors meeting was hastily convened and the termination agreement approved.

There was much discussion over Kennedy's exit—how to explain it with the minimum of embarrassment and, if possible, to the maximum advantage of the bid. There was no way that Tourang would divulge the real reasons behind Kennedy's exit, disclosing the bitterness and hostility behind the scenes.

The vetted statement on Kennedy's resignation went out using the line of unfair treatment of the syndicate. Kennedy decried that there would continue to be people who didn't accept that he was independent because he had been in the employment of Consolidated Press.

This is 'McCarthyism' the Kennedy statement said—'unjust and unwarranted':

> ... the task ahead for the new chief executive of Fairfax is going to be an extremely difficult one and in my view it would be impossible for me to carry it out if there are to be continued inquiries and investigations into my independence.

It was an inglorious end for Kennedy—his dream of returning to Fairfax to occupy the chief executive's corner suite on the fourteenth floor was dead. Thanks to a Canadian and an American Kennedy had unexpectedly fulfilled his life goal of retiring before fifty. He had been cut down ruthlessly. On the very day bids were due to be delivered to Burrows.

CHAPTER FOURTEEN

TOURANG UNDER SEIGE

MARK JOHNSON and Simon McKeon were silent in the elevator. As they walked out of the building and into Macquarie Place Johnson broke the tension. 'Our price was too low,' he said.

'Yes, I know,' Simon replied flatly.

Burrows had made no comment when he read through the AIN bid a few minutes earlier in the Baring Brothers boardroom. AIN's bid was the first to arrive on the deadline day (Tuesday, October 15) and they had expected some feedback.

Johnson hadn't been in corporate advice for over twenty years without learning a bit about body language. When an auction is under way every piece of intelligence you can pick up is crucial. You can tell a lot from human behaviour; there is a sparkle in the eyes when you are ahead.

The AIN bid handed to Burrows came in under the bank debt of $1.25 billion. The bottom line actually read $1.365 billion but $200 million of that was a share issue to be taken by the banks. This is known as soft equity.

Banks don't particularly like it. It means a part of their loan is not repaid in real dollars but in shares or notes that would be repaid when a stock exchange listing goes ahead some months down the track.

The only advantage of soft equity is that a bank can pretend it received 100 cents in the dollar for its debt and so doesn't have to take any write downs in its accounts. AIN's offer proposed a public listing of Fairfax on the stock exchange by May 1992. The banks would be entitled to be paid their outstanding $200 million plus interest at fifteen per cent out of the proceeds of that share issue.

If that issue could not fully pay out the banks, however, the banks would then have to take up shares in Fairfax to cover the difference.

The AIN bid price consisted of: $400 million in equity capital from AIN's institutional backers; $655 million in loans from the banks (known as senior debt); $200 million from the bank's underwriting agreement; and $110 million in zero coupon debentures. (These debentures were to be given to the unsecured creditors as a part payment of their debts. They would not be repaid in full.)

AIN actually presented four bids to Burrows that afternoon. One higher bid (outlined above), which had been approved by its top six backers, and one lower bid, which had been approved by its institutional backers. Each of these bids was for the shares in the John Fairfax Group company. The first bid was conditional on the approval of the other institutional backers. The second was unconditional. AIN had gone through this charade to ensure tight security for the terms of the higher offer.

Alongside the bid for the shares was a bid for the assets of the company. Burrows had requested the asset bid to pass around the problem of the junk bondholders and their exclusive deal with Tourang. If a bidder other than Tourang was to be the chosen purchaser of Fairfax, and that bidder could not come to an arrangement with the bondholders, then the banks would sell them the assets out of the company structure instead of selling them shares in the company itself.

AIN's asset bid came in at $1.303 billion.

■　■　■

Rowan Ross, Peter Hunt and John Reynolds sat quietly at Baring Brothers' boardroom table at 4 pm while Burrows scanned their share offer and asset sale offer. This was more like it, Burrows thought. The O'Reilly team appeared to have come in under the bank debt but was close enough to the wire to allow Burrows some leverage later.

Jeff White had spent hours going through the strategy with Ross a few days earlier—if Baring Brothers could get an asset offer for Fairfax which was higher than the bank debt, then the junk bondholders became irrelevant.

Ross had not been convinced and O'Reilly's asset offer came in just under bank debt. Burrows, nevertheless, felt that there was room for negotiation.

The bottom line of the O'Reilly share offer was $1.429 billion. It was made up of $120 million in equity from Independent Newspapers and $480 million from a share float. The float would be fully underwritten by stockbrokers J B Were & Son. In addition there was $600 million in senior debt, cash on hand in Fairfax of $48 million and $190 million in switching bonds. Of this $190 million, $108 million went to the unsecured creditors and the remaining $82 million was the soft section for the banks.

These switching bonds which made up the banks' soft section were a little unusual—but like all soft equity the bottom line was that the bank didn't get all of its money back immediately. They had to wait for some of it—in this case $82 million worth.

The switching bonds were a novel device. The cash interest for the banks would be four per cent less than that paid on the senior debt. The difference in interest would be paid as a lump sum when the bonds were repaid. The bonds had a life of ten years but would be repaid early if the company's interest cover was three times earnings at any stage or if Independent raised new equity at any stage.

The O'Reilly asset offer was for slightly less. It came in at $1.362 billion or $67 million less than the share offer. The banks had to take a higher level of switching bonds—$122 million under the asset proposal compared with $82 million under the share proposal.

The O'Reilly contingent left and, smiling, Burrows turned to White.

'We are in the money. We've got a game on here!'

*　*　*

The Tourang bid was late. At 6 pm Geoff Levy hand-delivered it to Burrows who took it into his office. It was a shocker and he was angry that his warnings to Tourang not to treat the banks as idiots had fallen on deaf ears.

Tourang's offer was below the bank debt by $200 million. Under the structure the banks would receive $400 million in cash and $850 million in reformulated bank facilities. Of the $400 million in cash, $162.5 million would be equity subscribed by the Telegraph, Kerry Packer and Hellman & Friedman.

The remaining $137.5 million would be equity from Australian investors—the issue fully underwritten by Ord Minnett. The $850 million in reformulated bank facilities would be made up of $400 million to be repaid with accumulated interest in five years; $200 million to be repaid normally over five years; and a $250 million ten-year loan with repayments and interest dependent on the performance of the Fairfax Group.

Without going through it too closely Burrows realised that this $250 million meant in fact that the banks would emerge with repayments of between $150 million and $200 million less than their outstanding debt. The variation depended on how well or badly Fairfax performed over the ten years. Throwing the offer into his in-tray Burrows knew this transaction had a long way to go—he still hadn't got the banks their money back.

There was nothing more he could do tonight. He locked the offices, wandered down to his 911 turbo Porsche and headed to the Tilbury Hotel in Woolloomooloo where he spent the evening laughing his way through the live comedy show 'Three Men and a Baby Grand'.

■   ■   ■

On the Wednesday morning, 16 October, Fairfax dominated the news bulletins.

It wasn't leaked details of offers, however, but a report of an extraordinary political coupling prompted by the sale of Fairfax. Former Prime Ministers Gough Whitlam and Malcolm Fraser had joined eminent ex-politicians to campaign against concentration of media ownership. This exceptional event had been set in train the previous Friday when former coalition minister Peter Nixon had pulled a crumpled piece of paper out of his pocket and handed it to Malcolm Fraser.

Since retiring from politics in 1983, Nixon had spent his days pottering around his cattle property in the Snowy River region near Orbost in eastern Victoria's high country. He had been listening intently, however, to the daily television and radio reports about the tussle for ownership of the Fairfax Group.

He was angry and alarmed about Packer's involvement in Tourang and the level of foreign ownership being considered. Running into AIN's chairman Jim Leslie at the airport recently he had commented how, for the only time since he left politics, he felt like writing a letter to the *Age*.

He made the decision to do something practical: he couldn't just sit back and watch Australia's press freedom threatened. As a former politician he knows the power that the media wields and the dangers of placing too much power in too few hands.

Nixon decided to put out a statement against media concentration with high-profile political names as signatories. He prepared a draft and showed it to his brother-in-law John Dahlsen to check for defamation problems. Dahlsen too had a keen interest in the print media. He had been chairman of the Herald & Weekly Times before it was acquired by Murdoch and is a lawyer with Corrs in Melbourne, the firm acting for Independent Newspapers. He is also a director of the ANZ Bank.

Following Dahlsen's clearance, Nixon showed the letter to Malcolm Fraser, the Prime Minister he had served under in the 1970s. Fraser was very receptive to the idea. For months Fraser had been telling friends and associates that he was appalled by the prospect of Fairfax, in particular the *Age*, falling into foreign hands or a consortium involving Packer.

Fraser had even telephoned Johnson at Macquarie Bank in March and offered his support for the AIN cause. The offer was passed on to Harley and McKay but rejected. Even then they had realised that AIN ran the risk of a Liberal Party taint—and Fraser was just a little bit too Western Districts Liberal Party branch for their liking.

Agreeing with Nixon that immediate action was called for, Fraser made an astonishing telephone call. He rang Gough Whitlam, the man he replaced as Prime Minister in 1975. Given the historic animosity between the two over Fraser's role in the sacking of Whitlam's progressive Labor Government in 1975, it was a surprising move.

Fraser was the man Whitlam dubbed 'Kerr's Curr' on the steps of Parliament House after the rosy-faced Governor-General Sir John Kerr caused a constitutional crisis by sacking the Government. Fraser was the man who had sparked the Labor Party election theme 'Shame Fraser Shame', and whose ascendancy to the prime ministership had deeply divided the nation.

Gough Whitlam had urged his followers to 'Maintain the Rage', but time had mellowed his bitterness towards Fraser. Without hesitation he joined Nixon and Fraser—he was well-aware of the power of media proprietors to make or break governments. Whitlam had spent the 1960s being berated by Sir Frank Packer's *Daily Telegraph* as it backed the Liberal Party; then there was Murdoch's support for Whitlam in 1972 followed by the dirty, slanted and concerted campaign by his Australian newspapers to oust him in 1975. Whitlam had had a few salutary lessons on why interventionist newspaper proprietors are an anathema to democratic societies.

Fraser faxed the letter through to Whitlam for his approval. 'Gough won't be able to help himself,' Nixon joked. 'He'll completely rewrite it.'

Whitlam faxed it back with two commas changed.

A letter boasting Whitlam's and Fraser's signatures would have been enough of an event to ensure widespread publicity but Nixon wanted to give the letter even further clout. He was after every major political party represented by a former leader.

By Monday afternoon Nixon had the support of Doug Anthony, the former Deputy Prime Minister and Leader of the National Party; Janine Haines, former Leader of the Democrats; Lance Barnard, former Labor Deputy Prime Minister; Frank Crean, former Labor Deputy Prime Minister and Treasurer; and Margaret Guilfoyle, former senior Liberal cabinet minister and senator. The letter read in part:

> The dangers of increased domination of media ownership are very real and very serious with major implications for the Government of Australia.
>
> As past senior political figures, we have a deep and realistic understanding of the powers and influence of the media.

We know of the mechanisms that can be, and have been used to influence policies. We know of circumstances in which such powers have been used.

Parliament must remain supreme, with its integrity and the public interest protected at all times.

It must not allow a power to be established in Australia which can challenge the supremacy of Parliament.

The implications of the decisions shortly to be made about the future of the Fairfax newspapers will affect the shape of Australian life for generations to come.

Parliament has the power to make sure that the right thing is done for Australia and that Fairfax shareholders and creditors are dealt with fairly and equitably.

It is not only a question of market domination by one or two powerful players. There is a second question of Australian ownership and control.

Present government decisions limit foreign ownership to twenty per cent of voting capital. With available corporate arrangements, that in itself is sufficient to give foreign control.

This is a matter for Government and for the Opposition. Government and Opposition must understand the importance of the issues they are dealing with—and the consequences for Australia.

Thinking the Kennedy resignation would lead the news that morning, Colson and Powers were perplexed about the amount of publicity given to this Fraser–Whitlam alliance. It had managed to capture the attention of millions of Australians not previously interested in the fate of Fairfax.

Powers and Colson were receiving a rapid lesson in recent Australian political history. They couldn't comprehend why this letter from a few politicians was being interpreted as extremely damaging for Tourang.

. . .

At 7.30 am that same morning groups of journalists began to gather at every major transport artery in Sydney—Circular Quay, Wynyard railway station, Town Hall station, North Sydney, Chatswood, Bondi Junction, Martin Place. They were tense. This was a last-ditch effort to stop Tourang.

A twenty-four-hour strike had been called by a meeting of journalists the afternoon before and they were hitting the streets to get their message out. Final bids were in and Fairfax could have a new owner within the month.

The ANZ Bank was the target of the day's demonstrations. A brochure handed to commuters included a form with a message for Will Bailey, the chief executive of ANZ. It read: 'Dear Mr Bailey, I believe in a free and independent press and a diversity of ownership of the media. If you sell the Fairfax papers to Mr Packer, I will close my accounts with the ANZ Bank.' Sympathisers were asked to send the completed forms to the Friends of Fairfax, which would pass them on to the bank's executives. Over the next week two thousand forms would be sent in.

At midday journalists began picketing the New South Wales headquarters of the ANZ Bank in Martin Place. Hundreds gathered waving mock newspaper posters with messages: 'Save us from Packer'; 'Stop Kerry from forming World Series Fairfax. It's just not cricket'; 'Don't let Fairfax turn into their facts'; and a Dick Tracy cardboard cut-out with gun blazing and Kerry Packer's photograph pasted over the face demanding: 'Hand over all your newspapers'.

Television networks turned out in force to hear journalists such as Matthew Moore and Peter Bowers accuse the Government of lying down like dogs over media concentration. In Melbourne journalists from the *Age* and the *Sunday Age* declined to go on strike but protested for two hours outside ANZ's headquarters in Collins Street.

It was Tourang's worst nightmare. The Fraser–Whitlam alliance, the Sydney journalists strike and Kennedy's resignation hit the consortium like a cyclone. Any hopes of the political outcry easing over time were shattered. The deal was fast becoming much more than a purely commercial transaction and Colson and Powers were in the eye of the cyclone.

It was now painfully obvious that the potential for widespread opposition had been grossly underestimated by Tourang's local 'experts'.

Walking up Pitt Street late Wednesday morning the two men were deep in discussion. Surely there was some way to get their side of the argument across, Colson argued.

As they approached Martin Place a casually dressed man thrust a pamphlet toward Colson's swinging hand. Stopping, he realised what it was even before he took it. It was a Friends of Fairfax pamphlet. Colson couldn't resist the opportunity to hear first-hand the arguments against his syndicate.

'So what's this all about'? he asked.

The journalist began a quick summation of the evils of media concentration, foreign ownership, Kerry Packer and Rupert Murdoch. Colson and Powers nodded. If this guy only knew who he was talking too, Colson thought.

'So what's this Conrad Black bloke like?' Colson asked.

'Oh, he and Packer are in bed together—and you can imagine what a sight that makes,' came the quick response.

Changing the emphasis, Powers suggested that the issue might damage Australia's international reputation—opposing foreign investment was bad for a small country like this. The journalist responded by explaining the need to keep key assets in Australian hands, an argument that Powers refuted on economic grounds.

Colson cheekily suggested that the Fairfax Group needed a strong proprietor to keep the journalists in line.

'That guy must think we are real dickheads,' Colson commented to Powers as they continued up the street. But his mood sank as he saw enthusiastic journalists milling on street corners and passers-by closely reading their handouts. This was bizarre.

At Freehills they were joined by Neville Miles, Carnegie and the Freehill lawyers. Conversation centred on the barrage of publicity against Tourang as they explained to the foreigners who Fraser and Whitlam were.

'Something has to be done,' Colson warned as he realised the gravity of the problem. 'This is starting to get out of control.'

Tourang was being denigrated in an unbalanced and hysterical campaign and it was all one-way traffic. It was decided that Tourang needed to counter the publicity and that John Singleton was the man for the job.

'Singo', the craggy-faced advertising man, is well and truly a member of the House of Packer—he is also a friend of Kennedy and Turnbull and mixes in the New South Wales right-wing Labor Party circles. He and Packer are long-time friends. They have known and liked each other since the early 1970s when

Singleton worked with Packer on advertising for the Australian *Women's Weekly*.

Singleton was in and immediately began to toss around some ideas on Wednesday evening. He thought Tourang was an evil name but still approached his task with enthusiasm. This was a major challenge.

The thrust of the campaign was to convince people that Tourang was a new form of rose—everyone should have one in their home. When it came to Packer, Singleton proposed a campaign to improve the image of his friend. Perhaps an advertisement featuring the face of Kerry with the catch-line:

'I may not be Robert Redford, but that doesn't make me Boris Karloff.'

. . .

Dan Colson had had enough of Sydney. He wanted to get back to London and regain some sanity. Burrows had been sitting on their bids for nearly two days now. He must have made a decision and it had to be Tourang—no one else could deliver the junk bondholders.

They met at 12.45 pm on Thursday. Colson was blunt. 'What's the decision?'

'There is no decision,' Burrows replied.

'I want to get back to London; how long will I have to wait?' Colson asked wearily.

'Well, go back to London. It will be at least a week before we are ready to talk again.'

Colson left vowing to get on the next plane and Burrows prepared to journey to Canberra. There was a Liberal Party dinner at Parliament House that night and Burrows was an invited guest of Opposition Leader John Hewson.

Later that evening Burrows found himself in a corner with Ken Cowley, managing director of News Limited. Although Murdoch was not a player in the Fairfax sale Cowley was unhappy about the prospect of Packer getting his foot into Fairfax—especially as it seemed the cross-media laws had a loophole that was bad for Murdoch.

Murdoch was allowed a five per cent shareholding in a metropolitan television station but Packer could hold 14.9 per cent of Fairfax. It was an anomaly and Cowley didn't mind pointing that out. There was also the fear that Packer might end up owning Fairfax—the prospect of a tough competitor like Packer didn't appeal.

Their conversation did not go unnoticed.

* * *

By 9 am the next morning Burrows was back in his Sydney office. He was linked into a conference call with four other parties— Citibank in New York; Karen Bechtel at Morgan Stanley, the adviser on the bondholders, in New York; John Atkin at Mallesons in Sydney; and lawyer Fred Cohen in New York, also advising on the bondholders.

Burrows carefully took them through the intricacies of the three bids. The call lasted two hours, each party questioning Burrows closely. At 11.15 that Friday morning there was another telephone hook up. This time it was just lawyers and Burrows in a detailed discussion of the strategy to be adopted. The bids were still too low but there was room to manoeuvre.

They were in to the 'bid enhancement period', an expression the bidders would become very familiar with.

* * *

The fury of the campaign against Tourang continued unabated in Canberra. The Caucus decision on foreign ownership was still the subject of enormous bitterness amongst Government ranks— the railroading of Cabinet votes had been dirty play.

The ructions and divisions within Caucus provided a wonderful opportunity for the Federal Opposition to embarrass the struggling Government in Parliament. The Opposition Leader in the Senate, Robin Hill, fired a question at Senator John Button, well-aware that Button had strong personal views on the fate of Fairfax. Asked whether Tourang's offer would increase media concentration, Button didn't disguise the anger he still felt over the Caucus vote: 'This is not a matter which goes to my portfolio responsibility, but I think the answer to the question would probably be yes.'

In the House of Representatives Beazley was on the back foot under a concerted Opposition attack on the issue. Beazley's answers sat uneasily with Button's comment and emphasised the rifts in the Cabinet. He argued that the only way Tourang's ownership of Fairfax could lead to an unacceptable level of media ownership was if Packer's 14.9 per cent holding was an instrument of control or influence rather than simply an investment.

Acting Prime Minister Brian Howe refused to answer Opposition questions. However, the following day he read a prepared statement: 'If the bid were to establish a control or influence over the operations of the Fairfax Group by Mr Packer, he would be in breach of the Broadcasting Act and be obliged to divest.'

The comment came as the Opposition finally approved the last few amendments to the Broadcasting Amendment Bill, which gave the ABT wider powers to examine potential breaches of the cross-media ownership laws.

On a trip to Japan John Kerin weighed into the debate and gave an outline of the factors he would be considering when he came to examine the Tourang and Independent offers. It was not good news for Tourang. Kerin said he would be looking at aspects of competition, quality, retention of the empire, journalistic and editorial freedom and other such matters, rather than just ownership *per se*.

This was the first enunciation of Kerin's views on the issues he deemed relevant to the national interest in exercising his sweeping discretionary powers under foreign investment guidelines.

The political pressure continued on the weekend as the Victorian Labor Party's State Conference considered the media issue, passing a motion calling on the Federal Government to take all possible steps to ensure that there would be no further concentration of media ownership in Australia. Australian Council of Trade Unions president Martin Ferguson also chimed in to remind all present that the union movement was very supportive of campaigns against further concentration of media ownership and greater foreign ownership.

Meanwhile a besieged Beazley appeared on Channel Nine's 'Sunday' programme and defended the Labor Party against allegations that it granted favours to media proprietors, or had any media mates:

Basically there are only sporadic social relationships which take place between people who are owners of the press in this country and Governments—I might say Governments of all political hue. Politicians, when it comes to friends, are essentially loners and the media in this country has decided from time to time to support one party or another and if they've been supporting you they are always likely to desert you. So there aren't any media mates.

Beazley's logic was odd—just because a proprietor deserts the Labor Party doesn't mean it wouldn't try to ensure the desertions were less frequent. Beazley also pointed out that other foreign countries don't restrict foreign ownership of newspapers:

I don't think a Britisher has owned the London *Times* for about seventy years. Of course, Conrad Black is a player in the British market as well as Rupert Murdoch. You go to the US and Canada, and it's the same story. There has always been an acceptance in every country with which we like to compare ourselves that there is a difference between foreign ownership in the print media and foreign ownership in broadcasting.

■　■　■

The theme music of 'A Current Affair' faded out. Jana Wendt, the presenter of Australia's highest rating news programme, began: 'Representatives from the John Fairfax Group will be joining us shortly, but first, the man they consider their foe, Kerry Packer. Mr Packer, thank you very much indeed for your time this evening.'

Kerry Packer, his half-glasses perched on the end of his nose, smiled. 'Pleasure, Jana.'

'You are the richest man in Australia with vast commercial interests. How much influence does your money bring with it?' Wendt asked her boss.

'Not very much,' said Packer.

The Tourang public relations fightback campaign was well under way. Singleton's advertising ideas had been discarded in favour of the big man himself coming out to defend his role.

The previous night—Tuesday, 22 October—Wendt had interviewed Conrad Black via a satellite hook-up with London. On

Thursday she would interview the two former Prime Ministers, Malcolm Fraser and Gough Whitlam.

On Tuesday Paul Keating had done his bit for the Tourang campaign at a National Press Club luncheon, arguing that if Fairfax was owned by Tourang, it would not lead to increased media concentration in Australia. According to Keating, sitting on the backbenches while his supporters conducted guerilla warfare to destabilise Hawke's leadership, Packer wasn't going to be anything more than a minority shareholder in Fairfax.

Therefore, Keating explained, you can't make the link that there would be a massive concentration of media ownership. It was a theme taken up that evening when Conrad Black made his hastily arranged 'A Current Affair' appearance.

Black stated that the opponents of Packer were guilty of an 'absolutely scurrilous campaign of defamation'. He vowed that he would not be deterred in his quest for Fairfax despite the opposition.

But Black's appearance was really only a warm-up for the main event—Kerry Packer on the silver screen. The Packer family hasn't owned television stations for three decades without young Kerry picking up a few tricks along the way. His television performance was magnificent.

'You are regarded as a very powerful man indeed. Do you see yourself as someone with a lot of power?' Wendt asked.

Packer answered ingenuously: 'No, I don't. I mean, I was brought up in a family that exercised a lot of power. I saw my father exercise power and he did exercise it. And I have never exercised it. And that's a deliberate intention on my part.'

Wendt: 'Never in any of your commercial interests, never exercised any power at all?'

Packer: 'Oh, I don't know what any power means. But by and large I do not exercise power. I do not try to exercise power and I certainly haven't used any influence that I have for my own benefit in running companies.'

Wendt: 'You provoke such ferocious opposition. Why do you think that is?'

Packer: 'Well, I don't know but I suppose it is because I don't often suffer fools gladly and I am prepared to stand up for what I believe in. And that's not always popular.'

Wendt: 'You inspire fear in lots of people including some of your employees. Is that the way you prefer it?'

Packer: 'It's not a matter of preferring it. If you're going to be a nice fellow and you're going to be the person everyone loves, then you're probably going to find out in life that the things that should be done, aren't done. Now, unfortunately ... I mean the Navy, all the places which have been used to authority over a long period of time separate the captain from the crew ... I have accepted the fact that I am the captain of my ship and I will do what I have to do to get things done, that I need to be done. And that doesn't make me popular. I know that, but that's the price of being successful. And that's a choice I made a long time ago.'

Asked how he reacted to being seen by some as an insidious force threatening the independence of a great newspaper group, Packer focused on the control issue:

'I have a problem answering that because it's such a preposterous suggestion, and it's been put forward by so many people who should know better that I find it extraordinary. Fifteen per cent will not control John Fairfax. Under the law, all I'm allowed is fifteen per cent. I have known that from day one. I will not control Tourang, which is the company that is bidding for John Fairfax. Why the big lie, why the suggestion I'm going to control it? I'm not going to control it.'

Packer stated that his interest in Fairfax was because the Group had been a competitor of his family for so many years: 'The idea that I can end up buying fifteen per cent of John Fairfax, and the Fairfax family have departed from Fairfax, amuses me.'

His face broke into a smile.

A panel of three journalists—Tom Burton from the *Herald*, Ken Davidson from the *Age* and Alan Kennedy from the Friends of Fairfax—were brought onto the set and there was no doubt who the captain was.

Packer went straight on the attack—it was like three schoolboys in the principal's office. Waving the Australian Journalists Association Code of Ethics menacingly, Packer attacked Tom Burton, challenging him to read out the code of ethics, thrusting it towards him and accusing the Fairfax journalists of breaching ethics.

It was a daunting sight; the large frame of Packer attempting to totally intimidate Burton, continuing his tirade about the 'Big Lie' which he claimed the Fairfax organisation was perpetrating over his alleged control of Tourang.

As the debate raged Packer also accused News Ltd of distorting the truth about Tourang: 'The truth of the matter is that News Limited don't want Conrad Black as a partner either.'

Packer then focused on one of the points that he and Colson had agreed was key to the argument. He claimed that the public shareholders would control Tourang since they would own sixty-five per cent of the shares.

'They can vote in or out anyone they like. They own the majority of the shares. That's how directors are appointed. Surely you know that.'

Under questioning, however, Packer was forced to concede that Conrad Black had appointed Sir Zelman Cowen and Sir Laurence Street to the board. He also admitted that he was involved in helping to get the bid going but maintained that after it succeeded he would only have 14.9 per cent.

As the interview went past 7 pm—with no attempt to wind up the boss—Packer vowed that he would continue to pursue Fairfax.

'Until this criticism arrived, it wasn't worth fighting for and it wasn't—I didn't really mind whether I got into it or didn't get into it. It's only now that it's become important.'

* * *

Mark Burrows didn't think Tourang was fighting hard enough. The next afternoon on Thursday, 24 October, David Gonski was told in no uncertain terms that the Tourang bid was lousy. Burrows had his own new term for lousy: 'Your bid is sub-economic,' he said.

'In your offer the banks have to take a haircut of up to $200 million. Why would they do that when you are paying the bondholders $125 million?'

Gonski was deputising for the Tourang team on negotiations with Burrows because Powers and Colson had left Australia. He didn't relish the prospect of passing on the message.

The O'Reilly team was given a better run by Burrows. At their bid appraisal meeting Rowan Ross and Peter Hunt were told:

'Your bid was the most professional of the lot, but there is not enough clarity.'

Burrows didn't say it outright but the banking syndicate had decided on Tuesday afternoon that they were prepared to accept a small amount of soft equity in the price as long as it was more defined than in either the O'Reilly or AIN first proposals.

AIN were the last to meet with Burrows. Mark Johnson was called in on the Friday and told the price was still way below bank debt.

'We are now into a bid enhancement programme,' Burrows told him.

Burrows was keen to screw down the bidding process but he knew that this was only one side of the equation. The political process was chaotic. Political history was being rewritten every day thanks to the Fairfax furore.

* * *

John Langmore and David Connolly sit on vastly different sides of the political spectrum; Langmore is left-wing Labor and Connolly a member of the Liberal Party. But they agreed on one thing— they shared the same philosophy on the dangers of further concentration of media ownership.

On Thursday, 24 October they met and reached an historic decision. They agreed to circulate a petition among MPs from both sides of the political fence directed at media concentration. Once signed, it would be presented to Hawke.

The move was brilliantly timed to capitalise on the widespread dissent among both Labor and Liberal backbenchers on the topic. It was today's parliamentarians attempting to achieve what yesterday's political leaders had achieved so dramatically with their letter earlier in the week.

Signatories to the petition asked the Prime Minister to:

... oppose the sale of the Fairfax Group to any individual or consortium that would result in a greater concentration of media ownership, and thus a diminution of competition and of the diversity of information sources in Australia.

There was a rush to sign. By that afternoon 128 of the 195 members of parliament who were not ministers had placed their names on the petition. The response was exceptional considering that some twenty MPs could not be contacted.

With the signatures rolling in, Langmore and Connolly called a press conference to announce the petition. Langmore admitted that it was directed at Tourang—based on the available evidence, he said, Tourang would add to media concentration.

Ministers didn't sign the petition and the New South Wales right-wing faction of the Labor Party was noticeable in its refusal to sign.

The petition did cause unrest among some of the Caucus members. Western Australian MP Dr Ric Charlesworth circulated a letter warning of the dangers of involving the Opposition since a bi-partisan approach could lead to disgruntled Caucus members trying to overturn other contentious issues.

A member of the Print Media Inquiry, Charlesworth added that he had heard little evidence before the inquiry to suggest that Black would represent an undesirable force in the Australian media.

In the Tourang camp the petition added to the growing sense of exasperation over the political fury whipped up against its bid. The momentum was maintained on Friday when Whitlam and Fraser appeared at a rally against media concentration in Melbourne's Treasury Gardens.

It was organised by the Age Independence Committee (AIC) and almost 2000 people attended. Among the speakers was ACTU President Martin Ferguson.

'It's now for the community at large, not just the union movement alone, to stand up and be counted on this issue,' Ferguson implored. To thunderous applause Fraser added that a sale of Fairfax to Tourang would be a 'crime against the Australian people'.

Trades Hall Council Secretary John Halfpenny; Janet Powell, a former Leader of the Australian Democrats; and David Wilson added their voices to the chorus against Packer.

The gathering ended with Whitlam and Fraser putting a motion calling on the Government and Opposition to do everything possible to prevent further media concentration and foreign ownership.

On Sunday, 27 October, the performance was repeated before a delighted crowd of 1500 at the Darling Harbour Convention Centre in Sydney. Fraser and Whitlam joined hands and held them high before the cheering crowd. For those with memories of the bitter events of 1975, it was an unbelievable and emotional event.

Fraser took up the anti-Tourang theme with conviction:

'If there are two media empires, and it's Murdoch and the Black–Packer consortium, there will be a power outside Parliament capable of challenging the integrity of Parliament.'

Calling on MPs to pass a resolution through Parliament as a private members bill he said any sale to Tourang could be blocked.

'If nothing happens we, the ordinary voters of Australia, will know to our cost how far the rot has already gone because we will know how intimidated the Parliament has already become.'

The crowd roared its agreement.

* * *

The following Tuesday, with October drawing to a close, it was the turn of the Baring Brothers team to cross the Harbour Bridge and front Peter Westerway at the ABT.

Until now Burrows had taken the line that he would not be part of the ABT process. He was very concerned about Foreign Investment Review Board (FIRB) and would consult with them frequently. The ABT matters, however, he was leaving to the bidders to clarify themselves.

Westerway had changed all that. He had taken the initiative and asked Burrows to meet with him.

Jeff White, Peter Breese, John Atkin and Burrows were spread around the leather sofas in Westerway's office. They sat stunned as Westerway outlined his demands. He wanted prior notice of everything Baring Brothers did and proposed to do regarding the Fairfax sale.

'What does that mean ... including how we think?' Burrows asked.

Westerway nodded. 'Yes.'

He wanted to know when Baring Brothers was going to make a decision and required at least forty-eight hours notice of it forming a view on the matter.

'I am not in the habit of doing that,' Burrows protested.

Westerway was unruffled. 'I can compel you with formal directions,' he said. Burrows backed off.

'Oh, we don't have to get into that,' he spluttered and undertook to place the ABT on the same level as his dealings with FIRB. 'We will make it our business to inform you when we make a decision.'

Westerway was cool and polite. He pointed out that Malcolm Turnbull was a problem for Tourang in some areas. Giles Tanner, the ABT lawyer sitting at the back of the conversation pit interjected.

'I can think of three of four issues.'

* * *

While Burrows was debating with Westerway, Langmore and Connolly were visiting Hawke's office with the bi-partisan petition. It now had 137 signatures. The level of support was incredible and an important indication of the sentiment within Parliament.

There was the telling lack of support from the New South Wales right-wing faction of the Labor Party—the faction of the pretender to the throne Paul Keating and his supporter Graham Richardson—but at least they had the Prime Minister on side.

Hawke asked Langmore if he could sign the petition as the member for Wills. This was not proper, since the petition was actually addressed to the Prime Minister. It was a damaging blow to Tourang.

The petition showed clearly that the majority of the elected representatives in a parliamentary democracy was against anything that potentially could leave Australia's media in the hands of just two men—Murdoch and Packer.

* * *

Colson and Powers returned to Australia early that week to face an even worse political situation than the one they had left behind a fortnight earlier.

This was unbelievable. Colson was not a political naif. He had worked at one stage for former Canadian Prime Minister Pierre Trudeau but he had never seen anything like this. Also the response to their bid by Burrows, as relayed to them by Gonski, infuriated them. What the hell was Burrows up to? He was stage-managing this like a Shakespearian play. They had the bond-holders tied up with the exclusivity agreement—how could Burrows deal with anyone else anyway?

Burrows was unimpressed. He was still considering what to do about the bondholders and wasn't convinced that the bondholder agreement was as strong as Tourang had persistently claimed. Since he hadn't been shown the exclusivity agreement, how could he know that it was as tough as Colson claimed?

■　　■　　■

That afternoon there was a call from Kerry Packer. Would Burrows come down to his Consolidated Press office in Park Street? Certainly, Burrows replied, he'd come for afternoon tea as long as there was cake. When he arrived Dan Colson was there as well as a gigantic plate of cake.

'There seems to be a problem, Mark,' Packer began. 'You want us to put all of our cards on the table. As a poker player, I am not used to that.'

Burrows repeated his statements of earlier that day—he could not assess the strength of the bondholder agreement without seeing it. Later Gonski rang. Packer had been on the telephone and told him to get Burrows a copy of the agreement.

■　　■　　■

Another more serious meeting was held at the Park Street office that evening on Wednesday, 30 October. The three men stood before Kerry Packer as if he were a Solomon figure to adjudicate on a dispute. It was a miscast role—he was too involved to be independent.

Turnbull was extremely agitated—he was becoming increasingly upset about Powers' and Colson's attitudes to his role within Tourang.

'They are trying to destabilise my position,' he said to Packer.

Listening as Turnbull outlined his defence, neither Powers nor Colson was particularly interested. They didn't like him and the frustration of the sales process and political and public opposition to Tourang was wearing them down. Each day gave more scope for disagreements and Turnbull was the main gripe.

The blow-up over the exclusivity agreement in late June had not been forgotten by either Powers or Turnbull and the sniping at each other continued.

Colson and Powers were increasingly worried about Turnbull's presence in the transaction. His involvement, just like the deposed Kennedy, was viewed as a potential problem with the ABT which, triggered by his prior relations with Packer, was still sniffing around Tourang. His proposed directorship of Fairfax would also be of interest to the ABT searching for a whiff of any arrangements or understandings that would give Packer more control than his stated passive 14.9 per cent shareholding.

Packer was acutely aware that an ABT inquiry before the sale would jeopardise his continued membership of the consortium because the delay of an inquiry could drag the negotiations on past the critical 16 January expiry date of the bondholders exclusivity agreement.

For all Turnbull's exasperation he wasn't finding any support from Packer. He didn't appreciate that the depth of the opposition to Packer's involvement in Tourang had made Packer more determined than ever to end up as a shareholder in Fairfax. Packer was determined to ride this one out. His ego and his family name were on the line. They were important considerations.

Turnbull, if Colson and Powers were right, jeopardised his ambitions. With the differences aired Packer didn't openly support Colson and Powers. They could sense, however, that when the time came he could be counted on. He certainly would not defend Turnbull.

So, despite the growing tension, the meeting concluded with an agreement to proceed on a more conciliatory note. An uneasy truce was struck—the three undertook to end the back-stabbing and work toward the common goal.

* * *

On the morning of Thursday, 31 October, Turnbull and Cass O'Connor were meeting with Michael Duffy, Federal President of the Printing and Kindred Industries Union (PKIU), and John

Cahill, the union's Federal Secretary, when Turnbull's receptionist rushed through to him an urgent fax.

The PKIU covers the printers who work for Fairfax. It has a reputation for militancy and its position was particularly sensitive within Fairfax because most bidders agreed that several hundred printers' jobs would have to be shed when they gained control.

What Turnbull didn't know was that one of the PKIU representatives at the meeting was a member of the AIC. Michael Duffy, as well as being Federal President, was the Father of the Chapel (the quaint name for the chief PKIU representative) at David Syme.

Turnbull was meeting with the PKIU representatives to argue Tourang's case, explaining why Tourang would be suitable to the PKIU in any staff reductions in the production area at Fairfax.

He read the fax and handed it across to Duffy with a wry smile. 'Look at this.'

It was a letter from Mallesons to Phillips Fox. Somehow Baring Brothers had found out that Turnbull planned a meeting with the PKIU. Burrows had cranked up the legal machine and Mallesons shot off a threatening letter to Phillips Fox demanding an immediate undertaking from Turnbull that he would not hold any discussions with any employees or union representatives of Fairfax. It was a breach of the confidentiality agreement. Mallesons had copied the letter to Freehills, Conrad Black, Gonski, Ords, Burrows, Kerry Packer and Des Nicholl.

When Michael Duffy left the meeting he still had the fax in his hand.

Colson was angry that the meeting had taken place. Turnbull had really landed them in a mess this time. Turnbull scoffed at the suggestion that his meeting would breach the agreement.

'I know what I can and can't do under the agreement,' he said to Colson.

The truce agreed to not more than twenty-four hours ago was now shattering.[1]

---

[1] Turnbull gives a different account of the PKIU meeting. He says that the meeting was held in the afternoon and that he was well aware that Duffy was on the AIC. Turnbull says no fax arrived during the meeting and the meeting had

• • •

The appearance of Packer on 'A Current Affair' the previous week was of enormous interest to Michael Lee and his colleagues on the Parliamentary Print Media Inquiry. Until Packer went public the inquiry had not intended to call him as a witness. Now, Lee decided, it was proper that Packer gave his views directly to the inquiry under oath or affirmation instead of the Committee relying on a video replay of his comments.

Packer's office was contacted. Yes, he would come. Packer would travel to Canberra on the following Monday, 4 November to face the Committee.

• • •

When Burrows heard that Packer had agreed to appear before the Print Media Inquiry he was sure there would be a revised offer for Fairfax on the way. As he saw it, Packer would only appear on national television under interrogation if he thought he was a strong player. That meant a higher offer for there was no way that Tourang was in a strong position at the moment.

Burrows was correct. The new bid came by letter on Thursday evening, the last day of the month. Burrows, White and Breese were staggered. This was a king hit. Tourang had increased its bid by up to $300 million in one swoop. The banks and all unsecured creditors would be paid out in full.

Under the new arrangement the banks would receive $450 million cash from equity contributions by the shareholders and $800 million in cash from re-financed loans obtained by the Tourang consortium. The banks themselves could make those loans if they wished (they would be normal, arm's length commercial loans with none of the repayments or interest rates tied to performance as they were in the previous bid) or Tourang would receive the finance from elsewhere. Tourang confidently said that it could make a fully funded bid and named Westpac as the likely

---

been discussed with Packer, Colson and others the day before. Colson's opposition to the meeting only developed on the morning of the meeting, when he (and Turnbull) learnt that Burrows knew of and objected to the meeting. Turnbull thought it was better not to offend the PKIU by cancelling the meeting. The meeting dealt mainly with issues of editorial independence, public access to media, etc; Turnbull claims staff reductions were not discussed.

bank. The decision was up to the banks; whichever they preferred. On top of the repayment of the bank debt, the bondholders would receive their $125 million and the unsecured creditors would be paid out in full.

The shareholders of Tourang were required to put up more cash under the new bid. The Telegraph would contribute $10 million more (up from $105 million to $115 million) and Kerry Packer and Hellman & Friedman would each contribute $7.5 million more. The amount to be raised from Australian institutional investors was up by $125 million to $262.5 million. The total amount of their bid was now $1.428 billion.

A very cocky Brian Powers and Dan Colson turned up at Baring Brothers at 5.15 pm on Friday afternoon, 1 November. Their message was clear. Tourang had driven over the bondholders and Turnbull and they had the exclusivity agreement. Now the bank debt and unsecured creditors were covered. Deal!

Burrows was delighted at the price. However, he knew it wasn't quite as simple as Tourang believed. There had to be approval from the FIRB before Tourang could complete. And there was still the ABT problem hanging over their heads.

Powers argued that the FIRB was not a problem. Freehills had told them they didn't need the approval with their present shareholding structure, which was within the strict legal requirements.

As for the ABT, they had officially notified the ABT on Wednesday of their intention to proceed on Fairfax. The way they interpreted the legislation, this meant that the ABT had to move within twenty-one days to announce an inquiry, otherwise it couldn't do anything until after the transaction had occurred. Then their only remedy would be to order divestiture.

Burrows was not convinced.

■　　■　　■

At the *Herald* that afternoon an extensive, uncut interview with Conrad Black was being laid out for Saturday's newspaper.

The accusation by Packer that there was a 'big lie' being pushed in the Fairfax press was viewed dimly by editor Max Prisk. He didn't like the challenge to the *Herald*'s credibility. The paper's New York correspondent John Lyons had been dispatched to Toronto the previous day to interview Black, to give him the chance to put his side of the case. The interview was to be run in full over a number of pages.

It was an odd decision for the interview to be run at such length, but Lyons had promised to discuss any editing with Black. Black, however, had been uncontactable before the paper was put to bed. In the wide-ranging interview Black attacked what he termed the almost 'relentless attempt to represent Mr Packer at 14.9 per cent as the author of the takeover' and the 'relentless and pernicious insinuation that Mr Packer is, in shareholders terms, an undesirable'.

The suggestion that he was an interventionist proprietor also rankled him as did suggestions that if Tourang secured Fairfax, there would be heavy job losses and a 'hit list' of journalists to be sacked.

> ... I suspect that if we chased it back far enough we would find the fine Machiavellian hands of my dear friends Rupert Murdoch and Tony O'Reilly. How can so many intelligent people be such unwitting credulous dupes? Do they really think serving Murdoch and O'Reilly is the answer to the Fairfax problem?

Black singled out Mr Ken Cowley's comments before the Print Media Inquiry for particular attack. Cowley had said that Packer should not be allowed to own fifteen per cent of Fairfax when News could only own up to five per cent of a television station under the cross-media rules.

> For Mr Cowley to go to the Lee committee and say that was just the most egregious hypocrisy almost of this whole episode. Rupert Murdoch is a citizen of the USA. He is one of the greatest cross-media owners in the world. The whole thing is almost surrealistic; it's such an obvious double standard.

> Some of those critical of the Tourang bid are so slavishly adhering to the Murdoch–O'Reilly line that they are either witting or unwitting dupes of Murdoch and O'Reilly.

Black said that he couldn't understand the fuss. He was: '... mystified that this story has become a band wagon and catchment for every charlatan and controversialist in the country.'

Repeating the line pushed by the Tourang camp since the whole issue exploded two weeks before, Black was adamant that Packer would not be dictating editorial judgement nor muzzling reporters. Packer would have the right to express his views but:

... he will not be sitting there either figuratively or, in fact, governing the management of those papers and promoting or demoting people.

I for one, at the risk of sounding sanctimonious, would never be a party to such a thing. If you asked me would Rupert Murdoch be party to such a thing, I would say yes. Rupert's a fine fellow but he's an authoritarian publisher and I'm being put in pillory of being some sort of virtual totalitarian intermeddler with my journalists.

This is absolutely scurrilous. This myth grew and grew and like a Frankenstein monster has achieved a life of its own that lurches around the Australian media every day. The fact is the working press of Australia is going to have to explain eventually how this happened.

■　　■　　■

The Friends of Fairfax and the AIC were delighted by the train of events. The strike had been a success, receiving saturation media coverage; the Whitlam–Fraser letter and the Darling Harbour rally had been incredible morale boosters and again provided invaluable publicity for the issue of media concentration.

Then the parliamentarians petition had really served to emphasise that this issue was important enough to cross political boundaries. It had presented the Hawke Government with a major headache at a time when it could least afford it, as the economy plunged further into recession. To the journalists the campaign was a success.

The day before the Black interview, however, certain journalists discovered that taking on Australia's richest man has its down side. At 6 pm the fax machine in the *Herald* news room began spurting out faxes from lawyers Phillips Fox. They were addressed to Alan Kennedy, Peter Bowers, Seamus Phelan and Colleen Ryan. Each one was identical: 'We act for Kerry Packer and Conrad Black ... we have instructions to commence proceedings ... to claim substantial damages for defamation.'

Phillips Fox was referring to a pamphlet handed out during the journalists' strike. The prospect of court battles pitted against the deep pockets of two rich media barons was a daunting one. Kerry Packer knew how to hit back.

CHAPTER FIFTEEN

PACKER HITS BACK

ON SATURDAY evening, 2 November, Colson and Powers sat opposite Packer in the sitting-room at Ellerston, the multi-million dollar polo complex at Scone in the Hunter Valley.

'I can't say this shit,' Packer said plaintively. 'That isn't the way I say things.'

'No, that's the way I would say it. You just put it in your own words,' Powers responded.

This was becoming difficult. Powers was trying to be diplomatic but Kerry Packer was not an easy person to coach. ABC TV was televising the Print Media Inquiry live throughout the nation on Monday, and the Tourang team were in overdrive preparing Packer for his appearance.

Packer had told Colson that he had not been pleased with his performance on 'A Current Affair' the previous week—this was to be a better effort.

In Sydney John Singleton and Mark Carnegie spent the day working with Freehills on the prepared statement that would be handed to committee members. Levy and colleague Stephen Chipkin handled the legal aspects and Singleton and Carnegie framed the lines to make the most impact.

This was Powers' and Colson's first weekend out of Sydney. It was principally work but Colson managed to get sunburned from trail bike riding around the property earlier in the day. It is a magnificent complex.

The polo grounds are considered the best in the world, better even than the Palermo fields in Argentina. Twenty grooms are employed to care for Packer's 160 polo ponies, which live in vast brick stables with high, cathedral-like ceilings. No expense has been spared on Ellerston.

In 1988 Packer doubled the size of the homestead through a two-storey extension. The additions included six guest rooms complete with en-suites, a kitchen and a huge games room to accommodate a billiard table, bar and open fire place.

During the Australian polo season Packer hosts a major tournament, one of the premier social events of the year. In 1991 it was exceptional: the eight best players in the world—the only ones with ten-goal handicaps—were present. In polo terms it was an extraordinary coup.

At Ellerston that Saturday night there hadn't been a lot of polo talk. Powers, Colson and Packer were trying to cover every possible detail that committee members could throw up on Monday. It was getting towards 2 am before they called it a night.

● ● ●

On Monday morning, 4 November, there was a fax from the Age Independence Committee (AIC) waiting for Mark Burrows in the Baring Brothers office. It was the next bullet for Turnbull.

The previous Thursday Turnbull had forgotten to collect from Michael Duffy the Mallesons fax warning Turnbull against any discussion with union representatives or Fairfax employees. Duffy had taken the fax back to Melbourne and shown it to his colleagues on the AIC. They realised immediately that this was pure gold.

David Wilson enjoyed penning his note to Burrows: 'We believe the following points require your urgent consideration and attention.'

It noted that the meeting with the PKIU officials had taken place and that:

> ... it was clearly the view of the respected union officials that Mr Turnbull was attempting to drive a wedge between employees at David Syme and Co. Ltd. We want to stress to you in the strongest possible terms that the ongoing good will and good faith of the staff of the *Age* and the *Sunday Age* is essential.

We firmly believe that the tone and discussion of the Turnbull meeting has the potential to dramatically devalue the
assets of the Fairfax Group.

Wilson pointed out that Turnbull was in clear breach of the
confidentiality agreement in meeting with the PKIU. He said
if Burrows sanctioned the meeting but would not give approval
for the other bidders to have similar meetings 'it appears to us
that the banking syndicate has some kind of private arrangement
with the Tourang syndicate'.

If Burrows had not sanctioned the Turnbull meeting, Wilson
asked that Burrows 'urgently take the appropriate legal steps to
prevent Mr Turnbull from possible similar activities being repeated'.

For good measure Wilson added: 'We can't stress to you the
depth of feeling of anger and despair by the committee'.

Burrows was quick to reply, alerting the committee to the
vulnerability of Turnbull's position. He asked permission for
Wilson's letter to be passed onto Colson and Powers and requested
details from Michael Duffy and John Cahill of the Turnbull
discussions.

Wilson rang Alan Kennedy of the Friends of Fairfax; they needed
to discuss strategy. This was a catch 22: if the AIC co-operated
fully with Burrows it was handing him a lever to pressure for the
removal of Turnbull from Tourang. Without Turnbull, Tourang
could be politically palatable and/or ruin the chances of an ABT
inquiry. The longer Turnbull stayed in Tourang, the better were
the chances of Tourang being knocked out of the game altogether.

Yes, this one was too dangerous. They decided to sit on their
reply for at least a week.

■   ■   ■

When Colson and Powers arrived at 12.35 for a lunchtime meeting, they were hit with the latest Turnbull debacle. Colson was
horrified. Now that the journalists were onto this, the implications
could be disastrous for Tourang. The stress was begining to tell on
Colson. He was very agitated. For the first time he and Powers
showed their true feelings for Turnbull in front of the Baring
Brothers team. The bitterness poured out.

Burrows went on to tell them of the ABT's comments at his

meeting the previous week—that Malcolm Turnbull was a problem for Tourang. An ABT official had referred to three or four issues without specifying what they were. This was the ammunition Colson and Powers needed to oust Turnbull.

* * *

Just after 2 pm on Monday Packer sat down at a long table facing the Print Media Inquiry members. The Parliament House committee room was packed with journalists and observers. The atmosphere was tense. Packer, peering over the top of the half-glasses, was making it quite clear that he was in a belligerent mood. He was visibly unhappy about the public scrutiny and barked at photographers that they had had enough time for pictures.

He opened his evidence: 'Kerry Francis Bullmore Packer. I appear here this afternoon reluctantly.'

Michael Lee and his fellow parliamentarians on the committee were left in no doubt that it was a formidable witness glaring at them from the other end of the room.

Packer's statement, handed out at the beginning of proceedings, was a gem. Singleton and Carnegie had delivered some memorable lines, the best toward the end with Packer outlining why he didn't want to control Fairfax:

Let me tell you why. I don't want to do the work and I don't want to have the responsibility that goes with control. Last year I suffered a major heart attack and died. I didn't die for long; but it was long enough for me. I didn't come back to control John Fairfax. I didn't come back to break the law. And I certainly didn't intentionally come back to testify before a parliamentary inquiry.

Throughout the statement Packer defiantly pursued the theme that he was doing nothing wrong in holding a 14.9 per cent shareholding in Tourang if it secured control of Fairfax:

My participation in Tourang is designed not to let me break the law. My participation in Tourang is designed to let me do what the law allows.

What does the law preclude me from doing in the case of John Fairfax Limited? Firstly it stops me from owning fifteen per cent or more of the shares. No one is suggesting that I will. Then it prohibits me from sitting on the board of Fairfax. I will not.

Then the Act further constrains what I can do. It says I am not allowed to control John Fairfax nor can I join with anyone else to do so. I won't. Please note that the law prohibits me from controlling John Fairfax or being a member of the board.

It does not stop me from being interested in it. It does not stop me from owning up to fifteen per cent of it and it does not stop me from doing anything else other than controlling it.

Packer explained that although he had had discussions with Conrad Black about the possibility of working together on Fairfax, the formation of Tourang was triggered by the Turnbull and Ord Minnett proposal.

Packer contended that it was understood that he would not lead the bidding effort nor, in fact, did he want to do any of the work. He said that he was consulted occasionally about the more important terms of the agreement with the bondholders 'but was otherwise not involved'.

He made no mention of his involvement in discussions with Fairfax management at Baring Brothers on 22 August during the due diligence process, nor the social contact with Colson and Powers but went on to outline his role in the appointment of Sir Zelman Cowen and Sir Laurence Street to the board—he was informed of both appointments and didn't object. He explained that he hadn't suggested Turnbull, who had made a board seat conditional on signing the exclusivity agreement.

The statement finished off with a stinging attack on cross-media and foreign investment laws:

The members of Tourang have entered into a commercial endeavour based upon Australia's laws and guidelines. What has happened is that what should have been a relatively simple commercial transaction under those laws has been hijacked by a group of self-opinionated and self-interested vigilantes.

What I can neither understand nor accept is how, as an Australian, I should be the victim of attempted one-minute to midnight changes of established and accepted cross-media laws.

Nor can I understand how such a transparent attempt to pervert the foreign ownership laws could have proceeded as far as it did. As I understand it, it is against the constitution to legislate against an individual. An attempt to legislate solely to thwart the legally proper aspirations of an individual just because some people may not like that individual has the same effect.

It was aggressive stuff. His theme was consistent: a victimised man under attack from politicians prepared to change the rules in the middle of the game.

As Lee and Western Australian MP Dr Ric Charlesworth tentatively asked the first few questions, Packer couldn't disguise his contempt. Charlesworth asked Packer what he could tell the committee about the formation of Tourang. Packer gruffly replied: 'It is all there in the statement.'

His short sharp answers quickly unsettled the committee. Michael Lee made scant attempt to play the role of chairman; Kerry Packer was running this show.

Langmore asked Packer whether he was saying that there was no arrangement, formal or informal, with Mr Black to control Fairfax.

'That is exactly what I am saying,' Packer barked. 'It is what I have said *ad nauseam* in that document. You are either going to have to believe me or call me a liar. I am telling you; there is no arrangement—and I am sick of telling people there is no arrangement. That is the situation. There is no arrangement. There is no agreement. I am not in the position ...'

His voice was high-pitched, aggressive, chiding. Langmore cut in with a question over the issue of formal or informal, and was curtly dealt with by Packer.

'What? Of course formal or informal, implied or anything else. I am sick of telling you all I am not going to run John Fairfax and, what is more, I do not want to.'

The comments struck at the heart of the issue: either Packer was lying or he wasn't. And the onus of proof lay with the accusers.

Peter Costello, a Liberal Party member of the committee and Shadow Attorney-General, tried the barrister's approach. Rubbing his hands together, speaking slowly and deliberately, he outlined the potential for Packer and Black to vote their respective 14.9 per cent and twenty per cent shareholdings together at an annual meeting or in any proxy war for the appointment of directors.

It was fair argument, but Packer replied bluntly: 'I do not accept that at all.' So much for Costello's carefully constructed argument.

Liberal Party member Warwick Smith raised the matter of pre-emptive rights over the junk bonds, whether Packer had any of these rights and what effect it would have on the Tourang shareholding structure. After answering that there would be no effect at all, Packer defiantly hit out at the committee: 'But if you think I am going to be railroaded and sit here and be told that you are going to change the laws and you are going to push me around, I may well buy them [the bonds]. And if I do, then the only way that Fairfax as a company will be able to be sold is individually as assets. I will not be able to buy it; I accept that.' But he could make it a lot harder for anybody else.

Ian Sinclair, the National Party member, gave Packer the opportunity to give his views on the new associates test. Packer said the rules were 'absurd'. Sinclair asked him if thought that they should be removed.

'Yes, I do. I think they are absolutely ridiculous. On that basis you could nearly knock out anyone any time you ever wanted to,' Packer responded.

Sinclair was smiling and obsequious. On numerous occasions he made the point to Packer that he agreed with him. He then raised the position of Turnbull. Packer admitted the associates rules could easily knock out Turnbull. Sinclair continued: after the junk bondholders were paid off, was there any role left for Turnbull?

'No, not really, except he wants desperately to be on the board of Fairfax,' Packer replied.

Commenting that where there are rules, 'let us all go through and abide by them', Packer left himself wide open for a question that left-wing Labor Party member Jeanette McHugh had been waiting to ask. She brought out some evidence Packer had given to the Costigan Royal Commission to show Packer would alleg-edly help people get around laws. She read out excerpts of Packer's evidence where he had said that he had bought shares in a company called Oceanic Equity: 'A friend of mine wanted to get control of that particular company. He was a foreigner, he could not get it through FIRB in that sense. It needed an Australian partner who was prepared to buy shares and hold them.'

'So you can be very helpful, can you not?' McHugh concluded.

Packer replied that he thought they were privileged documents. This unnerved McHugh; she said she was sorry.

'It's a bit late for that,' he snapped: 'You are giving me an example of something that I was exonerated from and hijacked into before the Costigan Inquiry, and you are sitting here under parliamentary privilege dragging that up again after I have been exonerated by the Parliament of this country. I think you have a damn hide.'

The thrust of her question was not followed up. Nor was the fact that the evidence she was presenting had come from Packer's own mouth and was not an allegation of the Costigan commission.

Firmly in control, Packer said it was absurd that Black was only being allowed to hold a twenty per cent shareholding in major Australian newspapers when, in countries like the UK, foreigners such as Black and Murdoch are allowed by the Government to own newspapers.

On the question of editorial independence, Packer dismissed the concept but said he thought the Australian Journalists Association Code of Ethics was a first class set of rules: 'As an owner, I believe that owners have the right to interfere in the running of a newspaper or in the running of a magazine. I make no bones about that.'

Packer revealed that his father used to dictate editorials when he owned Sydney's *Daily Telegraph* morning newspaper and said he did not think it was improper for a proprietor to do so.

'I do not see any reason at all why one group of people over here are the recipients of all the wisdom and all the right thoughts, and the other group over here, which is the proprietors, are all wicked, evil men who should not have their point of view put forward. I do not know who anointed the journalists to the position of being Christs.'

Towards the end of the session Packer admitted in reply to a question from Sinclair that, without cross-media ownership laws, he would have been interested in Fairfax and sought a shareholding of over fifteen per cent; he would have jumped at the opportunity to add the Fairfax Group to his empire. However, Packer said, he probably now wouldn't pursue Fairfax if in the future the share-holding restriction was raised above fifteen per cent.

'There are other things in my life which I would prefer to do. I would not have gone as far as I have gone in this matter if I had realised how controversial it was going to be to begin with.

'Having become controversial, I am not prepared to be rolled over on what I consider to be an unjust cause. I am not really that interested. There are other things that I would prefer to do. If I had the opportunity, I would still be in partnership with Conrad Black.

'I may have twenty per cent; I may have fifteen per cent. I would have liked to have been on the board and had some say on the matter, but I do not really want to run it.'

John Langmore changed his tack and pursued Packer on his low tax bill. He was Australia's richest man, yet he tried to contribute as little as possible to the Government's coffers to pay for services.

The left-wing MP's question met a curt response: 'There is nothing wrong with minimising tax. I do not know anybody who does not minimise tax.

'I am not evading tax in any way, shape or form. Of course, I minimise my tax. Anybody in this country who does not minimise tax wants his head read. I can tell you that as a Government you are not spending it so well that we should be donating extra.'

This gem of an answer was repeated again and again in talk-back radio programmes over the next few days.

The next few questions on tax were deftly shrugged off by Packer.

'The suggestion that I am evading tax—which is what you are putting forward—I find highly offensive. I do not intend to co-operate with you in the blackening of my character.'

Switching back to the central issue, Langmore had one last try to elicit a response on the question of whether Packer's participation in Tourang could lead to further reduction in media diversity: 'I expect that the central criticism of your bid for Fairfax is not to do with you or your companies but simply that many people believe that enough is enough; that with one television network and with a great many magazines, to extend further into the other arm of the print media is to increase the concentration of power more than is warranted. Do you have any sympathy for that point of view? Do you have any recognition of the reasons why people may feel that way ?'

The somewhat exasperated summation of the whole issue by Langmore cut no favour with Packer. He certainly was not going to admit anything and declined to deal directly with the issue raised. 'I have told you that fifteen per cent control is nothing. I do not accept at all the point of view that fifteen per cent controls, then it does not diminish the amount of media diversification.'

After over two hours of questioning Packer ended his appearance. To the television audience and those present in the committee room there was little doubt who emerged the victor. Packer's belligerence and intimidation mixed with disdain of the committee proved successful.

In Sydney the Tourang group watched the performance at Freehills and loved it. Colson commented that he could imagine mothers switching over to the ABC looking for 'Play School' and finding Kerry Packer's face beaming out at them. Packer had conceded nothing.

The politicians seemed totally overawed by his presence and time and time again declined to ask a follow-up question to put him on the spot. Such was his ability to brush off important questions of public policy on the media and foreign investment, it would have been easy for a viewer without an understanding of the issues involved to conclude that Packer was being dealt with harshly.

Only one answer was ominous for Tourang's future now that it had put in the highest offer. Packer said there was 'no way' Independent or AIN could top the Tourang offer and made a defiant, loaded comment: 'The only way it [Tourang] will be topped is by political interference and I do not hold that the political interference will actually happen.'

* * *

The following day Burrows could see that the afternoon's session was going to set a precedent for the style of negotiations from now on. It was bash-Burrows time, pressuring him to sell to Tourang immediately. Colson and Powers were emphatic—accept the Tourang offer now and a quick completion could be achieved.

There was no choice, Colson argued. Tourang had the highest cash offer and the junk bond agreement ensured that Burrows could not sell to anyone else. There was just no point in letting the process drag on any longer.

Burrows had a strong reply: the completion risks were serious for Tourang regardless of the fact that their offer was the highest and that they offered a clean sale covering the bank debt. He knew that the most important politicians—including the Prime Minister—did not want Tourang to own Fairfax.

Colson may not understand the opposition, Burrows went on, but that didn't change the situation. He had no intention of shutting off the process and risking a Tourang sale falling through. There was still AIN and Independent in the bidding, even if a sale to them involved selling the assets out of the Fairfax corporate shell to avoid the exclusivity agreement with the junk bondholders.

Had Tourang received FIRB approval for its offer? Tourang may believe that they had a strong argument in that Kerin couldn't reject Tourang under FIRB but there was no way that the banks would go against the Treasurer and sell to Tourang without his approval.

After all Kerin as Treasurer had the regulatory powers over banks. Citibank as a foreign bank was in an even more delicate situation than the ANZ and the other syndicate members. The Freehill lawyers could go on about black letter law for as long as they liked, but the commercial and political reality was that the banks were not going to go against the Treasurer's wishes.

Could Tourang guarantee that, if contracts were exchanged, the ABT would not go ahead and call a public inquiry, which would delay Tourang's ability to complete?

'It's okay for you to say to let you take care of the risks. Where does that leave us?' Burrows pressed. 'Are you prepared to give the banks an indemnity to cover us if anything goes wrong? What if you can't complete? We get stuck with Fairfax and have to sell it again.'

Colson knew that Tourang wouldn't give indemnity to the banks and that the banks wouldn't accept it anyway. It would be madness on the banks' part.

Moving on from the indemnity issue, Burrows raised the topic of Malcolm Turnbull. The AIC letter had raised serious issues. Mallesons had written to Phillips Fox twice on 31 October insisting that Turnbull not speak with the PKIU representatives; Turnbull had replied, assuring them he wouldn't do anything to breach the confidentiality agreement. It was clear now that the PKIU meeting had gone ahead. What was he playing at? Was this Tourang acting in good faith?

There were executives in the banking syndicate who were unhappy about the prospect of Turnbull as a Fairfax director. The banks intended to remain lenders to Fairfax and there was a lot of bitterness about Turnbull's litigation against the banks on behalf of the bondholders. His comments in March about the receivership—stating that the lunatics had taken over the asylum— still stung. On top of all that there were the comments made about Turnbull at the ABT meeting the previous week.

Burrows went on to say that he was still considering what to do about the bondholders. He hadn't seen the exclusivity agreement; Freehills and Mallesons were working on a suitable confidentiality agreement.

There was no doubt in Colson's mind that Burrows wasn't going to budge. He was adamant that there was no way he could recommend Tourang to the banks until the regulatory hurdles were cleared and he had a better idea of the terms of the exclusivity agreement.

Colson went straight back to Freehills to tell Levy and Chipkin to hurry along the release of the exclusivity agreement.

. . .

Relations with Turnbull were seriously deteriorating now. In a heated meeting on Tuesday night Colson told Turnbull that his directorship was a problem with the ABT. Burrows had warned him, he said, that Tourang would be injuncted by the Tribunal.

Turnbull was staggered. He had spent years on the other side of the ABT when he was Packer's lawyer; if anyone knew the Broadcasting Act, it was him. He also knew how Westerway operated. He couldn't believe that he would make such comments to outsiders.

The next morning Turnbull telephoned Westerway, who denied

the comments to Burrows. Turnbull felt besieged. That afternoon he decided to take action; he would put his grievances in a fax dispatched to Black, with a copy to Packer. He wanted to know if Black—rather than his representative Colson—held the same views about his involvement in Tourang.

Sending the copy to Packer was dangerous—if Packer got angry and declared Turnbull an enemy, he was on shaky ground. However, this fight was becoming personal and Turnbull, in his agitated state of mind, was prepared to take the risk.

The letter outlined the ABT issues raised by Colson and pleaded with Black that steps should be taken to bring the 'Chinese whispers' and 'destructive tittle tattle' to an end. The response came back: the Canadian—who had been diplomatic about the Kennedy saga—didn't think there were any major problems.

Over the next few days Turnbull decided that the only way to refute Colson's argument was to resort to the law books. He finalised his own legal opinion on the associates issue and fired off copies to Freehills and to Allen Allen & Hemsley, Packer's lawyers on broadcasting issues.

Always the lawyer, Turnbull mounted a persuasive case defending his directorship as an issue.

* * *

Burrows flipped through the agenda as he killed the last fifteen minutes before the Thursday morning meeting with ANZ and Citibank. This was the most crucial of all their monthly meetings.

It was 7 November—just three days after Packer's memorable evidence to the Print Media Inquiry. What had started off as a large receivership and reconstruction had turned into a national political issue dominating the news bulletins almost every day.

This meeting was to be attended by the full complement of people involved in the sale process: Fred Cohen, the New York lawyer, Karen Bechtel from Morgan Stanley, Jeff White and Peter Breese from Baring Brothers, John Atkin from Mallesons and Mary Reemst from Citibank. Each covering separate aspects of the auction process.

But the most important line on the agenda was the assessment of completion risk. Burrows realised that what he told the banks today had to be as much a political assessment as a financial one. There was absolutely no doubt about which consortium had the best bid, but should it be the one the banks accepted?

It was a year, almost to the day, since Burrows had taken on this job. He had succeeded in pushing up the price—from the $900 million estimated by Corrigan and Turnbull in February to towards $1.5 billion. A rising sharemarket, lower interest rates and ego-driven bidders in Tourang and Independent had given him the perfect environment. He had been lucky.

With Tourang's new offer the banks' debts would be paid in full, the unsecured creditors could be paid out and the bondholders sent away silent. But could they pull it off?

Burrows opened the meeting with a brief rundown of the current status of each bid. On a share acquisition basis there were Tourang at $1.428 billion; O'Reilly with $1.429 billion (but $82 million of that a soft portion for the banks) and AIN at $1.365 with a $200 million soft portion for the banks.

Jeff White had spent days working through each bid document. On a comparative basis his figures differed slightly from the originals: Tourang came in at $1.428 billion, O'Reilly at $1.438 billion and AIN at $1.369 billion. The asset bids by O'Reilly and AIN were around $65 million lower than the share bids in each case.

White and Breese explained the mechanics of the bids and Reemst outlined the banks' re-financing options. But the most important discussion was left until last—the completion risk.

For AIN the completion risk related principally to the lack of support from the bondholders due to the exclusivity agreement. If AIN were to be the successful bidder, it might have to be a sale of assets rather than shares with the extra complications on stamp duty and documentation that this would bring.

But there were other minuses for AIN—their $200 million soft equity left the banks exposed to the sharemarket—there was no underwriting commitment. Plus their price was the lowest of the three. On the positive side an AIN win would be well-received by journalists, particularly in Melbourne.

With the O'Reilly bid the completion risk centred on FIRB approval and the ability to provide the funds. Burrows said he was confident that Independent would be approved and that, in his view, it had political approval. He didn't anticipate any great problems with the Fairfax journalists with an Independent win. But, again, Independent didn't have the bondholders.

Tourang's bid was the best in terms of price and a clean deal for the banks with no more worries of bondholder litigation. But the completion risks on Tourang were serious.

FIRB approval was less certain than for O'Reilly—Tourang had a higher portion of foreign equity. The threat of an ABT inquiry was still very real and, while they could emerge unscathed, the time delay of the inquiry might take them past the expiry date of the bondholder exclusivity agreement.

Finally there would be strong staff opposition to a Tourang win. While the transaction remained incomplete, Burrows told the bankers, there were staff at Fairfax who would do everything they could to stop a Tourang win, including possible industrial sabotage. If the Saturday *Herald* or *Age* were prevented from being published this would have a damaging impact on cash flows. There was also the risk that industrial unrest could spread to the bank employees unions.

Following this sobering assessment, discussion moved on to the banks' assessment of soft equity proposals. They didn't want it at all but if at the end of the day they had to accept it, it would need to be a lot clearer than either the AIN or O'Reilly proposals.

Finally a process was discussed for the next round of bids. Each bidder would be given a final chance to bid and the political and regulatory process would be allowed to run its course.

* * *

The next morning appointments were made with each bidder. Independent and AIN were told that the banks were unhappy with their soft equity—it wasn't on. They would have to do better in the next round.

Mark Johnson could feel the pressure building up. Burrows was anxious. The auction was clearly under way.

'Your bid is well behind the others. Hurry up with your revised bid,' he told him.

It was easy for Burrows to issue his orders and expect them to jump.

But AIN had some twenty-seven institutions backing it. It could not go ahead without their approval—or at the very least the approval of the six members of the steering committee, representing the largest investors. AIN wanted its next bid to be a good strong competitor to Tourang's and this took time. Johnson and AIN's lawyer Colin Galbraith were also told that they must begin attacking the mountains of documentation, in particular the twenty-one volumes of loan agreements. The other bidders had started work on the documentation; now they wanted AIN to commence also.

The Tourang team was more belligerent when they heard the outcome of the bank meeting. Their line was becoming familiar—we have put in the show stopper; we will take the risk on the FIRB; we will take the risk on the ABT; we have the money to settle from Westpac—get on with it.

Burrows was getting sick of this belligerent, Clint Eastwood attitude. This was not Wall Street. He had no intention of moving without the approval of the regulators.

* * *

The pressure by the banks for Tourang to submit to the scrutiny of Kerin was irksome. The Tourang team had spent weeks working out methods to avoid the FIRB and Treasury approval process. Since a meeting with the FIRB in Canberra on 21 October, Freehill lawyer Stephen Chipkin had been poring over the Foreign Acquisitions and Takeovers Act and the Treasury booklet containing the policy guidelines for foreign investment in newspapers.

There was a strong case that legally Tourang did not have to submit its offer to FIRB provided it kept the Telegraph's voting shareholding to below fifteen per cent. If this was the case it wouldn't be classified as a foreign interest under the Act.

Tourang also disputed whether the proposed acquisition of Fairfax came under the policy guideline, as opposed to under legislation. The key sentence in the guideline stated:

All proposals by foreign interests to establish a newspaper in Australia or to acquire an existing newspaper business are subject to case-by-case examination irrespective of the size of the proposed investment.

If the Telegraph was below fifteen per cent, could it be classified as a 'foreign interest' to which the policy applied? Tourang further contended that the policy was aimed at a business asset acquisition below the usual thresholds and not a share acquisition which, if at all, was governed by the FATA.

This might be the legal position but among the Labor Party there was no intention to let legal arguments override the political process. Tourang was advised in no uncertain terms by FIRB's George Pooley that the Treasurer 'expected' Tourang to submit its proposal for scrutiny.

If there was any lingering doubts about what Tourang would be required to do, John Kerin dispelled them in Parliament on Monday, 11 November. The Treasurer emphatically said that the offers with foreign equity components would need to be submitted even if the shareholdings were below fifteen per cent and he referred to the policy booklet.

'Although this section of the policy is not enforceable under the provisions of the Foreign Acquisitions and Takeovers Act, the Government expects foreign investors to comply with the policy,' Kerin said in response to a question from John Langmore.

Tourang was acutely conscious of the danger of putting in its proposal after the political storm over the bid and the disagreements in Caucus about the acceptable level of foreign investment. The fact that their proposal was within the law was useless if Kerin decided to knock back the level of foreign equity proposed. Tourang had no idea if Kerin would allow its proposed thirty-nine per cent foreign economic interest and with Independent adamant it would be submitting an offer based on a foreign shareholding of only twenty per cent, it would ensure that Tourang's proposal was in stark contrast. O'Reilly was gleeful about this distinction and Hunt and the rest of the Independent lobbyists continued the task of highlighting this difference.

There was no way that Tourang could possibly submit a bid that mirrored Independent since it would mean Hellman & Friedman's proposed fifteen per cent holding would be slashed. Powers was particularly worried—a term of the exclusivity agreement stated that if there were any FIRB problems about the level of foreign equity, Hellman & Friedman had to reduce its holding before the bondholders.

After the time, money and effort spent pursuing Fairfax, Powers didn't fancy being the first casualty.

▪ ▪ ▪

Every Monday morning the six members of the Broadcasting Tribunal meet in Peter Westerway's bland office in North Sydney for morning tea and biscuits. Among the grey leather lounges and black modular bookshelves they discuss the Tribunal's current activities. This is Westerway's method of ensuring that all Tribunal members communicate with each other, that everyone is up to date on all issues. It might not be an MBA model of organisational behaviour but it works well enough.

For weeks the meeting had been dominated by the progress of the Tourang inquiries. The whole country seemed to be up in arms over the sale of Fairfax and the Tribunal members found themselves under an enormous amount of pressure. The amendments to the broadcasting legislation meant that they could confidently pursue a pre-transaction investigation for the first time ever, but there were legal quibbles about timetables and the exact operation of the new law.

The speculation that the ABT was going to hold an inquiry was growing and was making Westerway uncomfortable. He, in particular, was feeling the pressure, politically and publicly. It was a very difficult position for a long-serving public servant.

His shock of white hair seemed to be getting whiter, his manner even more serious and deliberate. Slowly over the last six weeks the ABT had been constructing, from information provided by various parties, the background to the formation of Tourang to determine if there was any evidence that Packer was exerting or likely to exert any control over Fairfax should Tourang be the successful bidder.

It was a long, tortuous process. It had begun in late September with statutory declarations from Turnbull and Kennedy on their past association with Packer. In early October letters were sent to Black, Packer, Kennedy, Cowen, Street, Barron and Turnbull requesting accounts of their involvement in the conception of Tourang and the development of the bid for Fairfax. This was followed up in late October by requests to Colson, Powers, Ezzes,

O'Connor, Miles and Mactier. All this information was provided voluntarily but then Tourang began to baulk. When a new batch of requests went out at the end of October, Freehill partner Kim Santow wrote to the ABT expressing concern about the notice requirements.

Tourang had hoped its voluntary provision of information had been enough and didn't want the requests to drag on forever. It was prejudicial to their offer, especially with Burrows constantly wanting to know if Tourang would be facing a lengthy ABT inquiry.

On Friday, 8 November Westerway, in a letter to Santow, made it clear the Tribunal might request further information; the previous day he had issued his first directions notice to Burrows— the first of many. The ABT planned to issue them every two days from now.

There were four questions—what is your current position regarding your consideration and assessment of each of the bids for Fairfax; have you made an in principle decision to recommend acceptance of the Tourang bid; when do you expect to finalise your position on recommending a bid; when do you expect that any agreement with the successful bidder might be concluded?

Westerway wasn't just being legalistic. At the next Monday morning meeting it was clear that the time had come to escalate the investigations into Tourang. There was now the evidence given by Packer at the Print Media Inquiry to consider and Conrad Black's answers in the *Herald* interview.

Many of the public statements made by the parties in Tourang were now becoming contradictory and confusing. Cracks were beginning to appear.

Black had stated that he wanted Packer's approval before Sir Zelman Cowen's appointment to the board, although he added it was showing courtesy to a small shareholder. He'd said that he asked Packer and Hellman & Friedman whether they objected to Sir Laurence Street's appointment and that Turnbull was going on the board as a representative of the bondholders.

Kennedy had told the Print Media Inquiry that Turnbull wasn't going to be a representative of the bondholders and Packer had said, when asked to confirm that he had no role in the selection of the directors of Tourang, that this was 'exactly' what he was saying. Packer had also admitted on 'A Current Affair' that he didn't have a record of making passive investments.

Then there was Colson, quoted in a Canadian magazine mid-year, stating Packer had approached Black to join Tourang rather than vice versa. This version was labelled incorrect later by Black.

The ABT legal staff was not convinced, however, that it had enough evidence to launch a public inquiry into Tourang on the information available. What was needed was evidence of Packer having an agreement, arrangement, understanding or practice with his fellow shareholders that would allow him control of Fairfax, despite keeping a shareholding below fifteen per cent.

Evidence of understandings about who goes on a board, who goes off a board and who a chief executive took instructions from would be some of the matters considered. Even matters like social contacts can be looked at under the legislation to ascertain evidence of control.

Westerway knew he had to be extremely confident about the strength of the case if he was going to call an inquiry. It would be high-profile and the commercial implications were shattering. Any inquiry would probably take at least two months and the delay would seriously prejudice Tourang's position, possibly forcing it to quit its offer.

On the other side of the equation though, extra pressure was coming from rival bidders—particularly Independent—and from public interest groups such as the Communications Law Centre and the Free Speech Committee.

The AIC had written to Westerway pointing out that it had the support of the Victorian Trades Hall Council, the Australian Union of Students, church leaders, the ACTU president, and the Victorian Attorney-General in its fight against further media concentration. There were over 15 000 signed letters of support.

Westerway knew the feelings of Hawke and other key ministers. If an inquiry was called Tourang would probably rush off to court challenging the ABT's right to hold it. If the ABT lost the case, and Tourang missed out on Fairfax in the meantime, there would be claims that the inquiry had been politically motivated. Westerway decided that calling an immediate public inquiry now was too dangerous but it was time to seek further information from Tourang. A fishing trip began.

A long list of questions about the formation and operation of Tourang was finalised over the next two days—seventy-one questions in all. On Thursday, 14 November the ABT's director, licensing Jennifer Stafford, sent out a one-page letter and annexure of questions to all the relevant parties involved in Tourang, utilising the Tribunal's information gathering powers under section 89X of the Broadcasting Act.

The shareholders, key bondholders, advisers, directors and lawyers were to provide answers by the following Thursday. If there was an association between Black and Packer or anything to show Packer had the capacity to influence or control Fairfax, the questions were designed to find out.

Issues canvassed included whether any director of Tourang reported or had given any information concerning their conduct or knowledge in the affairs of Tourang to anyone other than its directors. Or if anyone other than the Tourang directors had given a Tourang director, past or present, any directions or requests concerning the manner in which they conducted 'hemselves in the affairs of Tourang.

Other questions related to the financial arrangements surrounding Tourang. One key set of questions asked if there were any shares in Tourang held on trust for other parties or whether there were any understandings or arrangements on Tourang shares.

In simple language the ABT wanted to know if there were any warehousing arrangements between Black, Packer and Hellman & Friedman. Details were also sought about all the information brought to the meetings in London in early June and any minutes, audio recordings or other recordings of the meetings.

The extent of the section 89X notices was a nightmare for Tourang. Apart from the logistics, some people couldn't possibly answer all the questions because they were not involved in all the events. Colson demanded from Freehills advice on how to handle the situation.

With so many people involved and such a range of issues, Tourang knew that any answers that were contradictory would be of interest to the ABT. This was a case where one of Black and

Colson's favourite expressions was invoked: 'Everyone has to sing off the same song sheet.'

The next morning Santow and Levy telephoned Giles Tanner, the assistant director in the ABT's ownership and control division. They asked if it was possible for collective responses to the section 89X questions given there were, in many cases, identical questions to various people. They argued that it was common sense to take this approach and, in a later telephone conversation, suggested a new notice be issued enabling Freehills to reply for all the persons involved.

Taking legal advice from the Australian Government Solicitor's office and barrister Brett Walker, Tanner and Westerway decided that it would be acceptable for each person in receipt of identical questions to assent to a single form of words and for the answer to be consolidated into a single response. Tanner warned, however, that each person who assented should be aware of the responsibilities under the Broadcasting Act for the answers.

Colson was unhappy about the barrage from the ABT. It confirmed his worst fears. He knew an ABT inquiry would jeopardise and most likely kill the whole deal. It was just another headache—and his resilience was wearing thin.

Santow tried to trip up the ABT on legal grounds. He suggested that, under the new amendments to the Broadcasting Act, there was a time limit of twenty-one days from the date of notification on the Tribunal's ability to call an inquiry. Tourang had notified the ABT of its intention on Fairfax on 31 October. The twenty-one days ran out on Wednesday, 20 November—the day before the reply to the questions was due.

He added that the delays involved in holding an inquiry prejudiced Tourang's bid, the interests of Fairfax creditors and the Fairfax entities. In addition it was detrimental to future foreign investment in Australia.

Tanner penned a three-page letter refuting Santow's claims. Pointedly he denied that the ABT was proceeding at anything other than an appropriate pace given the seriousness and complexity of the circumstances.

He specifically rejected the description of the regulatory process as being 'drawn out' and the assertion that the ABT was not acting reasonably in the exercise of its powers.

The hint in Santow's letter that somehow Tourang may or should be given a 'provisional clearance' to proceed with the purchase of Fairfax was flatly rejected. Tanner made it quite clear that the ABT had not yet decided to have an inquiry. The ABT intended to go about its business methodically and ignore the angst from Tourang.

For Tourang the response from the ABT was another dead end. The belief that it was unwarranted and that Tourang would sail through it remained; the very fact that it was likely to occur, however, was enough to overshadow the rights and wrongs of it. The options, if an inquiry was launched, were becoming clearer.

At the top of the list was a request for Packer to withdraw. This was not palatable: Colson and Powers had staunchly defended Parker's involvement and the close friendships made it even harder.

At times, though, Packer had openly talked about pulling out if it became too tough and Black had admitted months ago that he might have to dump Packer if a cross-media problem arose. He hadn't, however, expected that to happen.

■　■　■

Jeff White, Peter Breese and John Atkin were becoming bored with this lengthy meeting with Mark Carnegie and the accountants from Ernst & Young. How exactly was this Tourang transaction going to work? Where was the cash coming from to pay out all the creditors, how was it being dispersed? What were the tax implications? The accountants were hedging.

This was confidential information but White and Breese were prodding. It was a game of cat and mouse, and Carnegie couldn't stand another second of it.

'What the fuck—if it speeds up the process, just tell them,' he said. The accountants detailed the whole plan.

The Baring Brothers team couldn't believe it: these guys were still just another bidder and here they were laying it all out before them.

■　■　■

As the group walked out of Westpac's headquarters in Martin Place on this sunny Friday morning, 15 November, each was totally perplexed at why the bank executives hadn't put up a more competitive deal to fund Tourang's offer for Fairfax.

It had seemed such a feasible idea: Westpac fund Tourang's offer so it could give Burrows and the banks a clean deal. This would leave Westpac in an excellent position, having secured Fairfax's banking business. Good corporate accounts in the banking world were hard to come by these days and they were particularly attractive to banks like Westpac, which were nursing the horrific fall-out from their heavy commercial property lending and loans to entrepreneurs.

The exploratory talks had been arranged by Turnbull who reminded Powers how well-known he was to Westpac executives particularly Iain Thompson, a senior executive in corporate lending with whom Turnbull had worked on the Ten Network deal.

The deal offered by Westpac was relatively expensive in both the fees and the interest rates to be charged. Powers was surprised that the bank wasn't more aggressive.

Later that day Neville Miles was alerted to the meeting at Westpac. He was furious. What was Turnbull doing rushing off to Westpac? Ord Minnett was Westpac's broking arm and if anyone made the approach it should have been Miles. Especially as he had worked within the banking group. Colson and Powers should have discussed it with him so that he could have nominated the right people to contact.

Miles simmered overnight and phoned Turnbull in the morning. Unable to get through, he rang Powers to air his grievance.

'It was inappropriate,' Miles fumed.

Powers couldn't really see the problem apart from Miles' hurt pride but his wicked sense of humour couldn't allow him to pass up this opportunity.

'Hmm. So Westpac is your parent, Neville,' he said.

'Yes,' Miles replied, puzzled. Powers already knew that.

'I suggest you find yourself another parent,' Powers said laughing.

Turnbull was on the telephone to Colson and Powers. He was angry. They were stepping up the pressure on him to leave the board and he felt he was being treated unfairly. He believed his presence wouldn't jeopardise the completion of the deal. As for Burrows' comments about the banks and not wanting him on the board, he was sure they were fantasy. He explained how he had telephoned bank executives in the syndicate and that they didn't know what Burrows was talking about.

Towards the end of the conversation Colson sternly mentioned Westpac and Miles' comments. 'Miles says that Westpac doesn't have a high opinion of you.'

Turnbull was annoyed with Miles. What was he trying to do? Join the people seeking to betray him? He got Miles on the phone immediately. How dare he say that! Malcolm had brought Ords into the deal.

'The next time I see you, you will be a Westpac superannuee,' he barked at Miles.[1]

Miles defended himself.

'I didn't say that Westpac didn't have a high regard for you.' He explained his concerns over Tourang going though the wrong channels, finishing by apologising to Turnbull. Miles agreed to send off a fax to Colson and Powers on Monday clarifying his comments. It was a ridiculous spat.

■　　■　　■

Jeff White stood before the heavy black iron gate at the entrance to Trahlee. It was just before 2 pm on Sunday, 17 November, and he was late. This deal was taking over his life. His squash game was lousy now—he'd had to cancel so many times in the past six months. He was unfit and tired.

This was an important meeting, though. Colson and Powers were joining them at 4 pm but he needed to talk over the flick pass option with Burrows before then. It was complex but it might just work.

If Tourang was so determined that its bid be accepted before the regulatory approvals came through, and it wouldn't or couldn't give any meaningful indemnity to the banks if its bid fell over, then one option was to arrange a flick pass. It was an idea Breese and White had come up with.

It revolved around Tourang agreeing, ahead of time, to flick its bondholder exclusivity agreement to the number two bidder should its bid fall through because of either broadcasting regulations or foreign investment rules.

---

[1] Turnbull denies having said this.

If this happened the banks could still go ahead with a share sale rather than an asset sale because O'Reilly—the number two bidder at this stage—would have the bondholders. As a bonus the banks' exposure to the bondholder litigation would be negated.

White walked into the large dining-room to find Burrows, Fred Cohen, Peter Breese and John Atkin with papers spread all over the table. An hour and a half later they knew they weren't anywhere near ready to put a firm proposal to Colson and Powers. They would have to cancel their meeting today and see them in the office at noon tomorrow.

Powers went berserk on the other end of the telephone when told the news. The frustration was becoming too much. Colson and Powers were showing signs of losing it—you don't attack the auctioneer or his executives.

■ ■ ■

Powers was determined to let Burrows know exactly what he thought about the previous day's delay. He had thought they were close to moving forward to negotiating a sale and Burrows ruined his day. It was not acceptable to arrange a meeting on a Sunday and then call it off at a few minutes' notice. This transaction had to be completed. They had the bondholders, they had the highest bid—there was no need for the theatrics.

Powers came in early for the Monday meeting and insisted on seeing Burrows alone first. He let it all pour out. Burrows listened patiently but was unperturbed.

'That is what today's meeting is all about, Brian. How we can move ahead?' he said quietly.

They walked back up the corridor and joined Breese, White, Colson and Steve Ezzes, who was back in Australia. Within thirty minutes Powers' antennae were picking up danger signals. This flick pass option could be a disaster for Tourang.

He pictured the scenario: O'Reilly is told that he is in second place; if Tourang falls over at either the ABT or FIRB, O'Reilly is told that he will be declared the winner by default. So what is the O'Reilly team going to put 100 per cent into now? Making sure Tourang gets knocked out by the regulators, of course. O'Reilly wouldn't have to increase his bid by even one cent.

No, they would have to be suicidal to agree to this one. He told Burrows that Tourang would consider the flick pass option only if there was an agreement with the number two bidder that it wouldn't attack the Tourang bid.

As the Tourang team left Burrows asked Fred Cohen and Steve Ezzes to dine with him that night. Burrows detected that Ezzes wasn't as close to Turnbull as he once was; this was his chance to find out just where the bondholders stood.

■　■　■

Ezzes had come back to Australia into the midst of the Turnbull row. He had known for months that Malcolm Turnbull clashed with Powers and Colson but he had no idea the situation had deteriorated so dramatically.

He had returned the previous week hoping that the transaction would be drawing to a close now that Tourang had increased its bid; he wanted to be on the spot to ensure that there were no hitches for the bondholders. Since he had arrived there had been a constant barrage of anti-Turnbull sentiment. Ezzes was staying at the Ritz Carlton—the same hotel as Powers, Colson and Cohen—so there were plenty of opportunities for informal chats.

Colson and Powers were convinced that Turnbull was a liability on all fronts—with the Government, with the ABT, with journalists and, most of all, with Burrows. He was working in his own self-interest. He clearly wanted to be on the board of Fairfax and he had totally lost sight of the transaction, they claimed.

Turnbull on the other hand was disgusted at the tactics of Powers, Colson and Burrows. He was bitterly opposed to the three of them. If they wanted him off the board, they would pay for it. He had a right to be there; he was the only independent board member who hadn't been appointed by the consortium. The Fairfax board needed him.

Ezzes couldn't resist a reply to this one when Turnbull raised it a few days before.

'Who appointed you—God?'

At the Ritz Carlton, Colson and Powers kept up the pressure on Ezzes.

This time they were more direct—Malcolm Turnbull's continued presence on the board would ensure that Tourang lost.

'I can't handle character assassination without corroboration,' Ezzes told them bluntly.

By the time Ezzes arrived at Burrows' home with Cohen just before 8 pm he was very tense. The atmosphere was stilted for the first half hour but over dinner he loosened up with Burrows prodding him about Turnbull. He joked about how Turnbull had been upset with Morgan Stanley back in April because it was trying to divide the bondholders. Turnbull, calling from a telephone in his kitchen, warned he would treat Morgan Stanley with contempt if it treated the bondholders with contempt. He was very aggressive.

Later Ezzes had to ring the Morgan Stanley executive Bruce Bockman to apologise for Turnbull's call.

Burrows hinted at the problems he saw for Turnbull and suggested that Ezzes meet with Jake Williams the next day to hear first-hand. Williams was non-committal on Turnbull. He didn't attach a great deal of importance either way to Turnbull's continued presence on the board. Burrows obviously believed that Williams was anti-Turnbull and would say as much to Ezzes. But he didn't. Either Burrows had misinterpreted Williams, or Williams was being circumspect in front of Ezzes. Burrows repeated Westerway's comments at the ABT and gave his assessment of the journalists' position. The rest of the Tourang team developed the case. Freehills took Ezzes through the broadcasting legislation and the new definition of associates—the section where Turnbull might trip them up.

Ezzes was beginning to come around to their way of thinking about the board seat although he felt obliged to talk to Turnbull about it. Sitting in Turnbull's office, however, Ezzes soon realised that it was a bad move to raise Tourang's objections directly with him. Turnbull exploded.

Ezzes was worried. Back at the Ritz Carlton he spoke to Powers and they agreed it would be a good idea to set up a conference call with some of the other bondholders the next morning. From the Freehill office they rang Ezzes' co-chairman, Doug McClure, at Drexels in New York. Ezzes took McClure carefully through each of the issues then Powers and Colson each gave their spiel.

McClure felt a certain amount of sympathy for Turnbull. He had a business to run in Australia, a professional reputation to protect, and resignation from such a high-profile board position would be humiliating, bad for business. It seemed to McClure that Colson's and Powers' desire to have Turnbull off the board had nothing to do with winning the deal. But on the other hand, Powers and Colson were representing the shareholders; they were the ones who were putting their money on the table for this transaction and they were going to have to run the business afterwards. If they didn't want Turnbull on the board that was their prerogative. The main thing for the bondholders was to make sure that Tourang won the bid. If there was any risk at all that Turnbull could affect this, then he should resign from the board.

* * *

While the Turnbull problem was the focus of attention in Sydney, Ezzes knew that McClure was handling another very delicate matter in New York.

In recent weeks Arthur Liman, a lawyer from New York legal firm Paul Weiss Rifkind Wharton & Garrison had been working overtime making approaches to the Fairfax bondholders. It was progressing well.

When Arthur Liman rings, you take the call. He is one of the best known lawyers on Wall Street. He was Mike Milken's attorney and the prosecutor for the Iran Contra hearings in Washington—televised nationally for weeks. He represented Steve Ross of Warner Brothers and was Tony O'Reilly's personal attorney.

O'Reilly had decided that it was pointless leaving the bondholders to Burrows and Morgan Stanley. From the beginning Burrows had advised not to worry about the bondholders, but then the bondholders had forged an exclusive deal with Tourang.

Now, months later, Burrows was still saying 'don't worry'. This time they didn't believe him; it was time to take matters into their own hands.

O'Reilly needed a top gun for the task—Liman had the credibility and contacts within the bondholder ranks to ensure a good hearing. He knew the Drexel people extremely well, thanks to his dealings with Milken. He was a perfect intermediary with the bondholders and Drexels was the largest.

Independent also made sure that the bondholders were aware that it was prepared to pay more than $125 million for the bonds. Liman spoke to Turnbull from New York and Cameron O'Reilly —who knew Turnbull socially—also spoke with him. The flirtation was well-timed, right in the midst of the deterioration of Turnbull's relations with Tourang.

Liman knew of Tourang's threats to sue anyone who tried to chisel away at the exclusivity agreement. The action would be based on a US offence—inducement to breach a contract. AIN had already had a taste of this attitude. They had hired Lazards for advice on the bondholders a few weeks before, also deciding to take matters into their own hands. This had prompted a swift threat of action.

So Liman trod carefully, but his message was clear: Independent was capable of improving substantially on Tourang's $125 million payment if it could somehow get the opportunity.

Ezzes and McClure felt the bondholders were probably entitled to more than $125 million and that there was a good chance the other bidders might pay it. The bidding process had pushed the Fairfax valuations well above the bank debt level. However, the fact that the bondholders had dealt exclusively with Tourang made escaping from the agreement seem very difficult. McClure was worried that there were inherent risks in flirting with another bidder. What if Tourang terminated the agreement because of a breach by the bondholders and then went on to win Fairfax anyway? It was possible. They did have the highest bid.

McClure shuddered at the prospect of trying to renegotiate with an angry Tourang at a decent price. And there was the Turnbull powder keg too. It was so difficult to judge the personality plays in Sydney from the perspective of an office in New York. McClure could only hope that it would settle down before too much damage was done to the deal.

CHAPTER SIXTEEN

GOODBYE MALCOLM

MALCOLM TURNBULL was pounding away at the keyboard of his computer on the morning of Wednesday, 20 November, carefully constructing his latest letter to Colson. He deliberated over every word. This letter was critical. It was Turnbull's reply to a monstrous betrayal.

Turnbull was being betrayed by everyone who mattered—his friend and client Steve Ezzes, his friend and mentor Kerry Packer, and his consortium colleagues Dan Colson and Brian Powers. Packer was not coming to Turnbull's aid. Turnbull tried to ring him in Argentina. Packer never returned the calls.

Turnbull had been told that Ezzes, Powers and Colson had tried to convince other bondholders in a marathon phone call the previous night that Turnbull should resign from the board. This would mean that he would have no role in Fairfax in the future— and after all he had done to secure it for Tourang!

Turnbull would not give up his board seat without a fight. All the allegations against him were unfounded, and he could prove it. Turnbull was adamant that if he left the board, it would be bad for the deal.

Turnbull's letter struck at the heart of the Tourang syndicate. It showed how serious this dispute had become. He was threatening to snatch Tourang's ace card—the exclusive support of the bondholders. He believed he had strong grounds to do it.

According to Turnbull, Tourang's offer for Fairfax didn't comply with the exclusivity agreement. The terms of the offer now exceeded the capital parameters set out in the original agreement. Not only was the level of debt proposed too high, but Turnbull also considered the exit of Kennedy a material breach. And even though the bid price had moved from the $900 million proposed in the agreement, the bondholders had received nothing extra.

'In short, from the perspective of the bondholders, Tourang is a less attractive proposition to the bondholders than it was [Perhaps the same comment could be made from the perspective of the Daily Telegraph.],' Turnbull wrote.

Suddenly the exclusivity agreement had become a weapon for Turnbull in his fight with Powers and Colson. The letter went on to focus on his directorship:

Despite the assurances given to me in Kerry Packer's office some weeks ago, and separately on the telephone from Conrad Black, both you and Brian Powers have continued to contend to my client Steven Ezzes, and as recently as today to my client Doug McClure, that my remaining a director of Tourang is 'an impediment' to the deal and that you have urged both gentlemen to apply pressure on me to step down from the Tourang board.

One by one Turnbull presented his arguments against the allegations, including that he was a political obstacle:

The only political issue in this transaction is the cross-media issue: put another way, Kerry Packer ... I am astonished that Kerry Packer of all people would lend himself to a campaign based on anonymous innuendo.

Gradually Turnbull built up his argument to the point where he made some of his most damaging statements:

In the absence of any apparent substance to the complaints, I can only conclude that your desire to remove me is motivated by another unspoken reason.

I have to assume your conduct is not motivated by mere personal animosity and that rather there is a real commercial objective which would be best served by my resignation.

That objective is, I assume, to control the board of Fairfax by the appointment of non-executive directors who, while notionally independent, are for all practical purposes going to act in accordance with the express wishes of yourself.

In short I must assume that you regard me as an excessively

independent director. I had hoped that matter would subside, however, your recent approaches to my clients necessitate that the back-stabbing cease.

The letter ended with Turnbull stating that he was willing to meet with Colson at his convenience to discuss the matter and he would listen with an open mind.

Turnbull knew that he would have to make Ezzes understand that what he was doing was right for the bondholders. It would be difficult—Ezzes couldn't be trusted any more. Turnbull was hurt that Ezzes could listen to Colson's arguments against him, and then behind his back try and promote them to other bondholders like McClure. Ezzes and Turnbull had become close friends during the Fairfax saga—Turnbull and his wife Lucy had been on holidays with Ezzes and his Australian girlfriend Deborah Huber, a lawyer who once worked with Turnbull.

Now Ezzes was acting as if he were the principal to the deal, which he wasn't. Turnbull had the power. He was the bond-holders' representative—it said so in the exclusivity agreement. It was his signature that was required under the agreement to sign off on any Tourang purchase of Fairfax. Colson and Powers needed to be conscious of that too.

Turnbull's letter was a warning, and the statements about the board were dangerous; they could potentially be used by the ABT as evidence to justify holding an inquiry into Tourang.

As Turnbull knew from his years spent dealing with regulatory bodies, when the thieves start falling out, it is a fruitful time for regulatory bodies to go hunting.

* * *

Colson was staggered when he received the letter at Freehills. Levy, Chipkin and Powers agreed. It was dynamite. There would be no compromise now; Turnbull had signed his execution warrant.

Turnbull was out of control, a loose cannon pointing at Tourang. Colson was sick of the disputes over strategy, of Turnbull's claims of superior knowledge on the political climate and how to run this frustrating transaction. The transaction was tough enough without this brawl.

Turnbull was a mercurial character, Colson decided. Very

clever, creative and intelligent at his best; at his worst—and Colson had now seen this side of his personality—he was stubborn and fiery. Turnbull was never a shareholder of Tourang, his role was adviser to the bondholders. If the shareholders wanted his resignation, that was it.

There was not unanimous support from within the Tourang ranks to sack Turnbull. Miles, despite his own blow-up with Turnbull over the Tourang funding on the weekend, argued against dumping him.

Colson and Powers were somewhat suspicious of Miles' stance —after all, Miles and Turnbull had come into this transaction together. Miles might be trying to be a friend to everyone, the voice of reason, but he needed reminding exactly who the shareholders were: just as Turnbull did.

Levy also wondered about the wisdom of sacking Turnbull before the deal was complete. At this bitter stage, however, even a suggestion of a moderate stance on Turnbull bordered on treason to Powers. He was blunt: some deals were worth walking away from if you were confronted with someone you couldn't stand working with. Powers was so opposed to Turnbull that he was prepared to lose the support of the bondholders, to walk away from the whole deal if necessary. Colson summonsed Turnbull to Freehills. He would be formally asked to resign.

• • •

Turnbull was fired up like a barrister going into a court battle. He was going to win this one. Colson and Powers could not possibly dispute his evidence that his board position was simply not the issue with the banks and with the ABT as they believed. This was persecution.

Turnbull's evidence was clear. Jake Williams had told Ezzes he was indifferent to Turnbull being on the board. Westerway had denied telling Burrows that Turnbull presented a major problem for the Tourang bid. But Colson and Powers were intransigent. Turnbull's evidence held no weight with them at all. It was hearsay.

Ezzes sat listening as the three antagonists interrupted each other, disputing every point. The verbal sparring bounced into sensitive areas as Turnbull targeted questions about Powers' relationship with Packer and the job offer at Consolidated Press. The innermost secrets of Tourang were aired.

But for all the words, there was only one important fact. Colson and Powers had the numbers; neither Black nor Packer was going to support Turnbull. This transaction was ruthless—nothing was going to stand in the way of the two media barons' victory.

Turnbull knew this. His long friendship with Packer was ending—the Costigan Royal Commission, the business deals, the staunch defence of Packer against the public barbs, some of them from the Fairfax newspapers—it was all over.

The bitter irony was that it had been Turnbull's own pursuit of Fairfax and his coralling of bondholders through the sheer weight of personality that might be an important factor in delivering Fairfax to Black and Packer.

There was no point in continuing the meeting. Colson and Powers demanded that Turnbull resign.

*   *   *

Later that night there was a three-way telephone link-up. Ezzes and Turnbull were in Turnbull's office and McClure was at Drexels in New York. Ezzes and McClure were both adamant that Turnbull should resign. Turnbull remained adamant that he should not.

'You are making your decision on an emotional basis, Malcolm. If the true investors want you off the board, you should leave,' Ezzes pleaded.

'You have to do the best thing for the deal,' McClure said.

Turnbull lost his temper and slammed down the telephone. He slammed it so hard the line to New York was lost.

Ezzes returned to the Ritz Carlton and called McClure again. They realised now that this dispute was dangerous—it had become extremely emotional. They wondered if they might have to ask Turnbull to resign as bondholder representative.

*   *   *

While Tourang was imploding the AIN team in Melbourne had quietly convinced its institutional backers to support a significantly higher offer. They had sound arguments. The recovery in the sharemarket and lower interest rates theoretically valued a quality group like Fairfax much higher than a few months ago. The irony was that the re-rating was occurring despite the continued slide in Fairfax's profits.

Fairfax's operating profit (before finance costs and tax) fell to $122.1 million for the 30 June 1991 year, compared with $195.6 million the previous year. This didn't deter the higher offers.

On Thursday, 21 November, Mark Johnson arrived at Baring Brothers and outlined the new bid. It was effectively $400 million higher than the previous bid and there was no soft equity. AIN would now take the banks out clean. Johnson outlined how AIN would pay $360 million up front in cash. This would comprise $200 million from the steering committee and $160 million from the other backers. There would then be a float underwritten by J B Were & Sons.

The support of Were was astounding considering it had also agreed to underwrite Independent's offer. As Australia's leading underwriter of share issues Weres was a logical choice for both Independent and AIN and the firm wasn't going to let the lucrative fees go elsewhere. It was now backing two out of the three bidders. To avoid potential conflicts of interest Independent's offer was being handled by the Sydney office and AIN's by the Melbourne office.

AIN was back in the bidding and arguably stronger than Tourang on price. There was one flaw—they didn't have the bondholders. However, they knew that Tourang's relationship with the bondholders was looking a little shaky.

Johnson stressed to Burrows that AIN wanted to keep this new offer very quiet. It was trying to maintain a low profile and wanted the press to think that it was out of the money. In the meantime it was revving up the institutions to pay the much higher price.

* * *

Colson and Powers returned to Baring Brothers in the afternoon, once again belligerent. This time there were lengthy arguments about re-negotiating the expensive newsprint contract at Fairfax and about access to details of defamation actions. How far down the track did they have to be before this crucial information was available?

Burrows assured them that there was a process under way and every bidder would eventually be given equal access to the sensitive material.

Burrows' hectic round of appointments continued.

Peter Thomas of CS First Boston came in to update Burrows on his progress. He was convinced a complete float of Fairfax was now a viable option more than ever, reminding Burrows that there was strong appetite for media stocks. He was confident he could offer the banks and unsecured creditors over $1.5 billion under the float proposal. After all, Burrows had done it successfully with QBE insurance group when its parent Burns Philp wanted to sell out. They had pulled off a $420 million price tag by selling it straight onto the market.

* * *

On Thursday morning Turnbull had a new plan. Talking over the details of the previous night's meeting with Wran, they came to the conclusion that they should take the matter over the heads of Powers and Colson.

Turnbull got to work on a lengthy letter that was to be signed by Wran and himself. If he was to resign, he wanted the shareholders to approve it directly. He addressed a letter to Black in London, Warren Hellman in San Francisco and Packer, who was in Argentina on the polo circuit.

The letter pointed out that the allegations had been investigated and in every instance had proven to be groundless. It dealt with each of them in detail.

He emphatically denied that some politicians thought he was an impediment to the deal:

Mr Wran, who unlike Messrs Colson and Powers is very well-acquainted with the Federal Cabinet and senior parliamentary members of the ALP, have [sic] told him that the proposition is nonsense. Further Mr Peter Barron, who is Mr Packer's political adviser, denied having ever told either Colson or Powers or anyone else for that matter that Mr Turnbull is a 'political issue'.

... Mr Turnbull doesn't believe his departure from Tourang will enhance the chance of closing, indeed, he believes it will diminish the chances ... [of Tourang winning].

Mr Turnbull's only motive in this transaction is to advance the interests of his clients.

We both believe that the interests of those bondholders who remain investors in Tourang will be enhanced by Mr Turnbull remaining a director.

Turnbull outlined his version of the meeting at Freehills, pointing out that he had agreed to attend as a way of 'bringing this unedifying exercise in character assassination to a close'.

'The only strategic asset Tourang has was brought to Tourang by this firm through Mr Turnbull. Now it appears Mr Turnbull is going to be rewarded for this by a humiliating dismissal.'

In what seemed to be a barely disguised warning of what might happen if an ABT inquiry eventuated, Turnbull and Wran continued:

In our view, Mr Turnbull's resignation will ensure the ABT inquiry. The ABT will undoubtedly view Mr Turnbull's departure as yet another example of dissension within the ranks of Tourang which could result in evidence being available contrary to the testimony of Messrs Packer, Black, Colson and Powers.

For this reason the ejection of Mr Kennedy (also at the hands of Messrs Colson and Powers) was similarly a huge strategic error.

Concluding the letter, Turnbull and Wran listed five conditions of any agreement to depart Tourang. First the three gentlemen must signify that they wished Turnbull to resign; then he would only resign on the completion of the purchase.

They turned to commercial matters. They were conscious of the fees Turnbull was due to receive if Tourang won. It was one thing to fight to the death, it was another to jeopardise the fee income. They demanded that the Ord Minnett–Turnbull fee of $4.2 million be put into an escrow account. This was designed to make sure Turnbull's share of the fee was safe from any legal action against him by Tourang.

Some claims were also made on behalf of the bondholders. These had been approved by Ezzes who agreed, after strong coaxing, to back Turnbull in his demands. Turnbull wanted Tourang to agree to a cash underwriting of the junk bonds for $125 million (up until now the bondholders had been offered $125 million in Fairfax debentures for their bonds) and to change the terms of the call option so that most of the bondholders would still get their cash if the call option was exercised. The final demand was ominous and reinforced the fears within the Tourang camp that the bondholders were under pressure from O'Reilly.

Turnbull requested that if Tourang's offer was rejected by the receiver the bondholders would be released from the exclusivity agreement.

Content with his efforts, Turnbull ended the day feeling somewhat better and got ready for his night's outing.

■　■　■

Senator Chris Schacht was enjoying the meal in the dining-room of the New South Wales State Parliament House overlooking Sydney's Domain. Over the years crowds have gathered on the Domain every Sunday to hear speakers argue passionately for their cause—from an end to conscription to Nazism and banning uranium mining.

The diners gathered in Parliament House that evening were also there to support a cause—the transformation of Australia into a republic. Schacht was a firm supporter of the republican movement, as was Malcolm Turnbull.

Schacht felt a hand on his shoulder.

'Hello, Chris. How are you?' Turnbull asked.

Schacht hadn't heard from Turnbull since the lobbying on the foreign ownership issue at the time of the Caucus debates in October. Their conversation soon came round to Fairfax.

Turnbull told Schacht he was in favour of a charter of editorial independence for Fairfax journalists but claimed that he was outvoted and had been told to be quiet about the issue. He then reassured Schacht that he wouldn't need to worry about Tourang.

'Packer's fucked, Packer will have to pull out,' he said before moving on to the issue closest to his heart.[1] 'They are trying to kick me off the board too. They are fucked, that's the end of Tourang.'

---

[1] Malcolm Turnbull denies that he made these comments to Schacht.

Schacht was surprised at the outburst and puzzled about why Turnbull had chosen to unburden himself. However, it was interesting gossip to take back to Canberra the next day.

* * *

That same evening Jeff White and Peter Breese headed toward the Harbour Bridge with Fred Cohen in the back of the car. Cohen was fed up with the hothouse atmosphere at the Ritz Carlton. It was like a school camp and there was no privacy. Ezzes' room was across the hallway; Cohen could hear him come in and out, he knew when he had visitors. Powers and Colson were on the floor above. He ran into them at breakfast in the lobby; he couldn't get away from them. White and Breese sympathised. They were taking him away from it all for the night. They would go to Armstrongs in North Sydney, which was off the beaten track.

The trio walked into the restaurant, chatting and laughing. Their laughter was silenced, however, by the sight of Steve Ezzes and his companion Deborah Huber. They too were trying to get away from it all.

* * *

Powers was angry when he picked up the morning newspapers on Friday, 22 November. Both Bryan Frith in the *Australian* and Mark Westfield in the *Herald* had columns stating that Turnbull had the power to drag out the bidding process for Fairfax until after the expiry of the exclusivity agreement on 16 January. Some of the lines explaining the loopholes in the bondholder agreement were almost identical to those stated by Turnbull the previous day.

To make matters worse, Frith revealed publicly that Powers had been considered as a replacement for Trevor Kennedy at Consolidated Press. His column then noted that Powers had worked for Wolfensohn, a director of Consolidated Press International, the group's Bahamas-registered ultimate holding company. Frith suggested that the ABT could examine the relationship between Packer and Hellman & Friedman. Powers was convinced that Turnbull had spoken to the press. Turnbull was finished as far as he was concerned.

* * *

Colson was in the shower on that Friday morning when his phone rang. It was a journalist. Did Mr Colson have any comment to make about the reported rifts between Turnbull and Tourang?

'No, I have no comment,' Colson said.

'Well, I've got one. I think it's great,' was the quick reply.

Powers laughed when Colson repeated the conversation, but they agreed that Turnbull must go. All it would take was one board meeting, one simple resolution passed around the table; Powers considered that it would be an embarrassing non-event.

Packer was informed of the latest problems.

'It's up to you to make a decision,' he said, but expressed amazement at Turnbull's behaviour as reported by Colson and Powers. Overseas, away from the day-to-day running of the bid, Packer could only form a dim view. He wasn't going to argue against dumping Turnbull. He was still determined to become an important shareholder in Fairfax and if it meant kicking out Turnbull, they could count on his proxy vote.

■ ■ ■

That afternoon Burrows and Peter Breese went to Canberra to brief the Treasurer. Kerin was pleased that the level of the latest bids meant that the unsecured creditors were now likely to be paid out in full. This had been one of his main aims in pushing through the Cabinet discussion on foreign ownership in October, keeping the non-voting equity level open so that the auction could continue untramelled.

Kerin was particularly sensitive to the views of foreign investors. It was important not to discourage outside investment, he said. But there were national interest questions too. Burrows came away from the meeting with the feeling that Kerin was particularly anxious not to be seen to be targeting Packer.

■ ■ ■

In Sydney the Tourang holy war was becoming surreal. Turnbull refused to meet with Colson at Freehill's offices and Colson wouldn't meet in Turnbull's office. They finally agreed on neutral ground. Turnbull also demanded that no one else be present.

Colson wondered as he crossed Macquarie Street whether

Turnbull was worried that their offices were bugged. That would be incredible paranoia.

Checking his watch, he stood at the entrance to Sydney's Botanic Gardens, the green oasis that nestles between the eastern side of the central business district above the Opera House and the Harbour. They were going for a stroll through the park. It was something right out of a spy thriller book.

It was at least a nice sunny afternoon for a walk and afterwards he planned to have a drink at the Ritz Carlton. Powers, Carnegie, Miles, Mactier and Colson's wife were waiting there with Ezzes and Huber.

Colson saw Turnbull stomping up the street towards him. This was it.

Exchanging terse greetings, they began their walk. Turnbull outlined his grievances yet again, how unfairly he was being treated. They stopped at a park bench and Colson sat down. He recalls Turnbull became increasingly agitated, pacing up and down, gesticulating wildly and raising his voice.

Colson couldn't believe he was sitting there listening to this wild-eyed man before him. This is like watching second-rate theatre in the park, he thought. What am I doing here?[2]

Turnbull was worried about the consequences if he resigned. Would he get an indemnity for any legal actions arising out of his involvement in Tourang? He didn't want his fees left vulnerable to be used as a set-off in any litigation against him by Tourang.

Colson wasn't able to give Turnbull definitive answers and Turnbull became upset again.

.   .   .

At the Ritz the Tourang crowd were up to their third round of drinks. There was no sign of Colson.

'Perhaps they have been arrested,' Mactier suggested with a grin.

The possibility of Turnbull and Colson wrestling on the ground in $1000 suits was raised and the crowd broke into laughter. Would the 6 pm news show footage of Colson and Turnbull, handcuffed and being thrown into a paddy wagon?

---

[2] Turnbull says that the meeting with Colson was cordial and calm.

Just before 6 pm a smiling Colson, shaking his head, walked into the bar—unscathed—to the cheers of the Tourang group.

Turnbull had finally agreed to resign.

■   ■   ■

Turnbull's agreement to quit was the only positive news in an extremely worrying day. The latest requests from the ABT were very pointed and seemed to be escalating the degree of attention on Tourang.

The ABT had plenty of assistance—representatives of Independent had that day made another journey across the Harbour Bridge to strenuously argue that Tourang was breaching cross-media laws. The Tourang team was becoming increasingly bitter about Independent's intense efforts to scuttle them.

There were real dangers inherent in the ABT's latest demands. The regulatory body wanted copies of all correspondence between Tourang and Turnbull by 5 pm on Monday, 25 November. Tourang knew that Turnbull would have received the same request.

Trevor Kennedy had also faxed in a request that he had received from the ABT. He had been asked to submit his diary notes from March 1990 to the present.

These two requests were the culmination of a flurry of specific requests received from the ABT in the last three days. Kennedy had been asked on Tuesday to send a copy of his employment contract to the ABT, along with any other documentation concerning the decision to appoint him as chief executive. He was also asked for a detailed account of the negotiations surrounding his termination agreement. Colson was also asked for any documentation concerning the decision to appoint Kennedy as chief executive. On the same day Packer was asked about the negotiations surrounding Kennedy's termination agreement from Consolidated Press.

For some reason the ABT was now really targeting Tourang. The questions were becoming incisive.

Colson and Powers understood the risks. Turnbull's nasty letter from Wednesday, laced with innuendos about independent directors, would be placed before the ABT. It was incredibly damaging material; the Tribunal was about to strike gold.

Arriving back at the hotel room after dinner with his wife on Saturday night, Colson leant down and picked up the message that had been left under the door. Just what he needed—a message from Turnbull.

It was getting late, but Colson still picked up the telephone. What was his problem this time?

Within a few minutes they were going over the same old ground. An hour and a half later Colson hadn't budged—unless Turnbull resigned, he would be sacked. It was as simple as that.

Colson went to bed hoping that was the end of the matter.

The next morning Colson's fax machine buzzed. He picked up the page—it was from Turnbull:

Dear Dan

As you know I spoke to Brian Powers this morning. He told me that he had 'teams of lawyers' getting ready to sue me, and that my refusal to resign from the board was 'professional and financial suicide'.

He said that I had made 'three powerful life-long enemies that would ruin me'.

In light of these remarks, I naturally sought advice from senior counsel (only one, I can't afford teams). I have been advised that not only should I not resign from the board, but I should not give any accommodation on short notice.

It is clear that despite the goodwill Conrad has extended to me, your partner Powers is planning to sue me—he said for defamation. In the circumstances I am advised that I should do nothing but await the actions under the Corporations Law.

If you wish to reconsider your position, please call.

Malcolm Turnbull

Having created a Mexican stand-off with Colson, Turnbull left for Malaysia on other business. Soaring thousands of metres above the desert there was plenty of time to stew over the events of the last few days. To fill in time Turnbull drafted a little missive to the receiver Des Nicholl. He faxed it through to Sydney from his hotel in Kuala Lumpur on Sunday afternoon, unsigned:

Over the past month or so my colleagues Dan Colson and Brian Powers have been reporting a series of comments made about me which they say were uttered by your financial adviser, Mark Burrows.

Turnbull went on to outline the allegations—that his (Turnbull's) relationship with Kerry Packer was a key element of the ABT's concerns; that the ABT was 'out to get' him; that his presence on the board was a 'major political negative'; and that the banks did not want to deal with Tourang if Turnbull was on the board. Turnbull stated that he would like to bring the matter to a head:

Has Mark Burrows had discussions with Colson and Powers and has Burrows told Colson and Powers that the Tourang bid would improve if I cease to be a director? Mark Burrows has said things about me which are calculated, indeed designed, to cause my colleagues to lose confidence in me and to do that which they have recently done, namely ask me to resign.

Finally, Des, I apologise for raising this matter with you at all. But the duty, I feel, to deal with these particular assets is your responsibility and Mark Burrows is at best your agent. Given the gravity of the matter I felt it best to approach you directly as the principal concerned.

Turnbull's fax was the first indication Nicholl or Burrows had had that Turnbull had been asked to resign. The fax was not signed. Nicholl's legal advice was not to discuss the matter with Turnbull until he was prepared to sign the letter. Turnbull said he had forgotten to sign it and would send a signed one.

• • •

On the morning of Monday, 25 November, Colson arrived at work prepared to investigate formally sacking Turnbull. The rift was now public following articles in the morning newspapers. This further airing of the battles within Tourang added to Colson's anger over the situation.

Colson and Tourang's advisers blamed Turnbull for this latest round of leaks and, since the row was already out in the public arena, it was agreed by mid-morning that a statement would be released later in the day confirming the intention to sack Turnbull at a shareholder meeting to be convened for Friday.

Both Miles and Levy were still not so sure about the wisdom of sacking Turnbull but Colson knew that Packer had no objections. It had to be done. A letter was despatched to Turnbull, responding to his correspondence of the previous Wednesday and Thursday and conveying Tourang's own warning.

Turnbull had spent the weekend on the telephone to bondholders, among others, as he conducted his guerilla warfare against Tourang. Even Warren Hellman had received calls. Powers, however, had kept Hellman briefed so he hadn't taken the calls.

Receiving the fax of the letter signed by Colson, Turnbull scoffed. The letter's threats didn't worry him.

'There seems little point at this time,' the letter read:

in traversing in great detail all the misleading and inflammatory remarks and statements made in your letter. This will be dealt with if necessary, at the appropriate time and in the appropriate forum.

. . . Nonetheless, there is a number of particularly misleading and objectionable statements in your letters which cannot go unanswered.

To begin, some of what you say appears to contradict your statutory declaration dated 25 September 1991 and to other related correspondence.

The letter then went on to refute Turnbull's claims that the 31 October offer was in breach of the exclusivity agreement. It also suggested that Turnbull's actions were not in keeping with the agreement:

. . . some of your actions to date do not appear to be in the best interests to advance the objectives set out in the exclusivity agreement, but instead dictated by personal considerations which we consider to be irrelevant and inimical to Tourang's offer.

You may leave us with no option but to deal directly with the bondholders.

Turnbull's comments regarding the independent directors issue were also refuted and the letter ended with Tourang's own warning:

Your suggestion that our request for you to resign stems from a desire on our part not to have independent non-executive directors is totally false and is evidenced by the proposed appointment of Sir Laurence Street and Sir Zelman Cowen.

Finally, I am of course aware of your threats to 'blow up the deal' and take various other actions in direct contravention of the exclusivity agreement.

Please note that the threats are taken very seriously by Tourang and in the event of any breach of the exclusivity agreement, we will naturally pursue our rights and remedies against you.

Colson's letter was a stinging comeback at Turnbull. If Turnbull wanted to fight Tourang, he would find himself in court. Such was the resentment about his apparent efforts to undermine Tourang's offer that both Colson and Powers vowed Turnbull would be pursued through the courts until the day he died.

CHAPTER SEVENTEEN

GOODBYE KERRY

ACROSS THE Sydney Harbour Bridge at the ABT offices there was a sense of heightened expectation among the senior ranks the same morning. They were about to strike the jackpot. A particularly pedantic notice had been sent to Trevor Kennedy that morning.

It superceded the previous Friday's request when Kennedy had been asked for his diary entries in relation to his departure from Tourang. This time he was asked for 'Diary entries or notes made during or after events relating to the circumstances surrounding your resignation from Tourang'. They were to be provided by 5 pm that afternoon, Monday, 25 November. The crucial words on this request were 'notes' and 'made during or after'. Kennedy had not kept a detailed diary during his time at Tourang. He had, however, later written out pages of notes about events that had occurred while he was there.

Mostly written after his acrimonious departure in October, the notes slammed Colson and Powers for their treatment of him. They outlined in graphic language his version of the weekend meeting at the Regent in October and the Monday afternoon meeting with Landerer, Levy and Colson at Freehills. They also noted Kennedy's unhappiness about Packer's support for Colson and Powers' stance—he had been rejected by the man to whom he had been faithful for most of his working life.

Kennedy's jottings, entitled 'The story of my departure from

Tourang: notes for possible litigation, memories etc' were sensational. They included his version of the chain of command at Tourang, which dealt with the question of who gave him instructions.

As evidence for a regulatory authority seeking to grapple with the question of whether Packer had the capacity for a degree of influence or control if Tourang secured Fairfax, it was critical information.

Kennedy discussed the latest request with Landerer and there was no dispute that his jottings could reasonably be construed to fall within the ABT notice. Kennedy's notes were promptly sent off with answers to other questions.

Kennedy still had his obligations under his termination agreement from Tourang to show Freehills a copy of anything he sent off to the ABT, however. A copy of his answers to the ABT request was therefore faxed to Freehills at 4 pm. By this time it was too late for Levy to do anything—the letter had already been delivered to the ABT.

Levy ran through the document and saw the answers to the specific questions. He panicked and frantically telephoned Kennedy.

'Has that letter gone?' he asked.

Kennedy was blunt. 'Yes it has.'

Levy groaned. It was all he could muster as he ran through the implications of the answers in his head. It was a crisis and he dreaded telling Colson.

■   ■   ■

Peter Westerway was finishing off a few urgent matters before rushing to the airport for a flight to Canberra. He had spent the afternoon making changes to the draft statement he intended to deliver to the Print Media Inquiry the following morning. Then he was briefed about the latest sensational responses from Kennedy.

A recommendation for an inquiry was now more likely. However, Westerway didn't intend to make a decision now; he wanted to read through the information provided by Kennedy more thoroughly first.

Sitting in the Australian Airlines aircraft, Westerway carefully perused Kennedy's notes. He had already seen Turnbull's letter

sent to Freehills the previous Wednesday and both matters were
very significant.

The pressure was really on now. Westerway knew that calling
an inquiry would either force Packer to quit Tourang or fatally
damage the Tourang offer for Fairfax due to the length of the
inquiry. Westerway's hand would pull the trigger on the gun that
blew Packer away—the gun a lot of politicians and others wanted
fired but weren't keen to leave their fingerprints on.

Westerway slept uneasily in his room at the Canberra Rex
Hotel. A senior public servant like Westerway could stay in a
plush, expensive room at the Park Hyatt rather than in the older
hotel situated adjacent to the bus station on the main road
into Canberra from Sydney. But he didn't. He had been staying
at the Canberra Rex since the early 1970s when Whitlam appointed the man who had been New South Wales Secretary of the ALP
to the Industries Assistance Commission—Westerway's first public
service post.

The next morning at 6.30 am Westerway pulled on his jogging
shoes ready for his morning run. As he jogged towards a park he
slowly came to grips with his decision. He would recommend an
inquiry into Tourang's offer for Fairfax—and that would require
a further statement to the Print Media Inquiry where he was due
to appear at noon.

Back at the hotel he contacted Fiona Chisholm, the public
relations manager of the ABT who had also come to Canberra,
and asked her to meet him in Beazley's office at Parliament
House. He would prepare an attachment to the statement there.

The statement was faxed to the ABT offices in Sydney and
Chisholm stood by the fax machine waiting for their reply. Staff in
Beazley's office could tell that something major was going to be
announced. But not until Westerway handed a copy of his speech
to the minister, just before he walked into the inquiry room, did
anyone know how big the announcement would be.

Westerway sat down after being sworn in and read out his
lengthy prepared statement, seeking to outline the role of the
ABT. Explaining that one minister had confessed that he didn't
understand the Broadcasting Act, Westerway said that many of
the representations made about Tourang had focused on the

wrong issues, that is, that Mr X or Ms Y was growing more powerful.

'But unless they provide evidence that in the course of growing more powerful the person concerned is potentially or in fact breaching the Broadcasting Act, the Tribunal has no legitimate role.'

After running through the ABT's powers, Westerway indicated the level of pressure that had been put on the ABT over the Tourang bid for Fairfax:

'There is a widespread misunderstanding of the respective roles of the Tribunal, the Trade Practices Commission and the Foreign Investment Review Board (FIRB).

'I do not speak for the other two bodies, but I am concerned that so many media and even political observers seem to see our role as "Stopping Packer". This is not our role, nor has it ever been.'

Westerway then read the attachment, stating that because of important new information received since the initial statement was prepared, he had convened a meeting of the ABT for that night to recommend an inquiry to prevent a breach of section 92JB of the Broadcasting Act. (This is the cross-media ownership provisions.)

Lee opened the questioning and asked about the time frame expected for the inquiry. For Tourang, the answer was devastating.

'It is a bit like saying how long is a piece of string, I am afraid,' Westerway responded. 'I do not expect that it would take a great deal of time; I should have thought a matter of no more than a couple of months at the outside, but probably less than that.'

Westerway was quizzed at length about the question of control. He pointed out that there could be a breach of the cross-media laws, not only if there was actual control, but potential for actual control: 'If you can establish that people have that capacity, whether they have exercised it or not, you are still able to act.

'It is not sufficient for us to say that if you did something in the future you might be in control. We have to show that the agreements or understandings that you have at the moment are such that there is a potential for you to do it. You have to have committed yourself to something.'

On this basis the information received by the ABT, especially Kennedy and Turnbull's answers and correspondence, was enough to convince the ABT that in its view, legally, there was sufficient evidence to investigate whether Kerry Packer was breaching cross-media laws. There were allegedly understandings in place that potentially gave Packer the capacity to exercise control as a shareholder in Fairfax.

Following the Print Media Inquiry Westerway returned to Sydney. By coincidence the ABT was holding a conference at the plush Peppers on Sea resort at Terrigal, the beachside town north of Sydney (famous for the 1975 Labor Party conference that occurred amidst the blaze of publicity over Deputy Prime Minister Jim Cairns' declaration that he had a 'kind of love' for his recently appointed office co-ordinator Juni Morosi).

The ABT conference was not due to commence until the Wednesday morning and there were frantic telephone calls to bring the Tribunal together that evening for a formal meeting to discuss Westerway's recommendation and the latest information from Kennedy and Turnbull. Westerway formally recommended an inquiry and members of the ABT agreed.

The meeting broke up and the members gathered in the Brasserie for dinner. A group of journalists and photographers, who had rushed to Peppers to seek comments, approached while they were dining, but Westerway was in no mood for a comment. He refused being photographed and was furious when a *Sydney Morning Herald* photographer took one despite this.

He stood up and followed her. 'No photographs,' he barked. 'If you publish that I will take legal action.'

He had visions of a front-page article: 'Tribunal Feasts in Luxury Hotel as Tourang Goes to Trial'. The photo didn't appear.

. . .

The ABT inquiry announcement placed a sense of despair over the Tourang consortium. It had lived under the cloud of an inquiry for months but the actual announcement was a tremendous shock.

Convening an urgent meeting on Tuesday, Colson, Powers and the lawyers grappled with the issues of how to respond, examining whether tactically a legal challenge should be launched in the Federal Court.

The inquiry stood to kill the whole deal; a two- or three-month inquiry, even if it made no adverse findings against Tourang, would drag everything past 16 January. Certainly Tourang's legal advice gave what it considered reasonable options to block the bondholders from going elsewhere. But the risk of everything breaking down into a barrage of litigation was a horrific thought.

The next morning Colson, Levy and Powers went to discuss the impact of a lengthy inquiry with Burrows. When they arrived, Fred Cohen was also sitting in Burrows' office.

It was made clear to the Tourang team that they had a major problem; why should the banks hang around for possibly three months while Tourang went through the ABT inquiry? Burrows reminded Tourang of its other regulatory problems—its offer hadn't cleared Kerin and the FIRB.

Colson and Powers were in a fighting mood, however. They would beat this inquiry. The bid was still on.

■　■　■

David Craig and Rupert Thomas from the ANZ came up from Melbourne for a hastily arranged meeting at Baring Brothers on Wednesday afternoon. They were worried. Packer was placing a degree of pressure on the ANZ to expedite the process. He had a number of valuable accounts with the bank. This complicated matters enormously. They wanted to know what the consequences of the ABT decision were going to be.

■　■　■

The next morning on Thursday, 28 November, Kerry Packer's voice boomed out of the speaker phone as Colson and Powers finished outlining the limited options now that the ABT had called an inquiry. He was very angry about the Westerway announcement and Turnbull and Kennedy's behaviour was considered treason. The main issue, however, was whether Packer would remain as a shareholder.

In his usual colourful language, spiced with plenty of four-letter words, he made it quite clear he had no intention of subjecting himself to another grilling in a public inquiry. Costigan and the Print Media Inquiry were enough for his lifetime. The prospect of a public ABT inquiry, where interest groups like the Friends of Fairfax and the Age Independence Committee or Australian Journalists Association could cross-examine him, didn't appeal.

No, Packer had had enough. He would quit Tourang so that its offer for Fairfax did not have to be put through the scrutiny of an ABT inquiry that would throw the bid into limbo.

The American and Canadian were both relieved and disappointed. A Tourang bid minus Packer still stood an excellent chance of winning Fairfax. However, they had become friendly with Packer and fervently believed that the manner in which he had been dealt with by politicians, Fairfax newspapers and others opposed to his participation in Tourang had been disgraceful.

Packer's withdrawal was a gracious act, for Colson and Powers had been prepared to stick by him.

The ABT was informed of Packer's decision and preparation began for a public announcement.

Packer was not going away empty-handed and it was agreed that a settlement would be negotiated in return for his forfeiting his shareholding in Tourang. Under the original Tourang formation agreement, Consolidated Press was to receive 30 million December 1993 $1.00 options in Fairfax if Tourang seized control.

It was now decided that on 30 December 1993, Fairfax would pay Packer out under an agreed formula. Fairfax would pay Consolidated Press 30 million shares multiplied by the average share price for the twenty days prior to 30 December 1993 minus $30 million. So if Fairfax shares were trading at $2.00 at the time, Packer would be paid $30 million. Even as a loser Packer was given a lucrative consolation prize.

The concern that Turnbull might be looking at ways to scuttle the bondholder exclusivity agreement prompted a serious look at the impact of Packer's exit on that agreement. His withdrawal meant that an original party to the agreement had gone and some of the bondholders might try to argue this was a material change that impacted on its enforceability.

Levy was relieved to see a clause that covered this event. Packer was allowed to assign his shares to a nominee.

It was agreed that Consolidated Press' 14.9 per cent would be assigned to Australian institutions. They would be placed by

Ords when it sought to raise the funds required from institutions if Tourang was successful.

The withdrawal of Consolidated Press put the pressure right back on Miles. Suddenly the consortium needed to find another $80-odd million for its offer from institutions and, before this occurred, Ords would need to underwrite the extra funds.

The stakes were becoming a lot higher for Miles. The turmoil within Tourang over the last two months was a great worry in terms of securing institutional support. In July Miles had confidently told institutions that Tourang was the best consortium available. Since then, however, everything had changed. Tourang now had no chief executive and no Packer. The financial community was abuzz with the gossip about the blazing row with Turnbull and newspaper articles about cracks within the bondholders' loyalty.

Miles had got Ords involved in the first place and now needed to secure the board's support to an underwriting exposing Ords to a commitment well over $300 million. The approval came through without any problems. Ords wasn't going to drop out of such a major transaction and allow some competitor to muscle in on its fees and the prestige of the deal.

● ● ●

It was 9.20 am on Thursday and Burrows was leaving his office for a Brambles board meeting when a call came from Powers. Could Powers and Colson come and see him? The matter could not be discussed over the telephone. Could they see him alone?

They came into Baring Brothers at 10 am. What would the consequences be for the Tourang bid if Packer were to withdraw?

Burrows was stunned. Only the day before these two had been in his office claiming they would fight the ABT to the end. Colson took Burrows through the plan in detail; they could win but there would be delays. They repeated their conversation with Packer: he would withdraw if it would give Black and Hellman & Friedman a good chance of winning.

Burrows' view was that all political impediments to the Tourang bid would be removed if Packer withdrew. He was excited about the development and said that Kerin and Hawke should be told. Colson replied that he would make a few calls to Canberra.

'No, I'll go down and tell them,' Burrows insisted. This strong desire seemed odd to Colson. What was wrong with the telephone?

Burrows wouldn't budge.

'Ruth, I have to get to Canberra,' he shouted to his Scottish secretary sitting outside his office. 'It's urgent. Look, hire me a jet if you have too.'

Entering his office a few minutes later, Ruth told Burrows that she had booked him a seat on a commercial flight that would get him to Canberra in plenty of time. Burrows appeared to be disappointed that he wouldn't be whisked away in a Lear jet.

Kerin agreed to see Burrows at short notice.

'Mr Kerin, there has been a significant development and we would like to know on behalf of the banks what the consequences are of that?'

Kerin was perplexed—yes, what was it?

'Well, Kerry Packer is in Argentina playing polo, but he has said he is out.'

The Treasurer was silent for a full minute. He was staggered but visibly relieved. A weight had been lifted off his shoulders: targeting Kerry Packer was no longer an issue.

'How confidential is this?' he asked.

'Only the Tourang team and those of us in this room know, but there is a press statement for release later in the day.'

Kerin rang through to the Prime Minister's office.

'I've got Mark Burrows with me. I have got some very exciting news. Can he spare a couple of minutes?'

Burrows repeated his news in the Prime Minister's office. Hawke spluttered: 'Can you say that again? He's out? There's no way he can come back? He's not going to appear after the ABT?'

'No,' Burrows said.

'Do you think he's gone because of a perception that Caucus was after him?' Hawke asked with a concerned note to his voice.

Burrows skirted around the answer to that one and Hawke smiled. 'Oh in life there are times when a little bit of sunshine is let in.'

He then began scrummaging in his briefcase beside him. 'I've got a letter to show you.'

After what seemed an interminable time, Hawke's head re-emerged above the desk and he handed over a letter dated April 1943. It was a copy of a letter from Sir A Clark Kerr, British Ambassador in Moscow, to Lord Pembroke:

My Dear Reggie

In these dark days man tends to look for little shafts of light that spill from Heaven. My days are probably darker than yours, and I need, by God I do, all the light I can get.

But I am a decent fellow, and I do not want to be mean and selfish about what little brightness is shed upon me from time to time. So I propose to share with you a tiny flash that has illuminated my sombre life and tell you that God has given me a new Turkish colleague whose card tells me that he is called Mustapha Kunt.

We all feel like that Reggie, now and then, especially when Spring is upon us, but few of us would care to put it on our cards. It takes a Turk to do that.

Yours etc.

There was laughter all around before Hawke asked for more details on what the withdrawal meant for the Fairfax bid. It turned out he had misunderstood and thought that Tourang was out completely. He seemed disappointed when it was explained that it was only Packer who had gone and Black would remain as the core shareholder.

With Packer out the media concentration problem with Tourang was over. Packer's desire to get his foot in the door at Fairfax had been thwarted. Neither Rupert Murdoch nor Kerry Packer could now, even if they planned to, have a game plan for the Australian media.

Packer's only way now of controlling his nemesis would be to sell Nine Network and make a takeover bid for Fairfax. This would involve buying out Conrad Black, who probably wouldn't be interested.

Now Black had the chance to own Fairfax in his own right. If Tourang secured Fairfax, Packer and Murdoch would have a new entrant to the Australian media baron club in the shape of Conrad Black.

• • •

The ABT inquiry announcement and the negotiations on the withdrawal of Packer only temporarily distracted attention from ejecting Turnbull. The feud continued to be outlined in newspapers all week as Turnbull spoke to journalists, first from Malaysia and then on his return.

In terms of leverage Turnbull still believed he had plenty of clout. Belligerently, he began to point out potential flaws in the bondholder agreement which could torpedo Tourang. As far as he was concerned the interpretation of various clauses in the agreement required that his approval and consent on various matters was required. Turnbull believed that effectively he was a principal, not an agent of the bondholders.

• • •

Caught in the middle of the brawl, Ezzes was very stressed by the time he returned to the USA. With the fears that Turnbull was actively working against Tourang, Ezzes was being hassled by the Tourang camp to give a commitment on behalf of the bondholders before he left Australia. Tourang must know if the bondholders were right behind it and would cut Turnbull out of the negotiations if necessary.

Miles took Ezzes to the Union Club, one of the institutions of the Sydney business community, for lunch. It is situated next to the Wentworth Hotel in the centre of the central business district. The sombre, old-style dining-room provides the perfect venue to rub shoulders with business contacts, while club membership can ensure a seat at the Rugby test matches with a pre- and post-match drink at the club.

More importantly, those ambitious young finance industry executives, merchant bankers, stockbrokers and corporate advisers who join the club have the opportunity to bump into the older guard they need to meet. The Union Club makes a nonsense of Sydney's jokes about the Melbourne Club and the networking that takes place there.

Miles knew from Ezzes' nervous state that he was being verbally battered by Turnbull who considered Ezzes guilty of treason for his apparent backing of Tourang in this row. The friendship between Ezzes and Turnbull, which had blossomed when they had a common enemy—the banks and Burrows, had ended and was poised to blow apart forever as the American moved toward a hard decision. He had sought legal advice on Turnbull's position under the bondholder agreement. Ron Sackville QC advised that Turnbull was only an agent.

Ezzes was aware that Tourang's legal advice also claimed Turnbull was only an agent of the bondholders. Colson demanded, as Ezzes prepared to return to New York, that he take a stronger role in the process and to make sure Turnbull didn't do any more damage to the transaction.

By the time he left Australia, Ezzes was no longer a Turnbull supporter—he wanted him fired. Just before he left he sent Turnbull a letter. From now on Turnbull was only to act on written instructions from the bondholders.

Turnbull was indignant about Ezzes' letter and his collaboration with Tourang. Ezzes might be chairman of the bondholder committee, and the Airlie Group might own a parcel of bonds, but that was it. Turnbull was the legal and financial representative with the power to speak for the bondholders.

Speaking to some of the bondholders, including the government body the RTC, and Executive Life, Turnbull was told that Ezzes had reported that he was running amok and acting without authorisation. Turnbull immediately convened a conference call for early the next morning. For hours he fiercely denied Ezzes' comments and, to make sure of his position, agreed that he would not do anything under his discretionary powers unless the majority of the bondholders approved it in writing.

'I don't want there even to be a hint of a suggestion that I am doing anything, or taking any decisions that are not completely approved by you,' he said.

With Executive Life and RTC supporting him, Turnbull ensured that although he was going off the board, Tourang hadn't seen the last of him.

* * *

On Friday morning, 29 November, Turnbull arrived at Freehills for the shareholder meeting called to terminate his board membership. He brought with him an unexpected guest. Neville Wran had come to mediate the dispute, giving a conciliatory speech that something ought to be worked out—a dismissal was unnecessary.

He found at first an uncompromising Colson who had no intention of backing down. Turnbull would have to go. However, in order to end the debilitating fight, Colson was later prepared to negotiate as long as the basic ground rule was Turnbull's resignation.

The meeting to officially sack Turnbull was then adjourned. Sitting in a conference room, Levy took notes as Colson, Turnbull and Wran worked out a settlement. At 3.45 pm they came to an agreement that Turnbull would be allowed to resign. The shareholder meeting to sack him was called off.

Tourang also agreed that if there was any litigation with Turnbull, his fee would not be held back and used as a set-off. In return Colson wanted Turnbull to sign an agreement that he wouldn't do anything that prejudiced Tourang's offer and would co-operate from now on. A one-page agreement was then typed up outlining these points.

As a parting shot Turnbull warned Levy that Ezzes and McClure, the co-chairmen of the bondholders' committee, could no longer speak for all the bondholders with any authority. He moderated the impact, though, by adding there was every reason to believe the bondholders would still support Tourang. To further boost his position Turnbull insisted that Ezzes write that day to the receiver, stating emphatically that Turnbull was still in control as representative of the bondholders.

So Turnbull joined Kennedy in becoming outcasts of Packer's fiefdom. They both knew that in Packer's domain you were either a friend or an enemy. The long-harboured goal of becoming an influential director of Fairfax had evaporated; the only solace for both men was that the ABT had ensured that Packer would not be part of Fairfax either.

■   ■   ■

From London Black went public over the traumatic events of the last few days in an interview published in the *Herald*. A confident Black claimed that Tourang was the overwhelming favourite and considered that all political obstacles had been cleared.

'It finally seems as if this long, degrading, grotesque charade is almost over. I think we are going to win. We are not complacent and we are not over-confident.'

Asked if Packer would make a comeback if Tourang won, Black said that this suggestion was the 'last gasp of the militant, dubious, unprofessional and wholly undesirable clique that is debasing this great company Fairfax'.

However, Black reserved most of his vitriol for Independent, slamming O'Reilly's efforts to push legal opinions suggesting the bondholders could desert Tourang:

I think if he's going to put that sort of charlatanism around Sydney, he'll just have to go back to selling ketchup in Pittsburgh.

O'Reilly and his acolytes have been putting around this appalling disinformation that I meddle, that I'm a domineering proprietor. It's not true, just ask any of my employees here.

They said we have a problem with the ABT. We don't. They said we had a problem with the FIRB and we don't. There are no other obstacles in our way.

Like his hero Napoleon on the eve of the Battle of Waterloo, Black sniffed a glorious victory within his grasp.

· CHAPTER EIGHTEEN ·

THE BATTLE FOR
BROADWAY

BURROWS STARED at the large bronze elephant on his sitting-room table. It was hand-beaten, over 100 years old and about forty centimetres high. It reminded him of the photographs in Kerry Packer's office. When you sit opposite Packer's desk there are large pictures of elephants on the wall behind him.

Everyone is into elephants, Burrows mused, and then drew his attention back to what Tony O'Reilly was saying. Yes, Fairfax is one of the great media assets of the world he agreed. Burrows was tired. He had just returned from Canberra. Also, quite apart from his pressured business dealings, Burrows was suffering tremendous personal stress. A few months earlier his wife of twenty years, Mary, had died tragically young of a rare form of cancer. As Burrows later told Caroline Jones on ABC Radio's 'A Search for Meaning', Mary was his best friend as well as his wife:

People asked how I coped in 1991. I coped by trying not to think about it. I became incredibly busy . . . I preferred working because I wasn't alone . . . But I went through a period for nearly six months of waking up at 3 or 4 in the morning and thinking and becoming incredibly upset with a sense of frustration and grief.

●   ●   ●

O'Reilly had brought his new wife Chryss with him on this trip to Australia. They had arrived earlier in the week and Burrows wanted to make her feel welcome. Tonight O'Reilly was friendly, a marked contrast to his demeanour at his first meeting at Baring Brothers on Monday.

There had been no rugby jokes then. O'Reilly was furious about AIN securing J B Were as an underwriter. Were was his underwriter; what were they playing at? It didn't show much confidence in the Independent bid if J B Were could say it would underwrite whichever bid won! How could Burrows let this happen?

There had been another spat with AIN too. Peter Hunt from Bankers Trust (BT) was claiming that at least two of AIN's major institutional backers were also supporting Independent. Burrows had passed this on to Mark Johnson who had replied that morning in writing: 'We have spoken to each of the members and they are unequivocal that the information given to you is false.'

His letter ended with a touch of humour: 'It is important that you have correct information on this aspect of the institutional position. What you have been given has more than a touch of blarney!'

Tonight, however, O'Reilly was enjoying the crisis within Tourang. He was upset with Black's comments about him, though not surprised—this was corporate war and there were few, if any, rules.

They sipped their pre-dinner drinks. This was Chryss' first visit to Australia. All she had ever heard about the country from Tony was Fairfax, she commented.

Chryss is a wealthy woman in her own right and has a very successful horse-breeding operation in France. They talked about horse racing before moving inevitably to Fairfax. Burrows had displayed his ignorance of the track by misunderstanding the price of one particular thoroughbred. When Chryss O'Reilly said 600, Burrows took it to mean £600—she had meant £600 000. Fairfax was safer ground for him.

For the first time O'Reilly disclosed his plans to expand Fairfax into South-East Asia and the USA to make it one of the great newspaper chains in the world. He still believed that Tourang wouldn't succeed, even after Packer's withdrawal. There was too much feeling in Canberra against a high level of foreign owner- ship. They talked until well after midnight.

•   •   •

O'Reilly's presence in Australia had an astounding effect on the morale of the Independent team. Always the super salesman, O'Reilly asked for one last effort to make sure everything possible—commercially and politically—was done to further the Independent bid. Independent might not win Fairfax, but the fees—now heading for $2 million—were not to going to be wasted. O'Reilly and his team would go down fighting.

In his first strategy session with Healy, Reynolds, Cameron O'Reilly, Ross and Hunt in his suite at the Regent Hotel the tasks for his visit were made clear. They must target the politicians and the institutions.

The only regulatory hurdle left to Tourang was political, therefore the Irish must escalate their only remaining blocking tactic: the successful killing of Tourang in Canberra. On a political level the exit of Packer had cooled some of the heat on Hawke regarding the media concentration issue and Tourang's chances of getting through Kerin appeared improved.

But Black's conservative views and his sniping at the politicians weren't making him any friends. The most important thing going for Independent remained its impressive list of politicians on side.

Hawke was their key supporter. His hold on the leadership was now extremely shaky but he was still behind them. The feedback was that Kerin was still under intense pressure from the left and centre left factions over Tourang's level of foreign equity compared to Independent's proposed strict twenty per cent.

There was a strong possibility that Kerin would block Tourang—and Independent was keeping up the pressure, contrasting its offer with Tourang at the political level at every opportunity. It had even taken the extraordinary step of criticising Tourang in its submission to the Foreign Investment Review Board (FIRB). It devoted four pages of its submission to a section headed 'Observations on the Proposed Tourang Acquisition of the Fairfax Group'.

This had been submitted prior to Packer's withdrawal. It claimed that the Tourang bid was in breach of both the Trade Practices Act and the Broadcasting Act and that it was contrary to the national interest. It criticised the Tourang attitude to editorial independence matters and noted that the important community role played by the Fairfax papers 'should not be compromised through the partisan intervention of proprietors'.

If Tourang won, Independent predicted a period of:

extreme industrial unrest, strikes and loss of valuable staff. In this regard, the Fairfax Group's unions have a great deal of leverage, as they are aware that fifty per cent of the total annual revenue of the *Herald* and the *Age* is derived from the Saturday edition of these papers, which, together, accounts for eighty per cent of the Fairfax Group's total earnings.

That FIRB submission was well-circulated around Canberra and Sydney by the Independent team. On the commercial side the underwriting from Weres gave Independent the clout to push the claim that it could better Tourang's $1.425 billion bid. But it still lacked support from the institutions. AMP and National Mutual hadn't budged from their backing of AIN and the lack of support from these two powerhouses was a sore point.

O'Reilly's return now allowed scope for some massaging of the key personalities, including Gil Hoskins at National Mutual and the troublesome Sir James Balderstone at AMP. The push on dividing the bondholders continued in New York where Liman was maintaining the pressure. The bondholders were now being told that they would receive $150 million or more from Independent if they could somehow extricate themselves from the clutches of the exclusivity agreement.

Independent's knowledge of the substance of the secret bondholder agreement gave hope that, if the bidding process dragged past 16 January, Tourang's advantage might disappear. The only way Independent would ever know if that was the case, however, was if the sale process went beyond the expiry date. On this front Independent lawyers Corrs had been briefed to put the pressure on Baring Brothers for a delay. A letter was fired off to Baring Brothers complaining about the sales process, claiming Independent was being discriminated against. There was a veiled threat of litigation.

On another tack Hunt could report how he was vigorously pushing the line to Baring Brothers and the press that the receiver wasn't obliged to accept the highest offer now that the banks were covered for their loans. The receiver had satisfied his primary obligation. With Tourang facing enormous problems getting past Kerin, it had serious completion risks and on this basis the receiver could be justified in accepting a lower offer.

The unceremonious dumping of Trevor Kennedy had given Independent an opportunity on the personnel side. Perhaps Kennedy could be given a position at Fairfax if Independent was the successful bidder? In the short term, however, there was one obstacle—Kennedy's termination agreement with Tourang restricted him from dealing with Independent at this stage. O'Reilly himself didn't speak to Kennedy but he decided that in the fullness of time, if Independent was successful, there may be a role for Kennedy. Also John Reynolds was enthusiastic about the prospect.

．　．　．

This was vintage O'Reilly. Standing on the podium, he was in full flight working the capacity crowd in the ballroom at the Regent Hotel. His self-effacing humour and carefully delivered lines were being devoured by an audience of rugby devotees.

The invitations to the sea of suits in front of him had not been random—Des Nicholl was invited and O'Reilly played up to his presence.

'How am I going Des?' he asked cheekily.

The lunch was in honour of the Wallabies, the Australian Rugby Union team, which had won the World Cup the previous month. In the quarter-final, the team had clinched a victory over the Irish team in the dying moments of the game.

The lunch ambled on into the afternoon. Financial journalists waited to secure a few comments about the Fairfax battle and O'Reilly was asked when he would have a moment to spare for a chat.

'This is a rugby lunch.' He smiled in astonishment at the question. 'It may never end.'

In this case the lunch did conclude. Dozens of red-cheeked finance industry notables slowly walked back up George Street to their offices while some of the less diligent headed into the hotel's bar for a cleansing ale.

The busy schedule continued over the next two days in Sydney as the Irish charm oozed over the fund managers. O'Reilly attended a lunch at stockbroker Prudential-Bache's office in Grosvenor Place, hosted by Wallaby and stockbroker Simon Poidevin. It was another opportunity, over nouvelle cuisine and a few bottles of white and red wine, to meet the men who controlled Australia's savings and explain why they should support Independent.

* * *

Sir James took the call from O'Reilly. They had met in 1983 at a US Steel dinner in Pittsburgh, a retirement dinner for Sir James McNeil who was stepping down as BHP chairman. Balderstone was his successor.

O'Reilly mentioned this and then came to the point of the conversation. 'Can I come and see you?'

There was a pause.

'No,' Sir James replied, deciding that there wasn't any point. He didn't wish to become involved in the Fairfax matter, particularly after the rumour that he had lobbied heavily for AIN and didn't like O'Reilly because of the Irish Sea episode. It would be improper.

'It is best if you contact Ian Salmon in Sydney and he will get you in to see Leigh Hall and the others on the investment team if you want to talk about your bid,' Sir James suggested.

O'Reilly decided to raise the sore issue.

'I know when you were at BHP we had a bit of a hiccup,' he began.

Sir James jumped in. 'Forget about that, Tony. It makes no difference. The AMP investment management team makes the decision on the merits of the investment.'

* * *

With the first round of the pressing of the flesh in Sydney out of the way, the Independent team converged on Melbourne. O'Reilly went to visit Gil Hoskins in National Mutual's bland, box-like head office in Collins Street. They shook hands and sat down in the deep, black leather lounge chairs. A painting from Sidney Nolan's Ned Kelly series caught O'Reilly's eye. The decor in Hoskins' office might be a little ordinary but the art is first class.

O'Reilly was direct. He wanted to know what National Mutual's attitude would be if AIN fell over; would it back Independent? Or was there another agenda?

Hoskins told O'Reilly that they had nothing against his bid *per se*.

'If AIN is out for some reason, we will consider supporting you on the merits of the case,' he told him.

O'Reilly asked if Hoskins had any advice on how they could woo more institutional support.

'Everybody is so straight-faced about this deal,' Hoskins said. 'They are all taking it so seriously. Why don't you try smiling?'

If there is one thing O'Reilly doesn't need tuition on, it is how to spread his charm.

O'Reilly made one other important visit on his Melbourne trip. He saw Michael Duffy, Attorney-General and staunch supporter of the need for a third force in the Australian print media. Duffy had supported the Age Independence Committee (AIC) and although he had not been a public supporter of Independent, behind the scenes he was discreetly behind his friend.

As a cabinet minister Duffy had good access to Beazley and Kerin. O'Reilly had seen Beazley briefly at his office in Sydney, but his attitude had been non-committal. Duffy and O'Reilly discussed where the political pressure would be exerted next. It was obvious that Kerin was the crucial man.

* * *

The members of the AIC stood by the reception desk wondering what the delay was. The staff were cagey and Wilson felt that the security was tight enough to handle a visiting foreign head of state. Finally, Wilson, Claude Forell, Robyn Dixon and Michael Short, an AJA representative, were escorted to a lift. A key was turned—O'Reilly's floor was inaccessible without it. The full O'Reilly contingent—Healy, Reynolds, Hunt and assorted other advisers—milled around the large suite.

After ordering coffee, O'Reilly began lamenting the cost of his bid.

'You have no idea what this is costing,' he complained. The irony of such a statement being made from a penthouse suite in the Regent was not lost on his guests. 'Look, he doesn't come cheap you know,' he added, pointing out various people in the room.

The discussion meandered on and the coffee arrived. This certainly wasn't the black water that passed for coffee in the canteen at David Syme's bleak headquarters. The waiter brought individual coffee plungers, complemented by individual servings of expensive cheese.

Unfortunately O'Reilly wasn't aware of the rules by which the AIC played. Just as it had refused his offer to fly to Ireland to look over operations there, the coffee was rejected. Nothing that would compromise their integrity was the sect-like motto, not even a cup of coffee. The plungers left untouched, O'Reilly mentioned that he had seen Victorian Premier Joan Kirner earlier in the day on a Heinz matter and he wondered why there wasn't more support for Independent on the political level.

'I can't understand why our bid hasn't been publicly supported by the Federal Government,' he said, deliberately underplaying the political victories in Canberra. Once again O'Reilly quizzed the committee about publicly backing Independent.

Wilson dismissed the suggestion.

* * *

By the time O'Reilly was ready to depart Australia he was convinced that AIN was still a serious rival. This would be the case even if Tourang was rejected by Kerin and the bondholders were somehow dislodged from supporting Tourang. With the backing of the two largest Australian institutions and at least twenty-five others, the unlikely team of McKay and Harley had the money that Independent needed in order to succeed.

An unpalatable option was eventually raised and discussed. For months Independent had fought to produce the best commercial offer and tried to derail and discredit its rivals at every opportunity. At this stage, for all its effort, it probably wasn't even ahead of AIN who it had attacked as not possessing any newspaper or management expertise.

Losing would be an embarrassment for Independent. A lesser version of losing, however irksome, was not. So O'Reilly's men decided to speak to AIN and see if they were willing to combine forces.

There had been the polite conversation between AIN chairman Jim Leslie, Rob McKay and O'Reilly in Melbourne in August. This had led nowhere and now it was time for O'Reilly to try again. After their battering in Canberra and the improved odds of Tourang succeeding with Packer gone, O'Reilly wondered if they might feel differently now.

Once again O'Reilly wasn't prepared to give too much away. Even if Independent didn't have the money, it wasn't going to stop pushing and acting as if it had the aces. Any link-up would have to be on terms that put Independent in charge.

* * *

Johnson wasn't surprised when Ross made the overture. He knew about the flirting between Independent and AIN and merger talks were always a possibility in any deal. This initial reaction soon turned sour as Johnson started jotting down the demands that Ross outlined as necessary points for any merger.

The first issue was the board and Johnson listened in amazement. If there was a merger, O'Reilly would be deputy chairman of Fairfax and John Reynolds would be the managing director. Then the rest of the board would be put together from suitable Australians. The proposed AIN board members would only be considered.

However, Ross went on, John D'Arcy could not be on the board. Despite his excellent credentials as a newspaper executive he was too hot to handle. Hawke hated D'Arcy and after massaging Canberra for so long O'Reilly's team were not going to risk losing this advantage.

When it came to the chairman, Johnson raised the position of Jim Leslie, AIN's proposed chairman. Ross responded that he would be a candidate. This was tough stuff—it wasn't a merger, it was a takeover!

The rest of the board composition was discussed, in particular Harley and McKay, the driving forces behind getting AIN going. Ross could give no assurances about their membership of a reconstituted Fairfax board.

Faced with such terms, Johnson wondered whether he should bother discussing this 'offer' with AIN. How could Independent put forward such outrageous terms? It was not as if the Irish were a red-hot favourite to get Fairfax—they were struggling badly on the commercial level to get as far as they had.

AIN knew that if Weres hadn't agreed to do an underwriting of Independent's offer, Burrows would have counted them out long ago. Johnson called McKeon to relay the news. As McKay,

Harley, Leslie and D'Arcy were informed there was disbelief at Independent's approach. What was the point of even mentioning a merger if the other side wasn't giving anything in return?

The more the terms were discussed, the angrier AIN's board became. All O'Reilly wanted was AIN's institutional backers. It was agreed that Johnson should at least meet Ross and put some counter propositions.

They sat down opposite each other at a secret venue—they couldn't let Burrows know about the meeting. The conversation became prickly within minutes as Johnson reeled off AIN's response. If Independent was serious, Johnson said, they would have to fold into AIN and hold less than fifteen per cent of Fairfax. O'Reilly could be a board member and, subject to discussions, perhaps Independent could have a second board position.

Johnson explained pointedly that Independent's overall board proposals were just not acceptable. If O'Reilly was deputy chairman and Reynolds left APN to become managing director, the Irishman would have a direct line into Fairfax. AIN had strong views on corporate governance and wanted a board of arm's-length, non-executive directors.

They would not accept Reynolds as the managing director; he could slot into Fairfax somewhere under Taylor and take his chances to be awarded the position when Taylor eventually retired from Fairfax.

Any chance of a merger was dashed as Johnson continued. Independent's deal to sell the *Newcastle Herald* to John B Fairfax for $32 million was to be cancelled. In addition AIN would want to be given full details of any other arrangements about Fairfax that Independent had made, including advisory fees or plans for management consultants, accountants or lawyers. Ross didn't have much to add as Independent's terms had already been outlined.

By the end of the fifty-minute meeting both men were tense. They knew it was a disaster. As advisers they were both living and breathing their respective clients' campaign for Fairfax. There could be no merger based on demands to basically sack each other's directors.

There was no follow-up call from Ross. Independent and AIN focused again on beating each other into the Fairfax boardroom.

On Tuesday, 3 December, Baring Brothers sent out the invitation for final offers. The deadline date for final bids was 11 December. The draft sales contracts were ready for distribution and each bidder was expected to make its presentation to the banks for financing before the end of the week. The final due diligence arrangements were now in place.

The pressure was great now—the bidders could sense that this would be the final offer. With the banks already holding discussions on financing facilities with each offeror, a decision seemed imminent.

Aware that their final offer wouldn't be able to compete on the ability to offer cash quickly, Independent became aggressive toward Baring Brothers over the next few days. Peter Hunt berated Jeff White and Peter Breese about the exclusivity agreement, suggesting that Baring Brothers had mislead Independent about the strength of the bondholder agreement.

The next tactic was to request that the offers that went in on 11 December were in fact final offers and that no variations would be allowed. That BT suddenly wanted an assurance on this point puzzled Burrows. It didn't make sense—it was in Independent's interests for the sale process to drag out past 16 January. The point on no variations also seemed odd. It would restrict a bidder such as Tourang changing its shareholding structure after 11 December.

The only situation where this might become an issue was if Tourang's proposed high level of foreign shareholding was blocked by John Kerin. Burrows was always aware this was a chance but knew Tourang could then restructure and cut the foreign component.

Perhaps Independent knew something he didn't?

■   ■   ■

John Kerin knew it was almost time to make his decision on Tourang's and Independent's proposals to own Fairfax. Over in the FIRB office Pooley and his staff were diligently working on a report, with the two foreign bidders pressing for early decisions on their proposals. Independent required an answer by 20 December in accordance with a statutory deadline that the Treasurer had to make his decision on an application within thirty days.

Over the next two days Kerin focused on discussing the two

bids with his fellow ministers and the convenors of the factions. He called in the major players from Caucus—Schacht, Langmore, Neil O'Keefe, Ric Charlesworth and Michael Lee to canvass their views.

'With Packer out, surely the major concern in the community about Tourang has been addressed,' Kerin said. 'Can't we now be more flexible on foreign ownership? I'm not going to allow fifty per cent. I may allow around thirty per cent.'

Neither Schacht nor Langmore were interested in this level. Kerin's desire for more discretion wasn't new—he had made it quite obvious when he was a party to that late-night Cabinet meeting in October that ruined Schacht and Langmore's motion seeking a twenty per cent overall limit. They hadn't spent hours vehemently arguing against a high level of foreign ownership in Fairfax since the forty-six–forty-one loss in Caucus to compromise now.

'No,' Schacht said forcefully and went on to warn: 'If you don't make a decision and stick to twenty per cent, you will find another fight in Caucus.

'And, anyway, it would be unfair to allow extra shares to Tourang when O'Reilly has stuck to twenty per cent.'

Schacht's defiance was a problem for Kerin. He didn't need to be reminded of the importance of the centre left's and the left's votes for Hawke in a leadership challenge. Schacht was one of Keating's strongest supporters. This wasn't any time to be cute; the Government was on the back foot and a challenge from Keating was considered imminent. He didn't want to put Schacht offside if he could avoid it.

Langmore remained fervently anti-Tourang and his strong support for Schacht's sentiments left Kerin in no doubt where the left faction stood.

The continuing strong push for a strict twenty per cent limit hardened Kerin's resolve. He was unimpressed with other aspects of Tourang's offer for Fairfax, although the exit of Packer had given him one less reason to send Tourang packing.

Kerin had publicly stated·the issues he would take into consideration in early October when he was in Toyko—would the new owner maintain the quality of the Fairfax Group and journalistic and editorial freedom? Tourang—as Independent and the journalists had constantly reminded politicians for months—wouldn't sign editorial charters. The more he thought about it, the more certain he became that Tourang was not acceptable.

A few days later Kerin's prospects of ever being the man to make the decision to strike out Tourang appeared doomed. Under the scrutiny of television cameras and before a room full of journalists—many salivating at the increasing chances of Paul Keating mounting another leadership challenge—John Kerin made a horrible mistake.

Running through the latest batch of national accounts figures, Kerin stumbled. Grappling for words, he came to GOS, economic jargon for profits. Kerin temporarily forgot the term.

'... The gross operating ... sorry, the gross, ah, share rose. Gross ... ah ... What is GOS?' he eventually asked no one in particular.

One of the journalists told him, and Kerin quickly corrected himself. But it was too late in the cruel world of television. The media seized on Kerin's mind block. Here was the Treasurer of Australia, the nation's ultimate economic master, asking journalists what an economic term meant.

■ ■ ■

Duffy finally decided to make the call. While he had never been Treasurer, this Thursday afternoon on 5 December, he was willing to cross portfolios. He picked up the telephone, not to give moral support to a shaken Kerin facing the sack, but to give Kerin some advice. This could get a decision on the Fairfax bidders before the axe fell.

'Kerin, this is highly political,' he said, referring to the FIRB decision on Fairfax.

'You can ask the FIRB to have a pre-examination,' he said, explaining that this would allow Kerin to make a decision on the two foreign bidders before Burrows made his selection of the winning bid.

This made a lot of sense to Kerin who, until Duffy's call, hadn't known that this was an option. The idea seemed to have a lot of merit. If Tourang's was the offer recommended to the receiver and the banks by Burrows, Kerin might find himself rejecting it after the event. Why not reject Tourang now and leave Burrows a choice of Independent—the Government's favoured candidate—or AIN?

On another level, if Kerin was sacked, it was also possible that a new Treasurer may not take such a hard line on Tourang. That would be a disaster for Independent.

The Irish needed Kerin as Treasurer for a while longer—they needed him to reject Tourang. Unfortunately this seemed extremely unlikely. Tourang's executioner was about to be executed.

Within a few minutes Kerin had telephoned George Pooley.

'Can I do that?' he asked, repeating Duffy's suggestion.

'Yes, Minister,' Pooley replied. 'In fact I have already prepared a minute. I will send it over straight away.'

'Will that help?' Kerin asked.

'No, two say yes and two say no,' said Pooley.

He was referring to the FIRB, which had considered the two proposals; the four members had split their vote down the middle. FIRB Chairman Sir Bede Callaghan and Pooley recommended to Kerin that he approve both proposals; Ken Stone and Des Halstead recommended he reject both foreign bids.

In reaching their conclusion, Callaghan and Pooley said they considered the prospect of foreign control to be outweighed by the benefits of foreign newspaper expertise such as higher quality journalism and more modern technology. The other two members of the Board were blunt in their reasons: they considered that foreign control of the Fairfax press should not be allowed.

Throughout the minute, FIRB bureaucracy's strong support for the foreign bidders and disregard for AIN's prospects were apparent, although this didn't sway Stone and Halstead.

The Independent proposal submitted by BT was based on a twenty per cent voting foreign interest plus an estimated six per cent non-voting debentures for the bondholders. All the key points pushed by Independent during the last twelve months were contained in the submission—the Irish would sign a charter of editorial independence, draw on the management expertise of the O'Reilly flagship, the *Irish Independent*, and introduce separate management structures in Sydney and Melbourne.

In the final proposal to FIRB, Tourang's submission was based on a total thirty-nine per cent foreign economic interest—the

Telegraph (twenty per cent voting), Hellman & Friedman (fifteen per cent non-voting) and the bondholders (estimated four per cent non-voting). In terms of plans if it achieved control of Fairfax, Tourang indicated that it would recruit high quality managers and journalists from overseas.

It outlined plans to cut staffing levels by seven to eight per cent over two years. There was no agreement that Tourang would sign a charter of editorial independence; in fact it submitted a two-page statement on Editorial Policy, which objected to the proposed charters put forward by journalists that denied the board any right or entitlement to express an opinion in the editorial pages of the newspaper. Tourang said this was a long-established proprietorial right, which has widely been acknowledged and exercised.

Discussing both bids' stance on editorial independence and management style, FIRB was a resounding advocate of foreign control of the Fairfax press. It concluded that both bids would bring valuable international expertise to Australia and result in higher quality journalism in the Fairfax papers.

In terms of Kerin's options the FIRB said Kerin could approve or reject both bids or approve one and reject the other; both bids complied with the basic Caucus proposition that not more than twenty per cent of the voting equity in Fairfax be foreign.

It then reiterated the management and technology skills the bids would bring. This view was slightly jaundiced in its broad brush claim that foreign management would improve Fairfax. The media group's Australian management during the mid- to late 1980s achieved profit margins that were the envy of major media groups throughout the world.

FIRB argued strongly against Kerin rejecting both proposals, citing that this option would signal to foreign investors that the Government was inconsistent by not sticking to stated policies, especially since it would be adopting a stricter approach than the Caucus resolution.

In a savage dismissal of AIN, FIRB stressed AIN had no newspaper experience and that it wasn't aware of any plans by the syndicate to acquire expertise comparable to that available to Tourang and Independent.

This was a serious slight on Fairfax's existing management.

Also AIN had made it clear that the experienced Greg Taylor would be chief executive and John D'Arcy a non-executive director—two of the most experienced newspapermen in Australia.

The issue of whether a foreign controlled Fairfax might appoint management which favoured overseas interests against Australian was dismissed. FIRB stated that if a foreign-controlled Fairfax published editorials unacceptable to the nation, this would doubtless be ignored or result in a loss of sales.

In terms of options, any rejection by Kerin of Tourang but not of Independent was considered by the FIRB to be unacceptable. The FIRB said it would be harsh to discriminate between the two bids when their respective economic benefits were similar and when Tourang had the exclusivity agreement. Rejection of Tourang could leave Fairfax in receivership, creditors unpaid and staff demoralised for many months to come due to the problems of a new arrangement with the bondholders and a delay that made bids vulnerable to a stockmarket downturn.

In conclusion the FIRB suggested a decision to approve both bids could be easier to justify. However, if Kerin was to reject both bids the FIRB warned that thought would need to be given on whether to do so under the Foreign Acquisitions and Takeovers Act or the policy guidelines.

A rejection under the Act could lead to a court challenge. The FIRB also warned Kerin that whatever decision he took would be criticised. A press release was suggested as desirable when Kerin made his mind up—and the FIRB said it would send a draft for his consideration.

Reading through the document, Kerin soon realised he didn't support Pooley's thinking on the subject. The FIRB had no problems with the difference in the level of foreign equity between Tourang and Independent, although it was a not inconsiderable thirteen per cent, and while Pooley might think that the option of rejecting Tourang and not Independent would be harsh and discriminatory, Kerin certainly didn't think so.

There was still fierce opposition to Tourang in Caucus and among the influential faction convenors and various ministers. Kerin also was acutely aware that O'Reilly had strong support among many of his fellow ministers.

Tourang's defiant perseverance with a high level of foreign economic interest made the decision so much easier for Kerin and this by itself would have been enough. However, Kerin thought about the other aspects. He didn't like the idea of staff cuts. After all, he was Treasurer and a few hundred extra onto the dole queues through staff reductions at Fairfax was a factor to consider.

Tourang was also refusing to sign the charters of editorial independence that staff at the *Age* and at the Sydney papers desperately wanted.

Kerin decided not to let Tourang through. He would approve Independent.

Picking up his pen, Kerin delivered Tourang a crushing defeat. For the O'Reilly proposal he put a line through the word 'rejected'; for the Tourang proposal he crossed out in one movement of the pen the word 'approved'. He then signed the document and dated it 5 December 1992.

* * *

Kerin's GOS gaffe was a mortal blow to Hawke's leadership—he had put Kerin in the job and Kerin had failed badly. For months Kerin had struggled to make his mark in a difficult portfolio as the Government's standing in the opinion polls plunged due to the recession and leadership instability. Kerin could not offer any hope for the end of the recession and made damaging mistakes for a Government seeking to reassure the public.

On 16 August Kerin was asked how long the economy would trip along the bottom.

'Well, basically your guess is as good as mine,' he replied honestly. His party didn't need such honesty.

Kerin's performance in selling the Budget in August and his impotent parliamentary performance against Opposition Leader John Hewson's radical proposals to introduce a Goods and Services Tax dashed his credibility. In addition he continued to make statements that were later retracted. After telling the International Monetary Fund that Australia was in the worst recession for sixty years, he was forced to retract the statement following howls of derision from his fellow ministers.

Kerin's latest mistake, at a time when the Government was

being embarrassed day after day in Parliament, angered Hawke. Over the past week the influential power brokers had been leaning on him to dump Kerin. With his government in disarray and the performance of other ministers under question, Hawke was lobbied by right-wing power brokers, Senators Robert Ray and Graham Richardson. The message had been simple: Hawke must act swiftly to limit the damage and sack Kerin as a starting point to get some credibility back.

With speculation of a challenge from Keating gathering force by the day, Hawke knew that he must consider it. He had stubbornly refused to stand aside for Keating in June. Never short on ego, Hawke convinced himself that he was the only person who could win the next Federal election for the Labor Party. He had no intention of retiring gracefully for Keating.

*　*　*

The following Friday morning, 6 December, Kerin's mistake on GOS screamed from the front pages of newspapers. So did the push by Richardson and Ray to dump the Treasurer. Hawke knew he had to act or his grip on the Lodge would weaken further. He spoke to Kerin by phone and asked him to meet when he returned to Canberra later in the morning.

Kerin walked into Hawke's office at 11.30 am. The message was brutal. Hawke had considered his options and Kerin must go. There would be a re-shuffle and Kerin had the option to accept the portfolio of Transport and Communications or another portfolio. He accepted Transport and Communications.

Within the hour Hawke had chosen his new Treasurer Ralph Willis, who moved from the post of Finance Minister. Amidst a major upheaval, suddenly thrust into the most sensitive position in the Government in a serious recession, Willis found he had inherited a political hot potato—the decision on Tourang.

Kerin told Hawke and Willis of his action on the Fairfax sale, that he had rejected Tourang and approved Independent, and then ran through his reasons, targeting the high level of foreign equity in Tourang.

'I don't think levels that high will or should be accepted by Caucus,' he said.

Neither Hawke nor Willis objected—the whole issue seemed to run a poor second to this current trauma.

Kerin told Willis he would send around the FIRB minute prepared by Pooley. Willis read it, deciding that it seemed a reasonable decision of Kerin's. He was well-aware of the strong feelings against Tourang by Hawke, other senior ministers and the majority of the Labor parliamentarians. The Kerin decision stood and Pooley was told to advise the two consortiums of the recommendations on Sunday afternoon.

As far as Hawke and the majority of his fellow pro-O'Reilly supporters in the ALP were concerned, the decision to reject Tourang on the grounds of the high level of foreign equity didn't leave too much blood on their hands.

In fact it was a sensational result. As far as they knew, O'Reilly was running second in the bidding process. Finally the Labor Government was on the verge of achieving something they had wanted for over 100 years: a media proprietor controlling Fairfax who might turn out to be a mate or, at worst, not an enemy.

. . .

Malcolm Turnbull was mounting a persuasive argument on why his clients would be entitled to consider requesting more than $125 million from Tourang. With key representatives of the bondholders plugged into this 9 am conference call, he laid out the case. The economics of the whole deal had changed.

Given the higher Tourang offer, if the bondholders were entitled to the same percentage—24.3 per cent—of Fairfax as agreed at the Savoy in June, $175 million was the more appropriate figure. Tourang was also being asked to pay the banks penalty interest of $25 million and it didn't flinch in handing over to Packer at least $15 million in options.

Everyone was getting more money in this deal except the bondholders. There was also O'Reilly on the fringe suggesting that he would pay the bondholders $150 million. Turnbull made it clear, however, that there was no express offer from O'Reilly, but he had no doubt that if the sale process dragged on past 16 January, either O'Reilly or AIN would pay more. He had legal advice that the right of first refusal of Tourang's other shareholders under the exclusivity agreement might not stand up in court.

There were risks, though, in brinkmanship. There was a good argument that it was still worth closing with Tourang to make sure the money came before Christmas.

'If Tourang falls over, you can forget any hope of getting a sale done before Christmas. I think the process will collapse and basically have to re-commence in February,' Turnbull said.

'If we are going to do this, we have to be very tough about it, because you know, we have to be prepared to formulate our arguments.

'The strategy of the exclusivity agreement has worked very well for us, to the extent that it has stopped the asset being sold, we have established a base price for our bonds.

'It is pretty clear if we don't do a deal with Tourang, we will be able to do a higher deal next year.

'But obviously, if we can get the right price from Tourang quickly and get it, it would be ideal. Why wait to hassle with people next year if we can get $150 million or $175 million from Tourang?'

The argument was logical, although there were some misgivings from some of the bondholders. Would the request for more money crater the deal—$175 million seemed too much to ask for.

While Turnbull took another telephone call, Cass O'Connor gave her succinct view on this concern: 'I really don't think a bondholder group asking for more money is going to be anything to tip it over the edge.'

Ho Wang from Prudential-Bache High Yield Fund later asked Turnbull for his rating of the likely success if Tourang was asked for $150 million or $175 million.

'Ho, I'm not a bookmaker. I would think our chances of getting $150 million are high; I think our chances of getting $175 million are not so high.

'I mean, a lot depends on what the other bidders are doing,' Turnbull surmised.

To further diffuse any opposition Turnbull reiterated his point about the low value put on Fairfax at the Savoy to justify why there was no harm in asking for more cash.

'In London we were talking about $900 million plus the bonds, perhaps going to $1 billion plus the bonds. If you had said to anyone in that room: "Do you think we will be paying the banks out?" Kerry and Conrad would have thrown us out the window into the Thames with contempt.'

Finally there was a feeling that it wouldn't hurt to ask for more; the leverage of the exclusivity agreement would be used as a potent bargaining tool. However, Turnbull wasn't going to ask Powers for more money unless he had the Committee's full support.

'There is no point me raising anything with Tourang unless I am doing it with the complete support of the Committee,' he said sternly. 'Because otherwise, they will just ring people on the Committee and then they will come back to me saying: "You haven't got the support of the Committee."

'I mean, they have made a real art form of trying to play the Committee off against me, and me off against the Committee, so you know, it is no point flying a kite because they will be straight back.'

The debate continued over conference calls on Saturday and Sunday, 7 and 8 December. Gradually everyone warmed to the plan. Ezzes was keen to ask for more: he didn't like Powers' attitude.

'Powers called last night. He thinks the bondholder agreement is cast in stone. I am concerned about this guy giving up $15 million in options to Packer but baulking at doing something as simple as underwriting money for bondholders.'

Doug McClure from Drexels was also keen to try for more money: 'I personally have no problem in asking for it, and find out what the response is.'

Conditions were agreed on, including asking Tourang to provide an underwritten cash offer for the bonds on completion. In addition the Committee demanded a condition stating effectively that Tourang had to execute a contract to acquire Fairfax by 16 January. If it was later than this, the bondholders and Turnbull would have to give their approval to a thirty-day extension. It was agreed that the bondholders would go for $150 million—it was about time Tourang shared its generosity around.

Mark Burrows sat in the school hall at Frensham on Saturday evening, 7 December, watching *The Sound of Music* unaware that John Kerin was about to drop a bomb into his carefully structured auction process.

It was 'Final Prayers', or speech day, at the exclusive girls school at Mittagong, south-west of Sydney. His sixteen-year-old daughter Sasha had a part in the play and his older daughter Tika, an arts law student at Sydney University, sat beside him.

Tonight was a sad reminder of Mary's death to Burrows and the girls as the Frensham headmistress, Miss Parker, spoke of those who couldn't be there. Burrows of Baring Brothers seemed a very different person to this caring father who supported his young daughters.

. . .

Quietly closing the door, Levy walked down the carpark at Peppers on Sea resort in Terrigal. The two nights with his family were a welcome break from the sixteen-hour days that he and the rest of the Freehill lawyers had put into this transaction in the last few weeks.

Heading down the freeway on a Sunday morning as the sun edged over the horizon, he thought about the draft contract that his colleague Warren Lee had faxed to him at Peppers the night before. At today's meetings at Mallesons, beginning at 8 am, they would put forward their views on each aspect of the contract. There was still a lot of negotiations to complete.

Levy knew that Mallesons was running these final stages very carefully. The Malleson team had to give the impression that each bidder was being treated equally. The worst thing that could happen at this delicate time was to destroy the confidence of the three bidders. If one bidder felt it was being neglected there was the risk, however remote, of a rush to court that would delay and jeopardise the whole process.

A contract had gone out to each bidder on Friday, with those sent to Independent and AIN covering the possibility of an asset sale to get around the exclusivity agreement. Each bidder now knew, or imagined they knew, how to detect signs of their progress. For months, as the principals and lawyers walked out of the marble foyer below Baring Brothers' office, they had talked about any strange reactions, any flinch or odd answer to a probing question put to Burrows, Breese or White. Any sign of favouring one particular bidder. At times, this bordered on paranoia. But the Freehill lawyers felt good this morning. They spent hours arguing about the wording of various clauses.

John Atkin was at the meeting and it was seen as a good sign. With Atkin there, Freehills knew it was dealing with the A-team. Of course no one expected Atkin every time. They suspected every bidder would see him at this late stage in the process to keep up the illusion of fairness. At some time, however, the illusion would vanish and the skill was to work out just when. You had to be able to detect the arbitrary point when suddenly you got the B- or C-team for any length of time or no invitation to meet at all. At these points depression would set in.

Late in the day the meetings at Mallesons and Freehills wound up. Levy, Chipkin and the rest of the Freehill team went home. Not long after Chipkin arrived, when he was just beginning to relax, the telephone rang. It was Pooley, who proceeded in his measured, unemotional tones to outline that Tourang's proposal had been rejected by Kerin as contrary to the national interest.

Hanging up from Pooley, Chipkin put aside the sick feeling in his stomach and dialled Colson.

The news was devastating. Colson had always known it was possible, although this knowledge didn't make it any easier. The timing appalled him—bids closed at 5 pm on Wednesday and Burrows had been adamant that he wouldn't entertain conditional offers. Tourang would have just three days to restructure and secure a new approval. It seemed an impossible task.

Colson's bitterness about the political process reached a crescendo. Colson and Powers had refused to face the reality of the strong sentiment stacked up against them; they had stuck to legalities in dealings with the ABT and the Treasurer. Kerin's decision might not be enforceable under the law. But sticking to the law wasn't smart in this transaction. The banks didn't care if the policy was enforceable or not. They would never contemplate pressing ahead on a sale that the Treasurer had rejected.

In defiantly persevering with Packer, resentment against Tourang in Canberra had snow-balled. Packer had only withdrawn when the ABT presented him with no option.

The blocking on foreign ownership over twenty per cent had been a strong possibility ever since the divisive votes in Caucus. However, Black had not been prepared to sell down to ten per cent to leave Hellman & Friedman in. And Hellman & Friedman declined to drop out completely, a decision supported by Packer. Tourang had decided on a crash through or crash strategy. It crashed.

Burrows was told the news of Kerin's decision in a 10 pm phone call from a panic-stricken Neville Miles. He was astonished. He thought that the October Caucus decision had settled the foreign ownership question. Without Packer the broadcasting legislation and the increased concentration of media ownership were no longer issues. This was extraordinary.

· CHAPTER NINETEEN ·

THE BID DEADLINE

THE IRISH had won their warfare against Tourang in Canberra. In a superb piece of timing Tony O'Reilly pounced on each of the bondholders on Monday, 9 December, with an extremely carefully worded and personally signed nine-page letter.

This was the end play in trying to sabotage the exclusivity agreement following the determined efforts of Liman in New York over the previous six weeks. Pointing out that final offers closed in just two days, O'Reilly advised them of Kerin's decision to reject Tourang.

Then the hard sell began. With Tourang out, O'Reilly said, the bondholders might now be free to enter into arrangements to participate in Independent's offer; they would have the opportunity to receive more than the $125 million cash offered by Tourang if they joined up by 5 pm on Wednesday—the day final bids closed.

As well as offering more money O'Reilly then, in no uncertain terms, tried to destroy Tourang in the minds of the bondholders. Pointing out that Tourang had been deemed as contrary to the national interest, he added that the Federal Government's policy on newspapers applied regardless of the level of foreign investment.

'Accordingly, there can be no assurance that Tourang could obtain approval for a revised proposal involving less foreign ownership.'

O'Reilly played up the intense public and political controversy and said that the Australian Broadcasting Tribunal (ABT) had not discontinued its inquiry (this was correct as it was still trying to satisfy itself that Packer was definitely out of Tourang): 'Consequently, we believe that it is most unlikely that Tourang will be able to obtain approval for any revised proposal it is likely to submit.'

The letter urged the bondholders that it was in their interests to enter into an arrangement with Independent if they were free to do so. O'Reilly claimed that the receiver wasn't necessarily obliged to accept the highest offer and pointed out that the receiver could sell the Fairfax assets without bondholder approval. He warned that if the bondholders failed to secure their position now, and Tourang withdrew, the Fairfax bidding process might become less competitive—to their disadvantage.

Making these sorts of allegations, and indeed seeking to deal with the bondholders, was a dangerous tactic. In November Tourang had threatened to take legal action if either Independent or AIN sought to deal with them. But the letter was careful and, in guarded language, O'Reilly stated that nothing in it was intended to encourage the bondholders to contravene their contractual obligations.

Concluding, O'Reilly advised the bondholders that if they wished to take advantage of the Independent offer, they should do nothing—unless obliged to do so—to facilitate Tourang's bid for Fairfax. Finally O'Reilly nominated his New York lawyer Arthur Liman and Independent adviser Peter Hunt as contacts.

The bondholders were still trying to work out the implications of Kerin's decision on Tourang's ability to continue. The letter was unsettling and to some extent it worked. That day the bondholders, through Ezzes, faxed a letter to Des Nicholl:

The interest in acquiring John Fairfax has reached the point where the value to be paid for the company has exceeded the level of the secured bank debt.

As a result it appears that the bondholders and the other unsecured creditors are the only parties for whom recovery is at issue.

Fred Cohen, who was back in New York now, told Baring Brothers that his feeling was that the bondholders might not go with Tourang. Meanwhile Steve Ezzes was trying to keep it all together. In an exasperating series of telephone conference calls, he maintained that nothing should be done to jeopardise the exclusivity agreement.

Early on Monday morning Colson explained to Ezzes that hurried efforts were being made to find out why Tourang was rejected and to urgently push through a reconstructed Foreign Investment and Review Board (FIRB) proposal. He also warned about the legal rights under the exclusivity agreement.

Colson had no option, however, but to relent over the payment of more cash to the bondholders. In different circumstances he would have played hard ball. But now it was a good tactic and would ease any lingering damage caused by the Turnbull split and the barrage of legal opinions about the enforceability of the bondholder agreement.

Ezzes and McClure were pushing hard for at least $150 million; Tourang remained adamant this was too high. Powers had been handling the negotiations to date, but Colson was now involved and saying $140 million would be the maximum. This carrot from Tourang was excellent ammunition for Ezzes to throw back at some of the unruly financial institutions interested in O'Reilly's letter.

The message was clear: Ezzes and McClure told the others that they must stick together. What would happen if Tourang still won, and they had breached the exclusivity agreement? They would then be in a terrible position to renegotiate anything with Tourang.

• • •

In the conference room at Macquarie Bank in Melbourne on Monday afternoon the mood was confident but not arrogantly so. Harley and McKay sat opposite McKeon and Kent, going through aspects of the final bid to be lodged in just two days.

This task was really a diversion from throwing opinions around about Tourang's demise. No one seriously thought that Tourang would be able to restructure to a lower foreign equity component and get through Willis in just two days. Willis didn't have to make a decision immediately. He could, hopefully, sit on the application for another thirty days.

In commercial terms the AIN team considered its final offer excellent. Running through the numbers, McKeon and Kent had nailed down an offer that valued Fairfax at $1.52 billion. It had been tough work in the last few days convincing some of the core institutions to back such a high offer.

However, the two-tiered structure (plus a sweetener for core institutions) was considered a clever ploy. AIN's core shareholders would subscribe for a total of 360 million shares at $1.00 each. In addition they would be issued with one free option on a one-for-four basis, exercisable in five years at $1.25 a share. Then early in the new year there would be the public float underwritten by Weres.

This float was aimed at giving the core investors an attractive entry price. It would involve the issue of an additional 370 million $1.00 shares at an issue price of $1.30, or $1.24 after deducting the five per cent underwriting fee payable to Weres. This would raise an additional $457 million to be handed over to the banks after the float.

Under the AIN plan $680 million in borrowings and leases would remain in Fairfax and the offer assumed a further $30 million in cash remained in Fairfax. A widespread public float at $1.30 a share immediately delivered the core investors who bought their shares at $1.00 with a profit, assuming that the float was fully subscribed.

The pricing was excellent, although everyone knew there remained one fatal flaw. AIN still didn't have the bondholders, and Lazard Freres was treading water in its capacity to work out a way for AIN to scuttle the exclusivity agreement.

The offer intended to match Tourang by giving the bondholders non-voting debentures but they also had a clever reset mechanism that would give the bondholders a share of the premium achieved on the sharemarket float.

The extra return to the bondholders would be calculated by taking the issue price plus fifteen per cent and then subtracting that from the share price three months after listing. Half of the difference would be payable to the bondholders, the amount dependent on how many bonds each held. Under AIN's proposal the bondholders could end up with $200 million.

●　　●　　●

A depressed group of men assembled in the conference room at Freehills mid-morning on Monday. Even though they had known for months that the anti-Tourang feeling was strong in Canberra, there was still astonishment at Kerin's decision.

The exit of Packer was supposed to sufficiently appease Canberra, but once again Tourang had been stepped on, thrown out just days before bids closed.

Still the sacking of Kerin was a plus if the rumours from Canberra were correct. One strong line was that Kerin had been forced to make the decision earlier than planned because of his sacking. He had, according to the whispers, intended to announce his decision on Wednesday, the day bids for Fairfax closed.[1] If this had occurred he could have ambushed Tourang by giving it no time to put in a new proposal. Even if Tourang had got an extension from Burrows, Kerin wouldn't have had to make another decision for up to thirty days, effectively dragging the sale process out past 16 January.

Suddenly an even bigger conspiracy theory began to grow. No wonder the Independent camp had been acting like winners— they must have known through their Canberra connections that Kerin was going to delay the decision. But Kerin was gone; it was now just history. The submission of a revised proposal was the issue at hand and there were still a number of potential hitches.

Where did Willis stand? He would have to be pressured to quickly make up his mind.

There was no need to discuss whether to slash the foreign economic interest in the new proposal. All the indications from Canberra were that the proposed thirty-nine per cent foreign economic interest was the primary excuse used by Kerin to justify knocking Tourang out. They had to make their proposal an identikit of O'Reilly's.

The new submission would involve Hellman & Friedman reluctantly cutting its proposed shareholding from fifteen per cent to five per cent. This was a debilitating option for them. It hardly seemed worth it to Powers. All this trauma, cost and time to end

---

[1] Kerin strongly denies that he intended to do this.

up with a paltry investment in Fairfax of $35 million instead of $103.5 million.

The new FIRB proposal would be based on the Daily Telegraph taking a fifteen per cent voting shareholding, Hellman & Friedman a five per cent shareholding in non-voting debentures, and the bondholders an estimated six per cent non-voting debentures. This twenty-six per cent total foreign economic interest mirrored O'Reilly's foreign shareholding.

Tourang's re-structured offer left it $103 million short on the cash component of its offer. Miles got his second approach from Colson and Powers. Would Ords Minnett underwrite the additional funds?

This time Ord Minnett was under pressure. Miles was still digesting the request from Tourang that Ords underwrite the $125 million cash pay-out alternative to the bondholders. (Tourang had decided to offer the bondholders the cash alternative they had been pushing for in a bid to ensure that they would not break ranks.)

Adding up the numbers for this latest request, Miles was worried: Ord's potential exposure was $462 million. These were serious numbers, especially with the sharemarket jittery after the Japanese stockmarket's fall in November. If something unexpected happened, the institutions might baulk at Tourang's fundraising, potentially leaving Ords to find the money to honour the underwriting. Certainly Westpac owned the firm, but the fall-out from an urgent loan to fund Tourang was too horrific to consider. And when the retribution swept through Ords, Miles might as well book himself a long holiday in a cheap resort back in South Africa.

If Ords was going to do it, the fee side of the equation would need to be adjusted. The extra risk would cost Tourang. Miles informed Colson that Ords would charge separately for the underwriting: Tourang would need to pay a net $8.4 million fee.

As the funding and fee for the re-structuring was being negotiated, Colson and Powers contacted Burrows to find out his reaction to Kerin's decision. He agreed that an O'Reilly identikit structure was their only option.

Since the final bids were supposed to be submitted free from any regulatory hurdles, Tourang would be unable to meet the conditions. Burrows was told that they would be putting in an offer subject to FIRB.

This wasn't Burrows' preferred option. He would now be receiving the Independent and AIN offers as unconditional and a conditional Tourang offer. The best he could do, he said, was consider their offer.

During the afternoon Burrows ran through the complex options. All things being equal, a conditional offer wouldn't rate a mention when, in two days' time, Baring Brothers would be receiving two other comparable bids of over $1.4 billion. On this basis Burrows would find it difficult to argue why Tourang should be considered, let alone selected.

It would be very difficult to recommend Tourang to Nicholl and the banks, except for one crucial factor. Tourang still had the scorpion. It was true that the bondholders had itchy feet, but the agreement they had signed with Tourang was tight. Baring Brothers, Mallesons and Cohen had concluded it was potent. No wonder Colson and Powers had been so smug for months and Turnbull absolutely gleeful.

There were, of course, arguable clauses in the document about what happened after 16 January on Tourang's rights and obligations. But even if the bondholders could be coaxed into dealing with which ever of the other two offers was selected, Black and Hellman & Friedman probably had enough ammunition to either fight the banks in court or buy twenty-six per cent of the bonds and torpedo the sale of the Fairfax corporate structure.

This would give the banks no option but to sell the assets into a new corporate vehicle, losing Fairfax's tax losses, incurring a multi-million dollar stamp duty bill and complicating the sale.

Clearly Burrows could be in trouble. If the sales process degenerated into litigation, it could drag on for months longer. And if, for some reason, any of the bidders he had carefully cajoled and nursed to this delicate point pulled out, the offers left might be revised downwards.

In commercial terms Tourang still had the aces. Driving home to Trahlee that night, Burrows mulled over one option that could clinch a sale instead of waiting for Willis to make a decision. When he got home he decided to give it a shot.

Johnson was surprised to be summonsed to Trahlee at 8 pm on a Monday night. Surprise gave way to shock as Burrows spoke. By the end of the monologue, Johnson was lost for words. What a bizarre idea, he thought. Consider merging with Tourang?

Speaking quickly, Burrows ran through the benefits again. AIN would be able to complete the deal since it might receive the benefit of the bondholder agreement. AIN could give Black and Hellman & Friedman a shareholding, perhaps up to twenty per cent.

'You could then work out the board,' Burrows added, running through some options. AIN was proposing Greg Taylor as its chief executive, and Tourang didn't have a chief executive now. There shouldn't be any problem giving Taylor the position and Black's newspaper expertise would be a great benefit to Fairfax.

'You've got to think laterally in deals like this,' Burrows told Johnson. Edward De Bono had another pupil.

The next morning Johnson telephoned McKeon and told him in a matter-of-fact manner of Burrows' suggestion. McKeon thought Johnson was joking at first, then got the same reaction when he in turn told Kent.

The key AIN people were contacted by the Macquarie Bank advisers. Harley and McKay rushed down for a meeting and D'Arcy and Leslie were informed. Initially the amazement at Burrows' idea was hard to put aside.

After twelve months of hard work to get themselves into the position of possibly winning control of Fairfax against all the odds, a merger with Tourang was not something ever contemplated. AIN's whole campaign had been fought on being an all-Australian offer, one that would keep the important Fairfax press in the hands of Australians and not foreigners.

AIN was staunchly in favour of maintaining editorial independence, ensuring a church and state division to lessen the opportunity for management intervention into editorial content of the newspapers. Now a decision had to be made about whether to pursue Burrows' request to open up discussions for a merger with Black, a foreigner who had been widely tainted, despite his protestations, as an interventionist proprietor.

Running through the commercial realities, it was obvious that the exclusivity agreement with the bondholders was very important. Tourang had it and AIN didn't. There would be a much greater chance of becoming the successful bidder, albeit through a merger, if AIN agreed.

The option of merging with Tourang wasn't ruled out immediately. AIN was prepared to flirt with the idea and Johnson was briefed on the ground rules. AIN would only be prepared to allow a maximum foreign shareholding of fifteen per cent in Fairfax. After taking account of the bondholders, this would leave around five per cent each for Black and Hellman & Friedman. And the two foreigners would only receive board representation consumate with this level.

Also AIN would need to know all the other financial arrangements and understandings that Tourang had entered into. Agreements or intentions to rebate fees spent during the acquisition process, for example, and full details of the generous termination agreement with Packer.

With the parameters set, Johnson walked up to Freehills for the 10.30 am appointment with Colson and Powers. Ushered into the Tourang war room by Freehill partner Kim Santow, he faced the two men who had been his fierce rivals for six months.

The atmosphere relaxed very quickly as they complimented each other on the fairness with which each side had conducted itself. Within minutes they even agreed on the identities of their common enemies: O'Reilly's group and some particular Labor politicians. Johnson then explained how AIN viewed matters.

'The situation is that you have a problem politically, and that we have an institutional structure that is in place,' he said, the other men nodding in agreement.

'We have respect for Black's position as a legitimate newspaper proprietor and we are willing to see if it is worth contemplating any more work to investigate whether we should join forces.'

Johnson then focused on the critical issue—if there was to be any discussions it would be on the basis that Tourang folded into AIN and not vice versa. AIN had a fully funded offer and expected to be able to offer the highest price to the receiver.

With the opening gambit set out, Colson could see a problem immediately. He acknowledged that Tourang was happy to talk in principle and then went on to explain that Tourang couldn't join AIN because of the contractual arrangements between Tourang and the bondholders. The exclusivity agreement was with Tourang; AIN would have to join them.

On top of that, Colson and Powers were not convinced that Tourang was dead, even with bids closing imminently. Tourang was determined to continue to fight Canberra and, if it succeeded, it wouldn't need AIN. Within an hour it was agreed that there wasn't much point in going any further.

'We will think about it,' Johnson concluded, 'but it seems we are both intent on going our separate ways.'

Walking out, he added one last suggestion: 'If conditions change dramatically, we may talk again.'

Returning to his office, Johnson telephoned McKeon and explained the outcome of the discussion. Later in the day he told Burrows the verdict. The conversation was short.

Burrows fumed. They are crazy, he thought. He had offered AIN the opportunity to possibly share in the glory of winning and they were not interested.

The rejection was also a blow to his ego. For months he felt he had the power to control the whole process—if you create the consortiums you can change them, he had confidently thought. From the time he had urged Hellman & Friedman to join up with AIN to form a consortium of institutions in April, until he assisted Independent to secure Were as an underwriter, Burrows had liked to call the shots.

* * *

Flicking through the four bulky documents on Wednesday night —11 December, bid deadline day—Burrows was surprised about the final offer from AIN. From throwing in the unwanted offer in August, which was well below the bank debt, AIN had put forward an offer that valued Fairfax at $1.52 billion. This was higher than Tourang and Independent.

The CS First Boston proposal was at the bottom of the pile and remained the fall-back position since it couldn't deliver a quick completion. As Burrows jotted down the differences between AIN and Independent he realised that the Melbourne consortium had produced a good offer in terms of a quick settlement.

AIN's proposal to pay up $360 million immediately was very attractive. Of course the rest of the funds—another $457 million—wouldn't come until the public float. But there was still a large amount of money on the table and their underwriting agreement for the float was solid.

He scanned Independent's offer. It was clear that it had fatal flaws when compared with those of Tourang and AIN. For all the political nous and corporate trench warfare to nobble its two rivals, O'Reilly didn't have the cash. Independent couldn't deliver its proposed $120 million in cash for its twenty per cent shareholding until it convened a shareholder meeting to approve the investment.

The final offer included information showing that Independent had already secured support from forty-eight per cent of shareholders—including O'Reilly's twenty-eight per cent shareholding. To convene an extraordinary meeting of shareholders would take twenty-one days. The remainder of the funds for the purchase would not be paid until the public offering of the other twenty per cent of Fairfax shares to institutional investors and the public, and this cash probably wouldn't come until March. Independent argued there was minimal risk because Weres had signed a tight underwriting agreement. The key escape clause was one that allowed the stockbroker to repudiate the agreement if the key sharemarket indicator, the All Ordinaries Index, fell more than fifteen per cent between the submission of the offer to the receiver and the registration of the prospectus with the Australian Securities Commission.

Burrows knew that there were major risks about Independent's ability to complete a purchase. If there was an unexpected dramatic fall in the sharemarket—similar to the Black October crash of 1987—Weres could pull out of the underwriting. This would kill Independent's offer before completion, leaving the banks to recommence a sales process in a shocking sharemarket environment. Suddenly Fairfax might be worth only $900 million again, putting the banks back where they were twelve months ago.

Overall, in terms of completion certainty, Independent ranked a poor third. Even the CS First Boston float proposal seemed almost as attractive.

Burrows knew that Tourang was the preferred option on commercial terms for a quick completion. They had political problems but commercially they had it all—the exclusivity agreement and the unexpected plus of the underwriting agreement with Ords.

If Tourang was accepted, Ords would immediately rush to secure a minimum of $412 million in cash from the sale of shares and debentures in Tourang to institutions. But only if Burrows sold to them immediately. Ords wanted one week to raise the funds and it must start by the following Monday morning.

To put the pressure on Burrows to recommend Tourang to the receiver, Ords would only keep open its underwriting offer for a limited period. Coupled with the immediate payment of $138 million in total to come from the Telegraph and Hellman & Friedman, Tourang was offering a total of $550 million on a completion date of only one week.

The message was clear: Burrows could accept Tourang by the following Monday to allow settlement to take place before Christmas or run the risk of the bondholder implosion.

This brinkmanship was fine, except for one catch that Burrows didn't know how to overcome. Tourang's offer was subject to Willis allowing them back into the sales process. Burrows had little feel for their chances. If they didn't get through, it would be an arduous Christmas.

* * *

It was late at night in New York as Turnbull convened the conference call and less than three hours before Tourang had to submit its final offer. Ezzes and McClure were joined on the line by Joe Guzinski and representatives from Resolution Trust Corporation, Ho Wang from Prudential, Dick Kuersteiner from Franklin Age and Pandora Pang from Executive Life.

Turnbull hurriedly outlined how Powers had refused to budge. The bondholders request that Tourang complete the purchase by 16 January was baulked at; Tourang wanted the date extended till 1 February. As a compromise, Powers agreed that Tourang would lift the payment to the bondholders to $140 million so it could close the deal. The debate began about the right of first refusal and the escalator clause.

If the bondholders didn't force the issue, after January 16 they ran the risk that if they tried to do a deal with another bidder, Black or Packer might buy some bonds and thwart any sale of the corporate shell. Powers argued strongly that he would need to get Packer and Black to agree to waive this clause and didn't hold out much hope of this happening.

Turnbull agreed with the argument but added he didn't think that either Hellman & Friedman, Black or Packer would block the bondholders if they were not going to win Fairfax.

'If Black walks now, he will never darken Australia's doorstep again,' he suggested. 'Kerry Packer is the only one likely to do something mischievous, but if he bought twenty-five per cent or thirty per cent of the bonds, he may find himself getting nothing.

'My impression is that Packer is likely, given his problem with cross-media ownership and so forth, not to get involved.'

Doug McClure and Ezzes were not convinced about giving up this point.

Turnbull pointed out that of course the right of first refusal was arguable, but did the bondholders want to risk litigation?

'Litigation is uncertain,' Turnbull added.

It was now 3.15 pm and Tourang's offer was to go in within two hours. Turnbull began to force the issue.

'The question is, do we make the release of the right of first refusal a deal breaker?'

Franklin and the RTC said no. Ho Wang at Prudential agreed. Ezzes remained unconvinced and showed some late toughness in his dealings with Tourang.

'We are not willing to crater the deal either. However, I would like the right of first refusal removed or I would like to see if $140 million can go to $150 million.'

Pandora Pang came back on the line adamant that she didn't want the date extended from 16 January to 1 February.

'January 16 is very important to us. I want to make sure ... I don't want to have anything to do with them after 16 January.'

Ezzes thought about the tactics of going back to Tourang and baulking on the 16 January date.

'I think we should call back at 4.45 pm,' he suggested.

'I think, Steve, you are playing with fire there. I really wouldn't do that,' Turnbull replied. 'I think that brinkmanship could backfire on you.'

In the end Turnbull agreed he would try again on the right of first refusal and push for an extra $10 million as the price for laying down on it. The call ended and negotiations began.

The meeting reconvened just after midnight, New York time. Ezzes reported that Powers wouldn't move on the $140 million or give up the right of first refusal without talking to Black and Packer.

'What are we going to do, basically? Are we going to live with what we have got? Is that the agreement?' Turnbull pressed to wind this matter up.

The RTC, Airlie and a reluctant Drexels agreed.

'I still think there is more money,' McClure said despondently.

Turnbull ran through the various clauses. They included that Tourang would be subject to a condition subsequent, the execution of a contract to buy Fairfax must take place by 5 pm on 16 January and completion by 1 February. The bondholders could extend the end date by thirty days.

Turnbull then called for a poll. Ezzes was still grumbling.

'I am in favour of going for $140 million, but I would like to go on record in saying that this is a marginal transaction and that the right of first refusal may come back to haunt us.

'We are getting a marginal amount of money versus what they are going to give to the free-riding bondholders [Janet Holmes a Court's company Heytesbury, and others] and we have not been dealt with in great faith by Tourang.'

Turnbull cut in: 'I agree with that also.'

Pandora Pang pipped in and said she gave a qualified support, a view that Turnbull wasn't happy with considering his efforts and anguish on their behalf.

'Pandora, I don't know where that leaves me. I don't want to sign off and get sued by Executive Life. If that were the case, I will literally just go home to bed.

'I don't think after what I have gone through in the last twelve months that I deserve to be told that I am to become the meat in the bloody sandwich.'

Pressing ahead, Turnbull summed up the issue.

'We either go on this basis or we don't. It is as simple as that. We really have to tell them in the next thirty-one minutes.'

Doug McClure reminded everyone that the vote would be decided by a majority in number of bonds. Pang grumbled about needing to talk to other people who were home in bed as Turnbull went for the vote.

'Is there anybody on the Committee who doesn't want me to give my consent in these terms to Tourang today? Speak now or forever hold your peace,' Turnbull implored.

McClure again suggested that Ezzes ring them back and try to wrangle another $5 million. Dick Kuersteiner from Franklin said he would back McClure but finally McClure gave up. It was really only nickels and dimes stuff now.

'We will take $140 million,' McClure agreed.

One by one the vote was taken. Airlie, the RTC, Prudential, Guarantee Security Life Insurance Co., and Franklin agreed. Pandora Pang from Executive Life mumbled something about needing to talk to different constituencies and said she had to vote no. The final vote was decisive—the bondholders agreed to stick with Tourang.

'Thanks and good night,' Turnbull finished off the conference call, leaving the tired bondholders to wend their way home well after midnight.

Tourang had tied up the bondholders. Neither AIN or O'Reilly were going to get the chance to offer the bondholders more money.

Burrows was informed of the decision and the need to have a contract executed by 16 January. As he headed home that evening, he knew only Ralph Willis stood in the way of closing the deal.

CHAPTER TWENTY

AND THE WINNER
IS ...

CONRAD BLACK almost spat out his words at the London journalist. 'It is sleazy, venal and despicable. I'm sure the Australian public are shocked and appalled by these tactics.'

He was referring to Kerin's rejection of Tourang and was beginning to warm to his subject. 'I've got a fair idea what happened last week. Names will be named at the appropriate time. In the meantime we press on gamely with the required accommodations and will make a bid that is superior economically, financially and politically than anything else on the table ... We have been in this for fourteen rounds. We'll do the fifteenth. We have to; it is a public duty.'

Referring to the political lobbying, Black said: 'I have been portrayed as a fanatical right-winger, an interfering meddler, and that is simply not true. Not true.'

Black's approach was full of machismo, but his intelligence from Canberra via Tourang was poor. He claimed, incorrectly, that the Foreign Investment Review Board (FIRB) had approved Tourang, but that 'something rather sinister happened between FIRB and Kerin's office ... When this game is up and it gets out into the open, there's a few people in Canberra that aren't going to look very statesmanlike.'

His contempt for Independent was not disguised, and he said he suspected that 'O'Reilly and his pimps' were behind the latest bout of political lobbying.

Slamming the politicians at a time when Tourang was desperately trying to re-enter the Fairfax battle didn't seem very wise. Black's outburst shocked the Tourang team at Freehills on Thursday morning, 12 December. They first learnt of it from front-page headlines in the *Herald*: 'Black lashes out: Sleazy, venal and despicable'. Black had released the equivalent of a Scud missile in the middle of an intense effort to squeeze the restructured proposal past Hawke and Willis.

Tourang had no option but to keep up the pressure and pretend Black had never spoken a word. The dealings with Canberra were still a disaster. George Pooley had agreed to rush the restructured Tourang proposal through FIRB. The problem, however, was Willis. He had attended his first press conference as Federal Treasurer on Monday but had then gone home to bed with a cold. It was impossible to contact him to stress the urgency of the approval. Tourang had confirmed that the FIRB papers and the bid outline had been delivered to Willis' home on Thursday and that he had received Treasury briefing papers on the new structure. It was another matter, however, to get an indication of when he could give them his consideration.

John Singleton was called upon to put pressure on Willis through Hawke's office. Singleton telephoned the Prime Minister's office and spoke to Hawke's senior political adviser Colin Parkes and press secretary Grant Nihill. He let them know that Tourang's restructured offer was urgently awaiting Willis' decision. 'You have got to give these guys a fair go; they have been treated poorly. Could you make sure Willis reads it,' he implored Parkes.

Parkes responded that it was unlikely that Willis wouldn't read it, and that he was aware of the urgency of the matter. By Thursday evening, there was still no response from Canberra. Fairfax was slipping away fast.

■ ■ ■

Colson and Powers had wandered into Baring Brothers on Thursday morning to reassure Burrows that the bondholders were no longer an issue. Tourang didn't want the process delayed. The bondholders had agreed to take the $140 million and the vote the previous night in New York was the evidence. Burrows remained concerned, however, that Tourang still didn't have FIRB approval.

Even though the bondholders were willing to back Tourang, Atkin, Breese and White had run through the remaining imponderables. If Baring Brothers ran with Tourang, what would happen if the bonds didn't come through? There was still a completion risk, and Powers and Colson were well aware that Burrows still had doubts.

Discussions at Baring Brothers that afternoon centred on the latest Plan B to handle the bondholders if Tourang remained dead. It was simply a question of how to close with Australian Independent Newspapers (AIN). Atkin explained again that the receiver could sign a contract with AIN, nominating a date of 31 December as an example.

AIN could then leave an offer open to the bondholders for one month, which would run through the critical 16 January date. If the bondholders didn't take an offer of $140 million from AIN, then the asset sale route would be followed. The receiver would have given the unsecured creditors an offer; if they rejected it that was their problem. The risk was that Tourang would commence litigation. Whether this would happen couldn't be determined.

* * *

At Mallesons the delicate task of keeping the three bidders bubbling along continued. Atkin had split the negotiations into two parts: the three contracts of sale and negotiations over the loan facilities.

Teams of lawyers were running the two sets of negotiations in tandem. Burrows had requested that Mallesons put as many people as possible on the deal earlier in the week. If it could be completed by Christmas, he was going to do it.

Burrows wasn't happy when he was told by Atkin that AIN was tardy on the sales documentation compared with Tourang and Independent. AIN had a strong offer, and if Tourang didn't get FIRB approval, the strategy to deal with the bondholders to accommodate the Melbourne group would need to be activated.

Late on Thursday afternoon Burrows received a telephone call from Pooley at FIRB. Tourang's new proposal would go to Willis that evening. Burrows asked Pooley how long he thought it would take Willis. Pooley was frank. He didn't know.

At 8.00 pm Burrows yelled down the hall to Breese and White to leave. The three were running late for the office Christmas Party at the fashionable Taylor's restaurant. Walking quickly across the marble entrance to Macquarie Place, they felt jaded. It was hardly the night or the week to relax and enjoy themselves.

∎ ∎ ∎

Trying to keep a straight line, McKeon pushed the mower purposefully through the thick grass. There hadn't been much time for family or sleep in the last few months, so McKeon had no qualms about coming home at lunchtime on Thursday for a break. The tension was becoming unbearable in the office. The bid was in and there was little that could be done on the financial side at this stage. The lawyers were poring over the twenty-one volumes of sales documentation.

That night McKeon received the call from Johnson that broke the tension. McKeon should come up to Sydney first thing in the morning. Johnson had heard from Burrows. The indications were positive. It seemed AIN was in front.

McKay contacted Colin Galbraith who was in Hawaii on other business. He must return as soon as possible to Sydney and spend the weekend at Mallesons. There was an air of excitement within AIN as McKay and Harley brought Leslie and D'Arcy up to date that evening. They knew they had offered an excellent price on Wednesday. It seemed the crucial ingredient.

∎ ∎ ∎

When Levy, Chipkin and Lee arrived at Mallesons on Friday morning and looked across the table at their counterparts they felt nervous. This didn't look like the A-team. In fact Levy wondered if it wasn't the C-team. If this was the team for Tourang on this side, then he assumed that Al Donald, the Freehill partner handling the awesome task of wading through the twenty-one volumes of re-financing documents, was getting the same treatment.

For the next few hours they slowly went through the contract. There were plenty of contentious issues, at least one dozen clauses they were unhappy with. However, the message had been clear before they left Freehills. Carnegie had revived a long-standing joke in the Tourang ranks. 'If they want to shove a pineapple up your arse, take it,' Carnegie had called out as they left the office. No lawyer likes conceding contentious legal points, unless their client orders them to.

At this stage of proceedings Tourang didn't want to spend time on anything but the most important clauses. It was also tactical. If the Mallesons team felt that it was walking all over Levy, Chipkin and Lee and winning points, it was more likely to concede a few later. So for the next few hours the Freehill lawyers winced as they followed instructions and took their pineapples.

In another room AIN's lawyers, led by Bob Santamaria, McKeon and Kent, were confident. They met with Atkin at various times, and felt that they were dealing with the A-team. It was a positive sign, and the adrenalin was pumping as they carefully examined the sales agreement.

From the speed at which the lawyers were moving, it seemed Johnson's feeling earlier in the day was correct. Burrows had called him in just before 10 am to tell him that he wanted the final details of AIN's bid. Johnson got the message into the meeting at Mallesons. Burrows was escalating the process and could be pushing for an exchange of contracts on the weekend.

■　■　■

Singleton was hopeful that the plea to Hawke would do the trick as he hung up the telephone. He had stressed that rejecting Tourang when its foreign economic interest mirrored O'Reilly's was unfair. Could Hawke also press Willis to make a decision?

On Friday morning Willis was giving 100 per cent of his time to the Tourang proposal. He received a telephone call from Hawke's office, asking Willis to speak to Singleton and get him off the Prime Minister's back.

Willis called Singleton but was dissatisfied with the outcome. Singleton told him nothing he did not know already. Willis did not need to be hassled. He was still feeling ill. He had officially been Treasurer of Australia for five days and had been sick for most of them—hardly a running start. He also had the Hewson Fightback package to respond to—the press was chiding the Government for not attacking the issues. This and the added burden of one of the hottest political issues of the year requiring an answer that day was a pressure he did not need.

He decided, however, to at least give Burrows a call to find out what the score was on the sale process.

■   ■   ■

'There will be no decision today,' Willis said emphatically when he finished exchanging pleasantries with Burrows. 'Black's comments have not helped and I haven't consulted with Caucus yet. I haven't spent any time on this one, so just bring me up to date.'

This wasn't what Burrows wished to hear. He wanted to close this deal now; if it wasn't completed this weekend, he might as well forget it until January.

Burrows dispensed with diplomacy. He wanted Willis to understand the gravity of the matter. 'I want to finalise this on the weekend,' he began, before launching into a lengthy outline of the reasons the deal had to be closed one way or the other. He drew on every reserve of logic and persuasive argument he could muster, explaining how the banks were nervous and the sharemarket conditions to sell Fairfax immediately were there right now. He outlined the potential bondholder instability.

There was, however, a real risk about the sharemarket. Tokyo was jittery, and if the process was hindered until the New Year, anything could happen.

He then explained why he felt he could recommend Tourang to the receiver if Willis approved their restructured offer. 'Tourang takes the banks out whole,' he said. 'The bondholders are satisfied and have been given an extra $15 million from Tourang.'

'The bondholders are aware others are offering more. This hasn't stopped them from taking the Tourang offer, Treasurer,' he continued.

Willis listened for another few minutes. By this time White had entered Burrows office and smiled as Burrows argued his case intensely.

'There are 2800 little unsecured creditors waiting for their money—Tourang will pay them out before Christmas,' he added.

White screwed up his face—the next thing Burrows would say was that there would be no Santa Claus if Willis didn't agree immediately.

Burrows also reminded Willis of Mallesons' legal advice that it would be difficult for him to reject Tourang under the foreign investment policy guidelines. Once again the issue had arisen: for all the uproar about foreign investment, legally it was hard for the Treasurer to reject Tourang—the policy was not something enforceable under the Foreign Acquisitions and Takeovers Act.

This seemed important to Willis. He could certainly reject Tourang, but the legislation might then need to be changed to ensure his decision was watertight. He was well aware of the blaze of publicity that it would create and the message to foreign investors: here was a government prepared to change the laws when Tourang mirrored O'Reilly on foreign ownership.

The conversation continued for nearly an hour. By the end of the commercial and emotional pleading, Burrows succeeded in convincing Willis.

When Willis hung up, he considered Burrow's argument carefully. He felt the weight of the decision keenly now. He knew it was more than just a decision on foreign investment levels. His approval of Tourang's proposal would deliver Fairfax to Conrad Black.

Willis could, however, make a decision immediately. It would be at least one less item on his agenda. Since Tourang now mirrored Independent in terms of foreign ownership level, he would find it hard to reject the submission.

However, even at the eleventh hour Willis felt Tourang was still unable to accept political realities. They wanted a twenty per cent foreign ownership level plus the bondholders. Tourang was also asking for discussions to continue on allowing the Telegraph to hold a twenty per cent voting shareholding and Hellman & Friedman a ten per cent non-voting shareholding. They required an answer on this aspect within thirty days of completion of any purchase of Fairfax.

Willis decided that he could see no justifiable reason why he should reject the revised proposal. Before he made the decision to approve Tourang, however, he had to consult with key Caucus people. The Beazley–Kerin motion that was pushed through Caucus in early October required that the Treasurer keep Caucus briefed on the Fairfax sale.

There was not the time take it back to full Caucus, so Willis did the next best thing and consulted with key Caucus members.

Chris Schacht was well-briefed on Tourang's latest position. He had been subjected to a hectic bout of lobbying by the Tourang camp all week. He had been speaking with Colson in a series of telephone conversations over the months, but in the last few days after Tourang was squashed by Kerin, Tourang's approaches had become more desperate.

Schacht had heard Colson's present concern that Tourang would need to restructure with Black only holding a fifteen per cent voting shareholding. Colson explained to Schacht that he was worried that such a small holding would allow the other Australian shareholders to collaborate against Black and out-vote him. For all the effort and outlay of $103 million, Black could in theory lose control.

In the last few days Schacht had been making his own suggestions to make Tourang more acceptable when he spoke to Colson and Powers. One name he pushed hard was Eric Beecher, the former editor of the *Sydney Morning Herald*.

Beecher had become friendly with Mark Carnegie, who was in the process of buying into Beecher's media business, Text Media Pty Ltd. With Tourang minus a chief executive, Beecher's name was circulated as a candidate with good credentials.

After the *Herald* Beecher had worked for Murdoch, undertaking the revamp of the struggling Melbourne *Herald*. Later he had joined the large club of ex-Murdoch editors after a falling out.

Schacht had suggested to Colson that Beecher was an excellent candidate and even suggested that an Australian chief executive like Beecher might assist Tourang's chances. Colson took the suggestion on board, although he was little acquainted with Beecher.

In a tight situation Colson even indicated that the charter of editorial independence for the Fairfax papers would be considered seriously. This removed some of Schacht's misgivings.

Colson did not enjoy these conversations with Schacht. He had little time for the man who was one of the key people to derail Tourang's initial foreign ownership plans. Now Schacht was sticking his nose into management issues, telling Colson how to run newspapers.

Shortly after midday Willis picked up the telephone and began making calls. First to Richardson, the influential power broker. Reiterating Burrow's arguments, Willis found no strong opposition to his intention to let Tourang through.

At this stage Richardson had little interest in the Fairfax saga. The kingmaker had too much on his mind, immersed in the secret strategy of pulling the rug on Hawke's reign as Prime Minister and installing his New South Wales right-wing faction's golden boy Paul Keating in The Lodge.

Willis spoke next to Duffy, and found his fairness argument won the day. He then moved on to the key Caucus figures. Michael Lee and Ric Charlesworth raised no objections.

Willis then spoke to Schacht.

'Tourang now has the same foreign equity level as O'Reilly. What is your present view?' He added that Tourang did want more.

As Willis spoke Schacht thought about his position on the issue in the light of his discussions with Tourang in recent days. For months his line had been that foreign ownership of twenty per cent was acceptable. He knew that his consistency on this point was supported by the motion that he and left-wing MP Langmore had put to Caucus.

Schacht was swayed by Tourang's restructuring and decided that he wouldn't object if the level was limited to twenty per cent. He mentioned to Willis that Colson had made favourable noises about editorial charters and raised Beecher's name as possible chief executive. However, his bottom line was clear, given the lower foreign shareholdings. 'I can't oppose it.'

Schacht warned Willis, however, that there would be problems if he agreed to Tourang's request for a higher level. Willis decided that he would call Colson to raise these two points. Colson confirmed both. On the issue of editorial charters he made some conciliatory noises but said that Tourang wouldn't sign the charter for the Broadway newspapers in their present form. On Beecher he confirmed that discussions were underway, but there was no firm commitment.

When Willis approached Langmore early in the afternoon, he received strong opposition. Langmore, as the mover of the defeated motion to limit foreign equity to a total of twenty per cent, couldn't argue against Tourang on that basis.

The level of foreign ownership wasn't Langmore's only concern and he strenuously argued against letting Tourang through. He didn't want Black to gain management control of Fairfax. Black's very conservative political and economic views—reflected in his strong support for the economic policies of Margaret Thatcher and Ronald Reagan—remained a major concern for Langmore and the left-wing of the Labor Party.

In Langmore's opinion Black's UK flagship the *Daily Telegraph* reflected his world view. The newspaper was an avid supporter of Thatcherism, attacking the welfare system and unions. Months later Langmore was still seething from reading a copy of an editorial that Black once authored in one of his newspapers. The editorial had been circulated anonymously, obviously from a rival bidder. Langmore was disgusted. He considered the views expressed to be outdated and more attuned to 1950s cold war McCarthyism thought. Even though the old Fairfax dynasty was not considered friends of the Labor movement, at least they were not vocal conservatives like Black. Langmore didn't want him to run Fairfax.

He was blunt with Willis, imploring him not to allow Tourang through. 'In order to have a diversity of opinions in the print media, it is inappropriate to allow a man who is a capital C conservative. You can't allow him.'

The plea didn't influence Willis; Langmore was the lone dissenting voice among the Caucus members he had contacted.

There was one last person to speak to. Willis walked along the corridor to Hawke's office. He discussed his analysis of Tourang's restructured proposal and said that he intended to approve it. 'Have you got any problems with this decision?' he asked Hawke.

The Prime Minister looked surprised and a little disappointed. His primary objection to Tourang was the involvement of Packer and the implications for further concentration of media in Australia. He was also not in favour of too high a level of foreign ownership. Now it seemed all issues had been addressed. 'You do whatever you think is right,' he nonchalantly told Willis.

The conversation was over in minutes. Tourang would be approved. Before he left Willis said that he was going to Melbourne and he would do the paperwork while in transit.

The short meeting with Hawke and conversations with Caucus

members did not do justice to the incredible furore the Fairfax sale had caused.

In political circles key power brokers in the Labor Party tried to ensure they chose the new proprietor at Fairfax. It had been the first chance in 150 years and might never arise again. None of them, however, got their first choice.

*   *   *

Just after 3 pm on Friday the Independent team were escorted into Baring Brothers' main conference room. Burrows rushed in after everyone was seated and ran through a few of the issues. He gave the same spiel he had given Johnson in the morning. Baring Brothers wanted any outstanding issues on their bids sorted out quickly.

There was no hint of the conversation Burrows had had with Willis. He wasn't likely to tell them that he had told the Treasurer three hours before that he felt he would be recommending Tourang if their FIRB application was approved. Right to the end Burrows was relentlessly pursuing his primary task to ensure the banks got their money back. Telling Independent that they had run a poor last wasn't his role. Things were never certain until a deal was complete—the other two bidders could still fall over.

Independent had its own views on what to do next. Hunt explained that Independent had been talking to the bondholders and that it had its own plans on how to deal with them. Baring Brothers was reminded that Independent needed approval from shareholders to provide its initial funds.

As the Independent group left, there were quizzical looks. Everything had gone too smoothly. Normally in a $1.5 billion transaction there are points that are argued strongly by the vendors.

There had been few searching questions directed at Hunt and Hoyle, the Independent lawyer from Corrs, and Bruce Teele from J B Were. Indeed nothing contentious had been raised for days. Independent's offer document was perused with barely a murmur. There was nothing to indicate that Independent's offer was inadequate.

Every confidence was had that an offer valuing Fairfax at

around $1.5 billion—including $150 million for the junk bond-holders—was a winning bid. Burrows need only demand that they close off.

* * *

Although Simon McKeon and Wayne Kent were mentally and physically exhausted as they sat in the taxi on the trip from Tullamarine Airport on Friday night, there was a certain sense of elation. They were close. Within two days their team could own Fairfax.

Burrows' message to Johnson that morning had been encouraging. He had all but given them the nod. The negotiations with Mallesons during the day were excellent; they felt they had the A-team of lawyers till the end. Tourang still didn't have the Treasurer's approval and might not get it for another three weeks. They had clearly beaten O'Reilly on price and certainty.

Kent and McKeon both planned to return to Sydney early the next morning. But tonight they had Christmas parties to attend. Their conversation in the taxi centred around their impending victory celebration. The 8 pm news on the radio, however, brought their celebratory mood to a quick end. Tourang had been approved by the Treasurer.

There was silence as the implications rushed through their minds. McKeon was the first to speak: 'I think that's all right. I still think we have beaten them on price.'

Also AIN's ability to put up the $360 million quickly must be a strong factor in its favour.

* * *

In Sydney Mark Johnson was preparing to leave for the Macquarie Bank Christmas party at Pavilion on the Park, a restaurant set in the Botanic Gardens opposite the New South Wales Art Gallery. Johnson's wife Sandra was picking him up directly from the office. She heard the news on her car radio on the way in. When she picked Johnson up in Pitt Street outside the Stock Exchange building she asked him what he thought of the Willis decision. His heart sank. He was worried now and couldn't relax at the Christmas party. They left early.

News of the Willis decision swept through the bidders over the next few hours. Rowan Ross was told at a dinner party by a late guest. Hunt heard in the office. They were also mystified at the speed of Willis' decision. He had a reputation for procrastinating.

For the Independent team the news capped off a strange day when everything had gone too smoothly with Baring Brothers and Mallesons. It didn't augur well.

． ． ．

Colson and the Tourang team were in the middle of a meeting when the call came through from George Pooley. There was enormous relief. Colson was elated. Finally the crisis-prone Tourang was back in the running and nothing could stop them now. This was the fifteenth round. Colson thought they could win; they could actually do it.

The resentment about the political upheaval over Tourang temporarily vanished. Colson and Powers ordered the lawyers to get everything moving urgently. Burrows felt harassed and telephoned Colson to lecture him. Tourang needed to be in a position to honour its commitment to complete by Monday morning at the latest.

Levy and Chipkin hastened the examination of the latest draft contract, putting aside the frustrations earlier in the day when they took the pineapples from Mallesons and dealt with the Australian Broadcasting Tribunal (ABT) over statutory declarations concerning Packer's withdrawal. Levy, who strictly observed the Jewish faith and wanted to be home before sunset on Friday, left Chipkin and Lee to handle the contract amendments for the rest of the night.

At Mallesons, Donald was poring over the loan documentation, reviewing the twenty-one volumes of legalese and banking jargon.

At Grosvenor Place Miles and Mactier were running around in circles after Colson hung up. They weren't sure what they should do first. Offering to underwrite a few hundred million was one thing. Now they actually needed to undertake the financial and legal tasks to ensure they could deliver the cheque.

If Tourang was going to exchange contracts by Monday, Ord Minnett had only forty-eight hours to prepare the Tourang offering memorandum required before the firm's dealers could begin the frantic telephone calls to the institutional investors to raise the required funds.

Mactier rushed through the preparation of a draft document with Simon Tripp from Ord's corporate division and Rick Ball, a corporate adviser at stockbroker ANZ McCaughan Dyson. Ords had to bring in the other firm because of a potential ABT problem due to Westpac being its parent. Because Westpac owned Ten Network after its collapse, this technically gave Ords a cross-media problem.

It was then time to go to Freehills for a meeting of the Tourang lawyers and advisers to establish where things were up to.

Leaving Grosvenor Place, Mactier and Ball looked towards the Regent Hotel and knew there was no chance of a taxi. George Street was filled with pre-Christmas revellers, and they knew they would have to walk.

Passing hundreds of faces in the street, most in high spirits and dozens intoxicated, Mactier felt self-conscious. Here he was, a young man in his late twenties, sober, dressed in a suit and carrying a pile of documents under his arm on a Friday night less than two weeks before Christmas. His only consolation as they walked quickly up the street was that they weren't getting mugged.

Arriving at Freehills, there were people running around everywhere. There was a full contingent as progress reports were given. Sipping cans of Diet Coke (Freehills had had to order it by the crate load over the past few months), Powers and Colson barked out orders. The offering memorandum was still the critical document.

Once the meeting had ended Mactier and Ball rushed back down to Ords to finalise the contents, working until 5 am. Mactier went home as the sun rose. He collapsed on his bed, setting the alarm for three hours later.

On Saturday afternoon the Freehill lawyers came down to Ords to conduct due diligence on the document, going through it line by line, marking each one off with a coloured pen. This tedious process was crucial—Tourang had to make sure nothing in the document was false or misleading.

By 6 pm the offering memorandum was ready for the printer.

Ords was to underwrite a total of $462 million, including those bondholders who had elected to take a cash payout rather than hold debentures in Fairfax. It was a large and risky underwriting for a stockbroker. The fees and glory of the deal made it worthwhile.

. . .

McKeon and Kent arrived back in Sydney on the 8 am flight on Saturday, unaware of the dramatic change in plans caused by the Willis decision. Tired after the parties the night before, they went straight to Mallesons. It was as if they had left a poker game for a few minutes—they had their antennae tuned to detect any change in attitude since they had last sat at the table.

When they saw the line-up of lawyers acting for the banks, they were relieved. It seemed like the A-team. Galbraith, the leader of their team, was already there. He had arrived on a 7 am flight from Hawaii. They sat down and began to go through the contract with the Mallesons lawyers.

As the day wore on there was some changing of the guard in the identity of the lawyers acting for the banks. This became worrying. The AIN team picked up the vibes—they were jumpy and paranoid, watching for every sign. McKeon left the room and rang Johnson to give him an update and conveyed his concern about the lawyers. Johnson said not to worry. He had telephoned Burrows, who said everything was progressing well.

As the day wore on it was clear that the Mallesons B-team was really taking over. Mallesons lawyer Robert Postema was checking the contract after lunch with Clay O'Brien from Baring Brothers. Atkin hadn't returned and it was a bad sign. As Galbraith raised contentious legal issues, it was becoming increasingly difficult to get any meaningful answers. Suddenly further instructions were required for everything.

McKeon thought these things wouldn't be a problem if only Atkin were there.

. . .

The Fairfax bankers and Nicholl assembled in the conference room shortly after noon on Saturday. Walking into the room, Burrows looked badly stressed. His eyes darted from Jake Williams and Jim Featherstone from Citibank to David Craig and Peter Meers from ANZ. Despite his determination to run with Tourang, there were outstanding problems.

He did not attempt to disguise his preference for Tourang. Tourang had FIRB approval and the ABT no longer presented a problem—Tourang had furnished various statutory declarations regarding Packer's exit and a decision had come through.

More importantly Tourang had the money. Ords would underwrite the offer and the cash would come in within eight days—but only if contracts were exchanged before the sharemarket opened on Monday morning.

Ords needed that clear week to tie up the institutions. The following was Christmas week (traditionally a wipeout)—Christmas Eve was a Tuesday followed by two public holidays. It is almost possible to fire a cannon in the Sydney and Melbourne central business districts that week without fear of a casualty. After those three days most of Australia goes on holiday for two weeks. So Monday was the deadline or all parties could forget about it until at least mid-January.

The issue was whether Tourang could exchange contracts by Monday. At this stage the bondholders, treated so derisively about twelve months previously when the bankers held a similar weekend meeting, were the key, Burrows explained.

If Fairfax was going to be sold to Tourang, could its claim that it had corralled the bondholders and secured their debentures into an escrow account in New York be believed? Atkin gave his opinion, although as he spoke Burrows felt he was being too negative.

Unfortunately, when the time came to hear from Fred Cohen in New York, his message wasn't much better for the Tourang cause. 'I don't believe the bondholders,' he said via the speakerphone. 'It's a risk if you deal with them before all their bonds are in escrow.'

These fears gave little support to Burrows. He decided that he would telephone Colson and ask him to explain in person on Tourang's behalf. He knew Tourang was desperate to close off and there would be plenty of positive views from Colson and Powers.

Half an hour later the two arrived and reassured them that all was well. There would be no problems with the bondholders, who had signed with Tourang on the $140 million and wouldn't back out.

'If you do an offer on these terms, we will close,' Powers said emphatically. 'The idea that one of the bondholders would not come in is preposterous. The bondholders' position could not be clearer. They are supporting us.'

'Malcolm was involved in getting them to agree and we should take his actions as an indication of his attitude,' Colson added.

Considering the public row with Turnbull, some of the bankers had to suppress laughter at the comment.

Both men then stressed the importance of going to the share-market to raise the funds and Powers tried to reinforce that the bondholders would not be a problem.

'I think we will have the bonds by Wednesday US time, or at the latest Thursday.'

Burrows had heard enough. He thanked them and said he would get back to them. After they had left Burrows was given the chance to usher Atkin from the room. As the lawyer walked outside he knew why he had been removed—Burrows didn't want him overstating the risks; it was no time to worry the bankers.

Burrows then asked Craig and Williams for their views and found they agreed that Tourang seemed the best offer. However, the bondholders were a risk. By mid-afternoon the meeting broke up.

Later the argument continued with Breese, White and Atkin on the risks of Tourang. Finally Burrows felt they had spoken enough. He left the small conference room and walked down the corridor to his office and sat down at his desk. Looking through the glass doors onto the balcony, he drew a breath and again ran through all the options in his mind.

What would he do if he were in the position of a bondholder? Here was a situation where they were virtually guaranteed of receiving their money or new debentures within a week. They had already voted to accept $140 million, although for all he knew some were still unhappy.

If he ran with Tourang and something went wrong, the consequences were horrific. He would be hung out to dry. This was the most gut-wrenching commercial decision he had ever made. There were legal risks that he couldn't argue with. However, if he became gun-shy, the deal might never be closed. If it dragged on past 16 January, anything could happen. He must be prepared to go out on a limb on this one.

Jumping decisively from his seat, he rushed back down the corridor and into the small room where Atkin, Breese and White were still seated. He was blunt: 'We must take the risk. Get on with it.'

■　■　■

Walking back into Freehills with the draft contract that had been sent to his home, Levy found Chipkin slumped in a chair. He looked like he was about to suffer a collapse.

Chipkin was pale and had dark bags under his eyes. He wore an overcoat, despite it being mid-summer with no air-conditioning in the office on weekends. The atmosphere was stifling. The sight of the overcoat was truly bizarre. The eighteen-hour days were finally taking their toll and Chipkin had been struck with a cold. On Levy's return he was ordered home and told to come back early the next morning.

Everything seemed to go smoothly throughout the rest of the day. Gonski and Carnegie wandered around overseeing some of the documentation. The offering memorandum was being final-ised and checked by Colson and Powers and finally went off to the printer by 6 pm.

The document was expected back from the printer by 9 pm, and Mactier waited around for its return. He had been invited to an engagement party but had to ring to cancel. As he waited he flicked through the document and suddenly saw a vital mistake that had slipped through. The numbers in an Ord Minnett table didn't correlate with those figures from Ernst & Young. He rushed across the room and telephoned the printer, ordering him to stop.

He then rang Ernst & Young and spent the next hour working it out. By 12.30 it had been solved and he staggered home.

■　■　■

By early evening on Saturday McKeon realised that it had got to the point where not much more could be achieved. Postema was saying again that he needed further instructions from his client. They would have another draft ready by midnight. Joining Johnson, the three went to Johnson's home at Bellevue Hill for a pre-dinner drink and then out to the Imperial Peking restaurant at Double Bay.

The mood was sombre. They were all worried over the decrease in intensity from Mallesons. In their hearts they knew that they had already lost.

Johnson left just before midnight. Galbraith and McKeon returned to the Hotel Inter-Continental. They checked at reception for the Mallesons documents. They hadn't arrived. This was infuriating.

Mallesons' office is situated directly opposite the hotel in the AMP Centre, so they both walked outside again and looked up to see if the lights were still on. Counting the floors to make sure that the lights were coming from the correct floors, they decided the Malleson team must still be there.

Back in Galbraith's room Galbraith and McKeon decided to find out what was going on. Picking up the telephone, Galbraith got through to Atkin. He asked where the contract was and tried to extract some information on AIN's position.

As far as Galbraith knew the documentation had to be finished by 9 am Monday morning as per Baring Brothers' instructions. Why then was Atkin being so obstructive? Earlier in the day, when it was clear that they were not dealing with the key lawyers, Galbraith had encountered Atkin in a corridor and asked him what was happening: 'It is extraordinary the way this is proceeding. Are you involved in discussions with somebody else?'

Atkin confirmed this. Galbraith demanded again what was happening and Atkin replied: 'We are not controlling the sale process. I will clarify the position shortly.'

Galbraith warned: 'We don't want to be played along.'

The afternoon's dealing had left Galbraith nervous. His team had worked up to eighteen hours a day for the last week, and if AIN was out, they deserved to know.

However, Atkin kept to the script and did not alert the other bidders to the state of play. He promised to ring back in a few minutes. Quickly he telephoned White and asked his advice. White said to tell Galbraith to continue; Nicholl hadn't made the final decision and anything could happen on Sunday.

Atkin rang Galbraith and told him that at no time had Baring Brothers suggested that documentation for AIN had to be ready by Monday, 16 December. His instructions were that AIN would not be prejudiced by the documentation not being ready to sign on Monday. Atkin then said: 'Do not read any more into that statement than the words themselves.'[1]

Atkin concluded that the draft wouldn't be ready until 5 am. Hanging up, Galbraith was left with the impression from the guarded conversation that AIN was still looking good.

It still seemed odd, however, that there could possibly be such a delay in getting back with the instructions on the contentious clauses. Unless Mallesons was busy on another more pressing contract, McKeon thought.

Meanwhile Independent hadn't been involved in any weekend discussions—Atkin had spoken for a while to Michael Hoyle, the Irish group's lawyer who was home in Melbourne, to keep the group warm.

On Sunday morning shortly before 7 am, the full Tourang group assembled early to go through the day's requirements. With victory in their sights, Colson and Powers were now calm— the whole transaction was firmly back on the commercial level.

This was the level they understood and thrived on—for months they had been out of their depth in Australian politics and time-consuming and traumatic personality and ego battles. Carefully the rest of the group—Levy, Chipkin, Lee, Carnegie, Miles and Mactier—calculated what was needed for them to be in a position to exchange contracts by late afternoon.

At Mallesons Al Donald was still leading the Freehill lawyers through the tedious process of re-working the loan documentation with the Mallesons lawyers. These lawyers had had no sleep in the last twenty-four hours.

● ● ●

As soon as Kent walked through the door into the conference room at Mallesons he knew something was horribly wrong. Returning from Melbourne—he had rushed back the previous afternoon because he was hosting a cocktail party for forty people

---

[1] Galbraith does not remember this sentence.

that Saturday night—the faces on the other side of the table facing McKeon and Galbraith were unfamiliar.

As Kent sat down, the Malleson lawyer, partner Chris O'Hehir, sitting forward and hunched over a pile of papers, glanced up momentarily. Kent nodded his head.

This wasn't Atkin. Continuing his dialogue, Galbraith asked about some point in the next clause. The Mallesons lawyer gave the same answer he had given for the last two hours. He needed further instructions. Galbraith sensed something was wrong.

Tired after the lack of sleep—he had spent Friday night on a plane from Hawaii, all day yesterday poring over legal documents and was up at 5 am to peruse the new documents—Galbraith was becoming very angry about Atkin's words the previous night: You will not be prejudiced. You will not be prejudiced. He decided that AIN wouldn't be prejudiced if they walked out now. He knew it was over. He came up with an idea to end this charade.

'Now look, this is a particularly critical point. It is probably a deal breaker,' he said seriously. 'There is one material clause missing, and my clients will not complete unless it is included.'

This caught the attention of O'Hehir, who looked up at Galbraith for longer than he had all morning.

'Could you take this one down,' Galbraith said sternly. O'Hehir nodded, and Galbraith ran the words through his mind before starting.

'Settlement of this contract,' he began as the lawyer began to dictate the clause, '. . . must take place in the Melbourne Club.'

Galbraith stopped as O'Hehir wrote down the final words. O'Hehir glanced up as the three men opposite smirked, then gave tired smiles, shaking their heads.

It was all over. They stood up and left the room and went back to the hotel. Johnson was telephoned at home and told what had happened. He agreed things looked grim and advised them to return to Melbourne.

On the plane McKeon couldn't get the final offer out of his mind. Perhaps greater certainty of completion would help, maybe an extra few million. He decided that the next morning he would work out a few changes to the bid and send them into Baring Brothers. AIN's final offer was about $30 million below the last one he had discussed with Baring Brothers. Maybe . . .

Burrows had a sleepless Saturday night and arrived at his office early the next morning, greeting Breese and White as he walked past their glass offices. It was quiet, and he had time to finalise the analysis of the offers and his recommendations.

By mid-morning Burrows was confident that the deal could be done by late afternoon. As he was worried that the imminent sale to Tourang would leak out quickly, he made sure there were preparations for a press conference. This was the deal of his life and he was going to make sure it was well choreographed. He telephoned Peter Gaunt and Greg Taylor and asked them to be at Baring Brothers' office at 4 pm. Taylor sensed this was important and immediately booked a seat on a plane to Sydney.

By late morning Nicholl and Chris Campbell arrived and were summonsed into the small anteroom. Sitting down, they were joined by Atkin, Breese and White. Burrows came in and handed around the analysis and recommendation. As Atkin read through it, he began to make a few pencil marks, which made Burrows nervous.

'What's he writing?' Burrows asked in a nervous tone, leaning over White, trying to decipher Atkin's words.

With the ever present threat of litigation from a bitter, unsuccessful bidder, these pages were critical. Each of the offers had been considered and comments made on their merits. Even the offer filed by a man called Hertzog, faxed into Baring Brothers from Hong Kong, was looked at. Mr Hertzog claimed to have a $2 billion fully funded offer.

The recommendation to Nicholl was clear. Burrows wanted Tourang. The intention of Tourang to put up $550 million within eight days was crucial. Ord's underwriting to provide $412 million of the funds was the clincher.

In addition the exclusivity agreement held a lot of weight since Burrows could sell Fairfax without resorting to an asset sale out of the corporate shell. With the bondholders agreeing to the terms of the Tourang offer and stating that they would put all the bonds into a New York escrow account, it was the best certainty available in the circumstances. Also the litigation against the banks would be dropped.

As for the other two offers, AIN's $360 million up-front was an advantage. At the end of the day, however, it didn't have the bondholders on its side.

Independent's offer was again dismissed on all counts. O'Reilly was unable to provide the cash quickly and despite his efforts, he didn't have the bondholders. It was ironic—some of the bond-holders in the end had contemplated dumping Tourang but then decided to vote for its offer. They decided against the sale becoming an open auction.

When Burrows finished, Nicholl asked a few questions. He then said that he would think about it and left the room with Camp-bell, disappearing into the third conference room.

Just on an hour later Nicholl emerged and caught White, asking that he convene a meeting of the bankers and whomever else was necessary. The bankers were spread through the Baring Brothers' office, working in small executive offices, fielding telephone calls from the Malleson lawyers.

Within minutes everyone was assembled in the main conference room. Jake Williams and David Craig headed the bankers. Nicholl was tense. It had been his toughest job yet, and the strain had shown at various times during the year. He began to read from a piece of paper, discussing the options before concluding.

'I will recommend Tourang,' he said, looking around the table as he finished.

Burrows asked White to go out and ring Colson and Powers. Hanging up, Colson yelled out: 'We have to speak with Nicholl.'

Colson and Powers and Chipkin rushed down to Baring Brothers just after 1.30 pm to face Nicholl. This was it. He was brief. Tourang had been chosen. Burrows was edgy, and when Nicholl finished he demanded that Tourang hurry up and be ready to exchange contracts later in the afternoon.

Levy and Chipkin joined Atkin to run through the contract again. There were still contentious clauses and they began to debate the wording of crucial clauses in the sale document.

When Taylor arrived at 3.45 pm, he knew the transaction was almost completed. People were everywhere; it looked like a news-paper office would on the outbreak of the Third World War.

He could see familiar faces of bankers through the glass in the main conference room—they had now been sitting there all day as the lawyers and Burrows updated progress. The mood in the office seemed happy—the bankers knew they had finally sold Fairfax and covered their loans.

The fifty-two months' saga of Warwick Fairfax—the young man they had encouraged and then deserted, pocketing some lucrative fees on the way—was finally drawing to a close.

As Taylor tried to discover what was going on, a hyperactive Burrows spotted Taylor from down the corridor. Approaching him, he grabbed Taylor by the arm and led him out of the office. Burrows ordered him to wait in the nearby Ramada Hotel—something would be finalised soon.

When Taylor got there Gaunt was already seated at a table, sipping a coffee. He had also received the order to wait.

· · ·

In the hot anteroom, the air-conditioning playing up, Levy and Atkin reached a stalemate an hour and a half later. There were six contentious points in the contract, and neither lawyer was going to budge.

Levy sought out Colson and Powers to work out what they wanted to do. Running through the points, the issues seemed outrageous. The banks were really trying it on. They wanted Tourang to give them an indemnity over their dealings in Fairfax during the receivership. It was a wide clause—Tourang would be liable even for gross acts of negligence.

The banks wanted Tourang to be responsible for any liabilities that arose from the sale process. Levy was deaf to this. What if, for instance, Burrows or Nicholl had told one of the other bidders that they had won? Why should Tourang wear such a liability?

The banks also wanted Tourang to buy Fairfax as a going concern. Basically the banks were saying that Tourang couldn't walk away between the exchange of the sales contract and settlement. To this Tourang responded that if the business wasn't there, if there was a major natural catastrophe, it would naturally walk away.

This wasn't seen as a major obstacle, since it was agreed that Tourang could go for a clause that it would not have to complete if the equipment needed to produce the newspapers was damaged or not there.

One very contentious clause was a warranty on title (guarantee of title). Tourang wanted this from the banks and used a Warwick analogy. What if the ex-proprietor had issued a large amount of shares that no one was aware of? The banks were only willing to insert a clause that there was a warranty on title to the best of their knowledge.

Levy told Colson that Tourang couldn't abide by that clause. Then Levy got onto the big issue. Something could probably be worked out on the other clauses without too much angst, but not on this one. In the end it was all coming down to fees. The last noses in the Fairfax fee trough had gone for that final jaw-stretching mouthful. Nearly $200 million had already been run up by Fairfax in professional fees to banks, lawyers, accountants and advisers.

Now the banks went for one more bite as they wanted Tourang to wear the fees incurred from the twelve months' saga to find a new owner for the media empire. The banks also wanted Tourang to pay $24.7 million in penalty interest for the loan document breaches caused by the plunge into receivership.

It seemed obscene to Colson and Powers. During the receivership Fairfax had not missed an interest payment. However, Levy's outline of the other sticking point upset them even more. The banks wanted Fairfax to pay all the expenses and costs associated with the receivership with no upper limit set on the amount. Shaking his head, Colson winced.

'That is outrageous,' he said, addressing Powers.

The other contentious clauses were secondary and quickly resolved. The banks agreed to give a warranty on the additional shares issue and accepted the disaster risk if, for example, the Broadway plant burnt down.

There would be no compromise on the fees, however. Colson and Powers went down the hall to confront Williams and Craig. Up to this point they had been occupying separate rooms and sending runners between them. They told the bankers the clause was a joke. For the next hour they argued.

Burrows walked in and as he realised the depth of emotion in this dispute he became despondent. His keenly awaited Sunday night press conference was off. Gaunt and Taylor were still at the Ramada, but they had now been joined by Breese and White—Burrows had sent his staff to keep them prisoners to ensure they didn't alert the newspapers of the impending sale.

Burrows had already been harassed by journalists who had learnt Tourang had won. He ducked the question and said no deal had been finalised that day. He neglected to mention that his plans to close the deal had come unstuck.

Around 8 pm Nicholl decided that there was no point waiting around as the deadlock continued and he headed home. Three hours later both parties were still in Baring Brothers' office, neither side conceding on the issue. It was too much money. If Tourang was forced to pay the penalty interest and the fees, Fairfax looked like costing at least another $50 million.

No one on the banks side, however, seemed to know if it was greater. What rankled Colson and Powers even more was that no one could give them an estimate of the likely receivership total professional fees. Was it $20 million or $40 million?

Just before 11 pm Colson felt exasperated by the banks' attitude.

'You're trying to turn the screws, and we are not prepared to be held to ransom,' he said defiantly.

Finally there was silence. Colson stood up. 'Sorry guys, this is a deal-breaker,' he said. 'Let's go.'

Powers and Colson went outside and told Levy and lawyer Warren Lee the deal wasn't happening. The group headed for the elevator. Walking out into the night, the group split up. Colson and Powers headed up the hill to the Ritz, while Levy and Lee walked up the deserted streets to Freehills to wait and see what happened.

It was decided to give the banks some time to think in private and then give them a call. Back at the office the two lawyers had nothing more to do than try to stay awake. Picking up the telephone they began to dial 0055 telephone numbers, ringing a service that offers black-jack.

About 12.30 am Levy remembered something. They hadn't told the Tourang lawyers working on the loan documents about the walk-out. He decided not to interrupt.

Meanwhile at the Ritz, Powers was worried. 'What will we do?' he asked Colson.

Running through the fee issue, they agreed that Williams and Craig seemed likely to compromise and agree to forgo the penalty interest, thereby letting Fairfax off. On the fee cap though, they seemed unlikely to budge and Colson was adamant he wouldn't either.

On the other hand Colson and Powers figured the banks knew that they must hurry to settle—Miles had told Burrows if he didn't close the deal before the sharemarket opened, Ords was out.

With enough time elapsed, Colson telephoned Williams at Mallesons' office, to which they had retreated, seeking to re-open negotiations.

'We are prepared to deal, if you want the deal closed. We are not prepared to budge on the fees, however; it isn't negotiable,' he said, before adding his Clint Eastwood-esque line. 'If you think I'm not serious, just try me.'

However, Williams was adamant there would be no backdown. After two telephone calls, Colson was so angry and tired he refused to talk again.

It was now after 2 am, and he hadn't slept since Thursday night. Powers took over the negotiations on Tourang's side; Craig on the bankers' side. They have reasonably similar personalities: forthright, tough, usually fairly unemotional. All negotiations were conducted by speaker phone. By 3 am they had struck a deal as Williams and Craig conceded to ensure the sale went through.

Fairfax would only pay $25.18 million of the banks' receivership fees and pick up some fees for Mallesons' legal costs from 6 December in finalising the new loan documentation for Tourang. The banks also agreed to forgo penalty interest of $24.7 million.

Exhausted, Colson telephoned Levy to finalise the whole thing. 'Get back down to Mallesons.'

There was still more legal work to finish off. Walking down to Mallesons, Levy knew there were not going to be any more pineapples. As the dawn came the lawyers continued to finalise the loan documents ready for the exchange of contracts.

• • •

On Sunday night Johnson sat at home convinced it was all over. A few telephone calls came through from AIN people and journalists. They were all bad signs. The O'Reilly people had been on the telephone all Sunday afternoon. Kevin Luscombe telephoned Rob McKay and Chris Tipler rang John D'Arcy.

The rumour that Taylor was in Sydney and the fact that

Burrows and his staff were answering telephones in their office didn't look good.

When he walked over and picked up the telephone again, it was a surprise caller—a very worried Tony O'Reilly.

'I have heard it on good authority that the Tourang group have concluded or are close to exchanging contracts,' O'Reilly said solemnly.

'I don't have that confirmed,' Johnson replied. 'But all the body language over the last thirty-six hours is consistent with that.'

There was silence—two men, who had lived and breathed Fairfax for twelve months or more, now faced defeat. Eventually O'Reilly suggested that Johnson attend a meeting early in the morning at Bankers Trust (BT) to work out what to do. Was it too late to join forces to stop it? As he hung up Johnson couldn't imagine how such a step would stop Tourang.

•　•　•

Honouring his undertaking to meet with the Independent group, Johnson walked into BT's foyer in Australia Square shortly after 7.30 am. He was escorted into a conference room where a group of stunned men sat quietly. Cameron, Hunt, Ross and Ted Harris acknowledged Johnson, who sat down.

Repeating the belief that Tourang was being chosen, Johnson nodded in agreement. 'All the indications are that way.'

The conversation turned to what could be done to stop Tourang now. Because Independent was so confident that its offer was the highest, it couldn't accept that Burrows had gone for Tourang. Commercial realities were being put aside: Independent and its executives, advisers and lobbyists had spent the best part of twelve months pursuing Fairfax as if a holy grail. Defeat was hard to accept.

Johnson couldn't see much point in fighting jointly; although he remained conscious that if they did, the AIN terms—not Independent's—discussed last time remained the opening position.

'I don't know what we could do, if it looks like we have to join to try and stop Tourang. It has to be on the terms AIN spelt out in the earlier meeting,' he said.

Picking a suitable break to depart, Johnson left after agreeing that each side would find out what was going on and perhaps take it from there. Walking across the street to the Stock Exchange building, Johnson caught the elevator to his office. He began making a few calls to get more precise information on the recent events.

■ ■ ■

Just before dawn Colson telephoned Black to tell him that Tourang had finally won. On the weekend he had had several conversations with his close friend, keeping him informed of the progress.

When Willis had allowed Tourang back in the sales process on Friday afternoon, Black was amazed and wondered whether his comments that the consortium had been the victim of sleazy, venal and despicable political conduct had done the trick. Colson didn't think so.

The Canadian then prepared to come to Australia—the country he said he had little wish to return to after his first visit in July—to add a fifteen per cent controlling shareholding in Fairfax to his growing media empire.

■ ■ ■

With the contracts set to be signed within the hour, Burrows was elated and running his speech through his head. He had contacted a few journalists and told them to be down at Baring Brothers by 11 am. His secretary Ruth buzzed to ask if he wanted to take a call from Mark Johnson. Johnson wanted to confirm that Fairfax had been sold to Tourang.

'Mark, I've had a dreadful night. I've got a 9.30 appointment with the physiotherapist. I'll ring you back,' Burrows said.

Nearly ten months later Johnson and the AIN group joke that they still don't know whether they missed out on buying Fairfax—Johnson is still waiting for Burrows to ring him back.

Just after 11 am that day, as a crowd milled in the reception area at Baring Brothers waiting for the press conference to begin, a telephone call came through. It was Tony O'Reilly wanting to speak with Burrows. Ruth asked him if he could take the call. 'Tell him I'm unavailable,' Burrows said.

Epilogue

THE BITTERNESS surrounding the sale of John Fairfax Group continued after Tourang was selected by the receiver. Both Australian Independent Newspapers (AIN) and Independent considered their offers were superior to Tourang. AIN claimed the effective price of its offer to the receiver was $1.52 billion and immediately sent out a four-page statement to institutions criticising the merits of the Tourang offer.

Tony O'Reilly has not been gracious in defeat, despite the weakness of his offer compared to those of Tourang and AIN. O'Reilly vented his anger at Conrad Black's comments about him and felt the sale process was not conducted fairly due to the bondholder agreement.

In the forty-eight hours following the sale, Independent considered its legal options. On Wednesday, 18 December 1991 Independent rushed into the Federal Court and tried to block Tourang's purchase, just as institutions were rushing to subscribe funds for completion of the Tourang purchase.

Independent's counsel Mr Charles Sweeney sought an injunction and a full hearing of the case the following morning. He requested a decision by the court before the 3 pm Thursday deadline for institutions to respond to Tourang's fund-raising. Justice Sheppard refused and suggested Independent seek an interlocutory injunction. Mr Sweeney declined the invitation and the case was adjourned.

Independent's action alleged Ord Minnett's underwriting of the initial $412 million in shares in Tourang breached the Broadcasting Act. It alleged that the issue breached media cross-ownership laws because it gave Westpac Banking Corporation—Ord's parent—a prescribed interest in Fairfax. Westpac already owned Ten Network.

The anger about the exclusivity agreement and its importance in Tourang being recommended by the Fairfax receiver Des Nicholl was evident in Independent's court action. It claimed that the Tourang offer breached section 47 of the Trade Practices Act. Independent alleged that the agreement between Tourang and the bondholders led to a substantial lessening of competition.

Tourang, Ords, the receiver and the Australian Broadcasting Tribunal (ABT) contested the cross-media ownership claim and Independent eventually dropped it. However, Independent has continued the Trade Practices Act action against Tourang and the receiver and eventually lodged a damages claim for $175 million. This upset Tourang (renamed John Fairfax Holdings Ltd) as it forced it to go to the expense of lodging a supplementary prospectus for its public issue of shares. The action is continuing.

* * *

Kerry Packer's fallout with Trevor Kennedy and Malcolm Turnbull is the lasting legacy of the Fairfax takeover. For two decades Kennedy's and Turnball's friendships with Packer gave them kudos in the business community. This friendship has ended.

Messrs Colson and Powers believe that Trevor Kennedy was a major factor in the ABT's decision to commence an inquiry into the consortium. A New South Wales Supreme Court action was commenced against Kennedy over his severance agreement and the case came before Justice Rogers on 21 February. Tourang sought the retention of $400 000 owed to Kennedy but held in an escrow account plus unspecified damages.

Tourang counsel Mr Peter Jacobson told the court on 21 February that there was a request for particulars (from the ABT) and stated that Tourang contended the information supplied was incorrect. The court was told that the information went to the question from whom Mr Kennedy was given instructions and that went to the question of the degree of influence or control of a particular party.

Tourang contended that Kennedy breached his severance agreement, *inter alia*, because he supplied information that hindered or damaged Tourang's bid and also didn't show it to Freehills in accordance with the termination agreement. Tourang alleged that the information provided in Kennedy's response to the ABT's requests of 25 November regarding the two people he reported to was inaccurate, citing Kennedy's earlier answers in a statutory declaration to the ABT dated 29 September.

Justice Rogers summed up the issue involved in the case and delivered a warning:

> I want everybody, and I do not mean counsel, but those people who are intimately involved in this case, to consider a bit more carefully just precisely what it is they are embarking upon.
>
> The information complained of in question 25 that throughout his tenure as managing director Mr Kennedy regarded Mr Packer and Mr Black as the two people to whom he had to report and that in fact he reported principally to Mr Packer and that whilst Mr Packer was not a board member of Tourang, he was influential in some of the instructions Mr Kennedy followed may, and I have no idea whether this is correct or not, be in conflict with some of the information which was otherwise supplied.
>
> Now, if there is going to be a contest about it and some judge is going to make a finding, the case may have consequences going quite beyond the $500 000 which is involved.
>
> If people want to litigate these issues, well that is fine, but I do not want anybody to be surprised at the last minute to find they are litigating issues that go far beyond those encompassed by this case.

The case returned to court on Friday, 13 March. Justice Rogers asked Mr Jacobson whether he was suggesting in the particulars of the case that someone told the ABT that Kennedy had made diary notes or entries.

Mr Jacobson said that if you looked at the ABT notices to Kennedy 'you can infer from them that Mr Kennedy or somebody informed the tribunal that there were other diary notes which would be ... The description in the 22 November notice was not sufficient to get the material that the tribunal wanted.'

Justice Rogers: 'Are you trying to tell me that you are going to try and assert that Mr Kennedy or someone on his behalf contacted the tribunal and said to them: "Listen, chaps, if I merely produce the diary notes from March 1990 until the present you won't get what you want, but if you call for the diary notes relating to my resignation then you might hit the jackpot?'

Jacobson: '... made during or after the event relating to the circumstances surrounding his resignation.'

The case was adjourned until May and was settled out of court on undisclosed terms.

* * *

Tourang prepared for its public float by appointing new directors to the board. Sir Rod Carnegie and the managing director of Brambles Mr Gary Pemberton became directors. Mr John Singleton was also appointed to the board, a decision that surprised the advertising industry, considering his ownership of an advertising agency.

John Fairfax Group was refloated to the Australian stock exchange on 8 May following an issue of shares to the public at $1.20 each. The listing was successful, and the shares closed on the first day at $1.38, delivering Conrad Black a $39 million paper profit on his fifteen per cent shareholding within five months.

* * *

Since the takeover the Telegraph adopted a slow approach to its role as manager and major shareholder of Fairfax. Mr Black agreed to sign editorial charters of independence. The Telegraph waited until the float was completed before implementing changes to the operations of the Group. Budget cuts of up to ten per cent in the editorial department of each newspaper have been sought. It is also expected that major retrenchments will occur on the production side of operations, particularly at the Broadway plant.

On 5 June John Fairfax announced the appointment of Mr Michael Hoy as deputy chief executive and editorial director of John Fairfax Group. Mr Hoy has broad experience in newspapers, beginning as a cadet in Orange, New South Wales, and later working for the defunct Fairfax Sydney afternoon newspaper the *Sun*. He travelled to London and after a stint in the USA as executive of the *National Enquirer*, began a successful Fleet Street executive career working with the Murdoch organisation, first as executive features editor of the *Sun* and then managing editor of the *Times*. In 1990 he moved to Hong Kong as general manager of the *South China Morning Post*.

Despite undertakings given to the Treasurer and the Foreign Investment Review Board that Tourang would attempt to appoint an Australian chief executive at Fairfax, Stephen Mulholland, a South African, was chosen for the position.

Mulholland, fifty-six and formerly chief executive of *Times Media*, a Johannesburg-based publisher, controlled by Anglo-American Corporation, took up his post in September 1992. He made it clear from the start that his primary aim was to tackle the group's $700 million 'cancerous' debt. Cost-cutting is at the top of his agenda.

Since his arrival, the board has agreed to a massive shake-up of senior editorial positions. The editor of the *Australian Financial Review*, Gerard Noonan, was sacked in November and replaced by John Alexander, formerly editor-in-chief of the *Sydney Morning Herald*. David Hickie, formerly editor of the *Sun Herald*, replaced Alexander at the *Sydney Morning Herald*. Andrew Clark, the *Australian Financial Review*'s European correspondent, replaced Hickie at the *Sun Herald*. Finance columnist Alan Kohler was appointed editor of the *Age*, replacing Mike Smith, who was given a management position. And Bruce Guthrie became editor of the Sunday *Age* after Steve Harris defected to News Ltd. Every metropolitan newspaper in the Fairfax stable has a new editorial executive.

Malcolm Turnbull's resentment at his removal as a director of Tourang remains. From being a staunch public supporter of Tourang until early November, strenuously arguing that Kerry Packer would have no influence at Fairfax under Tourang, Turnbull has made several inflammatory public comments. He said at a National Press Club luncheon on 18 March that he was 'thrown off' the Fairfax board because Messrs Colson and Powers 'believed I would be an unduly independent director'.

He added that there was no doubt that Packer had a great deal of influence and was really involved in the bid. On 30 April Turnbull was reported in the *Herald* as stating that the community should be suspicious of agreements struck with media proprietors: 'Proprietors will sign any agreement to secure industrial peace and then promptly ignore the conditions.'

Turnbull achieved a marginal revenge against the controllers of Fairfax when he joined the opposition to executive share proposals in October 1992. Fairfax had proposed to provide Michael Hoy with a $1 million interest free housing loan and a swag of free options to executives—3.5 million options to Stephen Mulholland, 2 million options to Michael Hoy, 500 000 to Dan Colson, 100 000 to Conrad Black and 75 000 to Brian Powers.

The Australian Shareholders Association criticised the share scheme as excessively generous. At the $1.00 issue price, the options when exercised delivered the executives with a windfall profit of 55 cents, based on the share price level of $1.55.

The Australian Investment Managers Group—comprising leading institutional investors—said the deep discount to the share price at which the options were issued raised questions about whether the options gave an incentive for the executives to perform.

Turnbull launched a Federal Court action to stop the executive share scheme after he found a technical breach in the drafting of the resolutions, which were to be put to shareholders at the annual general meeting.

He claimed that the notice of meeting was false and misleading, since it didn't make it clear that a special rather than an ordinary resolution was required to set up the executive options scheme. Under pressure from the Australian Stock Exchange, Fairfax withdrew the executive share scheme proposal.

Turnbull was delighted with his victory, and at the annual meeting delivered a prepared statement critical of the board, accusing it of poor commercial judgement.

* * *

The fight to secure control of the Fairfax empire was watched from the USA by Warwick Fairfax. Shortly after the receivership Warwick moved to Chicago. His reign at Fairfax and the subsequent receivership has set a new record for professional fees in Australia.

However, the new management has taken a tough line on fees in the wake of claims from former advisers. Mr Bill Beerworth began litigation in April, claiming $450 000 for breach of contract.

Lazard Freres and Macquarie Bank have not been paid about $1 million and $376 061 respectively for professional services.

John Fairfax is also defending an ACT Supreme Court claim by Lady Mary Fairfax that she is owed $150 million due to the sale of the Group to Tourang or the continuation of an annuity for life under the terms of an agreement with Warwick and John Fairfax Group executed in September 1988.

She alleges that a deed of indemnity signed in September 1988 entitled her to the first $150 million in the event of the winding up or sale of Fairfax. However, if she didn't receive the $150 million, she was entitled to the annuity for life. Fairfax receiver Des Nicholl sent Lady Mary a letter purporting to terminate the annuity in November 1991 and she responded with a claim for the $6.5 million she claimed was due for 1991. The matter is unfinished.

The junk bondholders dropped their litigation against the banks following the sale. The motion to the Federal Court by Malcolm Turnbull to have the cross-claim against him struck out succeeded on 12 December, just prior to the sale. However, Justice Sheppard granted the banks leave to file an amended cross-claim, stating that the success of the motion had relied on the form of the pleading and not the substance. No new cross-claim was filed.

* * *

Mr Black remains to some extent vulnerable as the proprietor of Fairfax due to the continued refusal of the Federal Government to the request to allow the Telegraph to increase its shareholding from fifteen per cent to twenty per cent and Hellman & Friedman from five per cent to fifteen per cent.

However, a takeover is always possible for a publicly listed company and Mr Black's current inability to raise his shareholding is an obstacle if an offer were ever made. The authors believe that a takeover bid from Kerry Packer after a sale of his shareholding in Nine Network cannot be ruled out. Sources remain adamant that Packer is bitter about the treatment he received from the Federal Government. He also believes Fairfax is a valuable business.

Packer is in a strong financial position with the ability for a $3 billion acquisition after a major asset sales programme during the first half of 1992.

The Telegraph remains hopeful that over time the Federal Government's attitude will change and it will be allowed to increase its shareholding to a strong controlling position. But the centre left and left-wing factions of the Labor Party oppose any higher foreign control of Fairfax and Mr Black's conservative politics means he faces difficulties in achieving his aim. The Federal Opposition, however, is more likely to allow Mr Black to increase his holding if it wins at the next Federal election.

18 December 1992

The Players

Anderson, Chris Jamison Equity's nominee for the Fairfax Group chief executive. Former chief executive and managing director of John Fairfax Group

Atanasio, Mark Finance executive of Drexel Burnham Lambert

Atkin, John Partner at Mallesons Stephen Jaques, lawyer for the banking syndicate

Bailey, Will Chief executive of the ANZ Bank

Barger, Matt General partner at Hellman & Friedman

Beazley, Kim Federal Minister for Transport and Communications

Bechtel, Karen Managing director of Morgan Stanley

Beerworth, William J Director of John Fairfax Group, appointed August 1990. Partner of William J Beerworth & Partners

Black, Conrad Chairman of the Daily Telegraph, a member of the Tourang consortium

Bowers, Peter Veteran *Sydney Morning Herald* journalist, spokesperson of the Friends of Fairfax

Breese, Peter Executive of Baring Brothers Burrows

Burrows, Mark Adviser to the banking syndicate. Chairman of Baring Brothers Burrows

Cannon-Brookes, Michael Ex-chief executive Citibank

Carnegie, Mark Adviser to Hellman & Friedman

Carnegie, Sir Roderick Adviser to Hellman & Friedman

Charlesworth, Ric Chairman of the Caucus Economics Committee

Chipkin, Stephen Partner at Freehill, Hollingdale & Page

Cohen, Fred Partner at Sherman & Sterling

Colson, Daniel Director of the Daily Telegraph and partner of Stikeman Elliott Solicitors

Corrigan, Chris Chief executive of Jamison Equity

Craig, David Chief general manager of Australian business banking, ANZ Banking Corporation

D'Arcy, John Director of Australian Independent Newspapers. Former chief executive of the Herald & Weekly Times

Davies, Anne Director of the Communications Law Centre

Dixon, Robyn Vice chairman of the Age Independence Committee

Duffy, Michael Federal Attorney-General

Duffy, Michael Federal President of Printing and Kindred Industries Union (PKIU) and Father of the Chapel, David Syme

Ezzes, Steven Co-chairman of the bondholder committee, representing the Airlie Group

Fairfax, John B Cousin of Warwick. Managing director of Rural Press. Proposed director of Fairfax if Independent Newspapers PLC took it over

Fairfax, Lady Mary Mother of Warwick; twenty-five per cent non-voting shareholding in the John Fairfax Group

Fairfax, Warwick Proprietor and chief executive of the John Fairfax Group; seventy-five per cent voting shareholding

Featherstone, Jim Vice president of Citibank

Forell, Claude Vice chairman of the Age Independence Committee

Galbraith, Colin Legal adviser to Australian Independent Newspapers. Partner of Arthur Robinson Hedderwick

Halkerston, Keith Director of the John Fairfax Group. Partner of William J Beerworth & Partners

Harley, Tom Director of Australian Independent Newspapers

Harris, Ted Chairman of Australian Airlines. Independent Newspapers' proposed director of the Fairfax Group

Hawke, Robert Prime Minister 1983–91

Healey, Liam Chief executive of Independent Newspapers PLC

Hellman, Warren Principal of Hellman & Friedman. Member of the Tourang consortium

Hoyle, Michael   Legal adviser to Independent Newspapers PLC. Partner of Corrs Chambers Westgarth

Hunt, Peter   Bankers Trust Australia, adviser to Independent Newspapers PLC

Johnson, Mark   Adviser to and director of Australian Independent Newspapers. Chairman of Macquarie Hill Samuel Corporate Services

Kennedy, Alan   Vice chairman and spokesperson of the Friends of Fairfax

Kent, Wayne   Executive of Macquarie Bank

Kerin, John   Federal Treasurer, June–December 1991

Langmore, John   Senator. Member of Caucus Transport and Communications Committee

Lee, Michael   Chairman of Print Media Inquiry

Lee, Warren   Solicitor at Freehill Hollingdale & Page

Leslie, Jim   Chairman of Australian Independent Newspapers. Former chairman of Qantas

Levy, Geoff   Partner at Freehill Hollingdale & Page

Liman, Arthur   Attorney at Paul Weiss Rifkind Wharton Garrison, New York. Independent Newspapers' negotiator with the bondholders

Lloyd, Simon   President of the Australian Journalists Association House Committee, Broadway, January–October 1991

McClure, Doug   Co-chairman of the bondholder committee representing Drexel Burnham Lambert

McKeon, Simon   Executive of Macquarie Bank

McKay, Rob   Director of Australian Independent Newspapers

Mactier, Rob   Executive of Ord Minnett Securities

Miles, Neville   Director of the Corporate Advisory division, Ord Minnett Securities

Moore, Matthew   President of the Australian Journalists Association House Committee, Broadway, October 1991

Nicholl, Desmond   Receiver of the John Fairfax Group. Partner of Deloitte Ross Tohmatsu

O'Connor, Cass   Executive of Turnbull & Partners

O'Keefe, Neil   Chairman of the Caucus Transport and Communications Committee

O'Neill, Ward   Chairman of the Friends of Fairfax

O'Reilly, Cameron   Director of Australian Provincial News-papers

O'Reilly, Tony   Chairman of Independent Newspapers PLC

Packer, Kerry   Chairman of Consolidated Press Holdings, a member of the Tourang consortium

Powers, Brian   General partner at Hellman & Friedman

Reynolds, John   Australian Independent Newspapers proposed chief executive of Fairfax. Now chief executive of Australian Provincial Newspapers

Richardson, Graham   Federal Minister for Social Security

Ross, Rowan   Adviser to Independent Newspapers PLC. Director of Bankers Trust Australia

Schacht, Chris   Senator. Member of Caucus Transport and Communications Committee

Scott, David   Manager of corporate finance at Bankers Trust Australia. Adviser to Independent Newspapers PLC

Tanner, Giles   Legal officer at the Australian Broadcasting Tribunal

Thomas, Rupert   Senior general manager of business banking at ANZ Banking Corporation

Turnbull, Malcolm   Financial adviser to the bondholders. Partner at Turnbull & Partners

Vaux, David   Executive of Jamison Equity

Westerway, Peter   Chairman of Australian Broadcasting Tribunal

White, Jeff   Executive of Baring Brothers Burrows

Williams, Jake   Chief executive of Citibank

Willis, Ralph   Federal Treasurer, December 1991

Wilson, David   Chairman of the Age Independence Committee

Chronology

30 October 1990 Malcolm Turnbull appointed financial adviser to the Fairfax junk bondholders.

31 October 1990 Bill Beerworth meets with junk bondholders in Los Angeles.

9 November 1990 Syndicate of banks lending to John Fairfax Group appoints Mark Burrows of Baring Brothers Burrows as their adviser on the restructuring of the Group. Warwick Fairfax and Bill Beerworth meet Conrad Black in Toronto.

15 November 1990 Bill Beerworth and Keith Halkerston meet with Mark Burrows and banking syndicate representatives.

30 November 1990 Warwick and Lady Mary Fairfax meet with Mark Burrows and bankers.

9 December 1990 Malcolm Turnbull and Steven Ezzes present bondholders' rescue plan for Fairfax to Mark Burrows. Banking syndicate representatives reject bondholders' plan and decide there will be no more concessions for Fairfax.

10 December 1990 John Fairfax Group applies for voluntary liquidation followed by an application by the banking syndicate to place the Group in receivership.

11 December 1990 Chris Corrigan announces that Jamison Equity will bid for Fairfax. Malcolm Turnbull and Steve Ezzes meet with banking syndicate representatives. Receiver Des Nicholl takes over reins at Fairfax.

24 December 1990 Banking syndicate members appoint Mark Burrows to advise on sale or re-capitalisation of Fairfax.

11 February 1991 Co-receiver Jim Grant demands correction in *Sydney Morning Herald* business story involving his firm Deloitte Ross Tohmatsu.

14 February 1991 Junk bondholders begin litigation against Fairfax Group, banks and Fairfax auditors, alleging misleading and deceptive conduct.

5 April 1991 Banks lodge cross-claim against Whitlam Turnbull.

24 April 1991 Tony O'Reilly arrives in Australia to speak to Burrows and institutional investors.

17 May 1991 Friends of Fairfax fund-raiser at New South Wales State Parliament House.

23 May 1991 Malcolm Turnbull and Neville Miles of Ord Minnett Securities complete documentation for consortium bid proposal.

3 June 1991 Savoy Hotel meeting to establish Tourang syndicate. Those present include Conrad Black, Kerry Packer, Brian Powers, Malcolm Turnbull, Neville Miles and Steve Ezzes. Paul Keating defeated in his challenge to Bob Hawke for the Prime Ministership.

7 June 1991 John B Fairfax decides to join with Tony O'Reilly's Independent Newspapers bid for Fairfax.

18 June 1991 Independent Newspapers announces Ted Harris, chairman of Australian Airlines, will be a director of Fairfax if their bid is successful. Conrad Black interviews Trevor Kennedy in Toronto for position of chief executive of Fairfax should their consortium be the successful bidder.

June O'Reilly team prepares dossier comparing Jamison executives with those of Independent.

24–27 June 1991 Labor Party Conference in Hobart.

28 June 1991 Prime Minister Hawke announces that a parliamentary inquiry into the print media will begin during the August session of Parliament.

15 July 1991 Malcolm Turnbull and Steve Ezzes lunch with Graham Richardson and Kim Beazley in Canberra.

16 July 1991 The Tourang consortium and its bid for Fairfax is announced.

17 July 1991 Conrad Black arrives in Australia for his first visit.

18 July 1991 Conrad Black and Trevor Kennedy meet with

Hawke and Treasurer John Kerin and lunch with Kim Beazley.

26 July 1991 Friends of Fairfax and Age Independence Committee delegates meet with Hawke, Kerin and Beazley.

31 July 1991 Colin Winter of Phillips Fox successfully applies for an injunction to prevent *Sydney Morning Herald* reporting existence or contents of a letter outlining junk bondholders' litigation against Fairfax and banks. The letter had been inadvertently faxed to competing solicitors Blake Dawson Waldron.

4–5 August 1991 Tony O'Reilly and Rowan Ross meet with Chris Corrigan and David Voux in County Cork to discuss a merger of Independent and Jamison bids.

8 August 1991 Australian Independent Newspapers (AIN) team makes its presentation to AMP.

14 August 1991 AMP and National Mutual announce their support for AIN.

23 August 1991 Mark Burrows' deadline for expressions of interest.

23 August 1991 AIN lodges a bid worth effectively just over $1 billion. After heated negotiations bid is withdrawn.

29 August 1991 Tony O'Reilly and Ted Harris dine with Hawke at The Lodge.

30 August 1991 O'Reilly meets with Jim Leslie and Robert McKay of AIN in Melbourne.

10 September 1991 Meeting of the Caucus committee on Transport and Communications. Beazley refers to AIN as 'uptown Melbourne establishment'.

12 September 1991 Transport and Communications Committee passes motion limiting foreign voting equity to twenty per cent of a print media company, but effectively allows unlimited non-voting foreign equity.

1 October 1991 Parliamentary inquiry into print media begins public hearings.

8 October 1991 Full Caucus vote on limitation of foreign ownership of print media deferred. The question is referred to a joint committee meeting—the Economics Committee and the Transport and Communications Committee.

9 October 1991 Federal Cabinet considers John Kerin's proposed Caucus resolution on foreign ownership of print media.

10 October 1991 At a joint Caucus committee meeting and a full Caucus meeting, the issue of foreign ownership of print media is considered. The rule remains with a twenty per cent limit on voting equity.

13 October 1991   Trevor Kennedy confronts Brian Powers and Dan Colson at the Regent Hotel.

15 October 1991   Trevor Kennedy resigns from Tourang. Malcolm Fraser, Gough Whitlam, Peter Nixon and five other political leaders release a letter calling for action to stop further concentration of both ownership and foreign ownership of print media. Bids close for John Fairfax Group.

16 October 1991   Fairfax Sydney journalists stage a twenty-four-hour strike and demonstrate outside the ANZ Bank.

23 October 1991   Kerry Packer faces his critics on 'A Current Affair'.

24 October 1991   John Langmore and David Connolly begin collecting Members of Parliament's signatures for a bi-partisan petition directed at stopping further concentration of print media ownership.

25 October 1991   Malcolm Fraser and Gough Whitlam address a rally of 2000 people in Melbourne's Treasury Gardens.

27 October 1991   Fraser and Whitlam repeat performance at Darling Harbour Convention Centre before a crowd of 1500.

31 October 1991   Turnbull meets with representatives of Printing and Kindred Industries Union. Tourang increases its bid by $300 million to $1.428 billion.

2–3 November 1991   Powers and Colson spend weekend at Ellerston coaching Packer for his print media inquiry appearance.

4 November 1991   Kerry Packer appears before the print media inquiry.

14 November 1991   Australian Broadcasting Tribunal sends out a list of seventy-one questions to parties associated with Tourang bid.

20 November 1991   Powers and Colson ask Turnbull to resign as a Tourang board member.

22 November 1991   Colson and Turnbull meet in Botanical Gardens. Turnbull agrees to resign from board.

23 November 1991   Turnbull changes his mind.

25 November 1991   Tony O'Reilly arrives back in Australia.

Australian Broadcasting Tribunal (ABT) chairman Peter Westerway receives critical new information on Tourang.

26 November 1991 Peter Westerway appears before print media inquiry and announces he will recommend that ABT hold an inquiry into the Tourang bid for the Fairfax Group.

28 November 1991 Packer announces his withdrawal from Tourang consortium.

29 November 1991 Malcolm Turnbull resigns from Tourang board.

early December Rowan Ross and Mark Johnson meet to discuss merger of AIN and Independent consortiums.

3 December 1991 Burrows announces the deadline for final bids is 11 December 1991.

5 December 1991 John Kerin decides to approve Independent bid for Fairfax under foreign investment powers but rejects Tourang bid.

6 December 1991 Hawke announces that Ralph Willis will replace Kerin as Treasurer the following Monday, 9 December 1991.

8 December 1991 Tourang consortium is informed that its bid has been rejected by Kerin.

9 December 1991 Tony O'Reilly writes to junk bondholders, canvassing an alternative offer.

10 December 1991 Mark Johnson meets with Powers and Colson to discuss a merger of the Tourang and AIN bids.

11 December 1991 Bids close. Tourang submits restructured bid to Foreign Investment Review Board. Bondholders vote to stay with Tourang consortium.

13 December 1991 Willis approves restructured Tourang bid.

16 December 1991, 3 am Deal is closed. Banking syndicate agrees to sell Fairfax Group to Tourang consortium.

The Cost

Fees paid by John Fairfax 1987–92*

Drexel Burnham Lambert: junk bond issue—$33.2 million

Citibank: financing/re-financing—$27.2 million

Bond Media: discounted success fee to Laurie Connell—$27 million

Baring Brothers Burrows: sale success fee—$18.6 million

The ANZ Banking Corporation: financing/re-financing fees—$17.9 million

Ord Minnett: gross fees on Tourang purchase and public float—$16.7 million

Whitlam Turnbull: asset sale advisory fees (1988)—$9.88 million

WSGP (Mr William Simon): junk bond issue advice—$8.64 million

Mallesons Stephen Jaques, Citibank solicitors: restructuring legal fees—$8.2 million

Chris Anderson, Peter King: termination payouts—$5.6 million

Freehill Hollingdale & Page: Fairfax legal advice pre-receivership—$4.8 million

Freehill Hollingdale & Page: solicitors' advisory work on public float—$500,000

Martin Dougherty: termination payout—$3 million

Deloitte Ross Tohmatsu: receivership fees—$3 million

Tourang: rebate loans/advances from shareholders for costs incurred in purchase—$2.5 million

---

* *Source:* John Fairfax Holdings Ltd and prospectus

Latham and Watkins: US junk bond issue attorneys—$1.8 million

Baker and Mackenzie, ANZ solicitors: restructuring fees—$1.3 million

Touche Ross, Fairfax auditors: $1.2 million

Lazard Freres & Co.: advisory fees—$1 million (disputed)

William J Beerworth & Partners: advisory fees—$857 267 (part subject to litigation)

The Daily Telegraph PLC: acquisition out-of-pocket expenses— $750 000

Hellman & Friedman: acquisition out-of-pocket expenses—$750 000

Minter Ellison lawyers, *Latham's local representative:* $500 000

Ernst & Young: accountancy advisory fees on float—$500 000

John Singleton: advice on advertising for Tourang takeover— $45 000

Estimated total: $196 million

Estimated final bidder costs

Independent Newspapers PLC: $2 million
AIN: $1 million

Sundry

Turnbull & Partners via 3.5 million debentures plus share of Ord Minnett fee: $6.3 million

Phillips Fox, bondholder lawyers: $2.6 million

Coudert Brothers, bondholder lawyers: $A966 000

Index

Also available in Mandarin

TOM BOWER

Maxwell
The Outsider

COMPLETELY REVISED AND UPDATED FOR A SECOND TIME

Robert Maxwell continues to make news even after his sensational and mysterious death. This book, which Maxwell tried to ban, now asks – and answers – the unresolved questions which remain. It reveals:

- the truth behind Maxwell's extraordinary links with the KGB, the Kremlin and Eastern Europe

- his history of shady dealings which shocked the City

- his conspiracy of public and private companies that concealed a staggering £3 billion in debts

- the scandal of the Maxwell pension funds

- the roles of his sons, Kevin and Ian Maxwell

- and the truth behind Robert Maxwell's death.

JONATHAN MANTLE

For Whom The Bell Tolls

Lloyd's of London is the world's oldest and most famous insurance market, traditionally a unique and respected British institution. But now, faced with record losses of over £2 billion, the chips are down for this last bastion of the upper and middle classes as it staggers beneath the worst man-made disaster in its 300-year history, its members taking legal action and locked into spiralling arrears of debts for years to come. *For Whom The Bell Tolls* tells the inside story of how complacency, negligence and possibly even fraud have catapulted Lloyd's into one catastrophe against which it has failed to insure – its own self-destruction.

'To thousands of members of Lloyd's the sound of the Lutine bell means more than the sinking of another ship – it signals the loss of a home, an end to their children's education and personal ruin. No wonder, then, that they believe they have been robbed. Jonathan Mantle charts how the gold rush went bust'
Harpers & Queen

'Candid and well written'
Independent

'The tale (Jonathan Mantle) tells is important and may never be heard in the courts'
Digest of Lloyd's News

DAVID MARSH

The Bundesbank:
The Bank That Rules Europe

'Ten years ago, the Bundesbank was an unknown quantity in Britain. Today, as ministers try to deflect blame from the ERM debacle, it is public enemy number one. And, for those determined to draw comparison between the pound's defeat and earlier military victories, there is plenty of material here'
Sunday Times

'With exquisite timing, the European Editor of the *Financial Times* has produced a fascinating guide to the soul of the institution which has suddenly become an object of bitter censure in Downing Street'
Observer

'David Marsh's excellent book . . . deserves a wide readership, both among those who see the Bundesbank as a dragon which has brought down St George; and among those who, as other nostrums fail, reach for an independent, central bank to perform the elusive economic miracle'
Financial Times

'A solid, erudite and engaging study that was certain to have been well received now promises to be a bestseller. The book deserves to thrive, not least because its author, David Marsh, has been consistently one of the best informed commentators on European (and especially German) affairs for the past dozen or so years. It demands to be read'
Yorkshire Post

ANDREW DAVIDSON

Under the Hammer

It was the biggest shake-up television had ever seen. The 1991 independent television franchise battle had everything; money, malice, intrigue, deception and a host of colourful characters that only the broadcasting industry could throw up. Richard Branson, David Frost, Phil Redmond, Bruce Gyngell, Michael Green, Greg Dyke and many other media figures joined the bizarre fray which left some of the losers in tears and made many of the winners millionaires overnight.

'It races ahead like a prime time soap . . . Davidson's tale makes compulsive reading with its startling revelations and insider anecdotes'
Broadcast

'Davidson is excellent on the wildly different rationales that were devised in this extraordinary business'
The Times

'An exceptionally well-informed account'
Literary Review

SIR JOHN HARVEY-JONES

Getting It Together

'Sir John is that rare animal, a businessman who makes business exciting . . . No businessman has ever written a memoir like it.'
Sunday Times

Sir John Harvey-Jones is one of Britain's most admired businessmen. His television series, *Troubleshooter*, with its clear-sighted look at ailing British companies, became a national talking point, and as chairman of ICI he topped the *Sunday Times* poll of captains of industry five years running.

Getting it together is the memoir of a remarkable man – and a fascinating account of the experiences that made him a hugely successful manager.

Rich in illuminating anecdotes, this is a memoir everyone working in an organisation should read. Frank, beguiling and full of the wisdom about people and business that has informed his working life, this is the autobiography of the year.

SIR JOHN HARVEY-JONES

Managing to Survive

Every decade produces fresh challenges for the manager – and the nineties look set to produce more difficult challenges than most. After the roaring eighties, most businesses are facing a very different world – a world in which some skills which were neglected in the last decade have suddenly become relevant. Sir John Harvey-Jones, who steered ICI triumphantly through some of its toughest years, and who became a household name with his brilliant *Troubleshooters* series, here isolates the key areas which every manager will have to confront in the nineties, and the key skills he or she must bring to the job. He looks at:

● Sustainable competitive advantage – how to get it, how to keep it

● Why verticality is the most dangerous form of organisation you can have

● How to be the 'fastest with the mostest' – and how 'activity costing' can transform your overheads

● The roles of the boss in the flat, non-hierarchical nineties organisation – and how the new structures can keep pace with people's need for personal growth

● Technology – why it hasn't worked for most companies, and how it can

● Why the customer is no longer the enemy – and how to construct your company around the links with the ultimate consumer

FENTON BAILEY

The Junk Bond Revolution

On 21 November 1990, Michael Milken, undisputed Junk Bond Guru and the man who created a 200 billion dollar bond market virtually single-handed, was sent to prison for ten years. In this captivating account of greed, power and corruption, Fenton Bailey shows how Milken was made an Icarus of Wall Street, symbol and scapegoat for an era where the art of the deal was practised at the expense of truth and justice.

'A partisan, revisionist account of the junk bond saga, Bailey's book concentrates on the disgraced financial wizard at the heart of the Eighties boom, Michael Milken. Bailey makes a convincing case for the cerebral Milken as simply the ideal scapegoat for the dumb, and finally self-destructive, greed of the whizz-kids who flourished in his wake'
Spectator

'An alternative history of the Age of Greed . . . profiles the rise and fall of arch capitalist Michael Milken, the Junk Bond King, by placing it in the context of American economic decline and moral confusion. Did he really fall or was he pushed?'
Time Out

'Provides convincing evidence that Milken's personal acts of charity were great, not merely in money but in time and personal commitment'
Financial Times

DAVID SPANIER

All Right, OK, You Win

National playground, sleepless city of supercharged excitement, gambling capital of the world, Las Vegas is the shiniest tableau in the American dream – and one of the country's most successful industries. From the tables to the slots to the ever-spinning roulette wheels, from mirror-lined hotel room to boxing ring and brothel, David Spanier explains what the winners win, what the losers lose, and how Las Vegas always comes out on top.

'Combine Spanier and Las Vegas and you have a work of superlative, witty reportage which will antagonise Puritans and have the rest of us shouting: "Hold me back." As Spanier makes clear from the outset, he loves Las Vegas: the lunatic razzle-dazzle, the vulgarity, the thronging, fat, devil-may-care punters in their fluorescent Bermudas, the city motto "If it's worth doing, it's worth overdoing" all act on him like champagne'

Val Hennessy, *Daily Mail*

'Spanier vivdly evokes the atmosphere and ethos of Las Vegas – the raucous, garish life along the Strip and Fremont Street, the tragicomedy of fortunes being flung away by eternal suckers, the crassness of room-service sex and the sinister controlling power that manifests itself across the whole madcap scene'

C J Fox, *Independent*

RICHARD LYNCH and
KELVIN CROSS

Measure Up!

Few areas are as important to the performance of
organisations as measurement, yet it remains one of the
weakest areas in management today. Leading consultants now argue that improvement in this area will be a
matter of survival in the 1990s. *Measure Up!* is based on
discussions with hundreds of managers in the US and
Europe and on case studies of three companies. Packed
with clear and practical examples it shows you how to:

measure what is important to your customers

*motivate your organisation to improve continually
against customer expectations*

*identify and eliminate waste, both of time
and resources*

*accelerate organisational learning and build
consensus for change*

*custom tailor new dynamic measurement systems to
suit your organisation.*

'Finally! a practical book from practical people about
management's most powerful tool – measurement. Hats
off to Richard Lynch and Kelvin Cross for a long
overdue job well done'

Tom Peters

A Selected List of Business Titles Available from Mandarin

While every effort is made to keep prices low, it is sometimes necessary to increase prices at short notice. Mandarin Paperbacks reserves the right to show new retail prices on covers which may differ from those previously advertised in the text or elsewhere.

The prices shown below were correct at the time of going to press.

All these books are available at your bookshop or newsagent, or can be ordered direct from the address below. Just tick the titles you want and fill in the form below.

Cash Sales Department, PO Box 5, Rushden, Northants NN10 6YX.
Fax: 0933 410321 : Phone 0933 410511.

Please send cheque, payable to 'Reed Book Services Ltd.', or postal order for purchase price quoted and allow the following for postage and packing:

£1.00 for the first book, 50p for the second; **FREE POSTAGE AND PACKING FOR THREE BOOKS OR MORE PER ORDER.**

NAME (Block letters) ....

ADDRESS ....

....

☐ I enclose my remittance for ....

☐ I wish to pay by Access/Visa Card Number ☐☐☐☐☐☐☐☐☐☐☐☐☐☐☐☐

Expiry Date ☐☐☐☐

Signature ....

Please quote our reference: MAND